AUGSBURG COLLEGE AND SEMINARY
LIBRARY - MINNEAPOLIS 4, MINN.

WITHDRAWN

IN THE CAUSE OF PEACE

THE MACMILLAN COMPANY
NEW YORK · CHICAGO
DALLAS · ATLANTA · SAN FRANCISCO
LONDON · MANILA

**THE MACMILLAN COMPANY
OF CANADA, LIMITED**
TORONTO

Fayer, N.Y.

Trygve Lie

IN THE CAUSE OF PEACE

Seven Years with the United Nations

THE MACMILLAN COMPANY - NEW YORK

1954

COPYRIGHT, 1954, BY TRYGVE LIE

PUBLISHED SIMULTANEOUSLY IN ENGLAND

All rights reserved—no part of this book may be reproduced in any form without permission in writing from the publisher, except by a reviewer who wishes to quote brief passages in connection with a review written for inclusion in magazine or newspaper.

PRINTED IN THE UNITED STATES OF AMERICA

First Printing

To

HJÖRDIS

FOREWORD

THIS VOLUME of recollections deals with the questions which concerned me most during seven years as Secretary-General of the United Nations. These very questions also aroused the greatest public interest and were discussed daily, demanding constant attention by governments and by the United Nations itself. And often I felt it was my duty to take a definite stand.

Lack of space and time has made it impossible to take up all the political questions with which the United Nations had to cope. Unfortunately, Kashmir, Indonesia, and the Italian colonies are among the subjects that have had to be omitted; and there are yet other matters which I should have liked to discuss more fully—for instance, the activities of the Economic and Social Council and the Trusteeship Council. The work of these two United Nations organs is very important; much of what they have done is of lasting value. There are also many administrative problems on which I have been unable to touch. Perhaps I may have an opportunity to deal with them all later, in one way or another.

Therefore, the present book is neither a history of the first seven years of the world organization nor a textbook, though I hope that teachers and students of international relations will benefit by reading it. It is written for ordinary men and women—in all countries—who are interested in the world in which they live and in the political climate of their own day.

It is based in large part on official documents and memoranda, and on my own diary (notes) and letters written when the issues were of immediate concern.

I am grateful for the counsel and aid rendered by old and loyal colleagues in the United Nations Secretariat, and thank them all for their contributions and support during seven long and strenuous years in the United Nations as well as for help during the writing of this book. I wish also to express my debt to many other friends, both at home and abroad, for active assistance.

It is my hope that this book, by making the United Nations better understood, may in some measure contribute to an increased support of the world organization in its striving for peace.

Lieset, April 5, 1954

CONTENTS

FOREWORD   *vii*

I   *HOW I BECAME SECRETARY-GENERAL*
A message from Adlai Stevenson.—Unwilling competition with Spaak for presidency of First U.N. General Assembly.—The Russians meet America halfway.—Persuasion by friends.—A final night meeting at Claridges.—Election with 46 to 3 votes.—What were the reasons.   1

II   *THE WARTIME ALLIANCE BEGINS TO BREAK UP*
The enigma of great-power unity.—First round offers hope for continuing accord.—Vyshinsky and Bevin clash in Security Council.—The Soviet casts its first veto.—"Iron Curtain" is sighted from Fulton, Missouri.—How to take things as they are?   22

III   *THE SECRETARIAT: OUTPOST IN THE STRUGGLE FOR PEACE*
The role of the Secretary-General.—Great powers agree on allocation of Assistant Secretaryships-General.—The problem of guarding a geographical balance.—Recruiting a crew for a ship already on her course.   39

IV   *WHERE IS THE CENTER OF THE WORLD?*
First round in London: contest over Europe or America as Headquarters site.—The Pacific raises its voice.—Shift of world political center of gravity across Atlantic finally recognized.—United Nations in New York.—Hunter College.—Lake Success and Flushing Meadow.   55

CONTENTS

V IRANIAN ENTANGLEMENTS
The question of Soviet troops in Azerbaijan.—Gromyko's walkout and Western insistence.—My legal opinion, and its consequences for the position of the Secretary-General.—U.N. still "seized" by a dispute settled in 1946.   74

VI THE CLEAVAGE HARDENS
The Baruch Plan and Article 43.—A year of serious negotiations followed by stalemate.—U.N. membership becomes a football of the cold war.—Greece and the Truman Doctrine.   89

VII PERMANENT HEADQUARTERS
Headquarters battle resumed.—Problems of a federal government.—Secretary-General forced to fight in the open.—All other alternatives defeated.—New York is chosen.—From Lake Success to Turtle Bay.—A miracle of international planning.—Workshop for peace completed.   107

VIII LATIN-AMERICAN NEEDS AND CONTRIBUTIONS
Pride and poverty at the threshold of plenty.—Groundless fears of rivalry between United Nations and Pan-American systems.—Economic Commission for Latin America launched and at work.—U.N. responds to technical aid requests.   125

IX THE CHALLENGE OF OUR TIME
Poverty still dominates the world.—A global welfare program takes shape.—Initial success for U.N. Technical Assistance to Underdeveloped Areas.—Large-scale capital investments needed for continued economic development. A threat to our highest values.   142

X THE PALESTINE CHALLENGE
The plight of Jews, and Arabs.—Partition decided but sabotaged.—Issue of the authority and power of the United Nations.—Shifting United States position.—Offer to resign.—"War" on the United Nations.   158

XI ARMISTICE ACHIEVED IN PALESTINE
Britain and America at cross purposes.—I work behind the scenes.—Security Council acts at last.—Count Bernadotte appointed.—The first and second truces.—Assassination of the Mediator.—Ralph Bunche moves in.—Armistice at last.—The visit to the Middle East. 174

XII MEDIATION IN BERLIN
The Soviet blockade and its impact. Conciliation in currency conflict attempted while airlift holds front.—Assembly's appeal to great powers carried further by President and Secretary-General. Conversation at Lake Success leads to solution. 199

XIII WHERE EAST MEETS WEST—MOSCOW, 1946—PRAGUE, 1948
Uncertainty confronts the border lands.—Soviet persuasion tactics at close hand.—My first conversation with Joseph Stalin.—Czechoslovakian tragedy, the last bridge burned. —Aftermath in Prague. 219

XIV THE BALKAN DILEMMA—BELGRADE, ATHENS, AND ANKARA, 1951
Yugoslavia in the vise.—Belgrade: "something big and inspiring halted in mid-motion."—Tito describes the plight of an ex-Soviet satellite.—Greece: saved by Western arms; supported by Western taxpayers.—The "sick man of Europe" is now strong. 237

XV THE ISSUE OF CHINESE REPRESENTATION
United Nations in danger.—Malik walks out.—Open breach divides the democracies.—Talks in Washington, London, Paris, and Moscow.—The future of Formosa.— Malik's unexpected return.—When Peking? 249

XVI MY PEACE MISSION—OUTWARD BOUND
My memorandum of points for a twenty-year peace program.—Why I decided to attempt it.—Visits to Washington, London, Paris, and Prague.—Arrival in Moscow. 275

CONTENTS

XVII MY PEACE MISSION—MOSCOW AND AFTER
At the Kremlin with Stalin.—Agreement to periodic meetings of Security Council.—Return visits to Paris, London, and Washington, and Publication of Peace Plan.—Korean aggression interrupts my efforts.—Progress after four years. 293

XVIII KOREA
The fate of an Asian borderland people.—I invoke Article 99 of the Charter.—Problem of participation.—The "Acheson Plan" is born. 323

XIX PEKING FAILS TO UNDERSTAND
The Yalu River is reached.—A new aggression unfolds.—Fruitless discussions with Peking representatives.—Nehru on "Asia first."—Status quo rejected by Communists but finally achieved. 349

XX MY TERM IS EXTENDED
Early decision to "quit while quitting is good."—Western powers' call to continue.—Soviet maneuverings and charges of "illegality."—Threat of an American veto.—My stand on Korea upheld. 367

XXI THE COMMUNIST ISSUE IN THE SECRETARIAT
"In an international organization that in most respects faithfully reflects the world as it is—a world of sovereign nations, the Secretariat has exclusively international responsibilities. The Secretary-General and his staff have in some respects been placed by the Charter in an advanced —and correspondingly exposed—position." 386

XXII RESIGNATION
Best kept secret.—Reasons for my decision.—Soviet boycott.—My hands are tied as dangerous cold war deadlock continues.—Lester Pearson nearly becomes my successor. —New Secretary-General takes over.—Home again at last! 406

XXIII REFLECTIONS

What is the United Nations?—The rule of unanimity.—The veto privileges and Soviet abuses.—Need for a general conference to review Charter in perspective.—Revision now, or better application first? 420

XXIV THE FUTURE—FOR PEACE WITH FREEDOM

A survey of conflicts threatening the peace.—Why have we chosen to risk the "cold war"?—No idea can be killed with arms alone.—The "have-nots": a threat and an opportunity.—Time now mobilized as an ally for peace.—Peace without freedom, a hollow shell.—Of what value is the threat of self-destruction?—"Somewhere between past and future." 435

INDEX 449

IN THE CAUSE OF PEACE

CHAPTER I

HOW I BECAME
SECRETARY-GENERAL

A message from Adlai Stevenson.—Unwilling competition with Spaak for presidency of First U.N. General Assembly.— The Russians meet America halfway.—Persuasion by friends. —A final night meeting at Claridges.—Election with 46 to 3 votes.—What were the reasons.

FOR ME it all began not in San Francisco or London, but in a cabin high in the Norwegian mountains on Christmas Day of 1945.

Norway was free again after five years of Nazi occupation. The separations, the anxieties and tribulations of the war were ended. My wife Hjördis and I had decided that we and our three children, Sissel, Guri, and Mette, should enjoy the traditional Christmas holidays with our old friends Mr. and Mrs. Ragnvald Bratz and their children. We had passed many Christmases together since 1920, but these had ended with the German invasion in April, 1940. Some of us had remained in Norway during the war years; some were in Sweden; others, in England and from time to time in America. Now we were all together again, resolved to enjoy this very special Christmas as in the old days.

The cabin, built of logs, lies high in the mountains of central Norway between Hallingdal and Numedal some 3,200 feet above sea level, and at least fifteen miles from the nearest railway station. We had driven up a winding mountain road to a farm at Rukkedalen, where we had put on our skis and shouldered our packs for the three-mile climb across steep slopes to the cabin. The lodge was soon warmed and readied, the Christmas tree was brought in and trimmed, and the struggle of getting there was at once forgotten in the excitement of preparing for a real Norwegian Christmas in the mountains.

The pleasure of being together again in these familiar surroundings seemed to lift us out of the everyday world below, and I cannot recall any Christmas Eve passed more in keeping with the true spirit of that holiday. Struggle, turmoil, and small troubles, all were left behind. Though 1945 had been strenuous and crowded with events, it had been a good and a happy year: we had much to be grateful for. Forgotten too were the problems of government and all the work awaiting me in connection with Norway's political and economic reconstruction.

Christmas morning, we had been out for a short ski trip in perfect snow before breakfast. Never had the mountains been more beautiful, with the glistening white of new snow on the hard-packed base of the open slopes and the yews and dwarf birches mantled with silver hoarfrost. We were all seated at the table with good appetites after this outing when one of the youngsters suddenly jumped up and ran to the window. Down near the edge of the forest a lone skier was making his way toward the cabin. He was soon identified as Knut Aaimellom, the farmer in Rukkedalen who took care of the cabin and saw to our comfort whenever we were in these parts. He was skiing hard, and we wondered what brought him here on Christmas morning. An illness, or a message for Ragnvald Bratz, or perhaps word for me from the Government in Oslo?

Reaching the cabin, Knut took his time; he brushed the snow from his shoes and placed his skis carefully against the wall. When he had been invited in and was seated at the table, he reported that a telegram had arrived from Oslo and he had been instructed to deliver it to me as quickly as possible. It was from the Foreign Ministry and contained the following message, which I read with surprise and consternation:

> The American Chief Delegate to the Preparatory Commission, Mr. Stevenson, has asked Colban * to determine whether Foreign Minister Lie would be willing to accept election as President of the General Assembly, which opens on January 10th next year. Mr. Stevenson could say

* Adlai E. Stevenson, Ambassador Erik Colban.

nothing about the prospects, as the matter had not yet been discussed with the other delegations, but, if Foreign Minister Lie is willing, the Americans intend to suggest him. Cable reply as soon as possible.

After examining the telegram I read it aloud several times for the others. My first feeling was almost resentment. The message was a kind of intrusion upon our happiness in these simple and peaceful surroundings. It was an unwelcome reminder of the pressure of problems that a world just emerging from a terrible ordeal would have to face without time for respite and recuperation.

It is true that at Oslo in August I had received a confidential query from the American Embassy as to whether I could consider the possibility of being a candidate for the presidency. The query was from Edward R. Stettinius, Jr., the first United States representative to the United Nations General Assembly, who, as Secretary of State, had presided over the San Francisco Conference. I had not taken it too seriously. First of all, I had replied, it was not certain that I should be the Foreign Minister of Norway in January, 1946. We were to have our first postwar elections in October, and, as a result, a new or reconstructed government would probably be in office. Furthermore, I had suggested, I could not in any case take a stand with regard to the presidency before acquainting myself with the situation in London when the General Assembly convened in 1946.

In the months that followed, I had given the American inquiry little or no further thought; and since I had heard nothing more about it, even after my reappointment following the October elections as Foreign Minister in Einar Gerhardsen's second Cabinet, I had dismissed it as a trial balloon that would not be followed up. I also realized what a difficult task the President of the first Assembly would have. In the complex procedures of formal international conferences my experience was limited to the San Francisco Conference, where I had been chairman for a short time of the committee which drafted the articles of the Charter concerning the Security Council. Although I had served continuously in the Norwegian Cabinet since 1935, my major political interests had been in the domestic field until the war, when I served first as Minister of Shipping and then as Foreign Minister in London. Since 1940 I had participated in many diplomatic negotiations and meetings of intricate character; but most of them had been in private, and nearly all were concerned with matters in which my country had a direct interest. What had been most important to me during those years was the common war against Nazism and the liberation of Norway. It seemed to me that presiding over the General Assembly of the United Nations would demand a profound experience in international relations and an expertness in the languages of diplomacy—qualifications I could not claim.

But a decision had to be made at once—a decision which would concern all of us as a family. At times like these, members of the Lie family have the habit of coming forward frankly with our own points of view, and now I found myself the most doubtful one present. The others were all but agreed that I could not possibly refuse permission to the American Delegation to suggest my name—a request which the Government of the United States now pressed a second time. So my answer was Yes. The message was scribbled out on a scrap of paper, and Knut was asked to send the telegram to the Foreign Ministry in Oslo.

Several hectic days followed my return to Oslo. I put the matter to the Cabinet, and it gave me authority to make a final decision in London on the American proposal.

After taking part in a conference of Scandinavian Social Democrats in Copenhagen, I arrived in London on January 8 and the American Delegation approached me that evening. In Oslo and in Copenhagen, following New Year's, I had had the impression that the United States, the Soviet Union, and Great Britain were agreed upon my candidature; but now I heard that Britain during the first stages actually had favored the Dutch Foreign Minister, Eelco van Kleffens, and for the last two months had been vigorously supporting Paul-Henri Spaak, the Foreign Minister of Belgium. Mr. Spaak's high abilities were unquestioned; moreover, he had taken part in the work of the Preparatory Commission, which had met in London in the autumn, with conspicuous success. I, on the other hand, had not been able to attend the Commission's sessions. After weighing the matter, I informed the representative of the American Delegation that I did not wish my candidacy to be considered further. Proposal of me as a candidate in opposition to my friend and associate of the war years, and to the wishes of Britain as well, would not serve Norway's interests.

On the morning of January 9 a special intermediary with the United States Delegation informed me that the Americans now regarded Mr. Spaak's election as certain, by a commanding majority. The United States would therefore refrain from trying to influence the Latin American delegations, who had 20 votes out of 51 in the Assembly and were in many instances strongly inclined to vote for Mr. Spaak; in fact, it had now decided against advancing my name for the presidency. I confirmed to my intermediary what I had told the Americans the night before, and added that I regarded the question of my candidacy as closed. My withdrawal, I explained, was determined by my conviction that Norway should not permit itself to be used as a football among the Great Powers.

On the morning of the 10th—the day on which the President of the Assembly was to be elected—Feodor T. Gousev, the Soviet Ambassador in London, sought me out. His delegation, he said, had been informed by the Americans of my withdrawal; nevertheless the U.S.S.R., together with its Eastern European associates, wanted to nominate me. He made it plain that Mr. Spaak was not acceptable to Moscow, and took no pains to conceal the reason why: the Soviet Union regarded him as an exponent of a Western European bloc. I suggested that conflict might be avoided if Dr. Eduardo Zuleta Angel of Colombia, who, as President of the Preparatory Commission, was temporarily presiding over the Assembly, were allowed to continue as President. But Mr. Gousev would have none of this. Rather, he reported, his delegation had conferred with the United States Delegation upon hearing of my withdrawal, and, as a result of the meeting, the Americans had agreed to revert to their original support of my candidacy. The Soviet Union would nominate me, he added, and the Americans would vote for me. I replied that I had understood that, if there were to be public nominations, it would be the United States that would propose me.

It should be explained that there had been a division of opinion in the Preparatory Commission as to whether public nominations of individuals for election to office by the General Assembly should be permitted. The provisional rules of procedure for the Assembly were not wholly clear on the point, but the consensus was that the provision for secret balloting was intended to rule out public nominations —on the theory, I suppose, that delegations would thereby have greater freedom from pressure by the Great Powers. The Soviet Delegation refused to go along with this procedure, and insisted on the right to make nominations, whereas the United States accepted the interpretation of the rules barring nomination. What happened, apparently, was that the United States had agreed with the Soviet Union to maintain its support of my candidacy but had not agreed to a public nomination.

This new turn indicated a rather alarming state of confusion about the election and especially about the position of the United States, hardly more than three hours before the Assembly was to meet. Delegation meetings were in progress in hotel rooms all over London, and I am afraid that many delegates had a picture of the state of affairs that was not at all clear. What was I to do now?

I left Gousev to attend the meeting of the Norwegian Delegation, already in progress. I put this question to my colleagues: In view of the reiterated support of the Soviet Union and of the United States, should I continue to oppose my being nominated for the presidency? The unanimous answer of the delegation was No; the U.S.S.R. or the United States might misinterpret such a refusal, to the damage of Norwegian interests. Thus it was decided that I should not object to the Russian or the American decision, and at the same time it was agreed that I should explain to the British why we arrived at this point of view.

The delegation came together again after lunch. I reported the dispatch of a message to the British Foreign Minister, Ernest Bevin, and Philip Noel-Baker, Minister of State, who were then in the midst of a cabinet meeting. At this stage, a telephone message informed us that the American Delegation was in conference as to whether it should recede from opposing public nominations to the extent of formally seconding my nomination should the U.S.S.R. in fact make it. The decision was not communicated to us until an hour later on the Assembly floor—by the action, or rather the inaction, of Secretary of State James F. Byrnes.

As we made our way to the Assembly hall at four o'clock, the whole question of nominations and seconds was still very much in

HOW I BECAME SECRETARY-GENERAL

doubt. The document which the Secretariat had circulated on balloting procedure tended to give the impression that public nominations would be out of order—that the procedure simply was for each delegation to inscribe its candidate's name on its secret ballot, but did not flatly say so. Neither I nor anyone else, I imagine, really knew what to expect; but I entered the Assembly hall resolved that, if Spaak were nominated as well as I, I would withdraw in his favor.

The opening day of a session of the General Assembly has since become a curious combination of pomp and circumstance with the very orderly and assured dispatch of purely procedural business. This occasion was a special one: the United Nations had been born in San Francisco, under the impact of the last victorious weeks of the war in Europe and amidst the highest hopes. Now the organization's supreme organ was starting its practical work, and in a few minutes' time it would begin taking its regular decisions, to be marked down in the records of the future as General Assembly Resolution number so-and-so.

It was both a climax and an anticlimax. Outside Central Hall, the open places and narrow streets of the City of Westminster had been filled with expectant crowds. Inside, even the foreign ministers and ambassadors could hardly conceal their personal interest in the event. The radio commentators were already reporting to the world from this new forum for world opinion; some newspaper correspondents had sent their preliminary dispatches on the likely course of the day's events, while the cameramen had directed their lights on the picturesque groups of Arab delegates, as became their habit thereafter. In the intense glare, the colors of the fifty-one Member States national flags came out beautifully, reminding us at once that the United Nations was to be an association of sovereign states as well as a joint force for achieving the purposes of the Charter. A handsome drapery in "Stettinius blue" of San Francisco days gave impulse to what later became the United Nations flag. It was an impressive and colorful scene.

Of orderly dispatch of routine business on this first day of the General Assembly's first session, however, there was to be little. Dr. Zuleta Angel opened the meeting, and Prime Minister Clement R. Attlee welcomed the delegates. The chairman then announced the next item on the agenda—the election of the President—but added that, before proceeding to the election, he would call upon Andrei A. Gromyko, the deputy chief of the Soviet delegation, who wished to make a statement on the subject.

Mr. Gromyko strode to the rostrum and declared:

"Weighing the candidatures which have recently been mentioned in connection with the election of the President . . . the Soviet Delegation has come to the conclusion that the most appropriate candidature would be that of the Foreign Minister of Norway, Mr. Trygve Lie.

"It is not necessary," he continued, "to dwell in detail upon the role of Norway in the war against our common enemy. Norway was one of the first victims of German aggression. The Norwegian people as a whole have shown that they are good fighters for democracy. . . . With regard to the personal qualities of Mr. Lie . . . I think that one would hardly doubt that Mr. Lie is a very capable and experienced statesman. . . . All this gives reason to believe that his candidature is quite suitable . . ."

There was a stir in the hall: Mr. Gromyko's characteristic seizure of the bull by the horns seemed to come as a surprise. The United Nations was still to grow accustomed to his matter-of-fact and rather stilted way of saying startling things. The press had been predicting the election of Paul-Henri Spaak: the British had, as usual, been quietly competent in spreading the word. Now the issue was in doubt.

Dr. Zuleta Angel retreated to the rules. He read out, *in extenso,* the relevant articles and the document which the staff of the Executive Secretary, Gladwyn Jebb, had prepared on balloting procedure. His choice of tellers was irreproachable: Dr. Ivan Kerno of Czechoslovakia, on the one hand, and Dr. Luis Padilla Nervo of Mexico, on the other. And then he concluded by saying that "the rules of procedure for the General Assembly do not exclude the presentation of candidates in the way that Mr. Gromyko has just done, but the view of the Assembly must be expressed by secret ballot."

The situation was tense. I remember looking at Mrs. Eleanor Roosevelt, sitting as one of the American delegates in the front row. This was her first appearance on the world stage in her own right—still in solemn black, reminding us of the world's irreparable loss in the death of her husband, who more than any other man deserved the name: "Father of the United Nations." The great role Eleanor Roosevelt herself was destined to play in the life of the United Nations was yet to be revealed to us.

Wincenty Rzymowski of Poland then rose in dutiful support of the nomination, and spoke of Norway and of me in generous terms. He was followed by Dmitri Z. Manuilsky, the "Old Bolshevik" from pre-Stalin days who was then Foreign Minister of the Ukrainian S.S.R., and was to be one of the United Nations' more dramatic personages in its first years. Mr. Manuilsky got off to an energetic start. Since no candidature had been put forth other than that of the Norwegian Minister of Foreign Affairs, he suggested, "the question of procedure is simplified. . . . I propose . . . that this election be made by acclamation." To the chairman's declaration a moment before that the view of the Assembly must be expressed by secret ballot, Mr. Manuilsky made no reference.

A moment's respite from this rapid fire of Soviet proposals was given by Gustav Rasmussen, the Foreign Minister of Denmark, who gracefully supported my nomination. Then the chairman, despite his injunction about the necessity of a secret ballot, announced that he would seek the Assembly's opinion on Mr. Manuilsky's proposal for election by acclamation. But he worded his question in the contrary sense: "Will those in favor of a secret ballot please raise their hands? Those against?" Before the vote could be counted, however, Dr. Zuleta Angel recognized Mr. Gromyko, who urged that the vote be taken on Mr. Manuilsky's motion to vote by acclamation. Dr. Zuleta Angel responded that this was precisely what the Assembly was in the midst of doing. The confusion was now complete; most people just sat on their hands, being quite unable to determine what they were voting for or against, while Mr. Manuilsky buoyantly voted both for and against his own proposal. The chairman announced the result as 15 voting in favor of a secret ballot and 9 for election by acclamation, with the majority not voting at all. He thereupon requested the chiefs of the delegations to write the names of their respective candidates for the presidency on the ballot papers which had been handed to them, and to deposit these in the ballot box one by one.

Tension mounted, and mine not least. I was pleased by the demonstration of Soviet good will toward Norway. I was embarrassed by the clumsiness of the Soviet attempt to push things through. I was disconcerted by the silence of my American friends. My candidacy was Washington's idea, but Mr. Byrnes had not made a move. I was not anxious to be publicly defeated by Mr. Spaak, and cared still less to defeat him. And yet I was the prisoner of events. I could hardly withdraw in favor of the Belgian candidate, because Mr. Spaak had not been nominated, and I did not know what might have happened to his candidacy in last-minute discussions.

The issue was quickly settled. Dr. Zuleta Angel announced that 51 Members voted: 28 for Mr. Spaak, and 23 for Mr. Lie. I was both relieved and discontented. It had been a tough day. I soon withdrew to evaluate the situation with a few friends, and we started speculating on the meaning of the events of the day.

There is no doubt that the results of that election were felt long after, and clearly influenced the subsequent election of the Secretary-General. The battle which followed over the rules of procedure, was of little importance. By a majority of one vote, the rules were amended so as to exclude open nominations; but, because of the secrecy of the preliminary diplomatic discussions, the procedures that day gave material from which the nonsensical tale was woven, by those who were interested in discrediting the United Nations, that I was "Moscow's man."

While I had many reasons to be glad of the result, I naturally ruminated over what might have been. It was a close election: a shift of 3 votes out of 51, and I, rather than Mr. Spaak, would have been President. *If* the United States had spoken out in the Assembly in support of my candidacy as it had spoken out to me in August, in December, and that very day, *if* Mr. Byrnes had not sat there tight-lipped, then, the result might well have been otherwise. American press criticism of what was called a United States "run-out" was severe, and after the election I was approached by Adlai Stevenson, who with his customary gentility expressed his regrets at the outcome. Even if a public word from the American Delegation might not have altered the election, it would certainly have removed the false impression that I was first and foremost the candidate of the Soviet bloc.

Equally, if the Russians had said nothing, if the Assembly had been spared their blunt maneuvers, the outcome might again have been different. It was suggested in the press that several smaller Powers so resented Soviet—and particularly Mr. Manuilsky's—railroading that they decided then and there to vote for Mr. Spaak; we both were Social Democratic Foreign Ministers of small Western European countries and in many cases equally unknown.

As it was, the first day of United Nations electioneering did not leave a favorable impression upon the public mind or upon me. I had not sought the presidency and was glad that Mr. Spaak and not I would now have to carry the burdens of that office; but I disliked having been trapped into a contest with him, and the way in which the whole affair had been handled that day.

I did not know then, of course, that had the outcome been different someone other than Trygve Lie would have been the first Secretary-General of the United Nations. The possibility that I might ever assume that office had not entered my head, and if it had, my personal reluctance to assume the great responsibilities of the post would have exceeded the doubts I had felt about the presidency. I paid no attention—at first—when, the presidency being settled, speculation in the press included me among the names mentioned for the office of Secretary-General. This had happened before, and I had put it down merely to the speculative capacity of industrious newsmen counting up the available possibilties. No delegate had approached me or my colleagues in the Norwegian delegation with any query as to my availability. On the contrary I myself took soundings on behalf of another.

During the war I had formed a warm friendship for Anthony Eden. I had known and admired his courageous stand against the prevailing mood of his own Conservative party in the later 1930's, his opposition to appeasement and effort to revitalize the League of Nations and make it a real force for collective security against aggression before it was too late. We had been together during the five years of war as well as the early days of the San Francisco Conference. Now he was out of office as Foreign Secretary, and I regarded him as an ideal choice for Secretary-General. I am not sure that he would have accepted, but he did not object when I told him I should like to sound out the Labor Government and Moscow.

However, the matter was never pressed, for I was quickly given to understand that the Labor Government in Britain was not favorably disposed.

In the Preparatory Commission days there had been many preliminary private discussions of other names among the delegations. During these discussions Philip Noel-Baker, the British chief delegate to the Commission, had strongly urged consideration of General of the Army Dwight D. Eisenhower. This suggestion at once attracted wide support; but it came to nothing for two reasons.

In the first place, the prevailing view was that the Secretary-General should not be chosen from any of the Big Five Powers. The Charter had given the office of Secretary-General political responsibilities in the promotion and preservation of peace that the Secretary-General of the League of Nations did not possess. In the exercise of these responsibilities the Secretary-General of the United Nations must use his influence, not for the interests of any nation or group of nations, but for the interests of the Organization as a whole as he saw them. Thus the Charter brought to the conduct of international affairs something unknown in the world before—an office held by one man who must be at once the symbol of the collective struggle for peace and spokesman for a world interest overriding any national interests in the councils of the nations. At best this would be a most difficult and pioneering role, calling for the exploration of much untried ground. Furthermore the Charter provided that all the Big Five Powers (the United States, the U.S.S.R., the United Kingdom, France, and China) must agree in the Security Council on the nomination of the man to be elected to the office by the General Assembly. All this pointed to the desirability of choosing the first Secretary-General from among the smaller nations not so directly involved on one side or another in the power struggles of the world. It must be said that this view became crystallized only in the course of the London discussions. England and France, the most important and influential members of the League of Nations, had in succession provided its first two Secretaries-General. This precedent no doubt was in Mr. Noel-Baker's mind when he proposed General Eisenhower, who, besides being immensely popular in Europe as the former supreme commander of the victorious coalition armies of the West, had gained a high reputation for devotion to the cause of

HOW I BECAME SECRETARY-GENERAL 13

peace and ability to conciliate and unite varying national interests and policies. My own advocacy of Mr. Eden indicates that I did not at that time necessarily rule out a statesman of one of the Great Powers. But the latter view prevailed as the discussions proceeded.

The second reason why the suggestion of General Eisenhower came to nothing was related to the location of Permanent Headquarters. No decision had been made on this question at San Francisco, and the Preparatory Commission had debated long whether the Headquarters should be in the United States or Europe. I shall return to this in Chapter IV. In the meantime it suffices to recall that the Preparatory Commission finally decided in favor of the United States. Once this decision had been made, it was generally agreed that the Secretary-General should not be an American, because this would give too much to a single Member nation. Indeed one of the arguments in favor of Europe during the Preparatory Commission discussions was that the Headquarters should not be located in the United States because that would rule out General Eisenhower as the Secretary-General.

The United States itself took the view that an American should not be Secretary-General. At General Eisenhower's request the United States Delegation announced that he was not a candidate; and it fell to none other than Adlai Stevenson, as the principal American representative in the negotiations over the Secretary-Generalship, to throw cold water on the proposal. "A candidate for Secretary-General seriously proposed at one time during the long negotiations in London by Philip Noel-Baker was General Eisenhower," Mr. Stevenson wrote later. "The United States, assuming that the seat of the United Nations would be in this country, took no part in furthering the appointment of an American as Secretary-General."

During the days that followed the opening of the Assembly session, the consultations about the post of Secretary-General became increasingly active. My name continued to crop up in newspaper speculation, but the first approach to me occurred at an American Delegation reception. Two Australian delegates, the undaunted war veteran with scars from Gallipoli, Colonel W. R. Hodgson, then Australian Minister to France, and Norman J. O. Makin, the Minister for Navy, intimated that the Australian Minister for External

Affairs, Herbert V. Evatt, had instructed them to put forward my name. Australia, it should be explained, had just been elected to one of the six nonpermanent seats on the Security Council and thus would have a direct part in the Security Council's consideration of nominations. The impression was conveyed to me that, while Evatt might have so directed for a reason of his own, the Americans were associated with the proposal.

I remained noncommittal, but then came other hints, suggestions, and attempts at persuasion. The deepest impression on me was made by a strong appeal from Peter Fraser, the Labor Party Prime Minister of New Zealand, and—like Field Marshal Smuts—Grand Old Man of the Commonwealth. He spoke up one evening in the home of a close friend of mine, William H. Stoneman of the Chicago *Daily News.* "You can't escape from this job, and you mustn't," he insisted. Mr. Fraser had been at the San Francisco Conference and was known by all as a stanch defender of the rights of the small nations. I not only respected the New Zealand Prime Minister; I had a warm affection for him. His advice was received as that of a father, and I trusted it the more because we shared a similar political background.

"This United Nations is the greatest undertaking of our time," he said. "People of our kind must support it and take on what is required of us." "What about yourself?" I asked. "Too old," he grinned, sadly. Several outstanding newspapermen were present at this party, all eager to give advice—or to sound me out.

There were other conversations in the whirlwind of meetings, dinners, and receptions of the London Assembly. Once, at the British Government's official dinner for the Assembly at St. James's Palace, Anthony Eden introduced me to Sir Ramaswami Mudaliar, the Chief Delegate of India, with the following words: "Mr. Lie would be a very good Secretary-General." I was embarrassed, though I appreciated his kindness.

One day I discussed the whole matter openly and honestly with Jan Masaryk, my wartime colleague and very close friend who continued as Foreign Minister of Czechoslovakia. He, too, had been suggested as a candidate; but, as he said: "My political skin is a good deal darker than yours." We finally agreed that this was an office none of us would seek, nor could we take it on—if pressed—

HOW I BECAME SECRETARY-GENERAL

with any particular pleasure. Aside from Peter Fraser, with his fatherly prodding, there was another person whose opinions carried considerable weight with me—especially with my personal views now beginning to take a more positive course. I refer to John G. Winant, former Director-General of the International Labor Office, and wartime Ambassador of the United States to the Court of St. James's. He earnestly counseled me to accept the Secretary-Generalship, if called upon. Mr. Winant did not hide his concern for the future of the world, or about the burdens of such an office. But, he maintained, I had no right to refuse. I should rather thank the Almighty for such an opportunity to serve.

The approaches and inquiries continued from many sides, and the interest of the United States in my availability was indicated to me in many ways, although I was not told directly that I was their choice. Much later I learned that the United States had long had a list of desirable candidates for both the Presidency of the General Assembly and the Secretary-Generalship. From this list they had selected me as their first choice for the Presidency of the Assembly. For Secretary-General their first choice was Lester B. Pearson of Canada, whose exceptional abilities were to lead later to his designation as Canadian Minister of External Affairs, Chairman of the North Atlantic Treaty Organization Council, and President of the 7th Session of the General Assembly. After I had been defeated for the Presidency of the Assembly I was made number two on the American list for Secretary-General. I did not know this at the time, nor did I know that in the private Big Five consultations Mr. Stettinius had urged the Soviet Union to agree to Mr. Pearson, and that Andrei Y. Vyshinsky had responded by proposing Stanoje Simič, a former member of the Yugoslav Government-in-Exile who had been appointed Foreign Minister in the original government established under Marshal Tito (Josip Broz) after the liberation of Yugoslavia, and that neither was acceptable to the other party. I have often wondered how the Soviet Government would have felt, after the break with Tito in 1948, if by any chance Mr. Simič had been acceptable to the Western Powers!

At all events, the information brought to the Norwegian Delegation meeting on January 25 was simply to the effect that the names of Messrs. Pearson and Simič, Foreign Ministers Eelco van Kleffens of the Netherlands and Wincenty Rzymowski of Poland, Henri Bonnet of France and Trygve Lie were under consideration in the negotiations among the eleven members of the Security Council. Australia had sponsored my name. This sounded serious. It was agreed that we could no longer let matters drift: a prompt decision as to whether I should accept the office, if offered, would have to be taken. I was authorized to fly to Norway to confer with the Prime Minister, and I did so the very next day. But before my departure I consulted among the Great Power delegations. Both the United States and the Soviet Delegations encouraged me to go and clearly indicated their favorable attitude toward me for the Secretary-Generalship.

After my departure, events seem to have moved even more swiftly. Political objections led to the elimination of all the main parties' first candidates, and agreement on a compromise was hinted in all quarters. It appeared that Mr. Pearson would have received eight ballots in a Security Council vote; but Moscow had made it clear that Mr. Pearson was not acceptable. So Mr. Stettinius, with the Soviet elimination of Mr. Pearson, could meet Mr. Vyshinsky halfway; the compromise candidate of both Washington and Moscow was the Foreign Minister of Norway. As a matter of fact, neither party compromised much. Certainly the Soviet Union did not see its Yugoslav, Mr. Simič, as a serious contender, and I think Washington would have been surprised if Moscow had accepted a Canadian as the first Secretary-General, especially in view of the Preparatory Commission's vote to locate United Nations headquarters in North America.

Mr. Stettinius took the formal initiative. On January 28, he called a meeting of the Big Five, and proposed designating me. Mr. Gromyko was agreeable; the Chinese did not object. The French accepted the Norwegian candidate provisionally, pending approval by the cabinet in Paris the following day. But it was not until twelve-thirty in the morning of January 29, 1946, in Mr. Stettinius' suite in Claridges that my wartime friend and old trade-union colleague, Ernest Bevin, was finally brought around to promising that he would recommend my candidacy to the British Government.

The venerable Joseph Paul-Boncour obtained the concurrence of Foreign Minister Georges Bidault by telephone during the night.

The British cabinet met the next morning and agreed to my nomination. On the afternoon of January 29, the full Security Council met at Church House, and unanimously adopted the motion of Mr. Stettinius nominating me as Secretary-General. I received a cable in Oslo asking if I would accept the nomination and requesting a reply to the Council president, Mr. Makin, at my earliest convenience. Under the circumstances I could hardly refuse. On February 1 the General Assembly met and appointed me, by a vote of 46 to 3, as the first Secretary-General of the United Nations. I was sworn in the following day.

I had been nothing less than catapulted into the Secretary-Generalship of this new international organization, to preserve peace and promote progress in a world beset by unrest, poverty, and great-power rivalry. It was a challenge beyond my wildest dreams; but it was a nightmare as well. I hardly dared to think of the days ahead. Instead, I asked myself again and again, Why had this awesome task fallen to a labor lawyer from Norway?

On the surface, the facts were clear and gratifying: my appointment was the product of a meeting of minds of Moscow and Washington and had been ratified by virtual unanimity among the Member states; furthermore, the original suggestion of my name for any United Nations office had come from the United States.

Norway had many friends in Washington. The two countries had always been on most friendly terms, and the Norwegian Government cooperated closely with the Americans during the war years. I myself had experienced that good will when I first visited America in 1940 as Minister of Shipping and received considerable American help toward arming the Norwegian merchant marine, through which we made our main contribution to the Allied cause; our fleet of 1,000 ships and 30,000 brave sailors was once generously described as equal in importance to an army of a million men. On a 1943 visit for my government to President Franklin D. Roosevelt, I found him surprisingly well informed on Norway's position—a fact doubtless in no small part due to personal friendship with the Norwegian Crown Prince Olav and Crown Princess Märtha—then resident in Bethesda, and to the untiring efforts of our Ambassador, Wilhelm Morgenstierne. It was easy for me then, as Norway's spokesman, to reach the necessary understandings with America.

After all, we did not come as beggars: our war efforts were a self-liquidating operation; we also took care of the interest and other payments on prewar loans. All the time, reports of achievements by our resistance movement at home found their way across the ocean and seemed to impress the Americans a good deal.

Norway, I concluded, had a good standing in American political circles, and the Foreign Minister of Norway—whatever his name— might not be an unnatural choice by Americans when candidates from small countries were sought for high offices in the United Nations.

As to my own position, I had loyal friends who might have given their opinion. My habit of frankness in discussions did not always please the British; but it may have disturbed Americans less. My political views, as a Social Democrat, were fully known. But as early as December, 1940, I had advocated extensive cooperation between Europe and North America in the postwar world. After becoming Minister of Foreign Affairs I had even drawn fire from some good Norwegians who were working for our cause in neutral Sweden for leaning too much toward the Western world. During complicated military negotiations toward the end of the war, I had met men like Generals George C. Marshall and Dwight D. Eisenhower and Harry Hopkins, and got along very well with them.

The Russian reasoning is always more difficult to understand. Even after seven years as Secretary-General, I cannot pretend to speak with assurance as to how the Soviet mind is made up. Let me simply make a guess as to the probabilities. First of all, Moscow had to agree upon a man whom the West—above all, the United States —would be prepared to accept. A Yugoslav, a Pole—any such proposal was a negotiatory device, and nothing more. Moscow would have to find a man who, without being committed to the East, was not hostile to it; and it felt that the Norwegian Foreign Minister was such a man. I had always been scrupulously correct toward the Soviet Union during the war, as of course any sane Foreign Minister of Norway would be. It was my hope that our huge Soviet neighbor would respond in kind.

In those London years, I dealt with the Big Three equitably, as far as circumstances would permit. Problems were sometimes delicate, as when we had to deal with American generosity, British military red tape, and Russian suspicion during the negotiations for Norway's liberation. It was mainly a question of determining when the military should withdraw and yield administrative power, allowing Norwegian civil authorities to take over. But once agreement had been reached among the British, the Americans and ourselves, I informed Soviet Ambassador Alexandre E. Bogomolov that Norway hoped to enter into a similar agreement with the Soviet Union. To our satisfaction, a reply from Moscow came almost at once. On May 16, 1944, I had the pleasure of signing identical agreements covering the liberation of Norway with the United States, the United Kingdom, and the U.S.S.R. The other signatory Powers were represented by General Eisenhower, Mr. Eden and Ambassador Bogomolov. Perhaps a mark of the Soviet appreciation of this equal treatment was Soviet evacuation of northern Norway in exemplary style in 1945.

But this relationship was nothing new. My country's traditional good-neighborly relations with Russia had lasted centuries. In fact, Norway is one of the few European countries which have never been at war with Russia. Furthermore, in 1922, during the critical period when the young Soviet Republics were still struggling for survival, the Norwegian Liberal Government under Johan Ludwig Mowinckel had extended diplomatic recognition to the new regime. For a time after the revolution and the subsequent wars of intervention, motor launches between the port of Murmansk and the old Norwegian border town of Vardö had provided almost the only communication link between the Soviet Union and the outside world. Russians during the war told me that they remembered this very well. Several of them had been terribly seasick during the crossing.

As to my personal position vis-à-vis the Kremlin—if an individual counts with the Soviet masters—matters were more complicated. Truly I had, in the period before my service as Secretary-General, an entrée into the Kremlin which few non-Communists have had. I met most of the leading Russian Communists, including Lenin, in the course of my visits to Moscow in 1921, 1934, and 1944. I had also been an ardent anti-fascist and anti-nazi during all my mature life, at every opportunity condemning the aggressive ideologies of these movements, not least as regards their first victims, the working classes and the Jews. The Norwegian quislings certainly had let me feel their wrath, both before and after their open treachery, and I had even received the distinction of being referred to as a dangerous subject in a memorandum from Herr Adolf Hitler. On the other hand, Moscow must have been aware of my long record as an anti-Communist. I had fought the Norwegian Communists wherever they appeared in the Norwegian labor movement. As legal consultant to the Federation of Trade Unions I had challenged, in and out of court, the Communists' attempts to take over meeting halls, printing plants, bank accounts, and the like. I had never been popular among Norwegian Communists; in fact, they made me a frequent target for attacks during the twenties and thirties. In 1937, as Minister of Justice, I had to expel Leon Trotsky from Norway for betrayal of the conditions for asylum there. Some critics later asserted that this showed I did Stalin's bidding; they forgot that, a year before, over Stalin's protest, I also had been responsible as Minister of Justice for admitting the hunted and sick revolutionary when he asked for asylum. Nor was there any doubt about my stand during the Russo-Finnish War of 1939–1940. I came out publicly in favor of Finland and, as Minister of Supply, repeatedly sought to give material assistance. In fact, I knew that my strong stand for the Finnish cause had displeased Moscow.

It must have been my wartime record, and especially the position of my country as represented by me, I concluded, that had been decisive—besides the Soviet willingness to make some compromises at the time in order to get the world organization going.

The United Kingdom's negative attitude was more of a surprise, particularly as I had become fond of the British during my stay among them from 1940 to 1945. I had enjoyed a most friendly co-operation with their great war leaders. I had made lasting, personal friendships in all fields. At the same time, I had frequently had good reason to contest British attitudes toward the smaller allies, mainly when the vested interests of the bureaucracy made themselves too strongly felt. Such questions had in most cases been solved amicably on a high level. But now my closest personal friends in the wartime Cabinet had been defeated in the 1945 elections. New people had taken their places. As the Labor Government was still new in the saddle, I concluded that it had to lean more heavily than its predecessor on the advice of the very civil servants who, I knew, had frequently complained during the war about Mr. Lie "by-passing" them and taking matters straight to Mr. Eden and even to Winston Churchill.

On the evening of my first day as Secretary-General I went out in the streets of London, together with my wife and our daughters Sissel and Guri, who had joined us when I returned from Oslo. It was odd to be in London again, on the way to another "exile." Here we had spent most of the five long years of war. We had joined the Londoners in the defense of their city, and had shared their sorrows of gutted homes and crippled lives. We had also shared their joys of victory. Now, as then, we felt ourselves one with the British people, who had been the first to come to Norway's aid when we were attacked.

It was from the hopes and faith of the people in all countries, I decided, that I might be able to draw the strength for the ordeal and the challenge that lay ahead.

CHAPTER II

THE WARTIME ALLIANCE BEGINS TO BREAK UP

The enigma of great-power unity.—First round offers hope for continuing accord.—Vyshinsky and Bevin clash in Security Council.—The Soviet casts its first veto.—"Iron Curtain" is sighted from Fulton, Missouri.—How to take things as they are?

A FEW days before the election for Secretary-General, during the General Assembly debate on the report of the Preparatory Commission, I had expressed Norway's attitude toward the United Nations. Some spokesmen for the smaller countries had criticized the special position and dominant role of the great powers, with permanent seats and rights of veto in the Security Council. My speech stressed the opinion that assurance of peace lay not in the division of the world into blocs, but in unity among the great powers. "The great powers must play the leading role in the Security Council . . . smaller nations should aim at making a sincere contribution to the mutual understanding and confidence of the great powers."

This had been the position of Norway at the San Francisco Conference eight months before. The chiefs of the great-power delegations alternated as presidents of the Conference, at the Opera House in that beautiful city, and Vyacheslav M. Molotov was in the chair on May 2, when my turn came to speak in the opening debate. Victory was in the air. Indeed, the unconditional surrender of Germany took place just six days later, and I flew back to London to join in discharging the many responsibilities that lay upon my government in connection with the liberation of Norway, the surrender of the Germans there, and the restoration of the country to civilian control.

My speech at San Francisco had begun by pointing out that the coming Allied victory and the liberation of Norway could not have been achieved without the immense contributions of *all* the great powers, especially of the United Kingdom, the United States, and the Soviet Union. Then:

"It is my firm conviction that victory, which will soon be ours, has only been made possible by the trustful cooperation and understanding between the great powers, and I believe it imperative that the future peace and security be built on the same foundation. As we stood together in the war, we must stand together in peace.

"We Norwegians have come here to assist and not to offer negative criticism. We know that the Dumbarton Oaks Proposals are not perfect, and we welcome a number of the amendments that have been suggested. But even if the Charter as molded at this Conference will not correspond to all our desires and ideas, we hope that the building of a new security order will be started under such conditions that in the future it may be further developed in a process of continuous creation."

I saw no intrinsic conflict of interests between the large and small nations. Reminding my colleagues among the small-power delegations that "in any new world order the great powers will have to shoulder the main burden of providing the military and material means for maintaining peace," I also stressed that strong international cooperation for economic progress, social justice, and human rights through the new Organization would be of equal importance.

In these words I expressed deeply held personal convictions as well as the views of the Norwegian Government. Naturally, even then, I foresaw a succession of problems and difficulties ahead—new challenges would always be rising in mankind's ceaseless struggle for peace, freedom, and progress; but I hoped strongly, with all the peoples and most of their leaders, that the great-power alliance would hold together in spite of some strains and stresses already beginning to appear. I hoped that the war would be followed by prompt peace settlements, firmly establishing the United Nations as the supreme authority for the maintenance of peace and as the center of international efforts for a new and better world order.

I had no doubt that the real interests of peoples all over the world were in this direction. Certainly there could be no doubt of the interests of the smaller countries, who are buffeted about in great-power conflicts and often are first to suffer in great wars; and it seemed to me that the interests of all the great powers, whatever their differences over ideology and spheres of influence, were equally engaged. Surely, after suffering such nearly mortal wounds and making such immense sacrifices, their overriding interest must be to settle their differences in a fair and sensible manner and see to it that no such terrible holocaust should visit the world again.

During the weeks and months that followed San Francisco my hopes faded somewhat; but they were still strong when the first Assembly began its sessions in London. After I had left San Francisco the fight over the veto developed—a three-way fight in which many of the smaller countries sought to modify the veto in important respects, while the Big Five remained firmly together on the Yalta formula but split when the Soviet Union attempted to assert so restrictive an interpretation that the veto could have prevented even the hearing of a complaint by the Security Council. I myself regretted that the Yalta formula applied the right of veto even to decisions by the Security Council concerning the peaceful settlement of disputes; but I was prepared to accept it as a great-power agreement essential to the establishment of the United Nations.

The United States Delegation, under the leadership of Mr. Stettinius and Senator Arthur H. Vandenberg, originated the provisions of Articles 10 and 14 of the Charter under which "The General Assembly may discuss any questions or any matters within the scope of the present Charter" and may also "recommend measures for the peaceful adjustment of any situation, regardless of origin, which it deems likely to impair the general welfare or friendly relations among nations." This was broad language indeed, a wide mandate to the General Assembly to exert its influence as the "Town Meeting of the World" should the veto be abused in the Security Council. Furthermore the Soviet Union agreed to these Assembly amendments. When Molotov and Gromyko could not be budged from their assertion of the right to veto discussion in the Security Council, Harry Hopkins went over their heads to Generalissimo Stalin in Moscow with an urgent message from President Truman. Stalin promptly overruled Molotov and accepted the position of the Western powers. The crisis was over, and the Charter was signed a few days later—on June 26, 1945.

Reading the dispatches from our delegation about all this in London and in Oslo, I was disturbed by the rigidity of Molotov's position and the stubbornness with which he held on almost to the point of forcing a last-minute breakdown of the San Francisco Conference. But the Soviet Union had yielded in the end and had, besides, willingly agreed to strengthening the Assembly's position. Here, I felt, was a warning of other difficulties ahead but also, and more important, evidence that sufficient cooperation between the Communist and non-Communist powers in the effort to make the United Nations fulfill its intended role would be forthcoming.

Further developments in the world situation during the summer and fall indicated future trouble for the United Nations; but others held out hope. On one side was the fact that the Soviet Union, in all the countries of Eastern Europe liberated from the Nazis by its armies, except Czechoslovakia, had gone back on the Yalta agreements for genuinely free elections under joint Allied supervision. The West had been shut out, and Soviet military control employed ruthlessly to put Communist governments into power. The Soviet conduct in Poland, for which Britain and France had gone to war in 1939, was an especially sore point to the West—and rightly so, for the Western great powers had made every effort toward reasonable compromise both at Yalta and at Potsdam in securing for Poland a coalition government friendly to Russia yet genuinely representative of the Polish people. But the Russians had military control, and they used it. The West had no countervailing power short of war by which to back up its protests.

The Potsdam Conference in July, and the first Council of Foreign Ministers in London in September, also were disappointments. Both ended in disagreements on the main issues. The prospects for an early final settlement for Germany were dimmed, though none of us then realized how many years were to pass without real peace in Europe, with Germany continuing to be divided East and West and occupied by armies facing each other in suspicion and hostility. There were other points of trouble and friction, too—in Greece, Trieste, Indo-China, the East Indies, Malaya, and elsewhere.

On the other side there were some hopeful signs. Czechoslovakia, although entirely inside the Soviet military line in Germany, had been left free. Those good and great democrats Eduard Beneš and Jan Masaryk, my long-time friend, were in power as President and as Foreign Minister. In the Government and people of Czechoslovakia the Soviet Union had a living and vital demonstration that it was possible to have a friendly nation on its borders that was free and not a satellite. I hoped that this experience would lead in time to an understanding on the part of the highly security-conscious and suspicion-ridden Soviet government that genuine friendship from its smaller neighbors was better and safer for Russia than the hatred and resentment engendered by satellite governments imposed and maintained by Russian arms. There was also Finland, left comparatively free although wholly within Soviet military power. And there was Norway's own experience with the exemplary manner in which Soviet troops had been withdrawn from the northern part of the country after our liberation, in strict conformity to the agreement I had signed with Soviet Ambassador Bogomolov in London in 1944.

I recall something that Andrei Vyshinsky said in the course of a conversation in London just before my election as Secretary-General. It was a most friendly talk in which Vyshinsky said that both the Soviet Union and the United States warmly advocated my nomination, and that Mr. Bevin could be "brought around." He emphasized his pleasure at the excellent relations between the Soviet Union and Norway, and I replied that Norway was free from Russophobia.

"You have no reason," Vyshinsky rejoined, "to entertain fear of Soviet imperialism."

Another hopeful development occurred at the second Foreign Ministers' Meeting, at Moscow in December, 1945. The atomic bombs that were dropped on Nagasaki and Hiroshima and brought the Pacific War to a sudden end had been developed by the combined efforts of the United States, the United Kingdom, and Canada. Troubled by the revolutionary implications in war and peace of the harnessing of this awesome source of energy, President Truman, Prime Minister Attlee and Prime Minister Mackenzie King had met in Washington and issued a declaration on November 15 proposing

THE WARTIME ALLIANCE BEGINS TO BREAK UP

the creation of a United Nations Commission which would seek the means by which atomic energy could be so controlled that it would be used only for peaceful purposes of benefiting mankind and not for war.

At Moscow the Soviet Union agreed to join the other three powers in sponsoring a draft resolution to establish such a commission.

The resolution was introduced at the First Assembly session and adopted unanimously on January 24, the day before I first realized how likely it was that I would be elected Secretary-General. Thus, on this greatest of challenges to the survival of civilization in the second half of the twentieth century—the capacity of mankind to prevent its own self-destruction in atomic war—the great powers, East and West, had joined hands at least in the first step of general principle and procedure.

But London was simultaneously the scene of a disturbing development in the opposite direction. First let me explain that there had been a general understanding that the first sessions of the United Nations in London should be primarily organizational in character. Political problems and questions of substance concerning future economic and social programs and the Trusteeship system, should be left to a later date, after the United Nations had been established in at least interim headquarters and the organization of a permanent Secretariat had been sufficiently advanced. Indeed, this was the way things had gone, at first, with a minimum of "East-West" controversy. With minor exceptions, the elections to the Security Council and the Economic and Social Council had gone smoothly according to agreed "slates" negotiated in advance. The results of these first United Nations elections, too, had shown the truly comprehensive character of the world organization. All the continents, cultures, forms of government and social structure, all the power and regional groupings of the world, were represented—as they have since been, though not always in the same proportions. I give here the results of these first elections because they formed a pattern that persisted through the events recorded in this book. The pattern, if given only the briefest reflection, shows the complexity and clash of attitude and interest comprehended within the United Nations efforts for peace, understanding, and cooperation.

THE SECURITY COUNCIL

PERMANENT MEMBERS
United States (North American and Western democracies)
U.S.S.R. (Eurasian Communist Empire)
United Kingdom (Western democratic Empire)
China (Asia)
France (Western democratic Europe)

ELECTED MEMBERS
Brazil (Latin America)
Mexico (Latin America)
Egypt (Arab-Moslem world)
The Netherlands (Western democratic Europe)
Poland (Eastern Europe)
Australia (British Commonwealth)

THE ECONOMIC AND SOCIAL COUNCIL

Belgium, Norway, France, Greece (Western democratic Europe)
China, India (Asia—third of world's population)
Lebanon (Arab-Moslem world)
U.S.S.R., Ukrainian S.S.R. (Eurasian Communist Empire)
Chile, Colombia, Cuba, Peru (Latin America)
Canada (British Commonwealth)
Czechoslovakia (still Western but Soviet ally)
Yugoslavia (Balkan Communist)
United Kingdom (Western democratic Empire)
United States (North American and Western democratic)

Besides the comparatively smooth sailing of these elections and of the Assembly action on the organizational report of the Preparatory Commission, there had been the agreement between the United States and the U.S.S.R. on me, the Foreign Minister of Norway, first for President of the Assembly and then for Secretary-General. But the plans for an organizational and procedural London meeting went awry in the Security Council.

The Council had held its first meeting—a purely formal affair on January 17—and was not generally expected to do much else in London. But then the hard realities of world politics intruded. Like gusts of wind warning of future storms to come, they blew in the door of the new-built house of peace before the workmen had finished. The first blow came from Iran (Persia). That ancient kingdom on the road to India had been for a century disputed ground between the spheres of influence of the British Empire and the outward-pushing Empire of Russia. The Russian Revolution did not change this for long. Iran continued precariously to maintain its integrity and independence by balancing predominant British influence over the southern part of the country with its immense oil refinery at Abadan and in the capital at Teheran against predominant Russian influence in the northern provinces where the Soviet and Iranian borders meet near the Caspian Sea.

After the Soviet Union and the United States came into the war, Iran assumed new importance to the Allied cause as the only possible land passage by which American Lend-Lease and British military supplies could reach the Soviet Union. Aside from Iran there was only the dangerous sea passage to Murmansk through Arctic waters around the top of Norway. To run this life line through Iran, and secure it, a Tripartite Treaty had been signed under which Russian troops moved into the north and American and British troops into the south. The treaty provided for the withdrawal of these troops within a fixed period after the end of the war. The deadline was March 2, 1946, a date to which we shall have occasion to refer later. In January, however, it was not yet a question of the withdrawal of troops. The Iranian government was concerned with a separatist movement in the northern province, Azerbaijan, and suspected the Russians, who were in control, of encouraging it as a first step in detaching the province from Iran and attaching it to the racially kindred and adjacent Soviet Republic of Azerbaijan.

The government probably consulted the British, and also the Americans, as to what to do. It had been exchanging notes with Moscow but felt it was being put off, and its fears and suspicions grew stronger. I do not know how the decision was reached, but on January 19 the Security Council received from the Iranian delegate its first formal complaint, charging Soviet interference in the internal affairs of Azerbaijan and a refusal to negotiate. The Soviet Union promptly denied any interference and asserted that it had always been, and continued to be, ready to negotiate with Iran; but its reaction was by no means confined to a defense. It saw that the Security Council of the United Nations would begin its work by considering a charge directed straight against the Soviet Union, one of the great powers upon whose unity the security provisions of the Charter were supposed to rest. Furthermore the Soviet leaders must have concluded immediately that the complaint was brought with the full support of at least the United Kingdom—and perhaps the United States.

The riposte was immediate. Two days later, on January 21, Mr. Vyshinsky filed a complaint by the Soviet Union against the United Kingdom, charging interference by British troops in the internal affairs of Greece. Simultaneously Dmitri Manuilsky of the Ukrainian S.S.R. filed a similar complaint against the United Kingdom, charging that British troops were used to suppress the nationalist movement in the newly liberated Dutch East Indies (now the Republic of Indonesia). Note that both complaints were against interference by British troops in the internal affairs of other countries. If the Soviet Union was to be arraigned before the bar of the world organization, then Britain should be arraigned too—and on a two-for-one basis at that!

So here we were, right in the middle of a great-power war of maneuver and propaganda in the United Nations before the "cold war" had started, before that term had even been invented. I was greatly disturbed, feeling that the Iranian government should have given direct negotiation a longer trial. After all, Norway had had a very positive and satisfactory experience with the withdrawal of Soviet troops. A little more private prodding would probably bring results. I had no sympathy with the Soviet counter complaints. The British were present in Greece only at the request of the legal Greek government; and later United Nations investigations were to show conclusively that it was not the British, but the Communist governments of Bulgaria, Albania, and Yugoslavia that were interfering in Greek internal affairs—in support of the Communist wing of the Greek partisans. As for the Dutch East Indies, Manuilsky had been an active promoter of the Communist movement there in the old Comintern days, and I looked upon his complaint as a reversion to that old role in behalf of Communist efforts to capture control of the Indonesian nationalist movement.

The Security Council had completed its consideration of the Iranian complaint before I took office as Secretary-General and assumed my seat at the horseshoe-shaped Council table in Church House. Thanks largely to the moderating influence of Mr. Stettinius, this first United Nations East-West debate ended quickly on January 30 in a unanimous resolution introduced by the United Kingdom and amended by the U.S.S.R. The Council simply noted and approved the expressed willingness of both sides to settle the question by direct negotiation and requested them to inform the Council of the results.

The Council then turned to the Soviet complaint against the British in Greece; and in this debate I received my baptism of fire. I shall not soon forget that first day at which I was present as Secretary-General. Mr. Vyshinsky attacked strongly. British troops, he alleged, were in Greece not by necessity, but to exert pressure on Greek internal political affairs—a "circumstance . . . frequently used by reactionary elements in Greece against the democratic forces of the country." Mr. Vyshinsky spoke of the "fascist scum which rule" in Greece; charged that they ruled with and by British support; maintained that "such a situation constitutes a grave danger to the maintenance of peace and security"; and demanded that the Security Council call upon the United Kingdom to withdraw its troops at once.

Mr. Bevin, the veteran trade-union leader, who had become His Majesty's Secretary of State for Foreign Affairs upon the great victory of the Labor Party in the 1945 elections, had a sound case. He frankly said that a civil war had been launched in Greece primarily by the Communists, seeking to obtain minority rule over that country. He affirmed that British troops had not imposed any government upon Greece, but had rather helped in resisting an attempt at an armed coup which would prevent the Greek people from freely choosing their rulers. All this was true and needed saying; but Mr. Bevin's manner caused me concern. He did not speak with the traditional British moderation. At times, and particularly when outraged, he would descend to the Soviet level of abuse; in the bitterness of his style of delivery, he competed freely with Mr. Vyshinsky. The Soviet spokesman—white-haired, florid, former state prosecutor—was expert in dialectical fencing. By provocative statements, he clearly tried to draw blood. He had the lawyer's readiness with words. Mr. Bevin was more accustomed to banging the table to the shipowners and dock managers, his usual counterparts in trade-union negotiations. He fought for what he thought was right, and he was brave. The lifelong career of this big and blunt labor leader had been admirable, but both his patriotism and his hatred of Communism were strongly charged with emotional feeling he took no trouble to conceal. Vyshinsky's calculated lunges maddened him: he was like a bull charging furiously at the red banner all over the field of debate.

Moreover, Mr. Bevin seemed to take the diplomatic duel as a personal battle, in which his own honor, just as much as the Empire's, was at stake. "Have I or my Government . . . been endangering the peace of the world?" he asked. "If that is true, you ought to tell me to leave this table, because you are established to maintain world peace, and I am branded, at the first meeting, as being the one person in the world disturbing and endangering world peace." This was the way Bevin frequently spoke.

Let me describe a bit more of the atmosphere of the debate, for that was important in the shaping of my outlook upon United Nations potentialities. Mr. Bevin, in indignantly rejecting the Soviet charge that British troops in Greece were endangering international peace, retorted that "the danger to the peace of the world has been the incessant propaganda from Moscow against the British Commonwealth." Vyshinsky cleverly replied, playing on chords of sentimental liberalism: "When these words were uttered here, in the Security Council, from the seat occupied by the British Delegation, all we Soviet representatives felt a sudden cold breath of the unhappy past." The substance of Soviet charges was of course ill founded. The British had every reason for feeling indignation, but equal reason for not responding in quite this manner.

It was a bad omen, and a chill descended upon my optimism. My great-power sponsors had just reached another agreement, involving myself; but if the atmosphere of this very first debate of the Security Council at which I was present was a sign of future events I feared that the prospects for further agreements on all the great issues to come might be much poorer than I had thought.

In the Greek and Indonesian cases, I did my best at conciliation behind the scenes. I made no substantive suggestions—I had, after all, just taken office; but I was deeply shocked by the bitterness of the debate, and alarmed at what the public reaction might be. I did not want popular good will for the United Nations to be dissipated at the very beginning. Accordingly, on several occasions when the debate was at its worst I suggested to Mr. Makin, the President, that he adjourn the public meeting of the Council, and that the Council members meet informally in the privacy of my office in an attempt to settle matters (at this time, the President did not have a private office of his own). I also personally suggested to Mr. Bevin and Mr. Vyshinsky that they moderate their speech. I did not want the Council to degenerate into a propaganda forum. The President took up my suggestion, and, with the help of delegates like Mr. Stettinius of the United States and Mr. van Kleffens of the Netherlands, succeeded in easing the situation to some degree. The Greek debate was ended by a short and simple statement of the President, referring to the various statements made. This was accepted by all, and the Indonesian issue closed with no resolution adopted.

A fourth case was now brought before the Security Council, but it did not involve a direct clash between the West and the Soviet Union. Syria and Lebanon complained about the continued presence of French and British troops on their soil despite their previous understanding that these troops would be withdrawn immediately on the cessation of hostilities with Germany and Japan. They complained that a Franco-British agreement of December 13, 1945, now made the withdrawal of the troops subject to conditions inconsistent with the spirit and letter of the Charter.

The complaint of Syria and Lebanon was one with which I sympathized. Syria and Lebanon had been League of Nations mandates, administered by France. During the war the Free French, who assisted the British in ousting Vichy from control in the Levant, promised them full independence. They were invited to San Francisco and were signatories of the United Nations Charter. Faris el-Khouri, the venerable Syrian, and Charles Malik, a cultured Lebanese of Christian faith, approached me for my advice. I confess that I felt the willingness of France and Britain to depart from the Levant could do with a little prodding. Accordingly I advised Mr. el-Khouri and Dr. Malik to bring their countries' case to the Security Council, for I was confident that London and Paris would respond. The Council received the plea of these two new and powerless States sympathetically. "It is certainly a historic event," the Lebanese representative later acknowledged, "when two small States can, through the action of the Security Council, obtain satisfaction for their claims solely because they have a right to it."

France and Great Britain both assured the Council of their intention to withdraw their troops promptly and of their readiness to enter into direct negotiations to this end without delay as requested by majority vote of the Council; and, in fact, the whole matter was brought to a happy conclusion shortly thereafter, and the agreed withdrawals duly reported to the Security Council by the parties concerned.

But the Syrian and Lebanese case has another and less pleasant aspect in United Nations history. It marked the first time that the Soviet Union exercised the right of veto. The circumstances of the casting of that first in a long succession of "Niets" are worth recalling. The resolution that settled the case received seven affirmative votes, with the United Kingdom and France abstaining as parties to the dispute. But the resolution was lost, because the only negative vote was cast by the Soviet Union. Why was this first veto cast? Not because Mr. Vyshinsky opposed the substance of the resolution, but because its language was not strong enough to please him. This first, almost lighthearted use of the veto that I hoped would rarely be exercised by any of the great powers disturbed me as much as the violence of the debate on the Greek question. Although I did not then foresee the long succession of fifty-odd Soviet vetoes cast during my term of office, the great majority of them for reasons no more substantial to Soviet interests and policy than this, here was another chilly forewarning of the "cold war" to come—the clumsiness, the rigidity of position, the refusal to participate, even in non-essentials, in the give-and-take and the hammering out of acceptable compromises that are the very lifeblood of politics and diplomacy among the Western democracies.

There was, however, a positive note at the Security Council's final London meeting on February 16, which followed by two days the adjournment of the General Assembly. Three weeks earlier the Security Council had requested the Permanent Members to direct their Chiefs of Staff to appoint representatives to meet in London for establishing the Military Staff Committee called for by the Charter. All five great powers acted promptly and sent their representatives to London. Before ending its London sessions the Security Council directed the Military Staff Committee to begin its work by examining, from a military point of view, the provisions of Article

43 of the Charter which is an important part of the security system planned at San Francisco. The Military Staff Committee worked for many months and made some progress before the whole effort broke down in 1947.

By the time the delegates left London and I began the final three weeks of preparation for the move to New York I understood much better than before the depth and danger of the split that had been developing between the Soviet Union and the West. I felt that in some respects it was like a crevasse in a glacier which might spread wider beneath the bridge of soft surface snow that was called great-power unity. The confident hopes I had shared in earlier months with most other statesmen of the smaller powers at least, and certainly with the great masses of people everywhere, were impaired but by no means lost. I saw the dangers more clearly, but I saw also, on the other side, much evidence that the situation was not beyond repair, that the wartime cooperation of the great powers might yet be revived through the United Nations, at least in the most essential things; and I hoped that I might assist in the process.

In a talk I gave to the Norwegian Association of Students when I returned to Oslo briefly to wind up my personal affairs, I did my best to prepare them for the difficulties I felt sure were to come. For the benefit of these young and ardently idealistic men and women I agreed that "the work of the United Nations cannot be advanced without idealism, trust, and faith"; but I warned that we could not start the work of the United Nations in a "paradise of unreality—we must begin by taking things as they are."

Other men had been pondering the deeper trend of events at this time. And one of them—one of the greatest men of this century—spoke out concerning his conclusions at the little town of Fulton, Missouri, on March 5. Winston Churchill had been out of office since the previous July. He spoke at Fulton as a private citizen; but what he said carried round the world on press and radio, and echoes still in the events and policies that followed. Not only did he speak with all the weight of his immense prestige as a wartime leader, but the circumstances of his address gave added significance to his words. Mr. Churchill first visited the White House, and President Truman accompanied him to Fulton for his talk at Westminster College.

Mr. Churchill's address, entitled "The Sinews of Peace," was the subject of much controversy and a great deal of criticism, especially among European liberals and social democrats and the strongest supporters of the United Nations almost everywhere. This was because he flung down a challenge to Russia at a time when most people hoped for the success of peacetime collaboration with the U.S.S.R. I shared this feeling at the time.

But as I now look back upon the world scene which Mr. Churchill then surveyed I see two compelling factors which he tactfully did not dwell upon in his speech. One was the precipitate demobilization and dismantling of the tremendous American military machine of men and weapons, the greatest the world had ever seen. The soldiers streamed home from Europe and Asia in response to the overwhelming demand of the American people. And all that vast outward flow of American military and economic supplies under Lend-Lease—$45,000,000,000 worth in four years and most of it to Western Europe and the British Commonwealth—came to a sudden end at the same time. This was one of the factors. The second factor was that Western Europe was prostrate from its terrible ordeal. England was nearly bankrupt; France and Italy, weak shadows of their former selves. Nowhere on the eastern side of the Atlantic could there be seen evidence of the power and resources needed for the recovery of the continent that was the cradle of Western civilization. I am sure all this was clearly evident to Mr. Churchill, though absent from the speech, when he spoke so strongly at Fulton of a third compelling factor on the world scene—the presence in the heart of Europe of massive Russian military power—a power used to spread totalitarian Communism westward. It was on this occasion that he coined the now famous simile, saying, "From Stettin in the Baltic to Trieste in the Adriatic an iron curtain has descended across the continent." He believed that the Soviet Union, without desiring war, sought "the fruits of war and the indefinite expansion of their power and doctrines."

At the time there was a good deal of talk—which still persists—of developing Western Europe into a "third force" between the Soviet and American giants. But Mr. Churchill saw Europe with no means, in his judgment, of recovering to become a force of any kind without American help and partnership, and urged instead "fraternal

THE WARTIME ALLIANCE BEGINS TO BREAK UP 37

association" among the English-speaking peoples backed by a Western security arrangement. He believed a settlement with Russia depended upon the strength of the West and warned that we "cannot afford to work on narrow margins offering temptations to a trial of strength."

"If the Western democracies stand together in strict adherence to the principles of the United Nations Charter, their influence for furthering those principles will be immense and no one is likely to molest them," he said. "If, however, they become divided or falter in their duty, and if these all-important years are allowed to slip away, then indeed catastrophe may overwhelm us all."

He saw no threat in his proposal to the future of the United Nations, in which he reaffirmed his faith. He said: "Special associations between Members of the United Nations which have no aggressive point against any other country, which harbor no design incompatible with the Charter of the United Nations, far from being harmful, are beneficial and, as I believe, indispensable."

In retrospect it is evident that Winston Churchill's Fulton speech was the forerunner of the Western policy that a year later produced the Truman Doctrine and the Marshall Plan and, soon after that, the North Atlantic Treaty. At the time no government was ready to proclaim his proposals as its own. Public opinion was not prepared, and governmental policy not finally fixed. However, President Truman refused all requests for comments that would indicate disagreement with any part of the Fulton speech; and when I passed on word to Mr. Bevin that the hope had been expressed by my new Russian Assistant Secretary-General, Arkady A. Sobolev, on behalf of Soviet officials, that the British Foreign Office would issue a statement disavowing Mr. Churchill, I was merely told that his statements as a private citizen were no concern of Mr. Bevin and that no statement would be issued. Two weeks later, in a speech at Port Talbot, Wales, after the displeasure of many Labor Party members had become evident, Mr. Bevin simply said that the government was not consulted about the speech and was not a party to it.

The Fulton speech and the first indications that London and Washington might be considering moving their policies in that direction gave me new cause for concern about the prospects for great-power collaboration in the United Nations. Mr. Churchill was right in his basic appraisal of the situation, that strength was necessary for succcessful dealings with the Soviet Union and Western Europe could not be restored to military and economic strength without massive aid from America—a reversal of the process of withdrawal and pellmell demobilization that was then under way. But I wished that he might have coupled his appeal for Western unity and strength with a more positive and conciliatory approach to the Soviet Union, seeking common ground upon which the U.S.S.R. might be persuaded to return to its wartime policy of collaboration and to join with the West in the United Nations in a genuine effort to build a common system of security. There was nothing incompatible, I felt, between such an effort and a policy of rebuilding Western strength, either then or later. The development and strengthening of the United Nations could not and should not wait upon the rejuvenation of Western Europe. They should go hand in hand. It was to this end that I resolved to devote all my influence as Secretary-General in the months that lay ahead.

CHAPTER III

THE SECRETARIAT: OUTPOST IN THE STRUGGLE FOR PEACE

The role of the Secretary-General.—Great powers agree on allocation of Assistant Secretaryships-General.—The problem of guarding a geographical balance.—Recruiting a crew for a ship already on her course.

NOTWITHSTANDING concern with the developing political situation on the world scene, most of my time in the hectic weeks in London following my election was occupied by the preliminary shaping of my views as to the role the Secretary-General should play, and with the first steps in the creation of the Secretariat. Both grave considerations of high principle and policy, and practical political realities of a somewhat less elevated but very human kind, had to be taken into account.

Article 99 of the Charter states:

The Secretary-General may bring to the attention of the Security Council any matter which in his opinion may threaten the maintenance of international peace and security.

This Article confers upon the Secretary-General of the United Nations world political responsibilities which no individual, no representative of a single nation, ever had before. Furthermore from it derived further rights that were soon to be written into the rules of procedure of the Security Council, the General Assembly, the Economic and Social Council and the Trusteeship Council. The Secretary-General was to be empowered to propose items for the agenda of these organs and to take part in the debates, rights that otherwise were reserved to governments and to representatives of Member States.

The Secretariat had a very special place in the structure of the United Nations in other ways as well. The Charter reserved for the Secretary-General power of appointment to all posts in the Secretariat and, in Article 100, spelled out in the following unequivocal terms the exclusively international responsibilities of this civil service for the world organization:

1. In the performance of their duties the Secretary-General and the staff shall not seek or receive instructions from any government or from any other authority external to the Organization. They shall refrain from any action which might reflect on their position as international officials responsible only to the Organization.

2. Each Member of the United Nations undertakes to respect the exclusively international character of the responsibilities of the Secretary-General and the staff, and not to seek to influence them in the discharge of their responsibilities.

Finally, the writers of the Charter confirmed the importance they intended the Secretariat to have by making it one of the six principal organs of the United Nations, along with the General Assembly, the three Councils, and the International Court of Justice. Only the court and the Secretariat were composed of men chosen as individuals. All the rest were composed not of individuals but of representatives of national governments.

In the Assembly and the Councils the primary duty of these delegates was to represent their respective national interests in the work of the United Nations. But the Secretary-General and the Secretariat were responsible solely to the Organization as a whole—to the collectivity of the Member governments under the Charter.

This role, with all its potentialities and its pitfalls for the future, had to be weighed against the hard political realities of a world by no means ready yet to accept either the outlook or the responsibilities of world citizenship. Under the circumstances, how far should the Secretary-General seek to develop his independent political role? The question is still debated, and may well continue to be for a long time to come.

On the one hand, some people say that the Secretary-General, who more than anyone else symbolizes the Organization as a whole, must be an outspoken public servant endeavoring to express the views of all peoples. He should not merely service United Nations meetings; he should seek to influence the course of the debates. The Secretaries-General of the League of Nations, this school of thought holds, were far too retiring. The Covenant of the League gave them little basis for political activity, and they did not develop adequately what basis there was. In contrast the Secretary-General of the United Nations should emerge as a bold leader of international thought and action, as a genuinely international figure stimulating the Member States to rise above their nationalistic dispositions. The national delegations (the argument runs) tend to look at problems from their national points of view—they are traditionally bound to see the international interest in terms of their national interests; but a solution to a problem which is truly in the international interest is more than the sum of the national positions which the delegations advance, and the Secretary-General is uniquely placed to perceive this higher international solution and propound it if he so wishes.

On the other hand, the minimalist school looks back admiringly to the practices of Sir Eric Drummond, the first Secretary-General of the League of Nations. Sir Eric played an important behind-the-scenes role as a conciliator among the Member States. He did not speak out in public at all. He did not advocate an independent League of Nations policy on the basis of the organization's international identity; he did not try to influence popular feeling one way or another; he did not symbolize the League, for relatively few people heard much of him. As an administrator, he was on a very high level. As an international civil servant, he lived up to the unsurpassed traditions of the British Civil Service. Indeed, the very concept of an international civil service composed of persons responsible not to their governments but to the impartial organization—to the international community as a whole—was primarily Sir Eric's. His decision to create the first truly international secretariat was a decision of profound significance—surely one of the most important and promising political developments of the twentieth century. His place in history is secure.

In my view it was clearly not the intention of the Charter that the limited concept of the office of Secretary-General which Sir Eric evolved in the League should be perpetuated in the United Nations. I also knew that there were—there still are—many traditionalists in the foreign chancelleries of the world who would like to see Article 99 of the Charter, and all the implied power deriving from it, consigned to an unused constitutional corner to gather dust.

The role which the framers of the Charter of the United Nations envisaged for the Secretary-General fell between the two extremes. The Secretary-General unquestionably would be under an obligation to play a great political part; but, I felt, there were limits to the extent of his initiative—the limits of the Charter's text and, even more, the limits imposed by the realities of national and international political life. The Secretary-General might be the symbol of the Organization as a whole—the symbol, in other words, of the international spirit. This, and his strategic situation at the very center of international affairs as confidant of the world's statesmen and as spokesman to the world's peoples, attached significant influence to his position; but it was a moral power, not a physical one, and moral power in this world is not conclusive. The Secretary-General, it was said, should be more the general than the secretary—but where were his divisions? Thus I inclined, from the beginning, toward a middle way—a pragmatic and open-minded approach. I would listen to all my advisers and be directed by none. I had no calculated plan for developing the political powers of the office of Secretary-General, but I was determined that the Secretary-General should be a force for peace. How that force would be applied I would find out—in the light of developments.

Fortunately, the servicing of the General Assembly had been continued, at my request, by Gladwyn Jebb and his temporary Secretariat staff. I had no trouble with the day-to-day problems at Church House and Central Hall.

During the weeks prior to the last evening of the General Assembly in London, when President Spaak's gavel finally dropped well after midnight to end the first part of the first session, much of my time had gone toward building a permanent international Secretariat. I needed the best possible staff, to share the burdens of my office and prove its worthiness of being a principal organ of the United Nations. Furthermore, I knew that the Secretariat, unlike a national civil service, would not have the policy-making executive

THE SECRETARIAT 43

officials of a government available on a day-to-day basis for guidance and direction. The General Assembly and the Councils would be the policy-making authorities, and there would often be long periods between sessions. The staff, therefore, would be entrusted with responsibilities in carrying out their tasks that would require a high level of judgment, ability, and devotion to the objective international standards of Article 100 of the Charter.

Nevertheless, I approached this phase of my new assignment with a good deal more confidence. I knew administration—to the extent, at any rate, that national administration bears upon international. I had served in the Norwegian cabinet for years, initially as Minister of Justice. Commerce, industry, and shipping also were familiar fields. In 1939, at the outbreak of World War II, I had been charged with organizing Norway's entire supply system; and I had had a similar responsibility for Norwegian merchant shipping when the government temporarily took it over after the German invasion in 1940. I even thought I could deal with bureaucrats.

I still recall a peculiar discovery I made when taking over the Ministry of Trade: the chiefs of departments had formed the habit of sending up only the last page of bulky departmental opinions for the responsible Cabinet Minister to sign on a dotted line! I had balked. Though I never loved administrative details, I insisted on knowing what went on in my Ministry and what was said in my name.

The disabilities of national bureaucracies are legendary and real. I was soon to find out that the difficulties in international administration multiply these many, many times.

The League of Nations had set us a standard in internal administration which it would not be easy to match. The Preparatory Commission drew upon the League experience in drafting its detailed plans for the structure of the Secretariat. The General Assembly accepted the Commission's recommendations for the most part, and presented me with a table of organization which it was my task to fill. Despite this help, my initial task was far more complicated than Sir Eric Drummond's had been, not to mention the fact that the instructions were so detailed that they limited my freedom of action.

The central problem was that the United Nations was already a going concern which had to be serviced continuously, and with no delay whatever. It had been different in Geneva. Not a meeting of importance was held during the first eighteen months of the League's existence, when the world was far too busy implementing the peace treaties which—fortunately for the League—had already been concluded. Sir Eric could take the necessary time. I could not.

The Preparatory Commission and the Assembly had agreed that the Secretariat should be organized in eight departments, each under an Assistant Secretary-General. Four of the departments corresponded to the main fields of activity of the United Nations. They were:

The Department of Security Council Affairs, to serve also the General Assembly in all political questions and the Atomic Energy, the Disarmament, and other commissions.

The Department of Economic Affairs, to serve the Economic and Social Council and its commissions as well as the General Assembly in all economic questions.

The Department of Social Affairs, to perform a like task on all social questions considered by the United Nations, including human rights.

The Department of Trusteeship and Information from Non-Self-Governing Territories, to serve the Trusteeship Council, and the Assembly in its consideration of problems of non-self-governing territories not included in the Trusteeship system.

Then there was *the Legal Department,* to advise the organs of the United Nations and the Secretary-General on legal and constitutional matters and the drafting of international agreements, and to be responsible for the registration of treaties.

A sixth, *the Department of Public Information,* had the role of helping to promote an informed public understanding of the aims and activities of the United Nations without which, the First Assembly recognized in a unanimous resolution, "the United Nations cannot achieve the purposes for which it has been created."

The Department of Administrative and Financial Services combined administration of the Organization's finances with central responsibility for personnel.

The Department of Conference and General Services provided such services to the Assembly and the Councils as interpretation, translation, and official records, and the "housekeeping" services required for the organization.

The choice of the Assistant Secretaries-General, who would constitute my "cabinet," was, of course, my first concern. It soon appeared that it was equally the concern of some of the great, and a number of the lesser, powers.

Mr. Vyshinsky did not delay his approach. He was the first to inform me of an understanding which the Big Five had reached in London on the appointment of a Soviet national as Assistant Secretary-General for Political and Security Council Affairs. Mr. Vyshinsky simply spoke of an "agreement"—he said nothing of its binding quality, of the right of the Big Five to arrive at it, or of the length of time it was meant to apply. Now, by the terms of the Charter, the Secretary-General has full authority in the disposition of the Assistant Secretary-Generalships, with respect both to their nationality and to their personality. The authority, in fact, was the point of a hard-won decision at San Francisco which rejected an attempt to prescribe that there should be four Deputy Secretaries-General, appointed by the General Assembly upon the recommendation of the Security Council in the same manner as the Secretary-General. Strictly speaking, therefore, the Big Five had no right to arrive at any understanding regarding the distribution of the offices of Assistant Secretary-General which was binding upon the Secretary-General.

This is not to say, however, that it would have been politic of me to resist the great-power accord. Moreover, I welcomed the understanding as a sign of good will and confidence between East and West. That the Soviet Union wanted one of its nationals to fulfill the premier Assistant Secretaryship could be taken as another indication of serious Soviet interest in the United Nations, and that the United States was willing to agree to accord this key post to a national of the U.S.S.R. was evidence of an American desire to encourage this interest for the sake of world peace.

Mr. Stettinius confirmed to me that he had agreed with the Soviet Delegation in the matter. In fact, the Big Five had agreed among themselves to ask me to appoint a national of each of them as an Assistant Secretary-General. But both Mr. Stettinius and the French stressed that their agreement to the Soviet post was a limited one, designed to get the Secretariat off to a good start. It was not understood that a permanent lien on the office of Assistant Secretary-General for Security Council Affairs was granted to the Soviet Union. My understanding of the arrangement, accordingly, was that it was meant to apply for the five years which I should serve as Secretary-General (five years was the term of office which the General Assembly had prescribed). It would not necessarily apply after that.

As became my custom in connection with filling of the highest posts in the Secretariat, I felt it was both necessary and desirable to secure nominations from the governments, in particular for positions of the rank of Assistant Secretary-General. The decisions were always mine; but I had to try to get the best talent, and that sometimes took persuasion, as good people can seldom be spared. I therefore conferred with Mr. Vyshinsky on whom to appoint to the post given to the Russians. Being favorably impressed by Alexis A. Roschin, whom I had come to know in London as an able and popular member of the temporary Secretariat, concerned with the Secretariat's services to the Security Council, I asked for him. Vyshinsky's reaction was that Roschin had not had enough experience for the job; but he promised to suggest another man who qualified. A few days later, he proposed Arkady Sobolev, a prominent official of the Soviet Foreign Ministry. Sobolev had been a delegate to the Dumbarton Oaks meetings at which the Big Four made the preliminary draft of the United Nations Charter and had later been political adviser to Marshal Georgi K. Zhukov in Berlin. I checked with various sources, and was assured that Sobolev was a man of high ability. I appointed him, and was to find that the recommendation was amply justified.

The preservation of international peace and security was the Organization's highest responsibility, and it was to entrusting the direction of the Secretariat department most concerned with this to a Soviet national that the Americans had agreed. What did the Americans want for themselves? To my surprise, they did not ask for a department concerned with comparable substantive affairs, like the economic or the social. Rather, Mr. Stettinius proposed that an American citizen be appointed Assistant Secretary-General for Administrative and Financial Services. This post would be concerned with the internal administration of the Secretariat rather than its external projection. It has been suggested that the Americans were influenced by the strong role played by the Bureau of the Budget in the Roosevelt Administration and that they thought the administrative tail would wag the dog. However, another and higher motive may have had a bearing on the American choice. With the influence of the United States in the Organization bound to be so great in any event, with Headquarters to be established in the United States, Mr. Stettinius sought to reassure the other delegates against the impression that the United Nations would be "an American show."

The choice of a qualified American to fill the post proved to be a disappointing experience. I turned to Mr. Stettinus for help, but it soon appeared that Mr. Byrnes wanted to handle this matter himself. Many well qualified Americans were suggested in private conversations, among them Adlai Stevenson and Milton S. Eisenhower, brother of the General. Not hearing from Mr. Byrnes for some time, I made preliminary approaches to both; but they indicated they could not accept. Mr. Byrnes finally submitted but one nominee, John B. Hutson, at that time Under Secretary of Agriculture. A native of Kentucky, he was originally an expert in tobacco products, a good friend of both President Truman and Secretary of State Byrnes, with a long record in the service of the Democratic party. I cannot say that I was pleased with this procedure of advancing a single name only. I appointed "Jolly Jack" as Mr. Hutson was affectionately called by his colleagues—and he served during the Secretariat's initial, and rapid, build-up until he resigned in the spring of 1947.

The British took an approach which was so solicitous of my right to appoint whatever British subject I chose as Assistant Secretary-General, as to be not quite helpful. The United Kingdom was diffident in its suggestions, and my requests for Englishmen either in government service or in prominent private positions failed to meet with any positive response. I thought of appointing an Englishman as Assistant Secretary-General for Public Information, and had in mind Francis Williams, the brilliant former editor of the London *Daily Herald;* he performed notably in the British Ministry of Information during the war and had recently been Chairman of the Preparatory Commission's Technical Advisory Group for Public Information. But the British needed him as press spokesman for the Prime Minister. In consultation with my advisers, I alternatively decided to appoint an Englishman head of the Department for Economic Affairs. I personally spoke with Sir Arthur Salter, wartime director of Allied shipping control and a high official with the League. Sir Arthur declined, as did Sir William Beveridge (of Beveridge Plan fame), with whom I also spoke. We sought Geoffrey Crowther, the editor of the *Economist;* he too could not accept. Finally I had to leave London without an agreed candidate. Weeks later, on the day before the opening of the first session of the Economic and Social Council where an Assistant Secretary-General for this department had to be present, I appointed Arthur David K. Owen, who was an economist by training and was then serving as my Executive Assistant. Sir Alexander Cadogan, the former Permanent Under-Secretary of State for Foreign Affairs who had been appointed the Permanent Representative of the United Kingdom to the United Nations, after distinguished service at Dumbarton Oaks and San Francisco, agreed to my choice—although the next day, when it was too late, he came to me with another nomination. Owen himself was a bit embarrassed at his selection; he felt that an older man, of more senior stature in the field, should have been chosen. But I never had reason to regret his appointment.

Andrew W. Cordier succeeded David Owen as my Executive Assistant. In this capacity and as secretary of the General Assembly he was my strong right hand throughout my term as Secretary-General and filled a significant role in many of the developments recorded in this book.

The decision to appoint a Frenchman chief of the Department of Social Affairs was, under the circumstances, a logical one. The French put forth a few possibilities—Jacques Rueff, a leading banker and economist, and Professor Henri Laugier. Mr. Laugier had a distinguished background in academic and social affairs. When he came to London for a talk I was impressed with his sincerity and imagination, and appointed him. He served with distinction until 1951.

The idea of appointing an Asian as Assistant Secretary-General for Trusteeship and Non-Self-Governing Territories had obvious appeal. China was the fifth member of the Big Five, and I sought her suggestions. I decided upon Victor Chi-Tsai Hoo, who had been Chinese Vice-Minister for Foreign Affairs, a delegate to the Preparatory Commission, and a member of the Chinese Delegation to the London Assembly. For many years he had been a delegate to meetings of the League of Nations. Incidentally Mr. Hoo had the decided advantage of being in London at the time—on the spot, so to speak—as did, indeed, four other of my appointments as Assistant Secretaries-General. He served ably, and ran his department in an irreproachable style. Besides, he spoke all five official languages. As China underwent revolution, his views and mine came to differ about United Nations policy toward China; but he never wavered in his wise and objective counsel, and our cordial relations were unimpaired.

So much for the Big Five. Three posts remained, and I decided to make the appointments from the smaller states of Western Europe and Latin-America. I had thought of appointing to the Legal Department Dr. Luis Padilla Nervo, a member of the Delegation from Mexico to the London Assembly and later Mexican Foreign Minister and President of the Sixth Assembly. However, the Latin-American states were virtually unanimous in supporting Benjamin A. Cohen of Chile, a versatile man who combined the careers of diplomat, jurist, journalist, and public speaker in four languages. I appointed him Assistant Secretary-General for Public Information. The name of Dr. Ivan Kerno was warmly put forth by Jan Masaryk for the Legal Department. Dr. Kerno was a Czech diplomat and lawyer of League experience; he had been a member of the cabinet of the Secretary-General of the League. Now a member of the Czech delegation to the Preparatory Commission and the London Assembly, he was by no means a Communist—this, of course, was before the 1948 coup. I appointed him, and he served well until he reached retirement age in 1952. He then decided not to return to his native Czechoslovakia, and remained in the United States with his two sons.

One more London appointment was made—that of Adrian Pelt as Assistant Secretary-General for Conference and General Services. Mr. Pelt, a Dutchman, had been director of the Information Section of the Secretariat of the League of Nations for many years.

During the war, he had been chief of the Netherlands Government Information Service. He was strongly supported by his countrymen, and served with great ability as Assistant Secretary-General, then as United Nations Commissioner for Libya, and finally as director of the European Headquarters of the United Nations in his "old home town," Geneva.

A drawback of this pattern, which resembled the agreed geographical distribution of the first Security Council, was its European emphasis. Five of the eight Assistant Secretaries-General were European, and so, of course, was the Secretary-General. It was just as important that the United Nations Secretariat should not tend to be the European club which the League of Nations in a sense was, as that it should not be an "American" show; there is no principle to which I have more doggedly adhered than that of universality. There was no reason why Europe should be overrepresented in the highest ranks of the Secretariat. Therefore I took the first opportunity to correct the overrepresentation.

This prompts me to relate here the changes made in the innermost, or rather uppermost, circles of the United Nations official hierarchy during the succeeding years. When Mr. Pelt resigned to go to Libya as U.N. Commissioner, I decided to appoint an Indian to succeed him. India submitted a number of suggestions, and I finally chose Shamaldharee Lall. Aside from Mr. Lall's personal capacities and his former services with the International Labor Office, his appointment was a recognition of the stature which a free India had rapidly assumed in international affairs.

But the first important change occurred before that, in 1947. At the time of the resignation of John B. Hutson, I again discussed the question of this particular Assistant Secretary-Generalship with Washington, and this time, to my pleasure, procedures were more fitting. The State Department submitted a list of thirteen acceptable persons—men of superior abilities like Adlai Stevenson, Chester Bowles, Wilson W. Wyatt, Milton Eisenhower, and Byron Price. I was hard put to know where to begin. But in Chicago I met with Milton Eisenhower, in another effort to persuade him to join us. He had in the meantime been prominent in the United States National Commission for the United Nations Educational, Scientific, and Cultural Organization (UNESCO); his devotion to the United

Nations was unquestioned. But other commitments still kept him from taking up my offer.

Two of my staff spoke with Adlai Stevenson on my behalf, and he came to my office at Lake Success after sending a most helpful letter, full of suggestions. Mr. Stevenson, too, was friendly in the extreme, but he had determined to settle down in Chicago to the practice of law and keep an eye on local and state politics. Wilson Wyatt also paid us a visit but he also turned out to be unavailable. The same was the case with Chester Bowles, who was already active in Connecticut politics and heading for the governorship. Of the possibilities I have mentioned, Mr. Price was the only one in a position to accept the post, and he was appointed. A former high executive of the Associated Press, and Director of the Office of Censorship during the war, he left a much higher salary with the Association of Motion Picture Producers to come to the United Nations. He proved to be an administrator of solid integrity and efficiency. His complete reliability soon won him confidence and trust equaled by few of my close associates.

When Mr. Sobolev resigned in the late summer of 1949, I replaced him with another Soviet national, Constantin E. Zinchenko, taking care to limit his contract to the period which I still had to serve. I viewed the London understanding as applying only to my term, but these precedents have a way of perpetuating themselves.

Upon the resignation of Henri Laugier as Assistant Secretary-General for Social Affairs, I consulted with the French; and, after considering a number of candidates, I appointed Guillaume Georges-Picot, a career diplomat who was then French Ambassador to Argentina and, in outward manner, appeared to be as reserved as Mr. Laugier had seemed outgoing. Some eyebrows were raised at the selection of a man who was neither experienced in United Nations matters nor expert in social affairs, but I made no happier appointment.

The group of Assistant Secretaries-General was to be my official "cabinet," available for advice on all matters—not least on questions relating to their respective "home areas." They were also the responsible heads of their departments. I delegated to them broad administrative authority from the very beginning. As the work developed, it gradually fell to their deputies, the top-ranking directors, to assume many of the administrative duties; and then they too were called in for my regular meetings. This division of work was intended to permit an extensive political liaison activity to the Assistant Secretaries-General; but I soon found that many Member governments, and particularly their permanent delegates, insisted on bringing to the Secretary-General's personal attention not only all major political questions but even such infinitesimal administrative matters as the proposed appointment of a wife's nephew or a Minister's protégé to the Secretariat staff. In later years, this practice went so far that one Ambassador insisted that it would be below his dignity to call on an Assistant Secretary-General! In other cases, not least in the Councils and Committees, very good contacts were established and maintained, as a part of the liaison work; but as time went on, and the pressure for greater economy was added to my other considerations, I eventually concluded that the number of my "deputies" might be reduced to three (or four) provided they were of the highest caliber and could be selected freely by the Secretary-General according to his needs—and without having to please everyone. This conclusion in no way reflected upon the chief lieutenants assigned to me; in fact, several among them had personal qualifications that would have enabled them easily to fit into the proposed new pattern. But the change never went into effect, for my resignation intervened before I had finalized my proposal for consideration by the General Assembly.

I have gone ahead of my story in order to give an account of the members of my "cabinet" over the years. Let us now return to 1946 and the wider problem of establishing and staffing the Secretariat, with no time to spare. The General Assembly in London had provided me with a table of organization, a set of principles and standards for the recruitment of the Secretariat, and a first temporary budget of $21,500,000 to cover estimated expenses until the end of the year. But I was faced with an almost impossible time schedule. I must be prepared to provide all the Secretariat services for the Security Council at a moment's notice, for the Charter stipulates that the Security Council shall be in "continuous session," always ready to meet at once in an emergency. The Economic and Social Council was to hold its first full session in New York on May 25. The Human Rights Commission and four other commissions of the Economic and Social Council were also to meet in the spring. The Atomic Energy Commission would soon start its work. The General Assembly itself had decided to reconvene for the second part of its first session somewhere in New York on September 3.

I needed to enlist skills and talents over a very wide field—diplomats and others with political experience, economists, lawyers, administrators, financial experts, statisticians, social scientists, experts in public information and the mass media, in colonial problems, in the organization of international conferences, and in many other fields, researchers and archivists, interpreters, translators, documents editors, précis writers, verbatim reporters. But I could not base my appointments solely on the best professional qualifications, for this was an international civil service and the Charter instructed me that due regard should be paid to "the importance of recruiting the staff on as wide a geographical basis as possible." The Secretariat must, so far as possible, be representative of the Member states.

The word "geographical" in the Charter of course covered much more than mere geography. It was not simply a question, as it would have been in a national administration, of picking people from the southern as well as the western and northern provinces of Norway or from Texas as well as from New England. It meant bringing together people of many languages, races, and stages of development, of all the great cultures and religions, from Asia, Europe, Africa, and the Americas. It meant harmonizing all this diversity into an efficient and unified force, with all differences of background and outlook subordinated to the oath of office to which every Secretariat member must subscribe:

> I solemnly swear (affirm) to exercise in all loyalty, discretion and conscience the functions entrusted to me as a member of the international service of the United Nations, to discharge those functions and regulate my conduct with the interests of the United Nations only in view, and not to seek or accept instructions in respect to the performance of my duties from any government or other authority external to the Organization.

The General Assembly had estimated that I should need to recruit a staff of 2,450 in the first nine months, so far as possible, from the area of the Headquarters or wherever they could be found. Surveying the task ahead of me, I recalled, as I have often done before and since, a favorite quotation from that great Norwegian explorer and humanitarian Dr. Fridtjof Nansen: "The difficult can be done immediately; the impossible takes a little longer."

I could, and did of course, draw fully upon the competent temporary Secretariat of 300-odd members that had been assembled in London. Here and there I found former members of the League of Nations Secretariat, whose earlier experience was most valuable. Nor were we lacking in applications for posts. In London and New York we were swamped with them—letters from thousands of men and women all over the world, the great majority, I am sure, not mere place-seekers but persons genuinely desirous of serving peace in the new world organization. In New York alone we received several packing cases full of 10,000 applications from Americans who had written to the State Department before we set up our offices in New York; these were passed on to us as received without any evaluation.

This was the difficulty—to screen and to choose at a time when the careful international recruitment procedures that we developed later were still in an embryonic state. Nor did I receive much help from the governments. They were naturally preoccupied with their own problems of recovery and readjustment following the war, and they were inclined to let me settle my problems as best I could. The theory of the international interest as overriding national interests was, and is, slow to be accepted in practice. It was obvious that the concept of the career international civil service which was strongly endorsed at the London Assembly could be applied only gradually, and that these first staff appointments would have to be on a temporary basis. This is the way it was done, and I appointed some 2,900 staff members in the course of 1946, predominantly from areas of the world where available persons of the necessary qualifications could be quickly found. It should be added that a high proportion of these temporary appointees fully proved their worth and later joined the career service. But I shall not soon forget the hectic activity of this organizational period in the life of the Secretariat. Besides, I had another problem of equal urgency on my hands at the same time: finding a home in which the United Nations could do its work.

CHAPTER IV

WHERE IS THE CENTER OF THE WORLD?

First round in London: contest over Europe or America as Headquarters site.—The Pacific raises its voice.—Shift of world political center of gravity across Atlantic finally recognized.—United Nations in New York.—Hunter College.— Lake Success and Flushing Meadow.

THE EXTREME political importance of the decision locating United Nations Headquarters in New York has, perhaps, not yet been fully understood everywhere.

The long and sometimes heated discussions which started in Church House, London, as early as September, 1945, did not clearly reveal that the battle, in the last analysis, actually concerned the establishment and consequent official recognition of the world's new political center of gravity. Indications to this effect were hotly disputed by the "losers," who contended that the main issue was one of practical necessity and administrative convenience; the "winners," on their side, were not too eager to press their points at this stage, because their victory had been a slim one indeed. The political impact of the decision to establish United Nations Headquarters not only in America, but on the northwestern shore of the Atlantic Ocean, was therefore not fully appreciated at the time.

The question happened to be one which I had studied and discussed long before the war came to an end.

It was clear to me that old concepts based on once dominating geographical, military, and political factors had been turned upside-down by the Second World War. Pearl Harbor and the ensuing battles throughout the Pacific had given this theater a significance it had never attained during the First World War, in which hostilities were limited to skirmishes between lonely men-of-war off isolated atolls. As the Second World War drew to a close, with the Axis smashed and the supremacy of two great powers—both bordering on the Pacific—more apparent by the day, a new world picture began to take form. When the roar of bombs and artillery finally subsided, there were two world powers of overwhelming strength: the one with interests extending across the immense Eurasian land mass from Eastern Europe to the Pacific shores of Asia; and the other with a field of interest now extending outward from the two American continents across the Atlantic and the Pacific. Furthermore, there were already many signs of change in the direction of political self-assertion and independence in India, Indo-China and Southeast Asia. Europe, in short, was no longer the sole contender for the role of the world's political center of gravity, as it had been for centuries—a role which had resulted in periodic internal struggles on the continent itself and in the imposition of foreign rule on other large areas not necessarily in need of tutorship. Now these days were over.

Awareness of the shift of the center of gravity away from Europe did not give me any particular ground for concern. My country's outlook on world affairs had always had a global slant. It is true that Norway also exercised extreme caution in the political field; in fact, an earlier Norwegian Foreign Minister had once said, during World War I, that the best foreign policy for Norway was "to have no foreign policy at all." Economically, however, our interests had long been world-wide. Our merchant fleet—the world's third largest —plowed the seven seas carrying goods between all continents, nine-tenths touching a Norwegian port only on rare occasions. Our highly specialized exports also required a world sale, and we were always interested in extending our markets. Lasting international peace, with consequent prosperity and progress for countries and peoples all over the globe, was therefore an accepted national Norwegian objective, commanding the support of the entire people. With these considerations in mind, we were not nearly so disturbed about the future as many of our colleagues from the European Continent appeared to be, in view of the obvious weakening of its relative position in the postwar world.

On the basis of these considerations I took up the question of where the United Nations Headquarters ought to be situated. A common denominator for all the varying interests had to be found in a geographical location that would meet the maximum of requirements, bearing in mind that for a dynamic international organ—with as many interests in the underdeveloped areas of Asia, Latin America, and Africa as in the political capitals of the West—it was of paramount importance that its nerve center be located as close as possible to the new economic and political center.

I was helped toward this conclusion by other considerations of both a political and a practical nature. My early interest in a strong European-American cooperation had only been strengthened by experience during the war years. As I saw it, the challenging question for the future was how to secure the fullest possible United States participation in whatever international organizations might emerge from the wartime alliances. A repetition of the tragedy of the League of Nations, stemming not least from the United States' refusal to join, could not be permitted. Under President Roosevelt's determined leadership, and with bipartisan agreement, the American people now showed signs of a growing understanding of their country's new position in world affairs. The need for defeating Axis attempts at world domination appeared to have awakened them. It seemed to have overcome at last America's traditional isolationism, the strongly held desire of a people fully engaged in settling and developing its own continental domain not to be mixed up, as some so often put it, "in other peoples' quarrels."

Long before San Francisco—in London at the height of the war—I had discussed America's future stand with my closest personal advisers, and put forward what I thought a daring and somewhat adventurous solution: Why not locate the headquarters of the future international organization within the United States' own borders, so that the concept of international cooperation could match forces on the spot with those of its arch-enemy, isolationism—utilizing at all times the American people's own democratic media? My advisers all agreed that the common sense of the American people could be relied upon to play its role in safeguarding the future of the world if given a chance like this.

Participating in these early consultations were Hans Berg, a most gifted Norwegian ambassador, Dr. Arne Ording, professor of modern history at the University of Oslo, Dr. Arnold Ræstad, former Norwegian Foreign Minister and experienced internationalist, Finn Moe (later to become well known as Norway's Permanent Delegate to the United Nations and chairman of the Norwegian Storting's Foreign Relations Committee), and Tor Gjesdal, head of Norway's wartime information services.

Our discussions were taking place in London, behind blackout curtains, in the bomb-shattered Capital. Across the English Channel, all of Western Europe from Norway's North Cape to the Spanish border was in the hands of the enemy. Of course these circumstances had an influence on our reasoning. What, I asked myself, would be the situation if disaster struck again? Were Europe again to be occupied, an eventual European United Nations headquarters could be completely cut off from the democratic countries overseas —isolated and impotent, as had been the League of Nations. Such a mistake could not be repeated.

This reasoning beyond a doubt was far from uncommon among government leaders at the time. I am certain that the considerations just mentioned must have weighed heavily with them as the various delegations took their stands on the Headquarters question. Nevertheless, not too much was said openly. Instead, numerous arguments were brought to bear against the obvious conclusions— many of them strong in their own right; none of them seemed to face up to realities involved.

As the Headquarters battle got under way in London it was clear, at any rate, that the rules of decorum would be preserved, and that the debate would not descend to the level later to be reached in the discussion of openly acknowledged political issues. At times, there was even a good deal of elegant fencing and a maneuvering so smooth and in such conformity with polite diplomatic tactics that a casual spectator could easily be deceived. The Americans declared their neutrality as soon as the Preparatory Commission opened its deliberations. The Russians disappointed most Western Europeans by coming out at once for a site in America. Aside from prevailing doubts as to the suitability of Europe and of Geneva—the main contender among the proposed sites in Europe—was the hesitant attitude of the Swiss government. The well known hospitality of the Swiss notwithstanding, they appeared to have real misgivings about their possible future role as hosts to the new world organization. The United Nations was going to have some teeth, which the League of Nations had lacked, and they feared this fact might infringe on traditional Swiss neutrality. In the end, however, the Swiss position crystallized in the following formula: Switzerland would welcome the establishment of United Nations organs in Swiss territory; but it would demand that any decision by the Security Council involving the use of military forces be taken outside the proposed Geneva headquarters and beyond the Swiss borders. When this attitude became known the issue was clarified for many.

Personally I had never—among all my other considerations—regarded a neutral country as the ideal site for an active, "troubleshooting" world organization. Outlook and reasoning in a neutral land, I had found, are apt to take on a shading somewhat different from that of the world at large. In subtle ways, this atmosphere could even influence the thinking of the personnel of international bodies located there. To put it bluntly, world peace, and the world I wished to live in, could not be won nor assured by the type of thinking which made neutrality its first concern during the last World War.

Before long, the discussions began to bring in other European alternatives, although the "Headquarters-in-Europe" faction never surrendered Geneva as its core of defense. Brussels, Paris, and London were also mentioned, as were the three Scandinavian capitals. But with the rejection of each alternative I became more and more convinced that United Nations thinking would have to come abreast of the times. The whole Western Hemisphere, once a parade ground for empire and the larder of Europe, was already in a state of flux, and was assuming an identity all its own. Its leaders, representing a vast new bloc of political aspiration, would be taking an important part in every United Nations decision from now on. London was no longer the world crossroads of determinative political forces. This point had moved farther west. We had to settle on new shores.

Then I began thinking seriously of New York City as the most appropriate site for United Nations Headquarters. The huge metropolis and international crossroads would in many ways offer the best contact with the world at large. New York's technical facilities were far superior to those of any other American city that was talked about—even the beautiful and cosmopolitan city of San Francisco, which had won the hearts of the delegates to the earlier Conference.

But these were still only my personal views, as were the broader conclusions attained long before the first meetings in Church House. Opinion in the Norwegian Foreign Office and among my fellow cabinet members was beginning to take the opposite direction—in favor of Europe. After all, Europe was far closer to Norway. Denmark, Great Britain, the Netherlands, Belgium, and France—our closest neighbors—all were for Europe, and it was difficult to start rowing our own course in splendid unconcern. There were many arguments on the opposing side—arguments which had to be met and refuted—and they came increasingly to light during November and December, 1945.

About that time, when the Norwegian Delegation to the Preparatory Commission left for London, I could only advise its members to await developments and to request further instructions from the government in event of disagreement on the site question. Despite my concern, nothing more could be done yet. Should the decision be in favor of America, the Delegation was advised to push for a suitable location on the east coast, with general instructions to use its own good judgment.

In the meantime, the pro-European forces had lost the first round. The Organization's Executive Committee had recommended to its successor, the United Nations Preparatory Commission, that Headquarters be set up in the United States. This step had been taken much against the wishes of Philip Noel-Baker, who loved the League of Nations if any man ever did, and had fought valiantly though unsuccessfully, for Geneva. But Andrei Gromyko of the U.S.S.R. had come out flatly for the United States. As to where in the United States, let the American Government decide, he had blandly told his colleagues. Later the Soviet Union modified its stand to support the east coast.

The battle was soon resumed with new vigor, and by early December, there were real grounds for concern. A final decision on what to recommend to the General Assembly had been further postponed; time seemed to be playing against the United States, and I heard that opinion was now swinging in favor of Europe. One reason for this has already been mentioned in Chapter I. "It is the prevailing desire here," reported the Norwegian Delegation, "that General Eisenhower be the Organization's first Secretary-General." Knowing this, Paul-Henri Spaak, Foreign Minister of Belgium and one of the leading backers of a European site, shrewdly called attention to the preferred status of the Big Five under the Charter, as well as its stress upon their mutual equality. Without mentioning any names, he warned against blocking the election of the man desired for Secretary-General by locating United Nations Headquarters in his homeland.

Other surprising shifts indicated the scope of the trouble ahead. Canada, which had voted for the United States in the Executive Committee, about-faced and came out for Europe. Britain, Canada, Belgium, France, the Netherlands, and Greece were now pushing strongly for Europe; and—to the amazement of everyone—Poland had appeared to risk Soviet displeasure by taking a similar stand.

Moscow, too, was sending up some remarkable trial balloons. Ukrainian Foreign Minister Manuilsky at luncheon with a close friend of mine, while reiterating the Soviet stand for an American site, ventured the highly speculative suggestion that Oslo might be a prospect. The ensuing discussion revealed that this was no mere courtesy gesture, and also that the Russians too might actually be open to a European solution—perhaps in return for some never disclosed concession.

But finding out where the United States itself actually stood was a far more difficult matter. Before the Preparatory Commission, Adlai Stevenson had declared repeatedly that his government would remain impartial and abstain from voting; but if the decision went in America's favor he would be most pleased to welcome the World Organization on behalf of the United States. Hectic activities toward this end soon became apparent. Notwithstanding the Federal government's "hands-off" policy, Americans skilled in the art of lobbying, and convinced that their respective home cities would make ideal Headquarters sites, had become so numerous on the London scene that a special subcommittee had to be set up to receive them. Be it said that they were liberal hosts in the Church House lounges.

Finally—after what I considered high time—the Commission's Committee Eight, by a vote of 30 to 14, concurred that "the permanent headquarters of the United Nations be located in the United States of America." But the division of opinion was closer than the vote indicated. Only a few minutes before, an amendment recommending Europe in place of the United States had been defeated by 25 to 23, with 2 abstentions. Although the Commission—through a motion seconded by the leader of the "European party," Philip Noel-Baker—had agreed in the end to make the choice of an American site unanimous, there was no hiding the closeness of the decision. Now that the die was cast, Adlai Stevenson could rise to extend the welcome of the United States, recalling the great honor conferred and the heavy responsibility with which his government and his people were now entrusted.

By December 22 the Commission had managed to breast the flood of American municipal deputations and agree that Headquarters be established in the "eastern part" of the United States. An Interim Committee, named to study proposed sites and eliminate unsuitable alternatives, at last settled on several possible sites—all in the New York or the Boston area. Following a month's visit and study by an inspection group led by a Yugoslav delegate, Dr. Stoyan Gavrilović, a formal recommendation was made. United Nations Permanent Headquarters, it was proposed, should be located in the North Stamford and Greenwich area, near New York City, with temporary headquarters in the city itself.

As the General Assembly gathered in London, many of us were waiting to go through the report of this field committee—not least to get an indication of how the American people were accepting the prospect of "new neighbors." The municipal deputations to London had indicated a most active and friendly interest—a feeling borne out by some of the correspondence with which the Inspection Group returned. Raymond Baldwin, the Governor of Connecticut, assured full cooperation, as did Governor Maurice Tobin of Massachusetts, who wrote that the Massachusetts State Legislature was "pledged to authorize the taking of whatever sites are necessary." Attorney General Nathaniel L. Goldstein of New York had assured Governor

Thomas E. Dewey that there was no "constitutional obstacle to acquisition by the United Nations of a site within the State." The General Assembly of Rhode Island had passed a joint resolution "extending an invitation to the United Nations Organization to establish Permanent Headquarters in the State." In short, it looked as if the Organization could expect a genuine and open-hearted welcome.

But this fair weather was of short duration. In London a new Permanent Headquarters Committee, established by the General Assembly, was again split, this time on a proposal to postpone the whole matter of site selection until the Assembly's session that autumn. The 19-to-19 vote by which the resolution to postpone was ultimately rejected indicated the strength of the pro-European forces, seeking every opportunity to hold the breach open at all costs. Representatives from Australia, Egypt, Syria, and Iraq came out strongly against New York and favored San Francisco. And on the same day that the Westchester County Planning Commission voted to extend a welcome to the United Nations, neighbors just across the state line in Greenwich and Stamford, Connecticut, gathered in protest meetings and voted two to one in favor of a referendum opposing inclusion of either of the two areas in the proposed Headquarters site. Meetings and gatherings sprang into being all through the proposed areas, and the controversy raged pro and con. Some feared that such a center would be "too European." Others, who feared that their own homes and property might be taken, described the whole matter of site selection as "un-American and unfair." Much of the trouble stemmed from the fact that the prevailing concept of the Headquarters at this time was that of a self-contained international enclave of up to 40 square miles. At all events, this was one occasion when the American "town meeting" had international repercussions. For the arguments echoed again and again in the London conference rooms.

In the end, the Permanent Headquarters Committee wound up the matter by reaffirming that Permanent Headquarters should be located near New York, in Westchester County, New York, and/or Fairfield County, Connecticut. Further, it authorized establishment of a new Headquarters Commission to draw up alternative plans for Permanent Headquarters based on areas of two, four to five, ten, twenty, or forty square miles.

Temporary Headquarters were to be set up in New York City, the Secretary-General being directed to "consult" with the Headquarters Commission or the experts assisting it "as he may deem necessary or appropriate."

With that, the London phase of the Headquarters struggle was over, and the temporary Headquarters problem was dumped squarely in the lap of the Secretary-General.

What pleased me was the decision locating Interim Headquarters in New York City. Men and women being what they are, I reasoned that once Headquarters were set up—even though temporarily—considerable effort would be required to move them again. Human inertia—and the high costs of moving—would go a long way toward quieting even such energetic "Pacific Shore" backers as Evatt, Makin, and Hodgson of Australia and that capable Arab representative from Iraq, Dr. Awni Khalidy. It was no less gratifying to see how the Russians had gone in for the New York area solution. Washington, too, had taken a wise stand, in my opinion: holding neutral when the choice was between Europe and the United States, and remaining so throughout the whole tussle of selecting a particular city or district—though, after all, it could have done little else as a federal government. After losing the "Battle of Europe," the British representatives held correctly and loyally to the approved resolution and lent full backing to New York and vicinity. They were indeed "good losers." Then, and later, I was impressed by the ability of the youthful M.P., Kenneth G. Younger, who deputized for Philip Noel-Baker in most of the Headquarters discussions. Both his approach and his statements reflected a remarkable thoroughness and fairness.

As soon as it was settled that temporary Headquarters were to be in New York City I sent an advance party across the Atlantic to look for office space and meeting halls. David Owen, then still my Executive Assistant, was in this group, and Adrian Pelt, the newly appointed Assistant Secretary-General for Conference and General Services, soon joined them. But the two most useful members of this advance group, because of their familiarity with the American scene and their knowledge that hard prodding was needed to make headway, were David B. Vaughan, principal director under Mr. Pelt, a man who knew how to cut through red tape and get things done, and Abraham H. Feller, whom I had made Principal Director of the

Legal Department and General Counsel to the United Nations. Dr. Feller was the only American whom Mr. Stettinius had recommended to me for appointment to the Secretariat. Formerly general counsel to the Office of War Information and the U.N.R.R.A., he had been Adlai Stevenson's deputy in the Preparatory Commission and an adviser to the American Assembly delegation. I had been much impressed by his brilliant mind and sound judgment when I first met and talked with him. He soon became one of my most intimate and trusted advisers and played an invaluable part in the first seven years of the history of the United Nations.

How this Secretariat group, and others who joined them from London at almost daily intervals, managed to survive those first four weeks, I have never fully understood. I can only recall that the prediction cabled to London by the delegates who made up the first "Inspection Group," that "certain difficulties" would be encountered, turned out to be an almost ludicrous understatement.

There was no place to work in the first few weeks except cramped hotel rooms. Several hundred Secretariat members were arriving from London and other places, and more hundreds had to be hired on the spot. All had to be paid and provided with places to sleep. And in the midst of this the search for a minimum of indispensable meeting and office space—preferably combined—continued day and night.

During these hectic weeks, quarters for the Council and the Secretariat remained the burning question. Space for the General Assembly, convening half a year later, rated only a second priority. With the help of Mayor William O'Dwyer and his associates, initial efforts centered on checking off the prospects suggested by the Interim Committee; but it soon became clear that no ideal solution was going to be found in midtown Manhattan. The metropolis was then in the throes of the most acute housing crisis in its turbulent history. Hundreds of thousands of veterans were returning home from all corners of the globe. There was simply no space to be had. Every single proposed solution was encumbered with objections and disadvantages which relegated it, ultimately, to the discard file. "I have been forced to follow the policy of not violating a single existing contract," I wrote to a Norwegian friend about that time; "nor can we risk taking a single house, building, or office occupied by others."

We were left with only a few offices in Rockefeller Center, inherited from the wartime United Nations Information Organization then under liquidation, and our scattered hotel rooms.

I remember one of the first meetings with my advisers in the former UNIO offices when the circumstances of the late arrival of my Chinese Assistant Secretary-General Victor Hoo, as explained by him, dissolved our worries into laughter. We had been working together in various rooms in the Waldorf-Astoria. A message had been left for Victor Hoo to come to this meeting at 610 Fifth Avenue, the UNIO address; but he had not got it straight and thought I meant Room 610 at the Waldorf. He went there at the appointed time and knocked at the door. An elderly lady answered, and when she saw my Chinese Assistant Secretary-General promptly told him: "Oh, no, there's no laundry today." This was by no means the only time Victor Hoo enlivened our "cabinet" meetings; his always keen sense of humor seemed at its best when he told such stories on himself.

About this time our attention began to focus on the Bronx campus of Hunter College, a women's institution under the City of New York. The campus had been taken over by the United States Navy during the war and had just been returned. It had a number of advantages, balanced by a number of less pleasant aspects. The place was a good thirty minutes from midtown Manhattan by subway or automobile. The buildings were not air-conditioned, and the prospective office space was largely in the form of oversized classrooms, difficult to partition off.

Nevertheless, the Bronx campus was obviously our best and, in fact, our only possibility. I authorized Mr. Pelt and Dr. Feller to ask Mayor William O'Dwyer to let us use three of the buildings for a short time. They did so on February 25, and the Mayor's response was immediate and favorable. A lease was formally signed on March 6. But now, once again, we became the target for the same kind of emotional outburst as had aroused Westchester and Fairfield counties. It had its source, I am sure, in isolationist, anti-European tradition and was exaggerated out of all proportion by some newspapers. It was alleged that the United Nations, by moving into the empty buildings of Hunter College for a few weeks, would deprive returned war veterans of the chance to resume their studies. But

Mayor O'Dwyer, wise in the ways of New York, lost neither face nor faith, and the transformation of Hunter College for United Nations use went on as planned.

For me, the Hunter College project has always stood as an example of what can be accomplished when a situation demands. In just two weeks the bare and empty gymnasium and swimming pool had to be turned into a Council Chamber suitable for the Security Council, the Economic and Social Council, and the Trusteeship Council. Oversize classrooms had to be partitioned into offices for the Secretariat, delegates, press, radio and film reporters, etc.

On March 21, while the workmen were still sweeping up the last of their chips and shavings, members of the Security Council were able to sit down for their first meeting. The job was done—on time. Welcoming speeches by Governor Dewey and Mayor O'Dwyer were no less appreciated than compliments in the press describing the work as the speediest remodeling job ever completed in New York. And a fitting answer was provided to the earlier outbursts of the isolationist press by the craftsman who fashioned the first ballot box for the Security Council. When the box was opened and examined before the first use by the delegates, a piece of paper was found on which was written:

> May I, who have had the privilege of fabricating this ballot box, cast the first vote?
> May God be with every member of the United Nations Organization and through your noble efforts bring lasting peace to us all—
> All over the world.
> PAUL ANTONIO, Mechanic

This, indeed, was the first ballot in the box to be cast for peace, and I am sure it represented the true sentiments of American people about the United Nations and its arrival on their shores.

Although the first hurdle had been surmounted in the search for interim headquarters there was no time to waste before the next step. Hunter College was only a temporary answer to tide us over the first few months. We had to find quarters for the Councils and the Secretariat that would be good for several years, as well as a hall for the forthcoming session of the General Assembly.

We looked into many prospects, but it was finally concluded that there were only two possible solutions as far as the Secretariat and the Councils were concerned: either to get more space at Hunter College and continue there or go to the Sperry plant at Lake Success on Long Island.

In terms of office space, the Sperry plant was preferable by far. It was owned by the War Assets Administration of the Federal government and had been built for war production. Half of the plant was no longer needed for this purpose. The whole plant was air-conditioned. The Administration Building had the most modern appointments, and the open factory area was so arranged as to make it quite feasible to build in the Council Chambers and all the offices we should need for the Secretariat.

Both alternatives were inconvenient for Manhattan—thirty minutes' travel to Hunter and forty-five to Sperry—and neither provided a solution to the housing problem, though Long Island would offer better prospects than the Bronx. Finally, neither alternative could provide a meeting hall sufficiently large for the General Assembly.

On April 8 I invited members of the Security Council to a private meeting and put the matter squarely before them. Their reactions were not enthusiastic; but when I asked for other suggestions they had nothing to propose except a solution in midtown Manhattan.

There was nothing to do but try again. This time, however, new meetings with the Mayor and his aides revealed that, while a solution in Manhattan was out of the question, another combination could provide an answer. On behalf of the City of New York, the Mayor offered for the use of the General Assembly the former Municipal Auditorium built on the World's Fair grounds in Flushing Meadow, provided the Secretariat were moved to the Sperry plant. Though since used as a skating rink, the Mayor assured me that the structure at Flushing would make an appropriate Assembly Hall, and that the city would provide it rent-free, plus $1,200,000 in repairs and remodeling costs.

This was unmistakably the solution, and I struck while the iron was hot. That same day, I informed Mayor O'Dwyer that we would take the Flushing Meadow building; and three days later, on April 15, I wrote to the War Assets Administration in Washington, stating the desire of the United Nations to lease half of the Sperry plant for three years from July 1 with option to renew for two years more. The lease was signed shortly thereafter.

Meeting rooms for the Councils and the committees and offices for the Secretariat were soon being readied at Lake Success; but unavoidable delays were cutting down our time margin. On several occasions the necessary steel for partitions had to be flown in. In a letter to my daughter in Norway, there was no hiding my own anxiety: "I must admit that it's impossible for me to see how we can build two Council rooms, six Committee rooms, and turn 200,000 square feet of open floor space into offices in the course of only four weeks. Let us hope the age of miracles is not yet past."

Though a solution, I still recognized this combination as far from ideal, and was prepared for protests and objections. While not the solution we had striven for, it was nevertheless the best obtainable under the circumstances. Of that I was convinced. Come fall, these complications would probably feed the flames of discontent with the New York area as a Permanent Headquarters site—an eventuality with certain serious implications. But we had exhausted every other possibility. Sufficient unto the day, I reasoned, are the troubles thereof.

The troubles of the moment were more than adequate. One of the most pressing was housing for the staff. Manhattan hotel owners had promised to take care of all Delegations and visiting journalists, but had gone no further. Long-term housing for our working force had to be found in other quarters; and, once again, Mayor O'Dwyer and Robert Moses, Park Commissioner and Coordinator of Planning, helped us find it. My aides and I were introduced to representatives of a number of firms then building, or planning, large housing developments in the New York area, and in less than thirty days we managed to secure 1,612 apartments—in Great Neck, in Parkway Village (Flushing), and in Peter Cooper Village (Manhattan)—all available for occupancy within eighteen months. The average cost of $25 per month per room seemed high to some at the time, but before a year had passed we found ourselves with some of the most reasonable housing in New York City. In what other city in the world, I asked myself, would it have been possible to work out a similar solution at that time? As a permanent site, New York was already beginning to show the United Nations what it had to offer.

New York City was not alone among the instances of public authority coming to our aid. Not to be forgotten was President Truman's personal intervention in the interest of cracking our housing problem. He sent Secretary of the Treasury John W. Snyder to help coordinate our building and housing projects, and arranged for a priority on all building materials for the apartments so urgently needed.

For me personally, however, getting acquainted with the ways and workings of the vast metropolis in which we should now be making our home, involved a long series of surprises. When meeting with diplomats, city fathers, bankers, real estate brokers, or contractors, I generally felt myself on safe ground—their world was my world; but there were other occasions when the new Secretary-General found himself in deep water indeed.

Long years with a schedule so cramped as to allow little time for the theater or the movies had hardly prepared me for the new social circle in which we were now moving. And there were so many little things, such as the significance—or the triviality—of the prefix "Miss," for example. In Norway, a "Miss" becomes a "Mrs." upon marrying, and stays that way regardless of what may ensue thereafter.

I remember one evening at Carnegie Hall when, with my wife and daughters, I was a guest of the society columnist Miss Elsa Maxwell, who returned to our box during intermission to introduce a number of her friends. One of these, a handsome fellow, was introduced as "My son"—at least, that was the way it sounded to me.

Strange, I thought; and even more strange was the furor which seemed to surround the introduction—a mark of respect, I assumed, toward the son of Miss Maxwell. But my confusion, and consternation, were complete a few minutes later, when my daughters stormed down upon me to ask why I had not introduced them to a world-famous singer with whom I had just been speaking. The handsome young man, they informed me, had been none other than Frank Sinatra.

A part of my confusion may have stemmed from an incident a few nights earlier when I had made the acquaintance of another "Miss"—a very famous one at that—who had proceeded to tell me all about her four-year-old daughter. It happened like this:

Representatives of the Big Five and a number of celebrities were gathered at the Hotel Commodore. Before we went to dinner there was a good deal of photographing—one attractive lady in particular claiming considerable attention. Though we had not been introduced, we were posed together, and we entered into a most pleasant conversation. She was evidently a celebrity, and when I found myself seated beside her at dinner I thought it best to ask her her name. It turned out that she was the famous actress Miss Lana Turner: a charming and most attractive young lady who mentioned, among other things, that she too had a daughter.

This surprising little episode should have taught me something of America's disregard for prefixes. Here, it seemed, "Misses" not only had children but talked about them openly. However, local folkways of this kind furnished relief from the political and administrative perplexities which were always with us.

Without the friendship and help of the municipal authorities and the most influential citizens of New York, my task would have been an impossible one. The great metropolis had sent no delegation to London; but it did not delay in making plain its welcome once the decision had been made. Of course Grover Whalen was on hand at La Guardia Airport to extend the city's official greetings when I arrived from London by way of Washington on March 21. New York is always a bit overwhelming at first. As I rode behind the traditional and noisy motorcycle police escort to the Waldorf-Astoria with sirens screaming I thought of the story I had heard on an earlier visit to America of a small boy with his mother who, seeing the President pass by with a similar escort, turned to her with the question, "What's *he* done, Mummy?"

When I recall our first months in New York, and the need for becoming acquainted with leading figures in the country where we should now be making our home, I am at once aware of the debt my family and I owe to Jörgine and Lucius Boomer. The name of Lucius Boomer is well known, both within and without the United States. He, together with his talented wife, created the Hotel Waldorf-Astoria as it is known today and managed that world-renowned institution until his death.

Jörgine Boomer was born in Böverdalen, Norway. During the German occupation there were no more steadfast supporters of free Norway than she and her husband. And when my family and I arrived in New York in 1946, these two dear friends received us with a warmth and enthusiasm which is hard to describe. Their faithful support was now extended to the new world organization, which during the succeeding seven years knew no more devoted friends than these two.

Especially during the first years of our stay, the Boomers seemed to regard it as their special mission to make us acquainted with many of their country's leading figures in business, politics, and industry—men and women whose support could mean much for the United Nations.

Through them I became acquainted with former President Herbert Hoover, a man whose views and observations were most valued, even though they did not always accord with mine. My friendship with Bernard M. Baruch, the financier and statesman, also stemmed from a first meeting at the Boomers. There was more than one ticklish situation when I found it wise to confer with these two men before making my decision. And finally let me not forget Thomas J. Watson, his wife, and their family, who always did so much for the United Nations.

What I remember best from my first day as Secretary-General in New York was the luncheon given in my honor by the United Nations Committee of that city. There I met for the first time Park Commissioner Robert Moses, Vincent R. Impellitteri and Robert F. Wagner, Jr. (successors in turn to Mayor O'Dwyer), and such influential and farsighted citizens as Arthur Hays Sulzberger, publisher of the New York *Times,* Ogden Mills Reid of the New York *Herald Tribune,* Winthrop W. Aldrich, Frederick H. Ecker, Nelson A. Rockefeller, and Joseph E. Davies (former Ambassador to Moscow).

"We are all in this thing together," I told the guests. "You are in it, I am in it, and hundreds of millions of other people everywhere are in it."

On that day began seven years of fruitful and heart-warming cooperation between New York City and the United Nations. Perhaps it was an advantage that I had begun my political career in the municipal government of Aker, now a part of Oslo, and had spent many years in local politics. On a smaller scale I had experienced the problems the Mayor of New York and his officials had to deal with. I understood the political pressures they had to take into account. I understood their way of thinking, and they understood mine. There were occasions when we had to battle it out; but it was always as between friends who respected one another, and we always found a solution. They were stanch friends of the United Nations from the beginning. And it was due mainly to those who greeted me at that first luncheon that the final solution to the question of the Permanent Headquarters was found nine months later.

CHAPTER V

IRANIAN ENTANGLEMENTS

The question of Soviet troops in Azerbaijan.—Gromyko's walkout and Western insistence.—My legal opinion, and its consequences for the position of the Secretary-General.—U.N. still "seized" by a dispute settled in 1946.

I HAD hardly entered the Blair-Lee House at Washington, where we stayed after our arrival from London on March 18, when the Ambassador of Iran sought me out.

Iran was in trouble: the Soviet Union, which was bound by treaty to evacuate its troops by March 2, 1946, was clearly violating its obligations. Its troops had stayed on, and the Iranian Prime Minister had so far been unsuccessful in effecting their departure. Hussein Ala asked for my views on an appeal to the Security Council.

Iran had applied to the Security Council during the London meetings, on the ground that the Soviet Union was interfering in its internal affairs through support by Soviet troops of an insurgent movement in the northern province of Azerbaijan. The Security Council had then called for direct negotiations between Moscow and Teheran. Now Iran had a complaint based upon violation by the Soviet Union of the Tripartite Treaty of 1942. In the treaty it was expressly and unconditionally agreed that the British and Soviet forces stationed in Iran should withdraw within six months after the termination of hostilities. British troops withdrew; Soviet troops did not. Moscow's failure to order its troops out caused a world-wide sensation. Washington protested formally. So did London. In these circumstances the Iranian Ambassador came to see me.

Mr. Ala had received instructions that morning to appeal to the

IRANIAN ENTANGLEMENTS 75

Security Council, and so actually he was seeking my reaction to his government's decision rather than my advice as to what that decision should be. He was aware that, in London, I had counseled direct negotiation with Moscow. He found my views to be unchanged. I was disturbed by the inexcusable delay in the Soviet troop withdrawal. Nevertheless, I thought that a debate in the Security Council now would probably intensify rather than ease the dispute. Moreover, I felt that the U.S.S.R. could be persuaded to evacuate Iran, as it had evacuated Norway and the Danish island of Bornholm, if it could do so without too much embarrassment. Cynical as Soviet policy might be, it was unwise to assume that considerations of prestige, of "face," meant nothing to Moscow. If the Russians were haled before the Security Council, I felt, they would strive to prove to the world that it was not their side that was in the wrong; rather than withdrawing, they might bend their energies to show they were justified in staying. On the other hand, there was a good chance of inducing them to evacuate, through sustained and serious private negotiation. I believed then, and believe now, that open disagreements openly arrived at are not necessarily preferable to processes of diplomacy of a more discreet and effective character. Naturally, I told Mr. Ala, Iran had every right to bring its case before the Council; but a further attempt at direct negotiation should be made first, and I promised my help to that end. I had as my deputy, I pointed out, Arkady Sobolev, who enjoyed much confidence in Moscow. He would provide an excellent channel for frank, informal discussions with the Soviet Union, which I should gladly employ on Iran's behalf.

Mr. Ala received my views politely; but he had his instructions from Teheran, which apparently had been endorsed in Washington. At the end of our talk he walked across the street to the State Department and communicated the thoughts I had placed before him in confidence. Accordingly, on the very day of my arrival in Washington, I succeeded in offending the Near Eastern desk of the Department of State, if not the Department at large. Washington did not in this instance seem to be disposed to recognize that the Secretary-General of the United Nations might in all honor and intelligence take a view of a problem legitimately at variance with that of the United States. This experience was to be repeated with many governments throughout my service. I soon grew used to it and even able to smile at the inconsistency of human nature in high places as well as low. When he agrees with us, governments tend to feel, the Secretary-General is within his rights, and is a good fellow besides; when his views differ from ours he clearly is exceeding his authority, his reasoning is bad, and even his motives may be suspect.

That afternoon, a letter from Mr. Ala was delivered to me, bringing to the attention of the Security Council "a dispute between Iran and the Union of Soviet Socialist Republics, the continuance of which is likely to endanger the maintenance of international peace and security." In accordance with its request that his government's appeal be placed on the provisional agenda of the Security Council, which was to meet on March 25, I listed it for that day. While still in Washington I received a request from the Soviet Ambassador, Mr. Gromyko, that I postpone the meeting of the Council until April 10, in order to give the Soviet government time to prepare its response to the Iranian charge. Simultaneously, Mr. Stettinius wrote that when the Council met on March 25 he would move that the Iranian question be placed at the top of its agenda. Then occurred the first of a series of peculiar incidents which raised some doubts as to how accurately the Iranian Ambassador represented the views of his government, and just what the policy of that government really was. Mr. Ala sent me a note earnestly requesting that consideration of his country's plea not be delayed—and within three days the Iranian Prime Minister publicly rebuked him in Teheran for his letter, stating that it was unauthorized.

I took no steps to urge postponement of the scheduled meeting of the Council. The Council itself, if it wished to accede to the Soviet request, could adjourn consideration of the Iranian item to April 10. The Council met and, by March 26, was deep in controversy about whether and when to take up the appeal of Iran. A series of dramatic sessions was to follow.

Mr. Gromyko announced that agreement had been reached with Iran, that evacuation of Soviet troops had begun and "will presumably be concluded in the course of five or six weeks, unless unforeseen circumstances arise"; he saw no justification for placing the Iranian item on the Council's agenda. But Secretary of State Byrnes, who had come up from Washington, demurred: Iran, he pointed out, had not withdrawn its letter, and it had to be heard to see whether it wished to withdraw its complaint. Sir Alexander Cadogan was of a similar view. Dr. Oscar Lange of Poland suggested that the Iranian item be placed on the Council's continuing agenda, but not be considered at that very meeting; rather, an official inquiry should be directed to Teheran seeking confirmation or denial of the Soviet assertion that agreement had been reached. He received scant support—Australia alone seemed sympathetic—and Mr. Gromyko received less. The item was placed on the agenda, after two days' debate, and Mr. Gromyko at once moved that its consideration be deferred until April 10. If it were not, he warned, the *Soviet delegation would be unable to participate in Council discussion of the Iranian question prior to that date.*

In a word, Mr. Gromyko threatened to walk out unless he had his way. This was a threat I took seriously. The prospect that he would get his way was very slim, and the damage to the United Nations prestige which would result from a walkout was obvious. I saw Mr. Gromyko privately and urged him not to carry through his threat. I made it clear then, as I was to state publicly and repeatedly later, that I did not believe in the boycott as a weapon for dealing with political differences. But Mr. Gromyko had his instructions, and of course he stuck to them. The Council, for its part, acted firmly against what Eelco van Kleffens charitably termed "a sort of pressure which I do not consider quite fair." It marched on, and Mr. Gromyko marched out.

Of course this was a sensation. The vivid impression of Soviet intransigence that this first Soviet walkout made upon the public mind was to be amply borne out by subsequent developments; but at the time it came as a shock. There is usually a lighter aspect, however, of even the most serious events, and so it was in this instance. As Ambassador Gromyko walked grim-faced from the Council chamber he was met by the chief of security, Frank Begley, who warned him that photographers were waiting at the foot of the stairs to take his picture. Begley's sharp eye had noticed that Mr. Gromyko was in that embarrassing predicament in which men sometimes find themselves in public places—he had forgotten his zipper. "Are you willing to have your picture taken, Mr. Ambassador?" Begley asked him as they paused in sight of the reporters and photographers massed below. "Yes, of course," answered Mr. Gromyko. "But . . ." Begley leaned close to the Ambassador. Mr. Gromyko's face broke into a broad grin, and the defect was repaired as they stood with their backs to the crowd below, apparently engaged in conversation. Afterward, when pictures had been taken with Ambassador Gromyko stern-faced again, the curious reporters wanted to know what Mr. Gromyko and Begley had been talking and smiling about on the landing. They did not find out.

Though Mr. Gromyko was now no longer at the table the Iranian issue was still with the Council. It had to be tackled. Mr. Gromyko had asserted that there was agreement between Moscow and Teheran on the withdrawal of troops: Hussein Ala had asserted the opposite. Whom should we believe?

There was considerable private concern among members of the Council, which I shared, over the degree to which Hussein Ala really represented his government's point of view.

In private discussions with him as well as at the Council table, where he was seated as his country's representative because Iran was a party to the dispute, we did not always feel at ease. Did he take his stand solely in accordance with instructions from his government, or was he acting partly on the basis of his own judgment or the judgment of others as to Iranian interests? We could only guess as to the content of the cipher cables between Teheran and the Embassy in Washington, and the question was never fully answered.

At this point Secretary of State Byrnes proposed, on March 29, that the Secretary-General obtain fuller information from Teheran and Moscow about the status of negotiations between the two governments: Was the reported withdrawal of Soviet troops conditional upon the conclusion of agreements between the two on other subjects? Everyone was in favor of this idea, and after some discussion it was decided that I should make a report on April 3.

I dispatched my inquiries, and—perhaps to the surprise of some —Moscow as well as Teheran responded in time. The answers were not altogether consonant, though Moscow did assure the Council that it was in the process of withdrawing its troops, and that the process would be completed within six weeks of March 24 and was not connected with Iranian-Soviet negotiations on other matters such as an oil concession and autonomy for Azerbaijan. Mr. Ala, in turn, stated that his government would not press its charge further in the Security Council if the Soviet Union pledged that its evacuation by May 6 was unconditional. Mr. Byrnes then moved that the Council take note of Soviet assurances and defer consideration of the question until May 6 when the parties should report to the Council as to whether the withdrawal of Soviet troops from the whole of Iran had been completed. His resolution was applauded and adopted, with only Australia abstaining (and the Soviet Union still absent).

With the Iranian item deferred, Mr. Gromyko returned to the Council. Had things ended there, as they gave every indication of doing, I might have escaped any further entanglement in the Iranian riddle. However, Mr. Gromyko was not satisfied: Soviet pride had been hurt. Moscow would withdraw its troops, and at the same time show that it had been innocent from the start. He wrote to the President of the Council on April 6 demanding that the Iranian item be removed from the Council's agenda rather than deferred: agreement had been reached on the withdrawal of the troops, leaving no dispute between Iran and the U.S.S.R., and so there was nothing for the Council to consider. Mr. Ala promptly retorted that his government wanted the question to remain on the agenda. However, when the Council met on April 15 his instructions were otherwise: "The Iranian Government," he read, "has complete confidence in the word and pledge of the U.S.S.R. Government and for this reason withdraws its complaint from the Security Council." Mr. Gromyko was, in his sober way, triumphant; but Mr. Byrnes and his colleagues were unmoved. Mr. Gromyko chilled any conciliatory feelings they might have had by not merely requesting the deletion of the Iranian item from the agenda, but insisting that this would confirm his contention that the Council's consideration of Iran's complaint, and its resolution thereon, had been "incorrect and illegal."

My own opinion, disregarding Mr. Gromyko's absurd contention of "illegality," may be summed up in the following way: the Soviet Union had clearly put itself in a vulnerable position by violating the Tripartite Treaty; it had now given assurance that this violation would be promptly repaired, and Iran had expressed its satisfaction and withdrawn its complaint; in these circumstances I saw no point in keeping the question on the agenda. The United Nations, I felt, should aim to settle disputes, not to inflame them. If both Iran and the U.S.S.R. agreed that their quarrel had been resolved, the Security Council should not indicate the contrary. Of course, if it turned out that Soviet troops did not in fact complete their withdrawal by May 6, or if some undisclosed conditions came to light that required looking into, the Security Council could immediately return to the question. Iran itself, or another member of the Security Council, or the Secretary-General in exercise of his rights under Article 99, might raise the issue. Should it, for instance, appear that the "agreement" between Moscow and Teheran had been produced at the point of a gun, naturally the Council would consider such a situation even if the Iranian government did not dare move. But this would be a case of the Security Council versus Moscow—a criminal case, so to speak, of the People versus the U.S.S.R., rather than a civil dispute of Teheran versus Moscow. I do not deny the possibility that Iran withdrew its complaint at the prompting of the Soviet Union. Still, the Iranian government remained the sovereign spokesman of its country; it had not been overthrown through foreign intervention. The same Prime Minister was in power. The State of Iran had made a legitimate request, and the Council should respect it.

These were my thoughts, and I was disturbed to find that the majority of the Council did not share them. The delegate of France, the very Gallic Henri Bonnet, and the delegate of Poland, Oscar Lange, held views similar to mine. The latter, of course—if I may say a word about him—was predisposed to agree with Moscow's stand regardless of its merits; but I think an objective observer will concede that Dr. Lange during his United Nations assignment displayed a degree of independence in his adherence to the policies of the Soviet bloc which no satellite delegate has dared to emulate since. He openly disagreed with Mr. Gromyko on matters which were not inconsequential, and I can recall Mr. Gromyko humorously grumbling about the trouble the representative of Poland caused him. Dr. Lange, an economist of note, had spent the war years in America, teaching at the University of Chicago, and had become an American citizen. Then he decided to give up his American nationality and devote himself to the new Poland. It was not long before

IRANIAN ENTANGLEMENTS

he was demoted from his attractive station in America and at the United Nations to an uneasy obscurity in Poland.

I should have liked to convey my views to the members of the Council as a body, in a private meeting; but the Australian delegation had received instructions not to attend closed meetings of the Security Council, nor did the United States seem to favor one. All the members of the Council expressed their views in public meeting, eight for retention and three for deletion of the Iranian item. I felt that I could not permit such a precedent to be set—a precedent which might well carry great weight in the later life of our young organization—without at least setting forth what I, as Secretary-General, saw as the wiser course for the United Nations. Accordingly, I decided to present my views to the President of the Council, for such disposition as he might wish to make of them. I anticipated that the President would bring my views to the Council's attention, but I did not expect that they would alter the stand of the eight-member majority. I saw the matter as one of law—of precedent—rather than of influencing the immediate treatment of the Soviet-Iranian request.

"I tried to look at the matter," I later wrote in a letter to a friend in Norway, "as might a Foreign Minister of Norway confronted with a hypothetical case such as this: Suppose a dispute had arisen between Norway and the United Kingdom (about, say, fisheries and the extent of territorial waters) which, because of a British declaration that H.M. fleet would protect British fishing craft, could be considered as giving rise to a dispute which might threaten international peace. Norway exercises its right to bring the matter to the attention of the Security Council. But, through bilateral negotiations, Norway and the United Kingdom reached agreement. Norway, as plaintiff, with the consent of the defendant, would have the right to withdraw the case of Norway versus the United Kingdom. But (since the Security Council did not accept my view in the Iranian case) it would appear that, in the hypothetical case I have submitted, the Council, or a member or members (for instance, the United States, or the United States and the U.S.S.R. jointly) backed by a majority of the Council, may decide to keep the Norwegian complaint on its agenda for a considerable time. Now the motives of those who decide to keep a case on the agenda need not be primarily consideration for the complainant country. It has been said that the heart may not be searched; their motives might be ones relating to their own political interests—interests which might not be the same as those of Norway or of the United Kingdom."

The issue promised to be disposed of on April 16. I had to speak out then or not at all. Early that morning I met with the Assistant Secretaries-General and laid my thoughts before them. The reaction was varied. Some agreed (Sobolev was naturally among them); some perhaps did not—at least they did not wish to take the responsibility of agreeing with me on my first public intervention in the Council's proceedings. My general counsel, Mr. Feller, and I closeted ourselves and drafted a memorandum to the President of the Council, beginning as follows:

"I feel it desirable to present to you my views with respect to legal aspects of the question of the retention of the Iranian case on the agenda of the Security Council. The decision taken by the Council in this matter may institute an important precedent for the future, and it seems to me advisable to consider it most carefully in order to avoid a precedent which may cause later difficulties. I submit the views herein expressed to you for such use as you may care to make of them."

The memorandum went on to set forth the various articles of the Charter pursuant to which the Council could be "seized" with a dispute or a situation, suggesting that it was "arguable that following withdrawal by the Iranian representative, the question is automatically removed from the agenda unless: a) the Security Council votes an investigation . . . or b) a member brings it up as a situation or dispute, or c) the Council finds a dispute or situation of a like nature to exist and proceeds to recommend methods of adjustment." I recognized that there was another side to the question: the contention that, once a matter was brought to the attention of the Council, it was no longer a matter solely between the original parties. The Council collectively had an interest; but I suggested that the Council, if it so wished, must exercise that interest by invoking the relevant Articles. If it did not, I concluded, "it may well be that there is no way in which it can remain seized of the matter."

Immediately upon completing our draft, Mr. Feller and I tried in vain to find the President, Quo Tai-chi of China. Just before the day's session was to open, I met him entering the Council chamber and said I wanted to submit to him a memorandum on the question of retaining the Iranian item on the agenda. Mr. Quo seemed to be surprised and muttered what may have been a diplomatic version of "What business of yours is this?" He did not accept the memorandum, and so, on the way to my seat, I sent it to one of his aides. As I sat down a latent aspect of my intervention came to mind: the status of the Secretary-General. I believed that Article 99, which empowered him to bring to the attention of the Security Council any matter which in his opinion might threaten international peace and security, was more than enough authority for intervening in the proceedings of the Council in this fashion; in fact, I felt it was the intent of the Charter that the Secretary-General should have not merely the right to submit legal opinions to the President, of which the latter would take notice, but that he should be able to address the Council on any question it might consider. Mr. Quo's attitude seemed to challenge this conception of the Secretary-General's authority. If the President did not acknowledge to the Council receipt of the memorandum, I decided, I would myself ask for the floor and read it into the record.

However, the President had the memorandum read aloud by an interpreter at the very opening of the meeting. He then proposed that it be referred to the Council's Committee of Experts for examination and report, and it was so agreed. Discussion on the Soviet motion to delete the Iranian question was resumed, and after a short time the President announced that he would put the motion to a vote. Before he could do so the delegates of France and Poland took the floor on points of order, Mr. Bonnet requesting that the Council await the report of the Committee of Experts before taking a vote, and Dr. Lange expressing his "astonishment at today's procedure":

> DR. LANGE: The Secretary-General has submitted to us a legal opinion . . . and then we went on discussing the matter quite disregarding the Secretary-General's opinion. I submit to the attention of this Council that the Secretary-General is an important official of the United Nations, invested by the Charter with special and important powers, and that we cannot vote now as if his opinion did not count or exist. . . .
>
> THE PRESIDENT: I am quite agreeable to the suggestion that we can-

not take a vote upon the U.S.S.R. representative's motion until we have heard from the Committee of Experts on the examination of the memorandum from the Secretary-General. . . . In regard to my Polish colleague's observation that the Secretary-General is a very important official of the Secretariat, there is no disagreement on my part. But I should like to point out to him that in Chapter XV, Article 97, it is expressly stated that "The Secretary-General shall be appointed by the General Assembly upon the recommendation of the Security Council. He shall be the chief administrative officer of the Organization." So whatever observations we may receive from him—and I am sure the Council will wish to give due weight and due consideration to his observations—the decision remains with the Council.

MR. GROMYKO: . . . Since we have decided that the memorandum prepared by the Secretary-General should be referred to the Committee of Experts, how can we vote or take a decision? As regards the functions of the Secretary-General—a question which has arisen in passing—these are, of course, more serious and more weighty than was indicated just now. It is sufficient to recall one Article of the Charter to realize the heavy responsibilities incumbent upon the Secretary-General. Article 99 states: "The Secretary-General may bring to the attention of the Security Council any matter which in his opinion may threaten the maintenance of international peace and security." . . . Thus, the Secretary-General has all the more right, and an even greater obligation, to make statements on various aspects of the questions considered by the Security Council."

In response, the President acknowledged his "mistake"—his "error" in proposing to dispose of the question of deleting the Iranian item before the Secretary-General's view on the question had been considered. Neither he, nor any other member of the Council, challenged the remarkably broad interpretation of the Secretary-General's powers which—of all people—Andrei Gromyko had advanced. Rather, discussion was quickly adjourned for some days, to await the report of the Committee of Experts.

Now this committee, despite its name, was not necessarily composed of experts in the ordinary sense—if, by "expert," we mean an authoritative specialist who arrives at his conclusions on the basis of independent judgment. The committee consisted of a representative of each of the eleven members of the Security Council, generally the delegation's legal adviser. These delegation members, in fact, act in accordance with instructions from their governments. I accordingly had every reason to expect that the 8–3 split which had appeared in the Council over deleting the Iranian item would be reflected in the Committee of Experts—and it was.

The committee clarified one point which was not sufficiently explicit in my memorandum. When I suggested that the question "is automatically removed from the agenda" unless certain other decisions were taken by the Security Council, it was not in my mind that the question would be removed from the agenda until the Council had taken a decision to that effect. The Council evidently was master of its agenda, and, because it had placed the item on its agenda, it would have to take it off. What I meant was that the decision to drop a question which the parties to the dispute requested be deleted from the agenda was one which the Council should take automatically.

I shall not set forth the legal intricacies with which the Committee of Experts dealt. As is commonly the case in matters of law, plausible arguments were advanced by both sides. These mirrored rather than influenced the decision of the Security Council. And, needless to say, the Council did not remove the item from its agenda. However, the affair by no means ended there. The repercussions of my Iranian opinion may, at least in so far as they affected the status of the office of Secretary-General, still be felt.

At the time, "my memorandum fell like a bombshell," as I described it to Halvard Lange, who succeded me as Foreign Minister of Norway. My intervention became headline news in the press of the world. Washington was irritated; after the meeting, Mr. Stettinius and I met in the delegates' lounge, and he complained about my position and my not having consulted him in advance. He was not mollified when I responded that I had exchanged views beforehand with his legal advisers. Secretary of State Byrnes went so far as to state at a press conference that, in advancing my memorandum, I had exceeded my powers. I met Mr. Byrnes the day after this had appeared in the papers, and asked him if he had read my memorandum. "No," he confessed. So I explained its contents to him, whereupon he conceded that he had not been fully informed, and asked me to disregard the reports of his remark at the press conference.

London took a less emotional approach: there, my intervention was regarded as more legal than political, and accordingly "all right." As for Moscow—well, Moscow could not help being pleased. I have referred to the generous views of the Secretary-General's authority which my intervention prompted Andrei Gromyko to propound. It may be that, as the man who was then the legal adviser to the Polish delegation suggested years later, "the Soviet Union, misled by Mr. Lie's intervention in the Iranian affair, favored granting him broad political powers and regrets now its mistake." At any rate, the Soviet Union strongly supported my subsequent request for writing my right to intervene in the Security Council's proceedings into the Council's rules of procedure. By the same token, the United States was cautious in defining the "capacity" in which the Secretary-General should act in the Security Council, and certain elements in Washington started "leaking" that I was "Moscow's man." I was never one to underestimate the importance of American support of the Organization and its Secretary-General, and I was unhappy over this reaction, though certain that I was right. In due course, Washington came to recognize that I had acted throughout in good faith and in full conformity with the powers of my office.

I have dealt at length with the Iranian issue, partly because of the influence my intervention had upon the position of the Secretary-General in future meetings of the Organization's principal bodies. As for the substance of the intervention, I would submit that events have borne me out. The Soviet Union did withdraw its troops, and its dispute with Iran disappeared. Yet, contrary to my advice, the Council has never recognized this fact. *The case of Iran versus the U.S.S.R. is still on the Council's agenda, some eight years after its settlement.*

As to the position of the Secretary-General, the provisional rules of procedure under which the Security Council was operating at the time of my Iranian intervention did not allow specifically for the Secretary-General's addressing written or oral communications to the Council, although they recognized, of course, that he could act under Article 99. Now, the Committee of Experts met to redraft the Council's rules, and also considered this deficiency. Mr. Sobolev, representing me, informed the committee that I was "considerably embarrassed" at the lack of a provision authorizing the Secretary-General to convey his opinion to the Council on matters under discussion. He proposed a rule similar to that which the Economic and Social Council had adopted, which would enable the Secretary-General to speak out upon the invitation of the President. Not that I wished to be limited in my interventions to invitations which the President might or might not choose to issue. The question was not academic. In the General (steering) Committee of the First Session of the General Assembly, Mr. Spaak, as President, twice had not accorded me the floor when I had indicated to him that I wished to speak. The Economic and Social Council, as well as the General Assembly, had empowered me to intervene only upon the invitation of the President. In view of this I felt it impolitic to press openly for a more extensive right in the Security Council.

However, I had authorized my chief lieutenants for Security Council Affairs, Arkady Sobolev, Dragon Protitch, and Ping Cha Kuo, as well as my legal counselor, Abraham Feller, to discuss privately with the Council delegations my belief that the Secretary-General should be empowered to intervene in the Council's proceedings at his own discretion. In the Committee of Experts the Australian, Soviet, and Polish representatives promptly took a stand in agreement with this view. Professor Boris Stein of the U.S.S.R. responded to Mr. Sobolev's limited formal request with the statement that it was "insufficient, since it gave the Secretary-General the right of intervening only upon the invitation of the President." The United States and China spoke out for a narrower interpretation of the Secretary-General's powers. Mr. Sobolev, amid a debate which ran on in this fashion for five meetings, kept quiet. The Australian Minister of External Affairs, Dr. Herbert Evatt, instructed his representative to maintain that the Secretary-General's right of intervention was "absolute and not limited." Acting on Washington's instructions, the delegate of the United States, Professor Joseph E. Johnson (later, President of the Carnegie Endowment for International Peace), expressed a contrary view—he was "not at all sure that the Charter can be construed as authorizing the Secretary-General to make comments on political and substantive matters." The British delegate at first suggested that the committee "let experience show how the powers of the Secretary-General should be put into practice." Later he shifted in favor of the Australian-Soviet view. I do not know what prompted the change in Britain's position, but it seems that that change altered the balance in the committee to favor the Secretary-General's unrestricted rights. Mr. Sobolev finally came forward with a new text, which the committee ended by unanimously adopting: "The Secretary-General, or his deputy acting on his behalf, may make either oral or written statements to the Security Council concerning any question under consideration by it."

As the committee's discussion was doubtless influenced by the precedent of my Iranian intervention, so the later revision of the rules of procedure of the General Assembly was influenced by the precedent set by the Security Council's subsequent decision to give the Secretary-General unrestricted rights. The Assembly deleted the "invitation" provision from its rules.

I may add here that the Trusteeship Council did not prove equally generous. Some of the colonial powers, I suspect, had special reservations about the approach which the Secretary-General or his representative might take to the issues in this Council. In the Economic and Social Council I had no such difficulties. The Secretary-General has enjoyed the fullest rights of intervention in the Council and in its several subsidiary organs, such as the Human Rights Commission.

I can understand the hesitancy of the governments in the early months in giving to the Secretary-General these broad powers of intervention in United Nations debates, even though they were implied by Article 99. As I have pointed out before, the political role of the Secretary-General of the United Nations is something new to the world. The concept of a spokesman for the world interest is in many ways far ahead of our times, when nationalism is stronger than ever and national sovereignty still the ruling force. It is for such reasons that I later used these powers with caution, because to have attempted to go too far, too fast, might have lost everything. I believe that the influence of the office of Secretary-General must be developed slowly and steadily over the years. But I am glad that these rights were secured at an early stage in the Organization's history when the fluid state of procedures lent itself to my initiative.

CHAPTER VI

THE CLEAVAGE HARDENS

The Baruch Plan and Article 43.—A year of serious negotiations followed by stalemate.—U.N. membership becomes a football of the cold war.—Greece and the Truman Doctrine.

THERE WERE many ominous signs of the developing cleavage between the Western powers and the U.S.S.R. during 1946. The ruthless Soviet violation of its solemn Yalta commitment to support the creation of genuinely free governments in Eastern Europe, the endless and bitter debates of the abortive Paris Peace Conference, the Iranian and Greek cases in the Security Council, and the first few in the long succession of vetoes that Soviet representatives were to cast so recklessly in that body were among these signs.

Yet the year began and ended with unanimous resolutions of the General Assembly on two of the greatest problems of our generation: the atomic energy resolution of January 24, and the disarmament resolution of December 14, 1946. Furthermore, the great-power foreign ministers who negotiated the unanimously agreed text of the second of these resolutions at Lake Success and Flushing Meadow simultaneously broke the deadlock on the peace treaties for Italy, Rumania, Bulgaria, and Hungary in private sessions at the Waldorf-Astoria.

In these months the die was not yet cast with finality for the long struggle of the cold war. I believe that most of the world's statesmen then shared the hope of the masses that a genuinely peaceful and mutually tolerable coexistence between the West and the Communist world could be worked out without long delay in spite of the danger signals that were flying.

In this mood the United Nations Atomic Energy Commission assembled at Hunter College for its first meeting on Friday morning June 14, 1946. Its terms of reference were those to which all the great powers and every other Member of the United Nations had assented in the January 24 resolution: *

The Commission shall proceed with the utmost despatch and enquire into all phases of the problem, and make such recommendations from time to time with respect to them as it finds possible. In particular, the Commission shall make specific proposals:

(a) for extending between all nations the exchange of basic scientific information for peaceful ends;

(b) for control of atomic energy to the extent necessary to ensure its use only for peaceful purposes;

(c) for the elimination from national armaments of atomic weapons and of all other major weapons adaptable to mass destruction;

(d) for effective safeguards by way of inspection and other means to protect complying States against the hazards of violations and evasions.

I shall not soon forget the scene that morning. As the delegates took their seats at the horseshoe table most eyes were turned toward

---

* The Charter provides:

"ARTICLE 11: 1. The General Assembly may consider the general principles of cooperation in the maintenance of international peace and security, including the principles governing disarmament and the regulation of armaments, and may make recommendations with regard to such principles to the Members or to the Security Council or to both.

2. The General Assembly may discuss any questions relating to the maintenance of international peace and security brought before it by any Member of the United Nations, or by the Security Council, or by a state which is not a Member of the United Nations, in accordance with Article 35, paragraph 2, and, except as provided in Article 12, may make recommendations with regard to any such questions to the state or states concerned or to the Security Council or to both. Any such question on which action is necessary shall be referred to the Security Council by the General Assembly either before or after discussion.

3. The General Assembly may call the attention of the Security Council to situations which are likely to endanger international peace and security.

4. The powers of the General Assembly set forth in this Article shall not limit the general scope of Article 10. . . .

ARTICLE 26: In order to promote the establishment and maintenance of international peace and security with the least diversion for armaments of the world's human and economic resources, the Security Council shall be responsible for formulating, with the assistance of the Military Staff Committee referred to in Article 47, plans to be submitted to the Members of the United Nations for the establishment of a system for the regulation of armaments."

the representatives of the United States and of the U.S.S.R. For the latter, Andrei Gromyko was a familiar face; but the representative of the United States was a new and historic figure on the United Nations scene. Bernard M. Baruch had emerged at the age of seventy-five from his chosen role of elder statesman and private adviser to Presidents and Congress in order to meet the grave and terrible responsibility that the invention of the atomic bomb had placed in his country's hands, and—for a short time—in its hands alone.

As Secretary-General it fell to me to open the meeting. I recognized that the problem would "require all human ingenuity and wisdom for its satisfactory solution," but rejected the view of "those who despair of the future and doubt if man can devise a system to control this new power."

"'It cannot be beyond the resources of the human mind which has made such enormous strides in its technical development, to control it, to prevent its abuse, and to use it for the good of all," I said. "People all over the world demand that atomic energy shall be made to lighten the drudgery of their working days rather than fill their lives with fear."

Then I turned to Mr. Baruch and asked him to take the chair pending the election of a permanent chairman. He did not wait upon the further formalities of organization but proceeded immediately to unveil in considerable detail the bold and dramatic proposal for an International Atomic Development Authority which will go down in history as the Baruch Plan. His opening words were meant to evoke a sense of urgency:

> My fellow members of the United Nations Atomic Energy Commission, and my fellow citizens of the world:
> We are here to make a choice between the quick and the dead.
> That is our business.
> Behind the black portent of the new atomic age lies a hope, which, seized upon with faith, can work our salvation. If we fail, then we have damned every man to be the slave of fear. Let us not deceive ourselves: we must elect world peace or world destruction.

These words have stood the test of years. They are true today, and they will remain true in the future. But we can see now, better than we could then, that the salvation of which Mr. Baruch spoke so eloquently that day is not to be found in any blueprint dealing with one artificially isolated segment of the problem of peace, like the control of atomic energy, no matter how imaginative and how nobly inspired. The Baruch Plan was all of that. The International Atomic Development Authority which he proposed went far indeed in the direction of real world government within the area to which it applied. It would be a supranational monopoly, controlling all production and use of nuclear fuel from the uranium mines to the finished product in all countries. To such an International Authority, once it was firmly established, the United States was prepared to turn over both its stockpile and its "knowhow." No more atomic bombs would be manufactured, and all existing bombs would be disposed of in accordance with the treaty establishing the control system. But the safeguards against violations must be immediate and automatic. "There must be no veto," Mr. Baruch emphasized, "to protect those who violate their solemn agreements not to develop or use atomic energy for destructive purposes."

Thus the Baruch Plan went far beyond the United Nations Charter in its call upon the national governments to yield substantial elements of sovereignty to supranational authority. It was a remarkable proposal for any great power to make, and especially remarkable for the United States. Here was a country for the time being in sole possession of what many considered as the "ultimate" weapon, proposing to give it up. And to whom would this country of "free enterprise," this country which was the symbol of capitalism to so much of the world, give up this knowledge and this power? To an agency that would represent a bold experiment in a world-wide cooperative movement, almost socialism. This would be a case not merely of one government taking over the means of production, but of all governments joining together to create a world monopoly of a revolutionary new source of power and agreeing in advance to yield all rights of veto over the decisions of the world authority.

This was, indeed, an unexpected challenge to the Marxist-Leninist doctrines professed by the leaders of the Soviet Union. That the United States, to them the very center of a doomed capitalism fighting for its life, should make such a proposal, was against all their dogma. I am sure it did not take them long to decide it was a devilish trick to open up the closed and secret Soviet system to Western agents. Non-Communists, it was true, would be in a majority in the International Authority. The Soviet doctrine and system were such that they could not permit the intrusion of so powerful an outside influence without a drastic change in the internal policies of the Soviet state.

There was an ironic aspect of the debate that followed, with the Soviet Union standing on the conservative side, upholding the thesis that national sovereignty must be preserved unimpaired, while the United States took the radical, internationalist position. I have often wondered what the fate of the Baruch Plan would have been in the United States Senate if the Soviet Union had by any chance agreed to it. It would certainly have required all Mr. Baruch's immense prestige and influence to persuade that body to ratify so radical a treaty; but this test was never to come.

The first move of the Soviet Union was a counterproposal, whose effect would have been the unilateral atomic disarmament of the United States. Ambassador Gromyko declared the first step should be an international agreement to prohibit the production and use of atomic energy weapons. Three months after the coming into force of the agreement, all existing atomic weapons would be destroyed. A system of control could come later. Such a proposal could not be taken seriously and was a discouraging sign of what appeared to be the Soviet tendency to approach the issue of atomic energy on the narrow basis of "East-West" conflict, instead of as a universal problem calling for statesmanship rising above all lesser differences.

Nevertheless, the Atomic Energy Commission went ahead with serious study and discussion of the Baruch Plan in which Soviet representatives participated. Its Scientific and Technical Committee did especially useful work during the summer. When the General Assembly convened for the second part of its first session at Flushing Meadow on October 24, 1946, the hopes that had been entrusted to the Atomic Energy Commission were by no means dead. The Assembly itself soon was dominated by debates on various proposals related to atomic energy control and the regulation of armaments and armed forces. Although the Soviet Union maintained its position that prohibition of atomic weapons should come first, and control afterward, it did agree to the principle of "strict" international control, with inspection, and to the establishment of "control organs" within "the framework of the Security Council" both for atomic energy and for armaments in general. On the matter of the veto in relation to arms control, the U.S.S.R. stated in the First Committee that "the rule of unanimity in the Security Council has nothing to do with the work of the control commissions. Therefore, it is incorrect to say that a permanent Member with its 'veto' could prevent the implementation of the control system."

In the end, a subcommittee of the First Committee succeeded in framing a resolution which was unanimously adopted by the General Assembly on December 14, 1946. The resolution was in general terms, but its language was such that the Soviet Union appeared to have modified its position so far as to accept the principle that the prohibition of atomic weapons should not precede, but be a part of, an international system of control and inspection with special organs of control for atomic weapons and for the regulation and reduction of armed forces and armaments in general. This resolution led to the establishment by the Security Council in February, 1947, of a Commission for Conventional Armaments to work side by side with the Atomic Energy Commission. Meanwhile, the latter adopted on December 30, 1946, a first report to the Security Council whose recommendations were substantially in line with the Baruch Proposals. The vote was 10 to 0, with the Soviet Union and Poland abstaining rather than opposing, on the ground that they were not authorized to vote on the substance of the Baruch Plan.

When the report came before the Security Council for discussion two months later Mr. Gromyko submitted a number of major amendments, and the whole issue was sent back to the Atomic Energy Commission. There, in June, 1947, the U.S.S.R. finally submitted its own plan for a control system. This made clear that the Soviet Union would not accept two main features of the Baruch Plan: first, ownership and operation of atomic facilities by an International Authority (these would remain, instead, in national hands subject to "periodic" and "special" inspections by an "International Control Commission"); second, while the veto would not apply in the day-to-day operations of the control authority, serious violations calling for punishment would be referred for action to the Security Council, where the veto would apply.

On these issues the Baruch Plan foundered in the end. It had overwhelming majority support, but it could never have reality without the agreement of the Soviet Union. Although the General Assembly in every year thereafter returned to the problem, there was no real change in the deadlock, no really new proposal from that day until President Eisenhower's speech on December 9, 1953. The Commission for Conventional Armaments made no headway at all, and it was finally abolished, along with the Atomic Energy Commission, in favor of a combined Disarmament Commission. This, at least, was a sensible procedural step forward, for I think the distinction between weapons of mass destruction on the one hand and mass armies armed with "conventional" weapons on the other has always been unrealistic in relation to the realities of power and politics in this world. The reduction of armaments and the international control of atomic energy, when they come, will come only hand in hand, and only as part of a wider political settlement.

One paragraph of the unanimous disarmament resolution of December, 1946, declared: "The General Assembly, regarding the problem of security as closely connected with that of disarmament, recommends the Security Council to accelerate as much as possible the placing at its disposal of the armed forces mentioned in Article 43 * of the Charter."

All through 1946, generals and admirals of the United States, the U.S.S.R., the United Kingdom, France, and China had met regularly together in private sessions of the Military Staff Committee. Many were of high rank—men like General Matthew B. Ridgway and Admiral H. Kent Hewitt of the United States, Generals A. F. Vasiliev and A. R. Sharapov of the U.S.S.R., Air Chief Marshal Sir Guy

* "ARTICLE 43: 1. All Members of the United Nations, in order to contribute to the maintenance of international peace and security, undertake to make available to the Security Council, on its call and in accordance with a special agreement or agreements, armed forces, assistance, and facilities, including rights of passage, necessary for the purpose of maintaining international peace and security.   2. Such agreement or agreements shall govern the numbers and types of forces, their degree of readiness and general location, and the nature of the facilities and assistance to be provided.
      3. The agreement or agreements shall be negotiated as soon as possible on the initiative of the Security Council. They shall be concluded between the Security Council and Members or between the Security Council and groups of Members and shall be subject to ratification by the signatory states in accordance with their respective constitutional processes."

Garrod of the United Kingdom, General Pierre Billotte of France and General Ying-chin Ho of China. Their main task during this period was to seek agreement on the recommendations they would make to the Security Council on the basic principles that should govern the organization of the United Nations forces.

On February 13, 1947, the Security Council asked for a report on the recommendations by April 30. The report, when it came, consisted of twenty-five unanimously agreed recommendations and sixteen on which there were differences. The main split was on the principle that should govern the respective contributions of the five great powers. The U.S.S.R. insisted on the principle that each should make equal contributions of land, sea, and air forces. The other four delegations supported the principle of comparability with allowance made for wide differences in the respective contributions of land, sea, and air forces.

When the Security Council began discussion of the report in June, this was the principal subject of debate. In the course of the discussion the Military Staff Committee was requested to submit estimates of the over-all strength of the armed forces that should be available to the Security Council to enable it to fulfill its responsibilities for the maintenance of peace. France, the United Kingdom, the United States, and the U.S.S.R., all submitted informal estimates, and China agreed to the United Kingdom figures. It is interesting, in the light of subsequent events, to recall these long forgotten estimates of 1947:

	FRANCE	U.K.	U.S.A.	U.S.S.R.
Air Forces				
Bombers	775	600	1,250 [1]	600
Strategic	(225)			
Medium	(150)			
Light	(400)			
Fighters	300	400	2,250 [2]	300
Reconnaissance	200	...	...	...
Miscellaneous	...	200	300	300
TOTAL:	1,275	1,200	3,800 [3]	1,200

[1] Strategic and tactical bombers only.
[2] Includes fighter-bombers.
[3] Air transport not included.

Ground Forces	FRANCE	U.K.	U.S.A.	U.S.S.R.
Divisions	16	8–12	20	12
Armored	(3)			
Airborne	(3)			
Motorized or mountain	(10)			
Naval Forces				
Battleships	3	2	3	...
Carriers	6	4	6	...
Cruisers	9	6	15	5–6
Destroyers	18–24	24	84	24
Escort vessels	30	48	...	24
Mine sweepers	30	24	...	24
Submarines	12	12	90	12
Assault shipping and craft for divisions shown	1	2–3 [4]	6	...

[4] 2 regimental combat teams or brigade groups.

It will be noted that the estimate submitted by the United States of the desirable total of available forces was by far the highest, while the Soviet and British figures were the lowest and closely corresponded to each other, except for naval forces. There was never any real discussion of these estimates in the Security Council because of the insistence of the U.S.S.R. that the principle of equality must be applied in the contributions made by each of the great powers in each category of air, ground, and naval forces. By the summer of 1947 the developing cold war had reached a stage in which it would, no doubt, have been impossible to reach agreement on these forces, even if the issue of equality versus comparability of contributions had not arisen. Nevertheless, I have often thought that even if the smallest figure submitted for each category had been agreed upon—for example, the United Kingdom's minimum estimate of eight divisions—the Security Council would have had at its disposal forces more than ample, not only to suppress, but to prevent any act of armed aggression except one committed by a great power. In the latter event, it has always been clear, of course, that the Security Council would be unable to act, and that the response of the United Nations would have to be undertaken through the General Assembly and such related collective self-defense arrangements as NATO.

For a few more months the Military Staff Committee went through the motions of discussion on implementing Article 43; but it soon suspended these efforts as hopeless in the circumstances. Since then there have only been formal meetings at which no substantive discussion has taken place. The Military Staff Committee remains in existence as a symbol of disappointed hopes which are not dead, but have been put aside for a better day. During the spring of 1948, when it was already evident that there would be no possibility of implementing Article 43 in the foreseeable future, I cast about with my advisers for a new approach that might provide the Security Council with some sort of armed force. The outbreak of hostilities in Palestine gave urgency to such thinking, and after much consideration I decided on at least floating a trial balloon for the idea of a small internationally recruited force which could be placed by the Secretary-General at the disposal of the Security Council. This would by-pass completely the great-power differences in the Council over Article 43. Without being too hopeful that the idea would be accepted in the prevailing atmosphere, I felt that it was my duty as Secretary-General to try.

I chose the Harvard University commencement exercises that June as the occasion for launching the idea. President Conant had asked me to speak, and it was from this very forum a year earlier that General Marshall had made the speech that was the beginning of the Marshall Plan. Of course what I had to propose was in no way comparable in scope and urgency with that, but the precedent made Harvard an appropriate scene. My speech made clear my opinion that Article 43 must remain the ultimate goal, but that it was wrong not to try to do something else in the meantime. Then I came forward with my proposal in the following terms:

It is possible that a beginning could be made now through the establishment of a comparatively small guard force, as distinct from a striking force. Such a force could be recruited by the Secretary-General and placed at the disposal of the Security Council. Such a force would have been extremely valuable to us in the past and it would undoubtedly be very valuable in the future.

Even a small United Nations force would command respect, for it would have all the authority of the United Nations behind it. I do not think of a single case that has been dealt with by the Security Council so far in which a large force would have been needed to act for the United Nations, provided that a small United Nations guard force of some kind had been available for immediate duty at the proper time. I include Palestine.

I hope that some preliminary action along this line can be taken very soon, pending settlement by the Great Powers of their differences over the final form of the Military Agreements they will make with the Security Council.

Such action would strengthen the United Nations, because it would add to the ability of the organization to exert its authority. It would also be a timely demonstration to the world that the Member governments are determined to make a beginning at least toward putting into effect the provisions of the Charter for the enforcement of peace.

The proposal immediately attracted widespread public interest and discussion and later received some preliminary consideration from the Member governments. However, the time was not ripe for attracting the necessary governmental support. Modest as it was, to carry it out would have required a degree of attention and imagination on the part of men in charge of the foreign policies of the principal Member nations that they seemed to be unable to give in the years after 1947 to projects for strengthening directly the authority and prestige of the United Nations as an institution. They were too preoccupied with the successive measures in the cold war like the Truman Doctrine, the Marshall Plan, and the North Atlantic Treaty, and with the domestic and foreign complications that all these entailed, to give time and thought to what seemed to them to be a less immediate issue. Yet, I continue to feel that this was one of those lost opportunities which, if seized, might have contributed substantially to building up the influence of the United Nations for the maintenance of peace.

During the summer of 1946 began the first of a long series of disputes over the admission of new members to the United Nations.*

* "ARTICLE 4: 1. Membership in the United Nations is open to all other peace-loving states which accept the obligations contained in the present Charter and, in the judgment of the Organization, are able and willing to carry out these obligations.
2. The admission of any such state to membership in the United Nations will be effected by a decision of the General Assembly upon the recommendation of the Security Council."

The Security Council considered the applications for membership from Afghanistan, Albania, Iceland, Ireland, the Mongolian People's Republic, Portugal, Sweden, and Jordan. The Western powers were opposed to admitting Albania and the Mongolian People's Republic; and the Soviet Union objected to admitting Ireland, Portugal and Jordan on the ground that it had no diplomatic relations with these three states.

Herschel V. Johnson, deputy United States representative in the Security Council, sought to break the deadlock by proposing that the Security Council recommend to the General Assembly the admission of all the present applicants. He stated frankly that the United States had serious doubts about Albania and the Mongolian People's Republic, but added: "In order to accelerate the achievement of universality of membership, we are prepared, on the basis we have suggested, to resolve the questions we have had in our minds as to the complete readiness of some applicants to assume the obligations of the Charter. The essence of our proposal is that the Council now, in a spirit of fair-mindedness toward all present applicants, and in the best interests of the Organization, recommend that the Assembly admit them all to membership."

Mr. Johnson and I had had many conversations on this subject. So when the United States finally presented its statement, I was already thoroughly informed. As soon as he had submitted his formal resolution, I therefore asked the President of the Council for the opportunity to speak in support of this approach, concluding with these words: "Many of the great tasks facing the United Nations remain to be accomplished. It is only one of our purposes to avoid war. If we are to fulfil our purpose, the United Nations must work for the improvement of mankind in every phase of life all over the world for time to come. This work will demand the active support and cooperation of every respectable nation and of every decent man and woman in the entire world. As I have already pointed out, the founding Members of the United Nations and all the great powers which form part of our Organization have agreed, on numerous occasions, that the United Nations must be as universal as possible. This is one subject on which there has never been a serious difference of opinion. For this reason, in my capacity as Secretary-General of the United Nations, I wish to support the admission to membership of all the States which are applying today."

My earlier conversation with Mr. Gromyko, when I informed him that there was now a chance of getting all applicants admitted, had awakened his personal sympathies; but he now received instructions from Moscow to reject the compromise proposal. No, he said, it would not be proper for the Security Council to admit the applicants *en bloc*. The Security Council should consider and vote upon each application separately and strictly on its individual merits. Mr. Johnson promptly withdrew his proposal. The Soviet Union then vetoed Ireland, Jordan, and Portugal, while Albania and the Mongolian People's Republic received only five and six affirmative votes, respectively, with the United States, the United Kingdom, and the Netherlands voting negatively. Afghanistan, Iceland, and Sweden ran the gantlet successfully and were admitted that fall by the General Assembly.

Thus began a dreary succession of deadlocks over admission to membership which continued to the end of my term in office. In 1953 twenty-one applications for admission were still pending, including Albania, Mongolian People's Republic, Bulgaria, Rumania, Hungary, Finland, Italy, Portugal, Ireland, Jordan, Austria, Ceylon, Nepal, Libya, Vietnam, Cambodia, Laos, Democratic Republic of Vietnam, Japan, Republic of Korea, and the Democratic People's Republic of Korea. A few nations did manage to secure admittance because the Big Five for one reason or another all voted in favor. These fortunate nations were Thailand, Pakistan, Yemen, Burma, Israel, and Indonesia.

Meanwhile, in the fall of 1947, the Soviet Union took a first step toward the position it had rejected so righteously the year before. After the peace treaties with Italy, Hungary, Rumania, Bulgaria, and Finland came into force, Mr. Gromyko proposed that the admission of all five should be approved by the Security Council. But now the United States, supported by the United Kingdom and some of the other Western powers, took the very line that Mr. Gromyko had pursued the year before. They strongly objected to the *en bloc* admission of these five nations and insisted that each be considered separately and on its merits. They supported the admission of Italy and Finland but opposed the admission of Hungary, Bulgaria, and Rumania on the ground that these countries had violated the human-rights provisions of the peace treaties. The result was that Soviet vetoes kept out Italy and Finland, and the other countries failed to get the requisite majority of seven votes in the Security Council.

Two years later, in 1949, the Soviet Union came full circle when Yakov Malik proposed that the Security Council recommend the admission at one stroke of Austria, Ceylon, Finland, Ireland, Italy, Portugal, Transjordan, Nepal, Albania, Bulgaria, Hungary, the Mongolian People's Republic, and Rumania. Once again the Western powers rejected this approach, and they have continued to do so since. Juridically they have a strong case. The International Court of Justice has given an advisory opinion declaring that a Member of the United Nations is not entitled to make its consent to the admission of a new member dependent on conditions not expressly provided for in the Charter, and, in particular, that it is not entitled to make its consent subject to the condition that other nations be admitted at the same time.

Furthermore, it is quite true that Article 4 of the Charter specifies that states desiring membership in the United Nations must not only accept the obligations of the Charter but be able and willing in the judgment of the Organization to carry out these obligations. It is very easy indeed to build up a case against the admission of the five Soviet satellite countries, for whose admission the Soviet Union has been bargaining so hard all these years with the veto power as its weapon. Nevertheless, it always seemed to me that it would have been wiser for the West to agree to the admission of these Communist states, along with the far greater number of non-Communist states that have been kept outside the door by this stalemate: From the practical political point of view, the West would have benefited far more than the Soviet Union; from the point of view of principle, it is surely evident that the most rapid possible approach to universality of membership is right if you accept the basic premise of any world organization at all. As for the standards of Article 4, the international behavior of some governments has certainly been far worse than that of others. But can any one of the sixty Members of the United Nations claim to have fully lived up to the obligations of the Charter since 1945, in all respects and at all times? The Charter sets

THE CLEAVAGE HARDENS

an ideal standard of international conduct which, alas, is still far from being realized in practice; but that standard has more meaning and more influence upon the policies of governments when they are inside the United Nations than when they are outside.

The progressive hardening of the cleavage between East and West which appeared in 1946 and became a permanent feature of the international landscape in the course of 1947, is also evident in the history of the Security Council's consideration of the Greek question. The offensive had begun from the Soviet side in London at the meetings of the Security Council where Mr. Vyshinsky had so enraged Ernest Bevin. It was renewed by Mr. Manuilsky of the Ukrainian S.S.R. in August, 1946. At that time the Security Council took no action beyond an inconclusive propaganda debate on the rights and wrongs of the struggle that the Greek government was waging against the Communist guerrilla forces. In December, 1946, however, Greece itself returned the question to the Security Council. It charged that Yugoslavia, Albania, and Bulgaria, all were aiding the Communist guerrillas inside Greece. Although the U.S.S.R. and its satellites indignantly denied the charges and renewed their attacks upon the Greek government and upon the small British force still in Greece, the U.S.S.R. nevertheless agreed to join with the Western Members in establishing a United Nations Commission of Investigation on which the U.S.S.R. and Poland were represented.*
The Commission went to Greece to undertake an investigation of the charges and countercharges of border violations.

Meanwhile, the Labor Cabinet in London came to a momentous decision. The United Kingdom, faced with simultaneous troubles in India, Burma, Malaya, Palestine, the Suez, and elsewhere, could no longer carry the burden of continued military and economic aid to Greece, a country which, by tradition, had been within the British sphere of influence and responsibility. Indeed, shortly thereafter, the United Kingdom government came to a similar decision with regard to Palestine. In the latter case the problem was tossed lock, stock, and barrel into the lap of the United Nations. In the case of Greece,

---

* "ARTICLE 34: The Security Council may investigate any dispute, or any situation which might lead to international friction or give rise to a dispute, in order to determine whether the continuance of the dispute or situation is likely to endanger the maintenance of international peace and security."

Washington was secretly notified early in 1947 of the British decision to get out.

This confronted the United States suddenly with the question whether it should move in to fill the vacuum of power that would be left in the eastern Mediterranean by the withdrawal of the British. It was one of several occasions upon which President Truman was confronted with the necessity of making bold and difficult decisions. Here as later in Korea, he demonstrated courageous leadership on great issues. Turkey was also in the picture. In bad shape economically, it had a large and brave but poorly equipped army and Moscow was subjecting it to a war of nerves, pressing for a revision of the Montreux Convention and reviving old Czarist claims to the border provinces of Kars and Ardehan.

Once President Truman had made up his mind, he acted swiftly. On March 12, 1947, he appeared in person before the United States Congress to propose a $400,000,000 program of military and economic aid for Greece and Turkey and to proclaim the Truman Doctrine, which brought American power for the first time face to face with the Soviet empire in this area. The later successes of the program in halting Communist expansion have amply proved the rightness of his decision; but President Truman's State Department served him ill in one important respect at the time. The situation in Greece was under active consideration by the Security Council. It would seem to be obvious that a government so strongly committed to the principle that the United Nations was the "cornerstone of its foreign policy" should first announce to the Security Council its intention of undertaking this program of aid, and the reasons for it. In fact, the Truman Doctrine burst like a bombshell upon the world with no advance notice whatever. I have been told that Ambassador Austin, the permanent United States representative, was himself neither consulted nor informed in advance. This was certainly true of many friendly Member governments in the United Nations, and of the Secretary-General. At all events, I remember that Ambassador Austin took the next train to Washington after the news tickers brought word of the President's speech to Congress, and I also know that Senator Vandenberg made publicly plain his own strong feeling that the State Department had blundered in completely by-passing the United Nations on so important a matter affecting the peace of the world. My guess is that these two stalwart Republican internationalists, who had long served together in the United States Senate, worked hard behind the scenes to repair the damage so far as they could.

At all events, Ambassador Austin promptly requested a meeting of the Security Council to consider the Greek question upon his return from Washington. At this meeting he informed the Council that Greece had urgently requested United States assistance on March 3, that the Truman Doctrine was in response to this request, and that the United States program of aid had the same objectives of restoring peace and security that had led to the establishment of the United Nations Commission of Investigation. Of course Mr. Gromyko responded by denouncing the United States for a "unilateral action" undermining the authority of the United Nations, although he went along for the time being with an American resolution calling upon the United Nations Commission to maintain a subsidiary group to keep watch in northern Greece while it wrote its report to the Council. Three months later, in August, 1947, the Soviet Union vetoed resolutions submitted by the United States and Australia based on the Commission's report. The United States resolution found that Albania, Bulgaria, and Yugoslavia had been giving assistance and support to the guerrillas fighting against the Greek government, and the Australian resolution declared the situation a threat to the peace and called upon Greece, Albania, Yugoslavia, and Bulgaria to enter into direct negotiations aimed at relieving tensions and resuming normal diplomatic relations. Both resolutions received nine affirmative votes, with Poland and the U.S.S.R. voting in the negative.

This ended the Security Council's consideration of the Balkan question. The issue had passed beyond the stage of possible negotiation between the West and the Soviet Union. But it did not by any means pass out of the hands of the United Nations. In the following September the Western powers were able to remove it from the Security Council's agenda, by a procedural vote, and brought it instead to the Assembly. This established a United Nations Special Commission on the Balkans, which the Soviet Union and its Balkan satellites refused to serve on or cooperate with; still the Commission nevertheless did very valuable work in the succeeding years. The presence of United Nations military observers on the northern borders, and of the Commission itself inside the country, proved to be an important deterrent to the flow into Greece of surreptitious aid to the Communist guerrillas. Gradually this flow dried up, while the massive American program of military and economic aid pumped new lifeblood, both in the material and in the moral sense, into a shattered country. Peace was restored inside Greece, and the future of a nation which had been on the verge of disintegration and collapse was saved.

CHAPTER VII

PERMANENT HEADQUARTERS

Headquarters battle resumed.—Problems of a federal government.—Secretary-General forced to fight in the open.—All other alternatives defeated.—New York is chosen.—From Lake Success to Turtle Bay.—A miracle of international planning.—Workshop for peace completed.

THE GENERAL ASSEMBLY had been scheduled to reconvene in New York on September 3, 1946; but when the Paris Peace Conference dragged on in disagreement during the summer the great powers requested a postponement. None objected when I polled the Members on a new date, October 23. This gave the Secretary-General and his staff seven more weeks—the extra time we needed to prepare for it.

Five days before the opening meeting, the new Assembly Hall at Flushing Meadow was ready. When President Truman rose to address the delegates that day, there was material evidence on every hand to bear out his welcoming assurance that the American government and people were ready to "extend the fullest measure of cooperation in making a home for the United Nations in this country."

For my part, I was reasonably satisfied with the new Headquarters arrangement. Addressing the Assembly the second day, I admitted the somewhat "wandering existence" which the Organization had been leading, but also pointed to the stones which were being added each day to its organizational foundation.

The new Headquarters arrangement, however, was still a stopgap, and the sooner a final decision could be made, the better. The report of the Headquarters Commission named in London now went to committee. It turned out to be a useful piece of work. The Commission had carried out its instructions in an exemplary manner; and—on the basis of the material collected—an early decision was indicated.

But this was not to be.

Once again, the embattled opposition to New York in the London debates was to push to the fore—armed with new and more telling weapons. During the summer, protests had continued to stream in from the New York and Connecticut countryside, decrying the decision to center United Nations' Permanent Headquarters in Westchester or Fairfield County. The protests increased in number as the date of the Assembly opening neared; and they made a deep impression upon delegates arriving in New York. Not least disturbing were the manifestations of antiforeignism and even, in some instances, traces of anti-Semitism. I knew that such an attitude was not representative of the majority of the people in these areas; but it sometimes appeared to be because the protesting groups were the most active and made the most noise. Many of the delegates with whom I conferred were outspokenly dissatisfied, and they strongly advised against moving into a district where we were obviously not wanted.

As I had feared, the travel time to and from meetings now emerged as a strong supporting argument against the London decisions. The long drives to Lake Success and Flushing Meadow were taking their toll. A sour note began to sound in the Secretariat as well, where older employees from the San Francisco and London days, and particularly those from Geneva, began to contrast New York with those localities. The climate, housing troubles, higher costs as compared even to other metropolitan centers—all tended to broaden the spectrum of discontent. And I was hardly surprised at the number of staff members who were in favor of moving Headquarters anywhere—as long as it was away from New York. I would be the last to describe New York City as an ideal residential area for those not born and raised there. But just how important was all this? Were we not concerned with more basic factors? A train of hard political reasoning had decided me in favor of this city. Under the circumstances, I should have to continue to place these considerations first, regardless of deficiencies in climate, personal comfort, and the like. None of us was here on vacation.

Once again it was difficult to ascertain where the Americans stood. I recalled Edward R. Stettinius's preference of San Francisco to New York—partly, perhaps, because he thought it would be better for the United Nations to be farther away from Washington. Nor was President Truman too keen on the choice of New York, as far as I could gather. While trying to hold neutral, he had mentioned to some close friends Boston and Philadelphia or, as I recall, some location in the Middle West. He may have had political reasons.

I was therefore most interested in sounding out Senator Warren R. Austin, the American First Delegate succeeding Mr. Stettinius, who had resigned in June. Our first meeting at his home in Burlington, Vermont, brought forth a wealth of information on the crossing and grafting of the apple trees in his beloved orchard, but not a hint of his stand on the Headquarters question. This came on November 5, however, when the Assembly's general committee met to consider the item and he proposed that the question be amended to read "'consideration of possible alternative sites for permanent Headquarters in the New York area *and in the San Francisco Bay area*, which may be available without cost or at reasonable cost." We seemed to have made a full circle, with San Francisco once more in the discussion and proposed, this time, by none other than the host country itself. United States neutrality on the Headquarters question was obviously being abandoned.

The Soviet reaction was prompt. While the U.S.S.R. maintained its position in favor of the New York area, Foreign Minister Manuilsky of the Ukrainian S.S.R. proposed that the agenda item be further amended to include "the possibility of fixing the temporary or the permanent Headquarters ... in Europe." Mr. Manuilsky's amendment was lost; but, whether or not this was only a maneuver, there was no doubt of Soviet concern over the Headquarters issue. When Soviet Foreign Minister Molotov rises to voice his country's views on a subject, that subject is important in Russian eyes. This time he had not been expected to speak; but speak he did—and forcefully too. What was most interesting, however, was that, while he came out strongly against San Francisco, not a word was said about a European site—only the offhand suggestion that the next General Assembly might be held there. Meanwhile the British succeeded in the Assembly in getting the agenda item further broadened to include other sites in the United States as well as New York and San Francisco. This opened the way for reconsideration of Boston and Philadelphia as east-coast alternatives.

During the next few days, New York's chances seemed to be fading by the hour. A subcommittee of the Assembly's Headquarters Committee was now named to study and report on San Francisco, Philadelphia, and Boston—earlier New York studies having been shelved at that point.

What was the Secretary-General doing during all of this? For better or for worse, I fear that my views on the Headquarters question were by then an open secret. Had there ever been any doubts, these were swept away in the course of an eleventh-hour meeting called by New York City officials. In a last-ditch effort they were prepared to offer the whole Flushing Meadow area—scene of the 1939 World's Fair and of the current General Assembly. Such members of the city's United Nations committee as Mayor O'Dwyer, Robert Moses, Winthrop Aldrich, and Frederick Ecker were among those present.

Municipal experts had assembled all possible information, and there was a lively exchange of questions and answers. Several subcommittee members, I recall, were inclined to doubt the city's contention that large, many-story buildings could be built at the Flushing site, in view of reportedly unstable ground conditions; and there were even some references to an occasional marsh odor and to a near-by cemetery. At this point my feelings got the better of me, and I intervened in defense of the city and its plan, going on record to the effect that I relied on New York's officials, that without them and their aid there would have been no General Assembly building for that session, and no Lake Success. Though these remarks were to bring the wrath of San Francisco, Boston, and Philadelphia supporters down upon me, my observations really consisted of a review of facts—just as they did some days later when, at the request of certain delegates, I reported that it would cost roughly $2,000,000 to move Headquarters to San Francisco, with added annual travel costs for the Secretariat and delegations amounting to another half-million dollars.

By December 4 the subcommittee had completed its latest investigations and had forwarded its report. Listed alphabetically, the

Belmont-Roxborough site in Philadelphia and the Presidio in San Francisco shared first place among their recommendations. The White Plains and Harrison two-square-mile site in Westchester came second, while New York City and the other earlier Westchester-Fairfield alternatives were out of the running. With this, New York and San Francisco backers had no more than set their heels for an all-out tug-of-war when the Soviet Union and the United Kingdom began to haul up their own heavy artillery. For them, San Francisco was out of the question. Kenneth Younger of Britain came out openly in favor of Philadelphia. The American Delegation countered at once with the statement that President Truman—subject to Congressional approval—intended to place San Francisco's Presidio at the disposal of the United Nations without cost. Aside from being an attractive offer in its own right, this latest revelation seemed to indicate the desires of the President and the Administration.

There the seesaw stalled in mid-air, and Delegate Georgi Filipovich Saksin of the Soviet Union stalled it. He held the United States responsible for splitting the delegations into three groups, and termed it "regrettable that the United States Delegation had disregarded the London decision." In closing, he made it clear that the "U.S.S.R. Delegation will not, under any circumstances, countenance the selection of the San Francisco site, and will not go there." He reaffirmed Soviet support for New York but indicated the U.S.S.R. might accept Philadelphia as a compromise. The British and, probably, a majority of the other delegations were equally opposed to the west coast as too far away, but could agree on little else.

With that, the Headquarters debate reached another impasse. Not one of us dared predict the outcome. But if confusion was rampant among the other delegations there was some consolation in knowing that the Americans themselves seemed equally confused. In a committee meeting on December 6 Mr. Austin back-pedaled rapidly. The offer of the Presidio, he said, had been made in response to inquiries from the Headquarters Committee and was not intended to influence the result. On the contrary the United States itself was opposed to the Pacific Coast as a site for United Nations Headquarters, as being too far from Europe; an Atlantic Coast site was preferred. But where on the Atlantic coast? Did the United States favor one of the new east-coast alternatives, or was it still holding to the New York area? An understandable silence prevailed. Admittedly, there are times when it must be difficult to be a federal government.

With the close of the meeting that day, it was clear that something drastic had to be done, and done at once. Flushing Meadow had won the support of but two delegates: Stoyan Gavrilović of Yugoslavia and Finn Moe of Norway. That same evening I telephoned to Mayor O'Dwyer and Robert Moses that unless they came up with a new and better proposal the whole thing would be over as far as New York was concerned. I had done all I could. It would be Philadelphia with San Francisco still an outside chance despite the new position of the United States Government.

Our telephone conversation was the turning point on the Headquarters issue. It started the series of events that ultimately raised the United Nations tower of glass and marble on Manhattan.

Turtle Bay, a maze of slaughterhouses and slum dwellings bordering the East River between Forty-second and Forty-eighth Streets, had been mentioned a number of times in conversations during the past ten days. I believe Robert Moses, Park Commissioner and Coordinator of Planning, was the first to mention it as a prospect; the solution appealed to him as a practical idealist and city planner. If there was no space on the island for United Nations Headquarters, why not make space by razing one of the city's most unsightly areas? For what greater purpose could such a civic betterment project be undertaken?

On the telephone that night, Mr. Moses, Mayor O'Dwyer, and I returned to the idea of Turtle Bay—a wildly remote prospect, it then seemed, but one which, even now, could turn the tide. What of the cost? Manhattan real estate was the most expensive in the world. The land alone in those six city blocks would cost millions. But there might be an answer, possible only in America with its tradition of private benefactions on an immense scale for the public good. Why not try to interest people possessing sufficient worldly goods and generous public spirit—such as the Rockefeller family; after all they had once given the League of Nations Library in Geneva. What had we to lose?

"Get in touch with Nelson Rockefeller tonight by phone," I advised O'Dwyer and Moses.

Later in the evening, the Mayor returned my call. He had just spoken with Nelson Rockefeller, then on a short vacation trip, and had also been in touch with Wallace K. Harrison, a close friend of the Rockefeller family and an ardent advocate of Headquarters in New York. Mr. Rockefeller, he concluded, would be returning to New York by air the following day.

This was on Friday December 6. Saturday and Sunday were among the most tense and exciting I can recall as Secretary-General. Reports which began to come during the week end indicated that momentous conversations were taking place backstage: steps were being taken that might snatch victory from defeat and crown these fifteen months of effort with success. Ambassador Austin and John C. Ross, one of his deputies, were now involved, along with Mayor O'Dwyer, Robert Moses, and Wallace Harrison. There were secret consultations with the Rockefeller brothers and with their father, John D. Rockefeller, Jr. But what was then happening was known only to a selected few.

By Monday morning our private hopes were rising. From the first, the attitude of Mr. Rockefeller fully reflected his great and generous spirit. But there was much to be done before so extensive a real-estate transaction as this could be assured. Normally it would have taken months of business negotiations with batteries of lawyers.

Warren Austin, rising in the Headquarters Committee on Monday morning, did not give the plan away. He merely admitted seeing no way out at the moment and spoke as if he were thoroughly tired of the whole wrangle. I think his suggestion that the committee's decision be postponed until the next Assembly was a bid for time. Whatever his motives, his proposal had the effect of delaying a vote on Philadelphia or San Francisco. The boring procedural debate that followed kept the committee in session until 11:15 that night. A few hours now were of incalculable value.

On Wednesday December 11, Mr. Austin rose once more—this time without a trace of fatigue. The first sentences of the letter he proceeded to read were enough to explain why, and to electrify the atmosphere of that Committee room. The letter was from John D. Rockefeller, Jr. It was short and to the point, offering the United

Nations a gift of $8,500,000 with which to purchase the East River property as a Headquarters site. "If this property can be useful to you in meeting the great responsibilities entrusted to you by the peoples of the world," concluded Mr. Rockefeller, "it will be a source of infinite satisfaction to me and my family."

With that the chips were down. A walk through the corridors or a glance at the 36 to 6 vote rejecting an Egyptian proposal to postpone consideration of the gift, were enough to indicate that the Headquarters issue was already settled. Within two days, the Headquarters Committee approved a resolution accepting the gift, and on December 14—just one week after my telephone calls to Mayor O'Dwyer and Robert Moses—the General Assembly sat down to ratify what was already a foregone conclusion. The vote of acceptance was 46 to 7, with only the Arab states, Australia and—oddly enough—El Salvador holding out to the end.

Turtle Bay had won.

With this lightning shift and the resulting decision, the five great powers were once more brought into agreement—in itself a strong justification for the outcome we had just witnessed. More important, the Headquarters of this new world organization were to be set up at the undisputed economic and political crossroads of our changing world. The United Nations would be at the turbulent center of twentieth century life, where, jostled by all the problems and all the challenges of struggling, swarming humanity, its work for peace would have a reality and substance unattainable in the relative tranquillity that so many had seemed to desire. To me, this meant victory after a long battle, and I wholeheartedly endorsed the expressed conviction of the Colombian Delegate, Dr. Eduardo Zuleta Angel: "The skyscrapers and chimneys of Manhattan will not hinder our work, as has been feared by some. On the contrary, they will continually remind us of realities and of life. With a profoundly human significance, they will be for us a constant warning not to lose ourselves in the byways of vain and sterile academic discussion."

During the nearly six years from the receipt of the Rockefeller gift to the completion of Permanent Headquarters in 1952, the planning and building of this great structure was among the projects closest to my heart.

Just as the location of the United Nations had concerned me from the first in London, so now I felt a personal responsibility for getting the building completed and occupied, a visible United Nations achievement. It was but one of the Secretary-General's countless problems during those six years, but it was the most cherished one. In contrast to the disappointments and the deterioration of the world political scene, the sight of Headquarters rising day by day was a source of strength and confidence. With expectancy I could send for the Headquarters file or attend a meeting of the Headquarters construction group. Its worries were good worries; its problems, healthy problems.

Headquarters brought new or deepened friendships of the kind only known to men or women who plan and build together. Three men were very close to me: Warren R. Austin, the first Chairman of the Headquarters Advisory Committee and one of the government representatives most responsible for bringing the structure to completion; Alexis Kyrou of Greece, another loyal and effective committee member; and Finn Moe, Norway's outstanding First Delegate. Their efforts, beyond the call of duty, helped assure a most gratifying cooperation between the Assembly and the committee, especially during the early years of planning and construction.

One of the initial moves of the Headquarters Committee was to accept the suggestion, made by New York City and the United States government, that Wallace K. Harrison be appointed Director of Planning. Mr. Harrison had been one of the chief architects for Rockefeller Center, for the Time and Life Building, and for a number of impressive structures raised by the Aluminum Company of America. We were never to regret our choice. His forthrightness, common-sense approach, and diplomacy with fellow architects, delegates, and building contractors alike were fully as valuable as his architectural skills; and he and his wife became close and admired friends besides.

Wallace Harrison had not been with us more than a few days before he proposed the creation of a Board of Design Consultants, to consist of prominent engineers and architects, some of them world-famous. In the course of but two meetings, the Advisory Committee approved the following as members: G. A. Soilleux (Australia), Gaston Brunfaut (Belgium), Oscar Niemeyer (Brazil), Ernest Cormier (Canada), Ssu-ch'eng Liang (China), Charles E.

Le Corbusier (France), Howard Robertson (Great Britain), Sven Markelius (Sweden), N. D. Bassov (U.S.S.R.), and Julio Vilamajó (Uruguay). They were a gifted group, with all the individualism and temperament that go with high achievement in the arts; but, under the leadership of Wallace Harrison, they worked as a well matched team.

A vast amount of legal spadework had to take place before we could begin clearing the jungle of tenement structures on the East River building site. The involved negotiations preceding transference of title were conducted by Dr. Feller in behalf of the Secretary-General. He had represented me in all United Nations contract dealings throughout 1946, and he enjoyed my absolute trust.

As is seldom the case with United Nations undertakings, our objectives were clear-cut; we were free from the numbing and unexpected slowdowns of international politics; we had our mandate and—not least—were blessed with an unusual degree of support and good will in all quarters.

In Washington and Albany, legislation was passed exempting the Rockefeller grant, as well as the U.N. property, from taxation, extending us the right of requisition and authorizing the city to control the posting of advertising in areas adjacent to Headquarters—an act of foresight which pleased me indeed.

There were Monday meetings at the Mayor's home—Gracie Mansion—informal gatherings attended by Wallace K. Harrison and Byron Price, Mayor O'Dwyer, Robert Moses, various experts, and myself. Soon a permanent fixture during the six years of building, these gatherings gave us a chance to coordinate the United Nations building program with the improvements which the city government planned for the surrounding area. Mayor O'Dwyer was able to report, on March 21, 1947, that the city had agreed to appropriate some $15,000,000 for improving and beautifying the area adjacent to Headquarters. What none of us knew then, however, was that New York City was destined to pay out closer to $25,000,000 before the job was done. Admittedly, the city would also reap considerable new tax revenues from the neighboring districts. In fact, it was later estimated that the city would recoup its investment from this source alone, entirely aside from the many millions spent annually in New York by the Secretariat and the Delegations. Still, $25,000,000 is a sizable amount, and, despite its own pressing financial problems, New York City was not to renege on a single promise.

After two months' work Mr. Harrison and the Board of Design Consultants presented us with provisional plans for the building. I recall the pride with which he reported that the plans were backed by fourteen architects from as many different countries. He concluded with the statement: "The world hopes for a symbol of peace. We have given them a workshop for peace." Such unanimity had not been foreseen. The exclamation of the Indian representative, M. J. Vesugar, that day, echoed our collective sentiments: "The accomplishment of this agreement might be considered a major miracle and should serve as an example to other United Nations bodies."

By mid-June of 1947 it was clear that work at the building site could soon begin. But it was equally clear that I should have to steer through a sea of figures more intricate than any with which I had previously worked, and should need expert advice. The Advisory Committee was prompt in approving my proposal of three recognized New York financial experts as advisers: George Spargo, Otto L. Nelson and John R. Kilpatrick. During the next two years they completed an assignment which all of us—not least Wallace Harrison and his associates—had every reason to appreciate.

Our lines of responsibility were cleared from the outset. Harrison, Price, and I were determined to avoid any and all charges of slipshod procedure, influence, or bungling; every move was to be thought out in advance, and the whole undertaking was to progress solidly step by step.

But the first over-all cost estimates came as a shock. I was prepared for a large figure, but nothing like the $84,000,000 presented by the Director of Planning. It was too high—far too high in my estimation—and I felt it had to be reduced by a good twenty million. Following a series of hair-tearing conferences where costs were cut to the bone in every possible quarter, we managed to get down to $65,000,000. But that fall, when the estimate was placed before the General Assembly, there was no avoiding a reservation on the final cost.

So far, so good: now we knew what we needed. But where should we get the money? All that summer, Ambassador Austin, Byron Price, and I went into every possible solution. Were there prospects for a loan from the Member states? Might they even consider a special assessment? What were the chances for a bond issue? These and many other suggestions were reviewed and rejected in turn. Apparently, the General Assembly would not receive a very cheering report on Headquarters financing when it met within a few weeks.

When my progress report on Headquarters came before the Assembly, however, I was surprised and encouraged to note how smoothly it was moved along. The work of the Assembly's new Ad Hoc Committee on Headquarters was in happy contrast to the experience of 1946. This was due mainly to the committee's officers, consisting of Warren Austin, Chairman, Finn Moe, Vice Chairman, and Alexis Kyrou, Rapporteur—all of them also members of the permanent Advisory Committee. The debate got off to a favorable start with none other than Dr. Evatt, the Australian Foreign Minister, coming out for acceptance of the provisional plans. With characteristic energy, he recommended that the Committee advise the General Assembly to launch building operations at the earliest possible date. Dr. Evatt was never in doubt. The deliberations took some days, and there were, as I recall, five meetings in all. Wallace Harrison made an excellent impression on the delegates. So did Robert Moses, with his reaffirmation of the city's intention to invest $15,000,000 in the area adjoining Headquarters. If there was any expression of feeling against New York at that time, I do not recall it.

Within a few weeks, the delegates had further grounds for satisfaction. I knew that Ambassador Austin and Mayor O'Dwyer and his aides had been active in Washington on the question of financing. There had been meetings with the President and members of his Administration. On October 29 I received a momentous letter from Mr. Austin, the steadfast and energetic Ambassador, reporting that President Truman had agreed to ask Congressional approval of a $65,000,000 interest-free loan to the United Nations, repayable over a period of thirty years.

All delegations were immediately acquainted with this offer, though, I must admit, it was not the first they had heard of such a possibility. I had been in close contact with Washington for a month and had passed a fortnight privately talking at Lake Success with representatives of the delegations.

On November 13 the committee voted a unanimous report to the General Assembly advocating acceptance of the loan.

The tone of good will and satisfaction, set in the committee, seemed to carry over into the General Assembly meeting a week later. There was a degree of unanimity which had become all too rare in United Nations proceedings. Not only was the committee's report unanimous, but the report of the Fifth (Budgetary) Committee had also been passed without a dissenting vote and was in complete agreement with the former. Hector McNeil, British Minister of State, and I were the only speakers that day. Recalling the magnificent example set by the fourteen architects, I could not resist expressing the hope "that the men of politics may be able to emulate the men of art and science in reaching common agreement also." Mr. McNeil's observations on that occasion were generous. "Like many of us," he began, "I was in the confidence of the Secretary-General. I know him as a most energetic man who knows no hours and no limits in hitting his target, but I must confess that my Government and I frequently thought he was overoptimistic in the plans he harbored for bridging this gulf between our desires and our capacity to pay. However, he has pulled off this financial miracle." Proud as I was of the "miracle," I was no less gratified by the fact that it was he who had put it that way.

Now to work. Wallace K. Harrison and his staff of architects and engineers turned to the detail planning. Drawings and specifications were examined meticulously, with an eye to the contract bids soon to be called for. Experts were named to study the latest building techniques and methods. Byron Price, whom I had named to follow the building operations, took over his new responsibility with a characteristic conscientiousness and determination. My own role, at this stage, was to lend assistance and advice, taking part in the numerous conferences and discussions, and seeing that the political wheels remained well greased.

Abraham Feller and Byron Price were put to work on details of the forthcoming loan with Washington, and their efforts soon led to an agreement better—from our point of view—than any envisioned in 1947. As we had expected, there was some difficulty in getting the loan through Congress; but the bill was passed on August 11, 1948, and President Truman signed it the following day in the presence of leading senators, congressmen and officials, including the United Nations Secretary-General.

The structures that cluttered the site were razed with dispatch. Excavating followed immediately, and foundation work was started during the late summer of 1948. Not much more than a year later, on United Nations Day, October 24, 1949, we laid the cornerstone of the United Nations Headquarters Building—the greatest event, until then, in the administrative history of the United Nations. President Truman was present that day, as were Governor Dewey and a host of other dignitaries, not to mention some 16,000 New Yorkers who gathered for the ceremony. With a trowel of mortar I sealed the cornerstone containing a copy of the United Nations Charter and the Universal Declaration of Human Rights. Behind us rose the thirty-nine-story steel skeleton of the Secretariat building. Only two weeks before, the last girder had been hoisted into place, and the workmen had paused in their labors as the blue and white United Nations flag rose for the first time over this workshop for peace.

My report to the 1949 General Assembly raised no new problems; progress at the building site now spoke a far more convincing language than what I put down on paper. The delegates had only to visit the scene of activity to see the distance we had covered since their last session in New York.

During 1950 the tempo of construction rose, now that completion was in sight, and on August 20 the first 450 members of the Secretariat were able to move in from Lake Success. The Conference Area —the section of the building that houses the Security, Economic and Social, and Trusteeship councils—was completed and occupied in the course of the following months. On January 1, 1951, less than two years after the first foundation form was placed, official Headquarters of the United Nations were formally transferred from Lake Success.

Headquarters on Turtle Bay were, at last, a reality.

As an international structure, it had long since been agreed that the art and design of the Member nations be incorporated into the building's interior. I was pleased when it was decided that decoration and furnishing of the Council Chambers should be entrusted to the three Scandinavian countries, which were the first to offer such assistance. The Security Council Chamber had been assigned to Norway, and my good friend the architect Arnstein Arneberg was charged with its planning and design. The Trusteeship Council Chamber was the responsibility of Denmark, under the able leadership of architect Finn Juell, and the Economic and Social Council Chamber was furnished and decorated by Swedish artists and designers under Sven Markelius—one of the architects responsible for the structure's planning in 1947.

This international participation idea soon won broad support, and many other member lands welcomed the opportunity to assist in decorating and furnishing the many chambers and committee rooms. Others offered statues, monuments, trees, and flowers for the planned park area. As the offers began to stream in, it became necessary to set up a Board of Art Advisers to assist me in handling the flow of gifts.

Of the hundreds received, I recall one in particular, and for a very special reason. One day, we were handed a check for $50,000 collected by American school children through a nation-wide ten-cent drive for a fountain fronting the entrance to the Secretariat.

Of course the new Headquarters had its share of growing pains. There were contretemps. A most spectacular one took place in April 1952. Vice President and Mrs. Alben W. Barkley, unexpectedly announcing their presence in town, had been invited to look around the new premises. Adlai Stevenson was also in New York that day, and so I had him join the party. The visit was a highly impromptu affair. Luncheon had to be prepared in all haste, and the hotel company managing our restaurant and cafeteria was not completely prepared with the necessary dinner service for serving the twenty guests that day. Our chef was offering his specialty: roast pheasant, with a mushroom gravy that had won him a reputation. Unfortunately, there were no gravy bowls, and there was nothing to do but serve the gravy in soup tureens—a most unfortunate makeshift, as matters turned out.

Mrs. Barkley was seated to my right; next to her, Adlai Stevenson. I was a bit nervous, noticing that our table was somewhat small for the number of guests, and that the waitresses had trouble in maneuvering; the huge soup tureens filled with gravy seemed to be difficult to handle. And then, as our waitress bent over to serve Mrs. Barkley, the catastrophe occurred. Slowly, the tureen slid to the edge of the tray; the waitress lost her balance, and in an instant several quarts of the chef's prized mushroom gravy poured out over the wife of the Vice President. Her white blouse, skirt, shoes and even her handbag were suddenly colored a rich, heavy brown. Chaos reigned; there were screams of horror. Servants rushed to our aid, trying to soak up the gravy with napkins, while stepping around their prostrate colleague, who had sunk to the floor in a faint. Mr. Stevenson and I saw that napkins were hardly enough, and went to work scraping gravy from the Second Lady with our table knives.

Mrs. Barkley was the only person to keep calm; smiling as if this were an everyday occurrence, she sat patiently as we removed what we could. But what then? How to get our unfortunate guest through the crowded restaurant and up to my apartment on the thirty-eighth floor without exposing the scandal? Frank M. Begley, our ever-ready Chief Security Officer, appeared with the Second Lady's fur coat, bundled her into it, and escorted her like a queen past hundreds of onlookers who had not an inkling of what had taken place.

Neither then nor later, to our supreme relief, was this incident mentioned by the Vice President or his gracious wife. Whether the waitress received a reprimand, I do not know; but the company procured regulation gravy bowls by lunchtime the very next day.

Though Headquarters was now up and occupied, one serious problem was still unsolved. From the very day we had begun to build, Wallace Harrison, Byron Price, and I had used every conceivable means to hold costs to a reasonable figure. Original plans and estimates, it will be recalled, were drawn up in 1947. Before the Headquarters structure was completed some building materials had risen 25 per cent in cost above the original estimates, and others also had risen. Harrison and his aides performed miracles. Costs were kept in line, but only by cutting into our original plans. Much had to be simplified or eliminated. In the end we found ourselves with buildings considerably less extensive than planned; but, despite all our care and saving, it was soon obvious that the $65,000,000 figure was simply not going to hold.

I made these facts clear in a special report. In the New York area, the cost of building materials had risen on an average of 19.4 per cent between December, 1947, and December, 1951. But because of our savings a far smaller increase, only $3,000,000 more, would be needed to complete the structure and its landscaping.

Most of the delegates to the Sixth Session of the General Assembly, then meeting in Paris, appreciated what had taken place. Only the Communist bloc, which, by then, was grasping at any opportunity to defame the Secretary-General, made an issue of my request for more funds. Its efforts, however, were unavailing. Despite a bitter and vociferous Eastern Bloc prelude, the Budget Committee rejected by a vote of 32 to 5 a Soviet proposal that my application be denied. It then proceeded by a vote of 34 to 5 to grant my request. Only two of the three million dollars were actually used.

With the opening of the Seventh Session in New York in October, 1952, all was at last in readiness for the Assembly. Only the landscaping remained. As I addressed the delegates, gathered for the first time that day in the General Assembly hall in the permanent home of the World Organization, I was deeply moved. Here, at last, was a United Nations program that had been completed. Here was a visible achievement in stone and steel. "When I became Secretary-General," I recalled, "the infant United Nations had no home except in the hearts of men. We did not know where the Headquarters would be, except that it should be somewhere in the United States. There was no money in sight to build it. There was not even a plan on an architect's drafting board. Through the years since then, the creation of the Permanent Headquarters has been one of my greatest responsibilities to you as Secretary-General. Now, here it stands, aspiring in graceful lines but solid upon the Manhattan rock."

For me, personally, this represented the end of a long, hard road. What had once been a dream was now reality. These mighty buildings would stand as visible symbols of years of hard and unrelenting effort. But, in reality, they were *our* achievement. Mine, and the loyal steadfast team of aids, advisers, and individuals outside the Secretariat without whom they would never have progressed beyond the aspiration stage. For me, the names and personalities to be linked first of all—and forever—with those towering walls require no tedious selection. The choice is immediate and clear: Harry S. Truman, Wallace K. Harrison, John D. Rockefeller, Jr., William O'Dwyer, Robert Moses, Warren R. Austin, Byron Price, and Abraham H. Feller. They are the men who, more than any others, raised United Nations Headquarters in New York City.

A six-year struggle had finally brought a roof over our heads, here in a land where government, groups, and individuals had proved to be able and willing to lend us the vast material support necessary to translate our plans into achievement.

Not only had we succeeded in building a workshop for peace, but the very strategy of peace had determined the structure's location.

CHAPTER VIII

LATIN-AMERICAN NEEDS AND CONTRIBUTIONS

Pride and poverty at the threshold of plenty.—Groundless fears of rivalry between United Nations and Pan-American systems.—Economic Commission for Latin America launched and at work.—U.N. responds to technical aid requests.

I PAID my first visit to Latin America in January of 1947. The decision to make time for the trip was motivated, in a measure, by experience in the previous summer, when United Nations business had taken me to seven European countries, including the Soviet Union.

That had been far from a pleasure jaunt. There were the Peace Conference in Paris, negotiations in Switzerland to straighten out United Nations status there and the transfer of the former League of Nations buildings in Geneva, and—not least—innumerable conversations with European leaders and statesmen on many subjects that bore upon our work. One result had been to confirm my judgment that it was very advantageous to the Secretary-General to talk over United Nations problems with responsible leaders of government in their own homelands. Reactions which might seem strange and obscure in New York, often were clarified by conditions witnessed at first hand.

Soon after my return from Europe, queries came through a number of Latin America's permanent delegates as to whether I might not pay a visit to their respective countries. I welcomed the invitations and the genuine interest behind them, and indicated the possibility of such a trip early in 1947—events permitting. The countries of Latin America interested me for a number of reasons, but what little I knew of them was entirely secondhand. Never had I been farther south than Washington—a serious deficiency, with a score of these countries among the members of the United Nations. There would not be time to visit them all on the same trip, and so I decided to start with Mexico, Central America, and the Caribbean area.

I recalled the resentment of the Latin-American countries at the near-stepchild status to which they had been relegated in the League of Nations. All were independent, striving for economic development and social democracy. A visit in the near future would, I hoped, strengthen their sense of "belonging," and bolster their faith in the United Nations. Further, I was interested in early ratification by these countries of the General Convention on Privileges and Immunities, and was set on securing their direct and active participation in the work of the International Refugee Organization and the United Nations International Children's Emergency Fund. Positive action by Latin America on all three matters would be encouraging, I reasoned—there being no better way to encourage a sense of "belonging" than the assumption of concrete responsibilities.

But there were other reasons for an early visit to the Latin-American countries. The end of the Second World War had left them in economic doldrums. Income from heavy United States wartime purchases of raw materials had now declined sharply. The national leaders were casting about for assistance. The Pan American Union had been a going concern long before the United Nations appeared on the scene, and it was only natural for the governments to seek aid and assurance first in that quarter. The Pan American Union had been revitalized at the Chapultepec Conference in 1945 in Mexico City, which paved the way for the present Organization of American States, and many persons felt that it was the ideal instrument for tackling a common problem. After all, the United States was the mighty member of that organization, and nearly all the most pressing problems were in terms of inadequate capital, techniques, and education. In short, they were much the same problems that economically underdeveloped countries faced in every corner of the globe. The most immediate route to American assistance, many of the leaders reasoned, was a reframed Pan American Union, building on the repeated assurances of the United States as to the seriousness of its Good Neighbor Policy.

Concern in Central and South America therefore seemed to be mounting, as certain Latin-American leaders began to eye with misgivings the United States' all-out support of the United Nations. They reasoned that this might be at the expense of the Pan American Union: hemispheric cooperation might suffer from emphasis on world cooperation. With such doubts superimposed upon unpleasant memories of their earlier role in world organizations, it was easy to foresee the direction their reasoning might take. While there was no real problem yet, the makings of a point of view far different from that which the United Nations was interested in encouraging among smaller Member states were admittedly present. It was a matter of acquainting leaders and officials with the responsibilities the new world organization was determined to assume. They would be deprived of nothing. On the contrary, the Pan American Union would be encouraged to new activity within the United Nations framework and—what was far more important—would be supplemented by new aid and resources from other parts of the world.

Yet another reason prompted me to make time for a visit to Central America. Most of the countries bordering the Caribbean still contain what can be termed economically underdeveloped areas. Here was an opportunity to observe conditions that extend beyond that region and are at the root of so much unrest in our time. I had never visited an economically underdeveloped area, and was convinced that an adequate understanding of its problems was impossible to me while that remained true.

I returned from the three weeks visit to Central America and the Caribbean in January of 1947 at once encouraged and disturbed: encouraged because it gave me a realization of peoples struggling toward a better life, which the United Nations could help them attain; disturbed because it gave me first-hand acquaintance with large-scale poverty and understanding of its full significance for the work of the United Nations for peace and progress.

For nearly every one of the ten countries visited, I felt the question was far more "How can we help you?" than "How can you help us?" Not many interviews were required to prove a general desire to participate—among the upper echelons, at any rate; but, the more I saw of the frail economic and social underpinnings that supported an often handsome façade, the more I was convinced that here the support that should be sought was primarily moral rather than monetary. The will to give should be encouraged; but the capacity, I feared, was lacking.

Early ratification of the General Convention on Privileges and Immunities was one of the first matters I took up with government leaders in the different countries. My first talk with Foreign Minister Jaime Torres Bodet of Mexico, revealed, however, that one of our own staff problems in New York was delaying ratification of this convention. A distressing shortage of experienced Spanish translators at Headquarters had forced us to distribute the convention text in English. In nearly every one of the countries visited I found they were ready to send the document to their parliaments for ratification as soon as the official Spanish text was prepared. I therefore cabled New York at once, and noted with satisfaction a few months later that each of the countries visited had ratified the convention, according to the Organization and persons connected with it the privileges and immunities essential for carrying out their work. Unfortunately, such openheartedness is not shared by all member states; and among those yet (April, 1954) to ratify this basic international document was one great power—the host country, the United States.

Foreign Minister Eugenio Silva Pena told me in Guatemala City that Guatemala had contrived to settle its pledge of $300,000 to U.N.R.R.A. by paying 10 per cent in cash and 90 per cent in coffee —a practical way out for many countries. I suggested to him that Guatemala might well be in a position to contribute dehydrated bananas for feeding undernourished children in countries which had suffered most. A similar suggestion was well received in Costa Rica, where both the President and the Foreign Minister thought it highly probable that their country could contribute various kinds of produce to the International Refugee Organization and the International Children's Emergency Fund. President Anastasio Somoza of Nicaragua was open to a similar suggestion, and promised to take action on my proposal that Nicaragua be opened for a certain number of refugees. Honduras had already signed the IRO Constitution and

President Tiburcio Carías Andino declared his country ready and waiting to do its share. In the Dominican Republic, I found that positive action had been taken on nearly every one of the issues, including the Convention on Immunities and Privileges. The Republic, I was informed, had already provided homes for a "large number" of refugees from Central Europe. Haiti, with its bedrock living standard, could not be asked to give. In conversations with President Dumarsais Estimé it would have been most unfair even to suggest help from Haiti at that time. On the contrary, his country was destined soon to receive its first United Nations aid, a complete survey of its economic and social potentialities which could provide the foundation for practical programs to follow.

From Mexico City on down the long arm of Central America, I sought at every opportunity to stress the vital role of the small Member states—noting that the experiences of these lands could serve as valuable guideposts for action on a far broader scale. Latin America, in particular, had already learned much from which the United Nations might benefit. "Your republics," I recalled at the foreign minister's luncheon in Mexico City, "have a better record than any other part of the world in the peaceful arbitration of boundary disputes." The century during which they had been "partly isolated from the conflicts of Europe and from the imperialistic expansion of the European powers over Asia and Africa," had given them time to work out their relations with one another. This observation drew an informal protest from the Netherlands Minister, who was present; but it was none the less accurate.

We had every reason to be gratified with the response of the Mexican public. Our visit received all possible press coverage, and the thoughtfulness of our hosts was often touching. I recall how, following my address at the City Hall, a large brass band solemnly played the national anthem of Mexico. The music for that of Norway was evidently unavailable; instead, the band broke into a refrain from the popular operetta *Song of Norway*—a gesture which, in the circumstances, I much appreciated.

Conversations with prominent Mexican leaders, on a variety of subjects, were most enlightening. I remember Foreign Minister Torres Bodet's explanation of Mexico's current economic crisis, caused by the outbreak of hoof-and-mouth disease, which had forced the cancellation of cattle exports. Such matters were seldom reported in the press of other countries. Mexico's leaders were forthright and outspoken, making no attempt to disguise their problems in the interest of making a favorable impression; but a fierce national pride was always in evidence and every effort was made to turn our visit into a memorable occasion.

This was true everywhere. In Tegucigalpa, the Honduran government took the occasion to dedicate a park under development on a height overlooking the city, as the "Park of the United Nations." Just before our departure from Guatemala City, nature had tried its hand at turning our presence into a "memorable occasion" of its own choosing. We were seated at an early breakfast in the hotel dining room, when we felt a slight tremor. Assistant Secretary-General Benjamin Cohen—himself a Latin American—and the Guatemalan *chef de protocol* promptly assured us that such tremors were most common and there was nothing to fear. However, both of them rose as one man and made for the door a moment later when the tremors became more pronounced—a most judicious procedure, I thought.

In Nicaragua I made the acquaintance of President Somoza—except President Rafael Trujillo Molina of the Dominican Republic, the only Caribbean "dictator" then in office. He appeared to be tough and competent. Our talks did not touch upon domestic politics, though a deputation of Nicaraguan minority leaders, visiting me the next day, failed to understand why I could not possibly take sides in their internal political disputes. President Somoza was proud of his country's material progress, and the schools, hospitals, and other public buildings of Managua were such as to bear him out. Uniforms, I also noted, were numerous. The President's son, a major in the army, had been assigned as my guide, and drove me around at breakneck speeds in a car with the most bloodcurdling siren I have ever heard.

Costa Rica was a pleasure, with neat green fields, well kept houses and streets, and it had a freer and more peaceful atmosphere than many of its neighbors. But finances were presenting serious problems, and it was obvious from conversations that it too would offer fertile ground for the work of the United Nations and the Specialized Agencies. Here the problem was clearly economic, and not educational. The literacy level was gratifyingly high, and Costa Rica is, perhaps, the only nation except Iceland (which has no military forces at all) with more teachers than soldiers.

Nevertheless, it was in Costa Rica that I met a most celebrated "soldier": Colonel Robert R. McCormick of the Chicago *Tribune*. We were introduced in the hotel lobby and found time for a chat over a glass of beer. I was impressed by his courteous demeanor in contrast to the fiery and bombastic editorials in his newspaper. He had the manner and appearance of a portly English lord, and his retinue of secretaries and journalists in no way disturbed the impression. A few days later we resumed the conversation in the Panama Canal Zone, where we met unexpectedly as guests aboard the launch of Willis D. Crittenberger, Commanding General of the Caribbean Defense Command. On a tour of Gatun Lake and a section of the Canal there was time for a longer discussion, which naturally turned to politics. I recall his measured recitation of old-school isolationist doctrine and his profound contempt for the city of New York—the latter subject having arisen in connection with certain remarks on Headquarters. While the Colonel apparently thought Chicago a far better city, I do not recall his suggesting that United Nations Headquarters be moved there. However, he did extend a hearty invitation to my wife and me to visit him—an invitation of which unfortunately we have not yet been able to avail ourselves.

Panama was in a somewhat different position from the other countries I visited. Basic problems were less acute, and conversations with President Enrique A. Jiminez indicated the possibility of Panama's contributing actively to an eventual Central American mutual economic aid arrangement under the United Nations.

The high point of our two days in Havana was a remarkable meeting arranged by the Cuban Association for the United Nations. This enthusiastic gathering of several thousand persons, including university students, intellectuals, farmers, industrial leaders, and representatives of women's organizations, labor unions and the press, provided the first real evidence of something which I had, until then, sought unsuccessfully in Central America. Up to that time governments had given me a series of splendid welcomes as representative of the United Nations; the type of welcome which any government might extend to the ranking representative of another, always on the diplomatic level. Here in Havana occurred my first real meeting with the people.

There were nine speeches that evening, and so I made mine short, expressing one thought I had voiced many times before, which seemed to take on a special significance against what I had just seen and experienced: "No international organization can act with success, no matter how strong may be the provisions of its charter, if the governments of the Member states do not give to it loyal and constant support. In turn, no government is in a position to give that support if it does not feel itself to be the faithful interpreter of the aspirations of its people."

Haiti presented few variations from the now familiar pattern. Its living standard was probably lower than that of any other of the lands I had just visited. Beyond a doubt, it would be among the most deserving candidates for United Nations technical assistance.

Ciudad Trujillo, capital of the Dominican Republic showed evidence of material progress similar to that noted in Nicaragua. However, I had not been there many hours before bitter complaints against the government began to come from newspapermen. I was also informed that university students had planned an anti-Trujillo demonstration to take place upon my arrival, but had been frustrated by a misleading report as to the hour.

Back in New York from the 8,400-mile journey with a bad case of dysentery, I had learned a lesson difficult to forget. Our group had left United Nations Headquarters three weeks before to bring a message to Latin-American Members bordering the Caribbean. Instead a message far more forceful and eloquent than any I was able to deliver had been handed to me—not by statesmen or other leaders, but by the thousands of dirty, ragged figures that never attended a reception or raised their voices in any fine declaration of faith. I was distressed by the sight of poverty and ignorance on such an unexpected scale—and on the very doorstep of the richest nation on earth. The contrasts to be seen in a single city, or in a single city block, were hardly to be believed.

This first visit to Latin America molded my thinking on the economically underdeveloped areas. From the day of my return, I took a new and consuming interest in the work of the United Nations Economic and Social Council and the Specialized Agencies. The creation of a firm and lasting structure that would preserve world peace implied all possible help to nations grappling with problems like those we had just witnessed. Here was a field where we should have to take the initiative; and we could not afford to wait. In a radio report I put it this way: "I have been impressed time and again by the realism and the candor shown by the statesmen of many of these countries in discussing their problems. I am glad and proud to say that these same statesmen look to the United Nations for leadership and assistance." At that early date, such an appeal had to be couched in careful generalities; but before many months we could speak out in terms more to my liking.

In the following August (1947) I visited Brazil, for the opening of the Inter-American Conference on Peace and Security in the luxurious Quitandinha Hotel at Petrópolis, twenty-six miles north of Rio de Janeiro.

Since the visit to Central America the need for dispelling any Latin American feelings as to the need for a division of loyalties between the United Nations and the Pan American Union had become increasingly apparent to me. The United Nations Charter had made provision for regional arrangements for the maintenance of peace and security, and it was to draw up such a treaty of mutual defense that the twenty-one American republics were now assembling at Rio de Janeiro. The proposed treaty would confirm and give permanent form to the Act of Chapultepec, subscribed to in Mexico in 1945, and would represent the first regional defense arrangement to be formed within the United Nations framework. As this meeting was called by the Governing Board of the Pan American Union, which together with the Republic of Brazil had invited me to attend, we had every reason to hope that a formalization of the positions of our two organizations would clear up a good deal of cloudy thinking.

Pausing only a few days at Headquarters in New York after a visit to Norway, I took off for Rio on August 26 with Benjamin A. Cohen, the Latin American Assistant Secretary-General, and William H. Stoneman and David E. Blickenstaff—both from my office. Though the General Assembly was to open on September 16, and a deskful of urgent United Nations matters was awaiting my immediate attention, the trip had to be made. In the first place, this meeting would set a precedent—one which would have a most important bearing upon United Nations status in time to come. The presence of the Secretary-General would—if nothing more—make it clear that the treaty drawn up was within the framework of the United Nations Charter. More important—a factor upon which I pinned considerable significance, in the light of the January tour— was the widespread conviction among Latin Americans that they needed economic aid more than a mutual defense arrangement. Latin-American delegates at Lake Success, I had found, were far more interested in Chile's proposal of an Economic Commission for Latin America—which was then up for decision in the Economic and Social Council—than in aid in the form of armaments. I intended, therefore, to make full use of my few minutes of speaking time to clarify the prospects for economic aid and technical assistance under the United Nations. This, I felt, could have certain results as far as United Nations support in Latin America was concerned.

The Hotel Quitandinha ("Little Market," to translate the name) proved to be an impressive, oversize Norman-Swiss chalet, set amid acres of recreational grounds and farms producing for its own tables.

There was time for informal discussions before the Conference opened. Talks with many friends among the delegates indicated that the right kind of United Nations "seed" planted here would fall in good soil. On the other hand, leftist organizations in South America—and elsewhere—were promoting the theory of potential conflict between the Inter-American system and the universal system under the United Nations Charter, arguing that the Inter-American system was built up for the exclusive purpose of coordinating the Americas against Soviet Russia, without mentioning the reasonable and genuine defense interests which any country or area will always have.

As the last speaker at the opening session, I lost no time in clarifying the United Nations' view of these meetings: "You meet here in Rio de Janeiro on this occasion to formulate a treaty between the American states for the maintenance of continental peace and security, based on the Act of Chapultepec concluded in March, 1945— and the Charter of the United Nations signed in June of the same year." I wished to make it clear from the very outset that the Charter was every bit as much a parent of the forthcoming treaty as was the inter-American Act of 1945. "So you come together," I continued, "not only as American states, with the interests of the New World in common, but also as members of the United Nations, with interests which transcend those of any nations or continent or group of continents." Later I returned to this point, itemizing the Articles of the Charter defining the relationship between these proceedings and the United Nations, and recalling that "they were carefully thought out and their implications are obvious to you and to the world."

Fully half of my speech that day was an appeal to the countries assembled there to join in the solution of their economic problems: "My travels in your countries and my discussions with your leaders have given me a clear impression of your problems as well as an impressive idea of your resources. You have a reservoir of wealth, which certainly can assure a good life to hundreds of millions. Granted true understanding and loyal cooperation between your nations, and between the American nations and the rest of the world, it can and it must provide a magnificent example of man's ability to make the most of his opportunities."

Though its full significance was not apparent at the time, Moscow's reaction to these remarks was destined to set the pattern for Russia's future stand on all regional defense agreements. A statement which Vyshinsky released through *Pravda* a few days after my address made it clear that the Kremlin considered the Rio Agreement to be illegal and in violation of the United Nations Charter. Soviet dailies expressed their surprise that the Secretary-General had even been present at the Conference. Then, however, we had yet to experience the discord which this first sour note presaged.

I returned to New York determined to work for the early formation of an Economic Commission for Latin America. David Owen and his staff in the Department of Economic Affairs agreed with me that what these countries desired and needed most was economic help: help to build up their industries, to develop their resources, to combat disease and raise their literacy level. It was within the capacity of the Members of the United Nations to organize such help.

By the middle of 1948 this Commission had been set up by the

Economic and Social Council and was a going concern, composed of the twenty Latin American republics, France, the Netherlands, the United Kingdom, and the United States. It assembled for its first meeting at Santiago, Chile, in June. It was the third regional economic commission to be organized, the others being the Economic Commissions for Europe, and for Asia and the Far East. Permanent headquarters of the Economic Commission for Latin America were set up in Santiago, where representatives of the various Specialized Agencies joined in a coordinating center with access to United Nations experts in every field. The Commission would act as a body responsible to the United Nations Economic and Social Council, and its activities, under the founding agreement, were to be coordinated at all times with those of the Inter-American Economic and Social Council.

Only a few weeks after the June meeting, the office of the Secretary-General began to receive an ever-mounting number of requests for technical aid from the Latin-American lands. One of the first was a request from Haiti in July to send a technical mission to advise the government on problems of economic development. Agreement was reached with no delay, and a team of experts was formed in consultation with four of the Specialized Agencies. By October the group was on its way, and within two months it completed a study which has become a landmark in economic planning. It was gratifying in the ensuing months to note the Latin-American countries' use of this new machinery. Ecuador, for example, asked for a team of experts to help organize its administrative and census system; Guatemala wished expert advice on economic development; Mexico needed technical advice for industrial and agricultural planning; Peru requested help in reorganizing its narcotics control.

One of the Economic Commission's first tasks was to launch an economic survey of Latin America—an area where reliable economic data had been sadly lacking. Another immediate task, undertaken in conjunction with the Food and Agriculture Organization, was the completion of a study of requirements for increased food production in these areas. An indication of the new interest in Latin America's capacities and problems is the fact that the United Nations *World Economic Report* for 1948 included a special section devoted to South and Central America.

With the Expanded Technical Assistance Program, authorized by the General Assembly in November, 1949, Latin America was brought more closely still within the working orbit of United Nations aid endeavors. Until then, our activities had been concentrated mainly in the war-ravaged countries of Europe, the Middle East, and the Far East. Now they would be extended to other areas, where centuries of poverty, ignorance, and disease had created even more deeply rooted problems—often far more involved than any we had yet faced. The man most responsible for the Assembly's taking this long forward step was Ambassador Hernán Santa Cruz, Chile's Permanent Representative to the United Nations and later President of the Economic and Social Council. His approach was direct and farsighted, and in harmony with his Latin-American colleagues' burning determination to expand United Nations activities in an area where concrete results could be achieved. This accorded perfectly with the conclusions I myself had drawn in Latin America.

Aside from economic aid and advice, Latin America was becoming a major area of operations for United Nations social, educational, and health organizations. By the middle of 1948 our advisory social welfare services had met requests for expert assistance from all the Latin-American republics, and scores of persons from those countries were receiving expert instruction abroad under scholarships provided by UNESCO, UNICEF, and other U.N. agencies. In March, 1949, the United Nations International Children's Emergency Fund voted to extend its activities to Latin America, and mass health campaigns for combating insect-borne disease, BCG vaccination against tuberculosis, yaws control, and immunization against diphtheria and whooping cough were drawn up. A plant for penicillin production was set up in Chile. A nation-wide BCG vaccination program, launched in Ecuador under the leadership of sixteen Scandinavian doctors and nurses, provided a training area for doctors from most of the Latin-American lands. Before long, these doctors were starting their own BCG programs in Costa Rica, El Salvador, Jamaica, and Trinidad. A laboratory for the production of BCG, equipped by this United Nations agency, was set up in Mexico, with others building in Ecuador and Uruguay. Programs for child feeding and milk conservation, and for the training of maternal and child-health personnel were also launched in Guatemala and Brazil.

Aside from the ever increasing number of technical assistance and health programs—each of them a joint endeavor by the receiving country and the appropriate United Nations organ—were the basic education projects. Thanks to the initiative of Jaime Torres Bodet, Director-General of UNESCO after his service as Mexico's Foreign Minister, Latin America was to play a leading role in this field. The Regional Fundamental Education Center opened in 1951 at Pátzcuaro, Mexico, was the first of its kind and was to serve as a model for similar centers in various parts of the world.

This summary account of United Nations aid projects in Latin America between 1947 and early 1951 is not meant to give the impression that any sweeping or far-reaching improvements were brought about in the course of four short years. Improvement in these and other underdeveloped areas is to be traced in terms of decades, not of years.

It was most fitting that the 1951 winter session of the Economic and Social Council should be held at Santiago, Chile. As I had received invitations from the governments of Chile, Peru, and Ecuador, I decided to pay yet another visit to Latin America—accompanied this time by Mrs. Lie, Tor Gjesdal, and my Ecuadorian adviser José A. Correa.

We arrived at Santiago late on February 18, with little time before the opening of the Council on the 20th, and entered immediately upon a series of official receptions. One of them, I have good reason to recall for its lesson value. We were dinner guests of President Gabriel González Videla, and he had sent his official plane to bring us to his summer residence at Viña del Mar for conversations shared by Foreign Minister Horacio Walker and other officials. Assuming that dinner would be at eight o'clock, we had changed to formal attire, only to find the other guests in tweeds. Dinner, we were informed, was to be at eleven, and the guests were expected to change to formal dress shortly before that. So for some three hours we circulated, conspicuous and hungry—victims of our own ignorance.

The following day, I was the last speaker at the Chilean government's inaugural ceremony for the Council. I recalled the significance of the gathering: "This first meeting in Latin America of a principal organ of the United Nations—the Economic and Social Council—gives evidence of the great importance the twenty republics of Latin America attach to the United Nations." There was reason for stressing this aspect, for I had ample cause to believe that the United Nations had gained stature in Latin America since my first visit, thanks—not least—to the efforts of the members of the Council assembled here. As the leaders charged with heading the fight against poverty, ignorance, and disease they deserved all possible credit. But the accomplishments—however substantial in themselves—were small indeed in comparison to the unanswered needs. "Let me remind you," I said, "that five hundred million people have achieved national freedom in the five short years since the United Nations was founded. These peoples live almost without exception in the less developed areas of the world. They, and all others in the many countries that have hardly begun to develop their resources, will not be content to live on in the grinding poverty that has always before been their fate."

From Chile we flew to Peru, where we made a new though now familiar circle of mansions, glitter, and formal attire, but again had only to turn our heads to see evidence of the problems of the indigenous population. Looking down from a mountaintop over Lima a few days later, we saw the city as a whole, with the slum quarters, the earthen huts and dilapidated shacks of the poor standing out alongside the beautiful avenues and villas; I could not but contrast with a feeling of guilt our own "discomfort" a few nights before, caused by nothing more than arriving for dinner in the wrong attire.

In Peru I was impressed by the country's ancient Inca culture. Evidence of the amazingly high degree of civilization to which Peruvians had attained so many centuries ago was to be seen on every hand, and I have never been more taken by the past than on a visit to the Inca collection in the National Museum of Archaeology and Anthropology at Magdalena Vieja, at the urging of Foreign Minister Manuel Gallagher and Dr. Victor Andrés Belaunde.

Peru appeared, too, to be comparatively prosperous on the surface. One seldom sees greater quantities of gold—outside a bank vault—than are used to decorate its churches and cathedrals. But the wealth has not been shared by many.

Quito, Ecuador, was too high for me. At the 9,300-foot altitude of this charming capital—still as Spanish in style as any town south of the Pyrenees—my circulatory system began to rebel. I thought that my years as Secretary-General were finally taking their toll, but after three nights sleeping in a sitting position, I was gratified to find myself still very much alive. President Galo Plaza Lasso was a most engaging person: a graduate of a California university, a former football player, and now a true fighter for popular government in a country which has often suffered from revolutions. There was no mistaking his appreciation for the aid rendered by United Nations teams sent to Ecuador following the earthquake disaster of 1949. I gathered, too, that Ecuadorians enjoyed a far greater degree of press freedom than some other South Americans.

I also had an opportunity to see how freedom of expression was respected by the government. Our last day in Quito, the Central University held the ceremony in which the degree of Doctor Honoris Causa was presented to me. I met President Plaza and Foreign Minister Neftalí Ponce at the Presidential Palace, and on the way to City Hall, where the ceremony was to be held, he told me of reports received to the effect that leftist groups would try to show their displeasure with the United Nations policies toward Korea and Communist China. He told me it was the government's policy not to oppose this type of demonstration. City Hall was so crowded that we had difficulty in reaching the rostrum, and my speech, which followed one by the President of the University and Dean of the Law School, was received with great applause; but as we went out the demonstration was in full swing. President Plaza and I walked in front of the demonstrators, took a car, and left the area. I remember this as a fine example of democratic practice.

Some of the most interesting conversations I recall from Quito were held with the sixteen members of a United Nations BCG vaccination team then working in the area. These Scandinavian doctors and nurses, headed by Dr. Osvald Osvik, described to me scenes and conditions they had witnessed during their months of work there. Later, during a short stopover in Guayaquil, on the coast, I accompanied Dr. Osvik in his jeep to see something of the bamboo hovels where the poorer people lived, and where these specialists spent much of their time. The mercury reached 105° that day, and my admiration for the doctors and nurses who were seeing this project through increased as the afternoon wore on.

My visit to the three South American countries was widely reported in the press and did much to raise public interest in United Nations problems. I received the newspapermen in every capital, and was impressed by their familiarity not only with United Nations activities, but also with international politics in a wider sense.

I returned to Headquarters encouraged. My 1947 visits to Latin America had left me with a sense of impotence, distressed by what I had seen, but even more so by the necessity of forever being forced to deal in terms of assurance and promises. Here were millions of people whose support we needed, and whose confidence in the United Nations could be strengthened, if only we were in a position to act. Their needs were not reflected in the vocabulary of military security that so fully occupied the world's statesmen. Their needs were for economic and social assistance in the countless areas where they themselves could not hope to make a start without outside help.

Now, we had at least begun.

CHAPTER IX

THE CHALLENGE OF OUR TIME

Poverty still dominates the world.—A global welfare program takes shape.—Initial success for U.N. Technical Assistance to Underdeveloped Areas.—Large-scale capital investments needed for continued economic development.—A threat to our highest values.

DURING my seven years in United Nations service, I visited as many countries as possible, trying to understand their problems and to assist in working out solutions. Delegates representing Member states at Headquarters often came to my office, explaining their difficulties and asking the same question: How can the United Nations help? Looking back now, I appreciate more than ever the unparalleled opportunity given me to gain a first-hand knowledge of the hopes, aspirations, fears, and uncertainties of peoples and their leaders in nearly every quarter of the globe.

One result of this experience was to strengthen my basic conviction that poverty remains mankind's chief enemy. Today, in the middle of the twentieth century, most human beings still are hungry most of the time; half the world's people have yet to be taught how to read and write, are constantly ill, and expect to die before the age of thirty-five. Calculations show that the per-capita income of almost two-thirds of this total is less than a hundred dollars a year; and other evidence proves that most of the world's population cannot afford decent clothing, housing, and recreation, while hundreds of millions still live in bondage and peonage not far removed from slavery.

Enlightened spokesmen and leaders of government were eager to correct these shocking conditions, and many countries were making real progress, mainly through their own efforts. But the advance was slow.

I concluded that here the United Nations faced one of its most challenging tasks—probably the most important, next to maintaining peace, and an essential condition for reaching that highest goal.

Fortunately, the basic need for extensive international economic and social cooperation had been recognized in 1945 when the United Nations Charter was drawn up at San Francisco. In fact, that document contains six full articles on such cooperation alone. During the first years, however, efforts toward a solution of urgent outstanding political issues claimed most of the United Nations' attention. In spite of being deeply involved in political matters, I remained uncomfortably aware of the somewhat slow start made by the Economic and Social Council, an organ which I once called "the General Staff for Peace." In Norway I had been mainly concerned with bettering the lot of the workers and other underprivileged groups. To me now there was a striking parallel between the national struggle in which I had taken an active part for more than thirty years and the present need for international action. To oversimplify somewhat, there was a repetition on a world scale of the familiar relationship between the rich and the poor, the haves and the have-nots. Years of effort in Norway had taught us that there could be no satisfactory long-term solution to the intricate problems through the mere adjustment of existing privileges; a general elevation of the living standard was possible only through economic expansion, which would bring an increase in production and in wealth. Around the world, however, there were not only underprivileged groups within a single fairly well-to-do society whose living conditions had to be improved but entire nations, even continents, subject to a degree of poverty unknown in Norway. Obviously, tremendous efforts were needed in order to make any headway at all.

The start might be slow, but it was systematic. This was a field where economic science and experience had to be applied with extreme care. World-embracing plans for production and trade were clearly necessary; but no great accomplishment was possible unless the country in need assumed the major burden itself. At the same time its legitimate interests had to be protected.

The first step for the United Nations, therefore, was to survey the world economic situation as it fluctuated from year to year. The annual volumes of the *World Economic Report,* prepared by our international team of economists, in close contact with national institutions of the Member states, soon became treasured documents; and they gradually promoted a more uniform approach to the great problems facing us.

With the different levels of industrial capacity and the varying national or regional trends in economic development, it also proved to be desirable to decentralize much of the work in this field. The first United Nations Regional Economic Commission, the one for Europe (ECE), was organized in 1946; the Economic Commission for Latin America (ECLA)—touched on in Chapter VIII—soon followed, as did the Economic Commission for Asia and the Far East (ECAFE). (A corresponding body for the Near East has yet to be established.) These three commissions, assisted by their own well equipped secretariats, headed respectively by Dr. Gunnar Myrdal of Sweden, Dr. Raúl Prebisch of Argentina, and Dr. Palamadais Lokanathan of India, were charged with general as well as practical economic planning in their areas; and their contributions over the years are already highly appreciated. The long-term value of their work may prove to be even greater.

Nevertheless, the real crusade against poverty requires a more active and immediate approach. Were we not only to plan but gradually to implement any plan on a global scale, we should have to offer real action which would capture men's minds and demonstrate the importance of the course we proposed to follow.

We pondered much over this problem during the early years. The United Nations had only modest funds for such undertakings, and these were largely tied to the Advisory Social Welfare Services—an assistance which many Member states requested and received. Neither did it have the authority to coordinate other efforts in these fields. It could not contemplate new large-scale financial or organizational arrangements requiring great outlays of public funds, on the scale of UNRRA's or any other emergency organizations. But we saw the need and gradually formulated the plans for what later became known as the United Nations Expanded Program of Technical Assistance for the Economic Development of Underdeveloped Countries. That was in 1947 and 1948.

Some first steps had already been taken in the right direction. What the United Nations itself did not succeed in starting, had been launched, piecemeal, by the Specialized Agencies—"close relatives" in the family of international organizations. These bodies are independent operating organs, with the right and duty to take initiative and action in their respective fields the world over. The right and duty was taken seriously from the outset.

We soon began receiving reports on their activities through the Economic and Social Council, to which they are tied by special agreements. The reports revealed that promising results were attained in many areas through specific technical assistance projects. But they also caused other questions to be raised.

I have always had the highest regard for the work of the Specialized Agencies. A few of them are several decades old, but most were set up after the Second World War. All include among their member states some that are still outside the United Nations—generally through no fault of their own. On the other hand, Eastern Bloc nations do not belong to more than a few; the Soviet Union, for example, belonged only to the Universal Postal Union, the International Telecommunication Union, and the World Meteorological Organization until early 1954 when it joined UNESCO and ILO and rejoined WHO.

The agencies administer their own funds, contributed directly by the governments; they have their own councils and assemblies where, on occasion, delegates even take positions differing from those expressed by their government representatives in the United Nations—particularly with respect to budgetary matters. One school of thought maintains that this relationship is too loose: that the Specialized Agencies with all their operations and undertakings should be fitted in directly under the United Nations administrative machinery. I have never agreed with this view. International cooperation gains added force if it can be kept functional; the pragmatic approach can go further than the bureaucratic. On the other hand, effective coordination of policy, planning, and actual operations is obviously needed, where these are in any way related.

Now, it appeared that a fuller coordination of the independent technical assistance projects undertaken by each agency was gradually becoming essential. A few journeys and discussions demonstrated to me that in order for all plans to be implemented with true efficiency, and the underdeveloped lands to receive the achievable maximum of the aid they required, a better coordination of efforts would be necessary. In 1947, I returned from my first visit to Latin America convinced beyond all doubt that the United Nations itself would also have to be brought directly into the technical assistance picture. There was so much to be done, and the instruments available could, I felt, be used far more effectively than they were.

It was therefore a gratification to me in 1948 that the General Assembly, meeting in Paris, approved the first plans which would make it possible for the United Nations to extend direct technical assistance to the underdeveloped areas: a special department was added to the Secretariat to facilitate the task. Until then, the Secretary-General had been forced to couch every reference to eventual United Nations aid in the broadest generalities. When shown projects—excellent projects—the completion of which hinged on outside aid, or when approached by representatives of one or another country in need, he could only voice general encouragement and express the hope of United Nations assistance at some future date. The Paris decision changed all this. We should soon be able to substitute action for words.

In the following January, the inaugural address of Harry S. Truman as President of the United States gave new life to the whole concept of technical assistance. This speech announced the now famous "Point Four" program. Technical assistance suddenly leaped into prominence as a major factor in international life and captured imaginations everywhere. The effect was quickly felt in the United Nations, and in November of 1949 the General Assembly approved the United Nations Expanded Program of Technical Assistance to be financed by voluntary contributions outside the regular United Nations budget.

At last we were in a position to start on the right course, and it is on the United Nations' achievements and my own experiences in this particular field that I wish to dwell briefly.

From the very outset it was clear that, in the first stages at any rate, the new technical assistance program would have to function as a world clearinghouse for skills and "knowhow," rather than as a purveyor of financial aid. It would work, largely, through the participating Specialized Agencies, whose heads would now be assembled as a coordinating Technical Assistance Board, under the chairmanship of the Secretary-General or his representative. Later, in July, 1952, the board was strengthened and David Owen was appointed full-time Executive Chairman with certain limited powers in connection with program review and the allocation of funds. The main purpose of the reorganization was to make possible a stronger over-all control of the program that would ensure proper coordination in the activities of all Agencies, and promote integrated country technical assistance programs. Early in 1954 six agencies were participating fully in the program: the Technical Assistance Administration, the International Labor Office, the Food and Agriculture Organization, the United Nations Educational, Scientific, and Cultural Organization, the International Civil Aviation Organization and the World Health Organization. Two other agencies as well—the International Bank for Reconstruction and Development and the International Monetary Fund—take part in the program to a limited extent.

The basic assumption of the United Nations technical assistance scheme is that there is available in the world today a wealth of technical skill, although unevenly divided among nations and peoples. The United Nations plan aims at expediting the sharing of these skills on a global scale—each country contributing the particular brand of knowhow that may be needed to solve a specific problem anywhere.

But do not let it be thought for a moment that this is a simple process of the "developed" countries starting out on a missionary venture to "teach" the "underdeveloped" lands. The United Nations is no supergovernment that can launch projects, or at its own whim make proposals and send out "teachers" to drag a poorer or less advanced member along against its will. Countries, whether rich or poor, great or small, are in this program on an equal footing; and here, I feel, is the one invaluable factor that distinguishes the United Nations program from all others. This element of the plan is essential for many reasons, one of the most important being that most countries in need of help are younger states, exceedingly conscious of their own national sovereignty. They are constantly on guard against "strings" that may be attached to aid proposals. The United

Nations' starting point, then, is to ask the government concerned to request whatever assistance it deems most urgent; secondly, the government has to explain in detail what it wants to do. In explaining, it will also have to bear in mind that the capital investment required to carry through whatever final plan emerges, will have to be provided from national resources or from any other quarter to which the government itself may have access. As David Owen, present Executive Chairman of the Technical Assistance Board, has so aptly put it: "The problem is rather to make available certain kinds of expert help, from any and every source, to those countries who are engaged in plans and programs for their own economic and social betterment, and to provide it only at their request and only in the fashion that they decide."

Some brief figures may illustrate the cost and scope of the program from the time of its inception in July, 1950—a time, be it noted, when the United Nations experienced one of its most serious political crises, the outbreak of the Korean War. I should also add that the program expanded rapidly until checked by the failure of contributions from governments to keep pace with the ever increasing requests for assistance from the underdeveloped countries. The amount spent rose from $6,436,000 during the first eighteen months to $22,968,000 during 1952 and, I am informed, to nearly $24,000,000 during 1953. As we entered 1954, a total close to $53,000,000 had been used. Experts employed rose from 765 in 1950–1951 to 1,626 during 1952 and approximately 2,000 during 1953. Over the whole period nearly 4,500 fellowships and scholarships were awarded and at least 97 countries and territories received some kind of assistance.

And where have the experts come from? Naturally, and especially during the early stages of the program, the bulk of them have come from the more advanced industrial countries. But a great many have come from such lands as India, Chile, Egypt, and Mexico—all classified as underdeveloped, and receiving assistance at the same time as they have provided it to others. In fact, this exchange is actually a common pooling of skills—a multinational cooperative effort—rather than a one-way flow. Let me again quote figures which should be remembered. During 1952, for example, some 1,600 technical experts from as many as sixty-four countries (not many of which would be classified as economically developed) were sent out to some sixty-two underdeveloped countries and territories, while seventy-six countries acted as hosts to fellows and scholars from ninety-two others.

One country may be far advanced in a certain field of agriculture, while lagging woefully in industry; but its agricultural experts may well be just the ones needed to help another underdeveloped country with problems in the same field. To illustrate the point, I will recount a classic example of how the word "underdeveloped" had best not be used carelessly.

I am thinking of the age-old practice of fish farming in Indonesia. Through at least five centuries, Indonesian peasants have become highly efficient in harvesting fish and rice from the same wet fields. The fingerlings—baby carp—are transferred from nursery ponds and planted in the flooded paddies together with the rice shoots. When the terraces are drained for the ripening of the rice, the fish, now about three months old, are the size of large sardines. Thanks to this fish culture, Indonesia has avoided the protein deficiency that affects about half of the world's population, mainly in the tropics. It was in the hope of sharing this skill native to Indonesia, that Haiti applied to the United Nations and received aid in developing fish culture.

Another phase of Indonesian fish farming has attracted specialists from other countries. By enclosing salt-water marshes within a sea wall, and keeping them constantly flooded with tidal waters for the breeding and culture of salt-water fish, any country with coastal swamps can develop a new and most economical food source. No less important is the fact that these fish are an invaluable means of controlling malaria, because they feed on mosquitoes. Fish culture in salt-water ponds occupies some 250,000 Indonesians—hardly a surprising number when one realizes that the yield of fish, in weight per hectare, is more than double that of rice.

Such skill is badly needed in other parts of the world. With the pond culture of fish in Israel accounting for two-thirds of the country's fish supply but proportionately only half the supply in Indonesia, it is hardly surprising that Israel should send two of its citizens to study the methods used in the other country. They were only two among many fellows sent to study under "professors"—

generally the cultivators themselves—who probably never had seen a modern city and perhaps were even illiterate, but who possessed a skill the world needed and could not acquire elsewhere.

This is but one of many examples proving that technical assistance knowhow is no monopoly of the highly developed countries. Knowledge can be "harvested and disseminated" wherever it is found.

Aside from illustrating how one underdeveloped country may have skills to share with another, the above example also underlines a second axiom supporting the concept of technical assistance. It is often just as important to bring the "fellows" (students) from the countries being helped, for training in a land where knowledge is to be gained, as it is to send out the experts. Haiti and Israel with their fish-culture problems sent to Indonesia the men they wanted trained as experts. There would have been little sense in sending Indonesian experts to either of these countries, where techniques and systems could not be demonstrated in action. Furthermore, it is always necessary to train teams of experts from the "receiving" lands who will be able to carry on at home under their own steam. As one of our specialists once put it, "Any short-term result, however gratifying, which cannot sustain itself without the continued presence of international experts is illusory."

A third axiom upon which the United Nations program of sharing skills is based, is that too sweeping or abrupt a change can often be more damaging than no change at all. Here the example of Afghanistan comes to mind—a country where natural resources are virtually undeveloped. Nine-tenths of its population is agricultural, and many are pastoral nomads, moving in tribes and families with all their worldly possessions strapped on the backs of donkeys or camels. Agricultural methods have advanced hardly at all in five centuries, and to remedy this state of affairs, the Royal Afghan Government decided to ask the United Nations for help. Both parties soon agreed that small beginnings would provide the most immediate returns. Though agriculture here could be revolutionized in time by the introduction of modern methods, a minor revolution could be produced immediately by introducing such simple tools as the European version of the scythe. Afghanistan is mainly mountainous, and the holdings are small; mechanized farming—even if it were not too costly for the farmers—could have only limited value in such a geography. For centuries, the average Afghan farmer has mowed his plot with a primitive sickle, sitting on the ground and grasping the grain or grass in his left hand. With "western" hand implements his efficiency could be increased five times without risking any violent disruption of his living pattern.

The project was as simple as it proved to be effective. A Swiss farm-implement expert, with two Austrian assistants experienced in the scything of high pastures, gave a series of demonstrations in the harvest areas, using scythes, forks, and hayrakes. One demonstration was generally enough to convince the farmer. The various tools were given to the local blacksmiths to copy, a distribution program was set up, and young Afghan farmers were sent to Switzerland for a year's training so that they could become instructors in the use of hand tools on mountain farms. The reasonableness of this program, which appeals to the practical bent of the local farmer and employs the local blacksmith, can be of far greater service to Afghan agriculture than any immediate attempt to introduce tractors or combines.

I have devoted some space to these two examples, among scores from every corner of the world, to illustrate how the simplest measures can often provide the best help to self-help—giving that little lift at just the right time and place.

To give a more rounded picture I quote from a report submitted by the Technical Assistance Board in early 1953:

A fifty-one day stay in Iran was sufficient for a team of UNTAA water resources experts using aerial photography to locate fifty sites for wells. Thai farmers, after learning from FAO experts of techniques developed accidentally in the Canary Islands, were able to cultivate pineapples as a year-round crop. Saudi Arabia exported packaged dates for the first time in its three thousand years of history after the introduction of assembly line packaging on the recommendation of a FAO expert. In India, the operatives in the Ambica spinning and weaving mills, with the help of an ILO expert in textile production were able to cut down by 50 per cent the number of cones which failed to empty completely, and greatly to reduce incidental damage. The output of an iron foundry in Pakistan was increased by 44 per cent as the result of technical advice given by an UNTAA mission. In Libya, scores of workers who would have received little or no education of any kind have now, with the assistance of ILO and UNESCO received basic training which has enabled them to undertake clerical and administrative duties. The first penicillin factory in any Asian country, near Poona in India, is an enterprise of the Government of India which has been made possible by equipment provided by UNICEF and by expert advice supplied from WHO. Production is expected to begin early in 1954. DDT plants are also under construction in Delhi and Ceylon as the result of help provided by WHO and UNICEF. These will be powerful weapons in the plan which WHO is developing in Asia for the control of malaria, yaws, syphilis and other diseases.

It is true that many of these successes are on a relatively small scale. But successes they are, and they are achieved within sight of, and with a direct bearing upon the daily lives of, the millions who are watching desperately for concrete evidence of the advances promised to them. They are taking place in the field, not in some distant conference chamber or ornate assembly hall. Their demonstration value, in days such as these, is of incalculable worth.

Skeptics in and out of government have asked if the United Nations technical assistance scheme, in all its modesty, is not really a device to start something which in the end will require billions of dollars of public funds. Experience from other public or private international investment undertakings, they contend, has not always been encouraging. Is it not really utopian therefore to think that all human beings can be provided with a certain minimum standard of living?

The answer is less complicated than one might think: There is a limit to the knowledge available in the world, and to the number of technical experts who can travel or teach. There is also a limit to the underdeveloped areas' own capacity to absorb outside assistance. Granted the most favorable conditions in all respects, I fail to see how this whole program of technical help could, in the foreseeable future, assume a total maximum annual cost of more than one hundred million dollars.

I remember very well how we planned it. We counted on some twenty million dollars for the first year and a half; thereafter, a scale of contributions increasing slowly, in accordance with the initial results, to thirty or forty million dollars annually. Fifty million dollars annually seemed to be a reasonable objective for years to come.

Of course this refers to technical assistance alone, and not to the consequent capital investments which should follow—a different matter, requiring a different approach. Thus far, capital has come mainly from the recipient countries' own meager accumulations of national savings. This is far from adequate, because their economies are mostly of an agricultural nature, yielding little surplus. In only the most isolated cases can this limited capital finance progress at a rate which can really count. Where larger construction projects are concerned, the United Nations is comparable to an architect handing the plans for a house to a penniless man: "Very well, here are your plans. Now you can go ahead and build." In short, technical assistance in terms of planning and advice has already gone far and can go much further. But a second step must be taken, in the provision of capital.

There are three general types of investment in underdeveloped areas. The first might be described as "investment in human beings" —in their health, education, the improvement of public administration, etc. The second type would cover basic equipment, such as transportation and hydroelectric development, while the third would include the various areas of production: fishing, farming, industry, forestry, mining, and exports.

For all these purposes, all types of investment are needed: public and private, national and international. In my opinion, it is an absolute condition to sound progress that the countries concerned, through whatever adjustments or arrangements they may make within their own national economies, provide the bulk of the investment capital, in the widest sense. Most of them, for instance, have huge resources in man power, which so far have not been systematically used. Furthermore, I believe firmly that large-scale private investments not only will be desirable, but will actually prove feasible. It is doubtful, however, that the necessary degree of "investment in human beings" will be generally possible unless the international community as a whole undertakes special responsibilities.

The United Nations has given much attention to the problem. As the Expanded Technical Assistance Program got under way, increasing consideration was given to the second phase of the program: the financing of economic development. The International Bank for Reconstruction and Development was requested to prepare a plan for organizing an International Finance Corporation. Such an organ would solicit or guide the flow of international private capital, which would supplement the national resources available for investment in revenue-producing or self-liquidating projects in industrially underdeveloped areas.

To deal with the type of investments which cannot show immediate returns in terms of production, the Economic and Social Council called in a number of international experts for advice. They met at United Nations Headquarters in early 1953 and proposed the establishment of an international development fund, with available capital up to a billion dollars. This fund, according to the proposal, would provide a part of the development capital required to follow up and implement a United Nations planning program, with the various governments entitled to request and receive such financial aid as an advisory international council might find reasonable and justified. The General Assembly has not yet reached a final decision concerning "SUNFED," as the proposed Special United Nations Fund for Economic Development has become known.

During the last period of my tenure as Secretary-General, I was actively engaged in soliciting support for the plan. Of course many governments which have already contributed heavily and generously over recent years to international or bilateral economic assistance programs may be somewhat reluctant to comply with this new demand, because by far the greatest financial burdens would fall on them. Nevertheless, I sincerely hope that they will realize in time the necessity of taking this step as well—a step so essential for the success of the whole effort to create a world not dominated by poverty.

Much has also been said in many quarters about the riskiness of investments in underdeveloped countries. In fact, this still seems to express the prevailing attitude in private financial circles; and the launching of the new underwriting institution, the International Finance Corporation, has been postponed. There are risks. Not all governments everywhere are equally stable. Furthermore, several countries have shown tendencies toward nationalization, whereas others have resorted to the direct and indirect confiscation of capital installations provided by foreign investment, even those backed or controlled by foreign governments.

But the United Nations' work in this broader field represents something new. Its plans have a broader moral foundation than foreign investments on a regular business basis have generally had. The United Nations program is built on mutual confidence and good will, with the donor organizations and recipient countries administering the projects jointly and sharing the responsibility. In such circumstances, the risks of exploitation on the one hand, and expropriation on the other, are reduced. Here, as has been so conclusively proven where the sharing of technical skills is concerned, the elements of cooperation and mutual interest would provide a milieu of surrounding circumstances that are new and unique. Once these facts are made fully known, it should not be too difficult to create a climate favorable for investments—not least of private capital—in economic development projects in the underdeveloped areas. Some countries realizing both the practical and the psychological factors involved have lately taken the lead in a move to have the whole issue fully clarified. I sincerely hope that they will succeed.

There is also the question of possible competition between the United Nations' plans for Technical Assistance and Economic Development, and the similar programs conducted by individual governments or groups of countries. Certainly there may be competition for the share of the tax dollar, pound, franc, krone, or whatever the currency concerned; but there, I feel, the competition ends—or should end. In the final instance the total amount of aid is the decisive factor, far more than the manner in which it is extended.

Of course it would be ideal for assistance of every kind to be channeled exclusively through the United Nations. But would the same amounts be forthcoming? With the many factors involved, including the political, I have strong doubts. In fact, I do not think so —at least at this stage. The United States' Point Four and "Foreign Operations" contributions have added very substantial funds to what otherwise would have been available. The same is true to some extent of the Commonwealth "Colombo" plan. Most of the funds for financing economic development, so far, have come from these sources. On the other hand, when the governments concerned decide to review their particular contributions in this field, they may be well advised to reallocate the proportions between their direct grants in aid and the United Nations common-pool scheme for help to self-help.

Dollar for dollar, I am convinced that more is obtained from the money contributed to the United Nations program than from any other similar scheme—for a number of sound reasons. It will not be denied that the world at large provides a wider basis for the recruitment of suitable experts than one country alone. Technicians from underdeveloped areas may also be able to work out simpler plans, easier to understand, costing less, than experts from a highly developed country. They may be able to supply just the type of skill required—a type of knowhow that may be as foreign to the highly developed "giving" country as to the problem area involved. The extensive cooperation the United Nations receives from recipient states can also make for far smoother operation, less hampered by bureaucratic waste. As has already been indicated, there is no avoiding a suspicion which—though often unfounded—is none the less real, wherever an attempt is made to inspire the faith of a backward people in a program conducted by one national government alone, particularly a great power. The United Nations program is hampered by none of these impediments. The "receiving" nations are themselves generally members of the agencies supplying aid, and the aspect of multinational cooperation constitutes a driving force toward self-help which no bilateral program possesses. In terms of value received, the United Nations Technical Assistance Program need fear no competition. For this reason, if for no other, it would seem to be to the advantage of nations operating their own aid schemes to begin weighing the advisability of tying these in more closely with the United Nations program in one way or another.

Recently, there have been tendencies toward stagnation in United Nations technical assistance activities. The expected increase in the governments' voluntary contributions did not materialize for 1953; there was even a decrease. I have learned that the trend seems to have been reversed for 1954. Nevertheless, the $24,000,000 pledged is substantially below the sum needed. I shall not dwell on the constant financial uncertainty which has inhibited long-range planning and forced a hand-to-mouth existence from one year to the next: What I am most concerned about is the fact that this is not enough money to go around. Because of the increasing popularity of the program, this means that nearly half the requests for assistance of various kinds now have to be turned down. Worth-while projects proposed by responsible governments cannot, in many cases, even be studied. Rich opportunities are going to waste. A good start is in danger of being frozen in frustration before the real harvest has been reaped.

I hope that this is only a passing stage, and that soon the right trend will again prove to be the accepted one.

But if we fail to act disaster may strike again, and for the following reasons:

First, the peoples of the world are today living so close together that they can observe at first hand how abundance is the privilege of the relatively few, while poverty remains the curse of the great majority. It would spell bankruptcy for our ethical and moral values for us now merely to ask, "Am I my brother's keeper?"

Secondly, we are living in a historical period marked by tremendous progress in science and technology, with means at our disposal which can eradicate poverty from the face of the earth. It would spell bankruptcy for our intellect and our talents for us to waste our energies and let our tools rest idle.

Thirdly, with rival ideologies competing for the souls of the hundreds of millions rising in search of a better life, it would spell bankruptcy for all free political thinking for us to permit age-old totalitarianism and international communism to gain new ground and establish violence as the philosophy of humanity.

That much is at stake.

CHAPTER X

THE PALESTINE CHALLENGE

The plight of Jews, and Arabs.—Partition decided but sabotaged.—Issue of the authority and power of the United Nations.—Shifting United States position.—Offer to resign.—"War" on the United Nations.

THE PARTITION of Palestine and the consequent creation of the state of Israel became one of the most dramatic chapters of early United Nations history. As Secretary-General, I put the full weight of my office consistently behind the Organization's decision from the time it was first taken. A corresponding consistency did not always prevail in every other quarter.

The problem was complex. Christianity, Islam, and the Jewish faith, all are inheritors of the ancient Hebrew civilization and tradition. Religious differences and rivalries were therefore bound to influence the discussions from the very outset. Then there was the human-rights issue, with its background on the one side of age-old persecution of the Jews, climaxed by Hitler's attempt to extirpate all members of the Jewish faith or "race" from European soil, and on the other side the problem of justice to the Arabs living in the ancient Jewish homeland. Extreme nationalism, always strongest in the youngest states, added fuel to the fire. Cutting across all this was the conflict between the old feudalism of the East and twentieth century social concepts. Finally, there were strategic considerations, there might be oil, and no great power appeared to be entirely disinterested.

It was not easy to remain objective on every one of these issues, but I feel that I managed. The religious rivalry did not disturb me much. I recognized the right of all creeds to enjoy equal access to Palestine's Holy Places. The persecution of the Jews concerned me more. Already as a child, I had been deeply impressed by the moving poems of Henrik Wergeland, Norway's great national poet of the early nineteenth century: "The Jew" and "The Jewess," written during his indefatigable fight for the free entry of Jews into Norway. I had read about the Czarist pogroms against the Russian Jews in 1906. Even fresher in memory was the fate of the seven hundred Norwegian Jews whom the Nazis deported in the course of World War II, of whom only twelve survived to return to their homes in 1945. This history of suffering naturally affected my conscience. About the Arab fellahin, I knew only that they were frequently oppressed by absentee landlords and would no doubt benefit from the great Zionist development projects already launched in the land: an orderly solution would provide for the fullest protection of their rights. The hostile attitudes announced at an early stage by the neighboring Arab states forecast difficulties. Still I felt that, in view of the United Nations will to help them preserve their newly won independence—as demonstrated already during the Security Council's London session—and their obvious need for outside help to solve their own internal problems, they would abide by the Organization's decisions. As to the attitudes of the great powers, I felt that here was a field where they should still be able to act in unison —the rapid deterioration in their mutual relationship notwithstanding. If they wished to do something positive through the United Nations, here was the place to do it. None of them would be interested in a breach of the peace in this area, with the consequent danger of becoming entangled themselves. I realized that Britain might be in a special position, because of her involvement as the Mandatory power; but the United Kingdom itself had placed the Palestine problem on the United Nations' doorstep.

Besides, the existence of a Zionist community in Palestine had been a recognized international responsibility ever since the League of Nations confirmed the grant of a League of Nations mandate over the area to Great Britain in 1922. One of the declared purposes of this decision was the establishment of a Jewish national home, with the necessary safeguards for the civil and religious rights of all the country's inhabitants, irrespective of origin or religion.

Now, in 1947, a permanent Jewish homeland seemed at least a partial solution to the problem of hundreds of thousands of refugees languishing in European camps and driven by natural instinct to seek haven outside a continent stained with Jewish blood.

The British, pressed by Arab opposition and Zionist insistence, harassed by acts of terrorism from both sides, finally threw up their hands. All efforts at reconciliation had ended in failure. "We have tried for years to solve the problem of Palestine," Sir Alexander Cadogan put it. "Having failed so far, we now bring the Palestine question to the United Nations, in the hope that it can succeed where we have not."

It was in March, 1947, that the British government first told me that it would request the inclusion of the Palestine problem on the agenda of the autumn meeting of the General Assembly. Informally it raised the question of calling a special, advance session of the Assembly, to arrange for the preparatory work which would be necessary for proper consideration in the fall. I was sensitive to the urgency of the matter, and, in fact, had already asked Ralph J. Bunche as director of the Department of Trusteeship and Information from Non-Self-Governing Territories to consider possible solutions and keep me informed; but I did not approve of a special session to set up a preparatory committee, and told the British I thought it impracticable and certainly costly. After considering the appointment of a study committee from the Secretariat, I finally proposed to the British that eight Member governments including the Big Five be requested to constitute themselves as a preparatory committee on the Palestine matter: if the five permanent Members of the Security Council were agreeable, I would inquire by cable from all Member states whether they had any objections to forming such a body. If fewer than one-third objected, I would act to constitute the committee. But the Big Five were not enthusiastic.

On April 2, 1947, His Majesty's government requested "the Secretary-General of the United Nations to place the question of Palestine on the agenda of the General Assembly at its next regular session." The government would submit to the Assembly "an account of their administration on the League of Nations mandate and . . . ask the Assembly to make recommendations, under Article 10 of the Charter, concerning the future government of Palestine." London further requested the Secretary-General to summon, as soon as possible, a special session of the General Assembly "for the purpose of constituting and instructing a special committee to prepare for the consideration, at the regular session of the Assembly, of the question.". . .

Time enough would be lost by this procedure, and I was resolved not to add to it. Cables to the states Members asking for their approval of a special session were dispatched at once. The machinery for servicing a great international meeting was promptly put into action, and on the morning of April 28 the representatives of fifty-five Members gathered at Flushing Meadow. After some sparring, the Assembly appointed the United Nations Special Committee on Palestine (UNSCOP) and adjourned. The terms of reference of the investigatory charge were broad, and the composition of the committee was equally so: Australia, Canada, Czechoslovakia, Guatemala, India, Iran, the Netherlands, Peru, Sweden, Uruguay, and Yugoslavia.

Placing some of the ablest members of the Secretariat at UNSCOP's disposal—fifty-seven in all—I appointed Assistant Secretary-General Victor Hoo as my personal representative to the committee, and designated Dr. Alfonso García Robles, a Mexican director in the Department of Security Council Affairs, as principal secretary. I was determined that the committee's secretariat should be above reproach—not only technically but politically.

For my own part I kept absolutely clear of UNSCOP, holding my thoughts about the fairest solution to both Arabs and Jews to myself. When the committee made its report as the designated United Nations organ, I would give full support to the solution it saw fit to recommend.

The committee failed to reach agreement in all respects. Agreeing that the British Mandate for Palestine should be terminated at the earliest practical date, and that independence should be granted in Palestine after a transitional period under United Nations auspices, it made further unanimous recommendations with respect to the Holy Places and religious interests, Jewish displaced persons, minority rights, peaceful settlement of disputes, and other matters. At this point, the committee split. The majority (seven) recommended the partition of Palestine into an Arab state and a Jewish state, which would be bound together in an economic union. The city of Jerusalem, as the Holy City for three faiths, would be separately administered as a United Nations trusteeship. The minority (three—incidentally, all with influential Moslem populations) recommended a single federal state, in which the Arabs would be the majority. Australia abstained from voting for either recommendation.

The majority found that the claims of both the Arabs and the Jews in Palestine were at once valid and irreconcilable: that to neither group could be granted all it wished. Conceiving of the conflict in Palestine as one between two intense nationalisms, they saw partition as the only means of granting each nationality expression. I shall not set out the plan in its impressive justification and detail.

What had emerged was a *clear victory for the principle of partition*. The international community, through its chosen representatives, had decided that two states should be created. As Secretary-General, I took the cue and, when approached by delegations for advice, frankly recommended that they follow the majority plan. Behind-the-scenes discussions soon became hectic, and some Arab spokesmen attacked me openly; but I could not yield. The responsibility for solving the Palestine problem had been transferred to the United Nations, and the Organization had to act in conformity with its best judgment.

After an epic struggle the Second Session of the General Assembly adopted the plan of partition on November 29, 1947, by a vote of 33 to 13, with 10 abstaining. The majority included the United States and the Soviet Union, Western Europe and Eastern Europe, most of Latin America, and the Commonwealth. Of the minority Members, all except two had substantial Moslem populations. The vote was preceded by a final series of vain efforts to bring the Arabs and Jews of Palestine together: spokesmen for the Jews indicated that they would accept partition, even though they said the plan would give them but one-eighth of the territory originally promised them in the Balfour Declaration; spokesmen for the Arabs made it clear that they would reject partition, and offered no hope for any compromise. When the vote was taken, the representatives of Syria, Lebanon, Iraq, Saudi Arabia, Yemen, and Egypt rose and filed out of the Assembly hall. Another walkout! The United Kingdom—the Mandatory power—abstained from voting for or against the resolution.

Great Britain had placed the matter before the Assembly with the declared conviction that agreement between the Arabs and Jews was unattainable. This did not deter the British representative, Arthur Creech Jones, from informing the Assembly that Britain would give effect only to a plan accepted by the Arabs and the Jews: Britain would "accept" the partition plan but could not implement it, as this might require the use of armed forces. All British reservations had been respected in the November 29 resolution, and so this attitude caused considerable surprise. Of course the partition plan failed to provide sufficiently for implementation; but most countries expected Britain as the original sponsor of United Nations action to do its utmost toward carrying the action through. Had it done so, need for an international force to restore peace in Palestine would not have become nearly as acute as it soon did.

It fell to "five lonely pilgrims"—the representatives of Bolivia, Czechoslovakia, Denmark, Panama, and the Philippines who together formed the new Palestine Commission provided for in the resolution—to plan the transfer of administrative responsibility from the Mandatory regime to the proposed Arab and Jewish government organs. The commission was to take over the administration from the Mandatory power and establish in each new state a Provisional Council of Government that would progressively receive full responsibility for the administration of its state. The commission was to supervise in each state the erection of the administrative organs of central and local government and the creation of an armed militia, maintaining general military and political control over this, which would include choice of its high command. Finally, the commission was to effect an economic union between the two states. I chose Ralph Bunche as principal secretary of the commission, and when it came together at Lake Success on January 9, 1948, that choice was almost the single bright element in the picture with which we were confronted.

From the first week of December, 1947, disorder in Palestine had begun to mount. The Arabs repeatedly had asserted that they would resist partition by force. They seemed to be determined to drive that point home by assaults upon the Jewish community in Palestine—assaults which brought considerable retaliation from the Jews. In response, I quietly set in motion Secretariat studies of the possibilities of creating an international police force, and undertook exploratory conversations with various Member governments. Publicly, I gave the Palestine Commission a calculated welcome. "You are entitled," I asserted at its first meeting, "to be confident that in the event it should prove necessary, the Security Council will assume its full measure of responsibility in implementation of the Assembly's resolution. You have a right to assume, as I assume, that in such a situation the Security Council will not fail to exercise to the fullest, and without exception, every necessary power entrusted to it by the Charter in order to assist you in fulfilling your mission." These were bold words, and admittedly hopeful ones. I prodded the Security Council so openly not because I was confident that it would act, but because I feared that it might not. There was no question now of veto. The Soviet Union and the United States stood together in support of the Assembly's partition resolution, and, as time passed, the former proved to be the more steadfast of the two. Other forces—Arab intransigence, British passiveness, American inconsistency—acted together to undermine the considered recommendation of the majority of Member nations.

The Palestine Commission energetically took up its task. It asked me to invite representatives of Great Britain, the Arab Higher Committee, and the Jewish Agency to sit with it. Sir Alexander Cadogan and Moshe Shertok * were promptly appointed, but the Arab Higher Committee cabled me on January 19, 1948, as follows:

> Arab Higher Committee is determined persist in rejecting partition and in refusal recognize UNO resolution this respect and anything deriving therefrom, for these reasons it is unable accept invitation.

The Arab response did not come as a surprise. The Commission and I could only endeavor to carry out the partition plan as fully as Arab opposition would allow, and we accordingly entered into the most intense consultations with Sir Alexander and with Mr. Shertok.

The British approach proved to be not in accord, in my opinion, with either the letter or the spirit of the partition plan: the United Kingdom could not progressively turn over authority to the Palestine Commission, as the Assembly resolution provided, but only abruptly

* Later, as Moshe Sharett, first Israeli Foreign Minister, and now Prime Minister.

and completely on May 15. Neither did it "regard favourably any proposal by the Commission to proceed to Palestine earlier than two weeks before the date of the termination of the Mandate." London would not permit the formation of the militia which the Assembly's resolution called for, nor would it facilitate frontier delimitation. The Assembly had further recommended that the United Kingdom endeavor to evacuate by February 1 a seaport and hinterland in the area of the Jewish state adequate to provide facilities for immigration. "It is not possible," Sir Alexander reported, "for my Government to comply."

The consultations with Mr. Shertok were more fruitful. The Jewish Agency in Jerusalem fully cooperated with the Palestine Commission, and he and I—for different reasons working toward the same end, namely compliance with the General Assembly resolution —had many useful consultations in the course of the meetings or in my home.

Needless to say, I should have been delighted to have an equally intimate collaboration with the Arab Higher Committee in implementing the resolution by which I was unreservedly bound as Secretary-General. Instead, the Arabs employed open threats. On February 6 the Higher Committee representative wrote to me: "The Arabs of Palestine . . . will never submit or yield to any Power going to Palestine to enforce partition. The only way to establish partition is first to wipe them out—man, woman and child."

It was not for the purpose of wiping out anyone, but rather for preventing an unrestrained civil and international war, that the Palestine Commission and the Secretary-General began to concentrate on the formation and dispatch of an international force to the Holy Land. In a special report of February 16 to the Security Council, on "the problem of security in Palestine," the commission noted that Arab interests both inside and outside Palestine were engaged in a deliberate effort to alter by violence the settlement which the Assembly had recommended. Armed forces from surrounding Arab states had already begun infiltration of Palestine. The report set forth the vast difficulties caused by the Arab and British attitudes, and cogently maintained that the armed assistance of the Security Council alone would permit success: "In the view of the Commission, a basic issue of international order is involved. A dangerous and tragic precedent will have been established if force, or the threat of the use of force, is to prove an effective deterrent to the will of the United Nations." Unless an adequate non-Palestine force was provided for keeping order after May 15, the commission warned, "the period immediately following the termination of the Mandate will be a period of uncontrolled, widespread strife and bloodshed in Palestine, including the City of Jerusalem. This would be a catastrophic conclusion to an era of international concern for that territory."

The stand of the Palestine Commission was unquestionably sound. It was responsive to the fact then dominating the scene: that the Arab states were making open preparations to invade Palestine and overthrow a United Nations decision. Any invasion would be aggression, in flagrant violation of the Charter. Its unlawfulness would be compounded by its design to upset the specific will of the United Nations. This was my reaction to the report, and I asked Ralph Bunche to draft a statement to the Security Council which I would hold in readiness. As he and I worked it out with other advisers, it would have stressed that, despite the disagreement between East and West on providing the United Nations with armed forces, a sufficient degree of agreement had been reached for the establishment of a United Nations land force—an emergency international force composed of those minimum units which the Big Five were committed to placing at the Security Council's disposal. Such a force would be more than adequate to cope with the Palestine challenge. Secondly, the draft statement took the view that the Organization could not permit violence to be used against its decisions and organs; that, if the moral force of the Organization were not enough, physical force would have to supplement it. Drafting such a proposal was one step; the other, and the hazardous one, was presenting it to the Security Council. I postponed the second step until it was possible to sense better the trend of the Council's discussion and action: it would be futile to speak only for the record, even if I were quite prepared to act granted a substantial possibility that the Council would follow.

My caution proved to be well justified. The Security Council met on February 24. Karel Lisický of Czechoslovakia, as chairman, made an impressive presentation of the Palestine Commission's report. The response of the Council rested above all in the hands of the

United States and Britain—here, as so often, affirmative action by the Organization required the support, if not the leadership, of those two great powers which were its originators.

Britain's response, through Arthur Creech Jones, "loyally accepted" the Assembly's partition recommendation—except that, "faced with specific threats by the Arabs," His Majesty's government could not promise the particular kind of cooperation now requested.

I hoped for more from the United States. Washington had outspokenly supported the partition decision at the General Assembly. At American suggestion the Assembly had adopted a resolution which spoke in strong terms of the Security Council's role in implementing partition. But now the United States spoke with a different voice. The Security Council, Warren Austin maintained, could take action to maintain international peace, but lacked the power to enforce partition or any other type of political settlement. He contented himself with proposing that the Security Council establish a committee of its five permanent members to look into "the question of possible threats to international peace arising in connection with the Palestine situation."

Ambassador Austin's doctrine that the United Nations did not have the power to enforce any type of political settlement is sound as a general proposition. Indeed, much later, I used it myself in the case of Korea to answer persons who asserted that United Nations forces should go beyond repelling armed aggression and unify Korea by force. But the constitutional position was very different in the two cases. The United Nations does not have the power to impose a political settlement, whether it be unification or partition, except in special circumstances. Such circumstances exist when all the parties in control of a territory hand it over to the United Nations to determine its fate. In the case of Korea all the parties did not do that. In the case of Palestine, on the other hand, the United Kingdom was the sole Mandatory power, and it had handed over the whole territory to the United Nations for disposition. Clearly, I felt, the Organization in these circumstances had full constitutional power not only to maintain order inside the territory but, even more, to resist any attempt from outside to overthrow its decision. The same circumstances would prevail for the Territory of Trieste if the Security Council had been able to agree on a governor and take over responsibility, as the Peace Treaty with Italy provided. All the signatories to that treaty had agreed to this, so that the juridical position was, in my opinion, fundamentally the same.

Be that as it may, with Ambassador Austin's statement and the subsequent arms embargo, Washington took the heart out of any support which the Security Council might have mobilized to enforce peace and maintain the decision on partition. This attitude, I feared, would prejudice fundamentally the powers of the Organization, in addition to damaging its prestige. I was opposed in principle, as well as on practical grounds, to the position taken. Now the Palestine Commission requested a paper from the Legal Department on the rights of the Security Council relative to the Palestine question. I was in Norway when the paper was prepared, but of course it took a position consonant with my desire to uphold the Organization's authority generally—as I had previously gone on record as doing in earlier cases. It recalled my Trieste opinion, early in 1947, and contended that the Council had already at that time "recognized the principle that it has sufficient power, under the terms of Article 24 of the Charter, to assume new responsibilities, on condition that they relate directly or even indirectly to the maintenance of international peace and security, and that in discharging these duties, the Security Council acts in accordance with the purposes and principles of the United Nations." When I returned from Norway I had the Palestine opinion circulated to the Members of the Security Council. The Council met in a private session on March 9 with the eternal question of appointing a Governor of Trieste on the agenda, and Dr. José Arce of Argentina, who espoused the Arab viewpoint, took the occasion to attack the opinion in extreme terms. Its substance, he maintained, was the "bastard" product of "unbalanced minds," and, in principle, the Secretariat had no business producing such a document. I replied to Dr. Arce's criticism by affirming that, as long as I was head of the Secretariat, it would have the right to give any opinion requested by organs of the United Nations. I added that I might have a further opinion on legal aspects of the Palestine question which I would present directly to the Security Council. The Members of the Council supported me, and took no action on Dr. Arce's attack.

The Palestine Commission carried on as best it could, and I gave it all possible support. On February 22 I dispatched an advance party of the Commission's secretariat to Jerusalem to establish contact with the Mandatory Administration and to consult on the spot regarding the problems of the take-over. The advance party arrived in Jerusalem early in March and left on the very eve of the expiration of the Mandate in May. In view of the attitude of the United Kingdom, this effort produced no result. Although the members of the party lived in Jerusalem as guests of the Mandatory government, the conditions in that city gave me serious concern for their personal safety, and I took all possible measures to ensure that they were safely evacuated. In the meantime the Security Council, after an interminable debate, requested its permanent Members on March 5 to consult together regarding the instructions it might usefully give to the Palestine Commission "with a view of implementing the resolution of the General Assembly." This resolution was a much watered version of the one Mr. Austin had put forth in February, which had been weak enough.

The United States, the U.S.S.R., France, and China thereupon entered into consultations. The meetings took place as a rule in the offices of the delegations, and sometimes in my Manhattan office. I was present throughout. The United Kingdom declined to take part, but Sir Alexander Cadogan did appear a few times to answer questions. From the start, the consultations were a frustrating affair. Only the Soviet Union seemed to be seriously intent upon implementing partition; the United States clearly was not. Rumors were flying that the United States was seeking to moderate the Arab stand even at the price of abandoning partition; and, in such an atmosphere, firm action by the Council or its permanent Members was out of the question. As it turned out, the United States would in effect repudiate partition on the very day, March 19, when the committee of permanent Members reported on its recommendations for "implementing" partition. With new instructions Mr. Austin took the floor to call for "action by all means available . . . to bring about the immediate cessation of violence" in Palestine. It was on this occasion that some sarcastic correspondents coined the imaginary Austin quotation: "We must do nothing—but at once!" To fortify his arguments for nonaction, he reverted to an old suggestion: The United States government now believed that a temporary United Nations trusteeship for Palestine should be established "to maintain the peace. . . . It would be without prejudice to the character of the eventual political settlement. . . . Pending the convening of a special session of the General Assembly, we believe that the Security Council should instruct the Palestine Commission to suspend its efforts to implement the proposed partition plan."

I had met with Mr. Austin and representatives of the four other permanent Members of the Security Council just before the Council session. He had told us then of Washington's trusteeship proposal. I pointed out that the possibility of trusteeship had been raised in UNSCOP by Australia, and had been withdrawn in the realization that the idea would be fought by both sides rather than one. It would, I maintained, require more military force to carry out than partition—and the objection to partition was that military force was needed to effect it. As Secretary-General, I stated, I had to ask whether the great powers, in adopting the American proposal, would accept responsibilities for implementing it. Mr. Austin replied that the United States was "ready, of course, to back up a United Nations decision." I could not help wondering if he meant backing as "stanch" as that which Washington had lent to the partition decision.

The American turnabout on partition has never been explained. Perhaps Washington, in voting for partition, expected milder opposition from the Arabs and more substantial cooperation from the British; perhaps, as has been charged, some quarters feared the effect of Washington's support of partition upon the oil concessions American interests held in Arab territories; or perhaps there was a belief that forcing partition through would arouse a bitter resentment that would turn the Arab states toward Moscow and thus promote Soviet interests in the Middle East.

In any case, the American reversal was a blow to the United Nations and showed a profoundly disheartening disregard for its effectiveness and standing. I could not help asking myself what the future of the United Nations would be, if this was the measure of support it could expect from the United States.

I brooded the night in this fashion, amid radio reports of United Nations depression, Arab jubilation, Zionist despair, and British self-righteousness. After lunch the next day—a Saturday afternoon, I recall—I telephoned to Mr. Austin and asked to see him. He invited me to his apartment in the Waldorf-Astoria Towers, where I bared my thoughts—my sense of shock and of almost personal grievance. Washington well knew where I had stood in the struggle over implementing partition. Its reversal was a rebuff to the United Nations and to me, because of my direct and deep commitment. I said to Mr. Austin: "You too are committed. This is an attack on the sincerity of your devotion to the United Nations cause, as well as mine. So I want to propose to you that you and I, that both of us, as a measure of protest against your instructions, and as a means of arousing popular opinion to the realization of the danger in which the whole structure of the United Nations has been placed—I want to propose that we resign."

"Trygve," Mr. Austin came back, his emotion rising, "I didn't know you were so sensitive."

In his warmhearted, upright Yankee way, he gave me his full sympathy. I think he respected my reaction; but—whether because he was less attached to partition, or was more skeptical of the impact which our resignations would have, or just thought it was not the right thing to do—he did not share it. He would not resign, and he advised me not to do so either. I should not, he remonstrated, take Washington's reversal in a personal sense.

Parting cordially from Mr. Austin, with whom I have always had the most friendly relations, I went to see Mr. Gromyko. He could receive me without reservation—his government's Palestine policy had been commendable. I announced the feeling that I should resign in protest at the American shift of position, and I have never found Ambassador Gromyko more friendly. His melancholy features lit up with sympathy. But he seemed half alarmed at my idea. "Speaking for myself," he said, "I hope you will not resign, and I advise you against it. What good will it do? How will it change American policy? In any case, I would be grateful if you would take no action before I have time to consult my government."

Tuesday, Mr. Gromyko took me aside. He had cabled Moscow, he reported, and Moscow's reply was: "No, definitely not." In view of the advice from both Washington and Moscow, I did not resign.

The second special session of the General Assembly opened at Flushing Meadow on April 16, 1948. In the weeks preceding, I had been careful not to give public prejudgment of what the Assembly would do—of whether it should, or would, adopt the United States plan for trusteeship. When asked, I could not, of course, conceal such obvious facts as that trusteeship had been proposed almost a year earlier and judged unworkable.

The Assembly debated for a month, not without confusion. The American proposals for trusteeship won slight support, despite Washington's announcement that it was now prepared to allot a fair share of the troops needed to push it through; in view of the *de facto* partition of Palestine which already was dissolving British authority, this amounted to proposing that the United Nations take enforcement action *against* partition. Other Members made no offer of troops. Skepticism about the practicality of trusteeship was everywhere, and a considerable body of states maintained that the United Nations should still undertake to implement partition, rather than go on talking while time ran out. Sir Carl A. Berendsen, the salty New Zealander, in one of his many penetrating United Nations addresses, compellingly voiced this view. He so well expressed the thoughts and feelings closest to my heart that—the first time I ever did such a thing for a speech—I sent him an admiring bouquet of roses! Sir Carl called upon the Assembly not to abandon partition in a capitulation to threats and violence. Partition was the right solution in November, and it was the right solution in April; but, in not making adequate plans for enforcement, the Assembly had done "the right thing in the wrong way." New Zealand, for its part, would continue to support enforcing partition. "What the world needs today," he concluded, "is not resolutions, it is resolution."

The Assembly, at any rate, did no more than adopt three resolutions. One affirmed its support of the Security Council's efforts to bring about a truce in Palestine, and empowered a United Nations Mediator to use his good offices, in cooperation with the Truce Commission which the Council had appointed, to promote a peaceful adjustment of the situation in Palestine, arrange for the operation of services necessary to the well-being of the Palestinian population, and assure the protection of the Holy Places. It relieved the Palestine Commission from further exercise of its responsibilities and, in a separate resolution, thanked it for its efforts. But the Assembly did *not* rescind or amend its resolution of November 29, 1947. The partition decision remained and remains valid.

As the Assembly debated on its closing day, May 14, word came that Jewish authorities had, with the expiration of the Mandate, proclaimed the existence of the State of Israel. While going beyond the November 29 resolution, this was essentially in accord with the partition decision. But the report was bound to increase the tension, already high. What would happen next?

The bombshell came from an entirely unexpected quarter. Minutes later, as the Assembly discussed a Franco-American proposal for the establishment of a temporary international regime for Jerusalem, the news flashed through Flushing Meadow that the United States had recognized "the Provisional Government as the *de facto* authority of the new State of Israel." Another reversal of policy! The press spread the story before the United States Delegation had been informed of President Truman's action, and the mortification of the American representatives was understandably acute.

During the next hours and days, events crowded upon us. The Arab states launched their invasion of Palestine with the end of the Mandate. This was armed defiance of the United Nations, and they openly proclaimed their aggression by telegraphing news of it to United Nations Headquarters. The Security Council, when it met on May 15, had before it a cable from the Egyptian Minister of Foreign Affairs, which brazenly announced, "Egyptian armed forces have started to enter Palestine to establish security and order." . . .

CHAPTER XI

ARMISTICE ACHIEVED IN PALESTINE

Britain and America at cross purposes.—I work behind the scenes.—Security Council acts at last.—Count Bernadotte appointed.—The first and second truces.—Assassination of the Mediator.—Ralph Bunche moves in.—Armistice at last. —The visit to the Middle East.

THE INVASION of Palestine by the Arab states was the first armed aggression which the world had seen since the end of the war. The United Nations could not permit that aggression to succeed and at the same time survive as an influential force for peaceful settlement, collective security, and meaningful international law. This was my view, and I acted upon it. The Arabs had threatened to invade Palestine some time before. Accordingly, as early as May 3, the Legal Department submitted a memorandum which I had earlier requested under Article 99 of the Charter in the event of an invasion of Palestine by armed forces of foreign states. The memorandum, after examining the legal elements of the problem, unqualifiedly affirmed that I should be entitled to bring to the attention of the Security Council my view that the invasion of Palestine constituted a threat to international peace and security. I then asked the Department to draft a letter to the President of the Council, drawing the Council's attention under Article 99 to the invasion of Palestine. I held the letter in readiness and, with May 15 and the invasion by Egypt, Jordan, and other members of the Arab League, was fully prepared to use it. But first I resolved to see if the United States would take action. If the United States, which would have to lead in any move by the Security Council to halt aggression in Palestine, was equally prepared to bring the question to the Council's attention in the appropriate terms and with appropriate forcefulness, then it would be wiser to let it have the public initiative.

But at the Security Council meeting in the afternoon of Saturday May 15, the day of the Arab invasion, the United States did not say a word; and in the Council as a whole (with the exception of the Soviet Member) there seemed to be a conspiracy of silence reminiscent of the most disheartening head-in-the-sand moments of the Chamberlain appeasement era.

That night I called my closest advisers to meet at my home in Forest Hills. Andrew Cordier, Abraham Feller, Dragon Protitch, and Tor Gjesdal were present; and I also invited the newly appointed Assistant Secretary-General for General Coordination, Commander R. G. A. Jackson, the dynamic Australian who had been selected to be my "trouble shooter." Our "council of war" that evening threshed through the problems. When it broke up at a very late hour, I had decided to throw Commander Jackson and Mr. Cordier into the front line of the struggle to uphold United Nations integrity in the face of the sharpest challenge which so far had been leveled at the Organization.

I think I can best portray the sense of urgency, of determination, of excitement and of high stakes, which May 15 and the days immediately following involved, by quoting from their reports.

Commander Jackson reported:

Following the instructions of the Secretary-General, and in agreement with the decision which we had taken late on the Saturday night, I saw Ambassador Austin in his suite at the Waldorf-Astoria at 11:20 A.M. on Sunday 16 May, 1948.

I described the Secretary-General's position in this matter. Having received the official communication from the Egyptian Government the Secretary-General felt that he could not fail to act. I told Ambassador Austin that the Secretary-General felt the future usefulness of the Security Council and the United Nations itself could be prejudiced by this most recent development. If the Security Council failed to take quick and effective action the Secretary-General believed that a precedent would be created which could easily encourage other nations at some later date to take aggressive action—when it suited their purposes—in complete defiance of their pledges to the United Nations.

The Secretary-General felt that there was an even greater and more immediate danger in that other governments which had so far accepted the authority of the Security Council in settling their disputes (e.g., in Indonesia and Kashmir) could easily decide to ignore the Security Council completely if Egypt were permitted to "get away" with this incident, and indeed all the effort which had been expended in the past in preventing the spread of civil war in Indonesia and Kashmir could be lost and a disastrous condition quickly develop in both those parts of the world.

For all these reasons the Secretary-General believed that it was imperative that the Security Council should take quick and effective action in this matter. He realised that some governments—for their own political reasons—might be quite content for action to drag in the Security Council on the assumption that by allowing the Arab forces and the Jewish forces to come into contact a situation would be created where both elements would be willing to negotiate. The Secretary-General felt that this was an exceedingly dangerous course. Not only could there be no reassurance that the fighting would die down after an initial period of conflict; it was quite possible that it might spread and some incident could easily occur which would involve one of the Big Powers and the whole scene in the Middle East could then develop into a world-wide threat to security. In any case it was very probable that Jerusalem would provide a stumbling block to any real settlement between the Jews and the Arabs.

There was an even greater danger than this. If the Great Powers accepted that this situation in the Middle East could best be settled by leaving the forces concerned to fight it out amongst themselves whilst at the same time those Great Powers sat in the Security Council of the United Nations, it was quite clear that they would be tacitly admitting that the Security Council and the United Nations was a useless instrument in attempting to preserve peace. It was here that the Secretary-General felt that the greatest threat to the future usefulness of the organization existed. He felt that it was essential, therefore, that the Great Powers should see that action was taken quickly to bring this problem under the authority of the United Nations.

It was for these reasons that attempts have been made during the evening of Saturday, 15 May, 1948, to bring about personal contact on Sunday, 16 May, with Mr. Marshall and Mr. Lovett in Washington in order that—since it was clear there were special difficulties between the United States and the United Kingdom Government in this matter—the Secretary-General could initiate discussions with the United Kingdom Government if it appeared that his good offices would be of value in bringing a closer understanding between the two governments; and especially in

ARMISTICE ACHIEVED IN PALESTINE

trying to bring this matter effectively under the control of the Security Council and seeing that effective action was taken to deal with it. As Mr. Austin probably knew, it had not been possible to arrange this meeting and as a consequence the Secretary-General had asked me to wait upon him and seek his advice in the matter.

Ambassador Austin . . . explained the difficulties of his own position and went on to describe the difficulties which the United States Government had experienced in dealing with the United Kingdom Government on this subject. After general discussion and checking the various points with me, he telephoned Mr. Rusk in the State Department and from that conversation they agreed that the best policy would be to "wait and see" what happened. There could be no meeting on Sunday with Mr. Marshall and Mr. Lovett. There seemed to be some inclination to suggest that in fact aggressive action had not yet been taken and there was a tendency to seek cover under the juridical questions which could be raised in connection with the problems. I told Mr. Austin that I felt that this view was unrealistic.

It could not be denied that the Secretary-General had been informed by a Member nation that it was using force in a dispute and it was quite clear that this act was contrary to the spirit of the Charter. That being accepted, it followed that if the Security Council did not take prompt and effective action then the consequential dangers which I had described would most certainly arise.

Ambassador Austin seemed to be tired and to some extent discouraged and I did not press him further on this point. I told him that I would communicate his views to the Secretary-General and that it might be possible for the Secretary-General and Sir Alexander Cadogan to have discussions on this matter. After the Secretary-General had decided what further action it might be possible for him to take, arrangements would be made for Ambassador Austin to be informed of the trend of these discussions.

The main impression which I gained from this discussion was the very wide gap which existed between the United States Government and the United Kingdom Government in approaching this problem, and it might well be that because of this divergence in view, effective action in the Security Council would not be forthcoming. It was clear to me that we would have to work very hard to try and bring these two governments together if we wanted action taken in the Security Council.

I then proceeded to the Secretary-General's house and discussed with him and with Mr. Cordier and with Mr. Feller the further action which might be taken in this matter. We agreed that a formal letter should be sent to each of the five Permanent Members of the Security Council making clear to them the Secretary-General's position in this matter.

In addition a personal letter would be sent to Secretary Marshall pointing out why the Secretary-General had hoped that personal conversations could have taken place with him with a view to easing the position between the Governments of the United States and the United Kingdom. In addition it might be desirable—after consultations had been completed with Sir Alexander Cadogan—for Mr. Cordier to go down to Washington first thing tomorrow (Monday) so that the State Department could know Mr. Lie's position in this matter, and possibly prepare the way for discussions with Messrs. Marshall and Lovett. We agreed on this line of action. . .

The text of my letter to each of the permanent members of the Security Council was as follows:

16 May 1948

My dear . . . :

The Egyptian Government has declared in a cablegram to the President of the Security Council on 15 May, that Egyptian armed forces have entered Palestine and that it has engaged in "armed intervention" in that country. On 16 May I received a cablegram from the Arab League making similar statements on behalf of the Arab States.

Since this matter is now before the Security Council, it is not necessary for me to invoke the provisions of Article 99 of the Charter, under which the Secretary-General may bring to the attention of the Security Council any matter which in his opinion may threaten the maintenance of international peace and security.

I consider it my duty, however, to emphasize to you that this is the first time since the adoption of the Charter that Member States have openly declared that they have engaged in armed intervention outside their own territory.

Moreover, this armed intervention has taken place in a territory which has been the special concern of the United Nations. A Truce Commission appointed by the Security Council has been active in Palestine for some time and it is only a matter of hours since the General Assembly adopted a resolution establishing a United Nations Mediator with the mandate of seeking agreement of the parties to a peaceful adjustment of the situation in Palestine.

The very first of the purposes of the United Nations is to maintain international peace and security. In Article 24 of the Charter the Members conferred on the Security Council primary responsibilities for the maintenance of international peace and security "in order to ensure prompt and effective action by the United Nations."

The opening discussions of the Council on 15 May have shown that there is danger that such prompt and effective action will not be forthcoming unless Members of the Council take a decisive stand in support of the authority of the Charter and of the United Nations.

Hostilities have already begun. There is grave danger that they will increase in intensity, and there is likelihood that other parties will become involved to the menace of the peace of the Middle East.

A failure of the Security Council to act under these circumstances can only result in the most serious injury to the prestige of the United Nations and the hopes for its future effectiveness in keeping the peace elsewhere in the world. Moreover, it may undermine the progress already made by the Council in other security problems with which it is now dealing.

I most earnestly urge that your Government should take account of the extreme seriousness of the situation which now faces the United Nations and of the necessity for prompt action at this crucial moment.

I have sent similar communications to each of the five permanent Members of the Security Council.

Yours sincerely
TRYGVE LIE

It is also useful to quote some paragraphs from the text of a second memorandum drawn up by Commander Jackson.

NOTES ON A CONVERSATION WITH SIR ALEXANDER CADOGAN
16 MAY 1948

Following our discussion with the Secretary-General, I proceeded as agreed to see Sir Alexander Cadogan.

I explained to him generally the Secretary-General's position in this matter. Having been addressed by the Egyptian Government, he could not fail to take action. Indeed, as his letter to each of the five Permanent Members of the Security Council indicated, the Secretary-General would have brought this matter to the attention of the Security Council under Article 99 if the Security Council had not already been convened to consider the matter. . . .

The Secretary-General appreciated that present divergencies in view between the United States and the United Kingdom could easily lead to a delay in the Security Council taking action, and for this reason he was anxious, not only to make his own position as Secretary-General absolutely clear in this matter, but he was also willing to assist in trying to help governments to come to an agreement about action which might be taken.

At the end, I emphasized again that time was the essence of the problem and that the longer the Security Council delayed taking action, the greater the danger would be.

Sir Alexander clearly understood the point which I had made and appreciated the position of the Secretary-General in this matter.

He went on to say that of course the whole problem could be confused by starting a legal quibble over the present status of Palestine. . . . He went on to say, however, that he accepted the realistic approach of the Secretary-General and realized that to indulge in legal quibbling could easily create a very dangerous situation to which the Secretary-General had now drawn the attention of the five Permanent Members.

He agreed that this case of aggression could well be regarded as the most dangerous crisis which had yet come in the life of the United Nations. He agreed that if not properly handled, the future of the United Nations might be prejudiced and that the disastrous experience of the League of Nations could easily be repeated. At this stage he expressed great regret that the United Nations had not yet been given the armed forces at its disposal which could so easily have dealt effectively with a situation such as this. He said, however, that it was necessary to avoid talking about an ideal world and to concentrate on what was practical. . . .

He foresaw great difficulties in coming to an agreed line between the United States and the United Kingdom, but equally appreciated that if that was not done then delay would be caused in the Security Council with all the most dangerous consequences which had just been discussed. He asked what specific steps the Secretary-General had in mind and assumed (which I confirmed immediately) that an immediate requirement would be to get a standstill order sent to all concerned. I agreed that this would be the first practical step. Sir Alexander then pointed out the danger of the Security Council issuing such a standstill order and then finding it ignored by the parties concerned. Could this not do even more harm to the prestige and authority of the Security Council? I pointed out that we felt that by accepting such an argument and failing to set the proper machinery of the Security Council in motion we would be acting in an even more dangerous way. It was essential—especially as far as the Secretary-General was concerned—that the proper procedure should be followed in this case even if one of the parties failed to comply with the Security Council's instructions. In that case the responsibility would be where it belonged and could not be wrongly placed either on the Security

Council or the Secretary-General. Sir Alexander accepted this point of view. . . .

Sir Alexander then prepared a telegram to the Foreign Office with which he forwarded the letter from the Secretary-General which had been circulated to the five Permanent Members of the Council. . . .

He then went on to say that he assumed that the Secretary-General would be discussing this problem with the United States Government and possibly other governments and that later either the Secretary-General or I might wish to propose further action. I confirmed that this was the case.

Now permit me to quote some excerpts from Mr. Cordier's report:

Upon arrival at the State Department on Monday morning I immediately delivered the letter [which the Secretary-General had addressed to the Big Five] to the office of the Secretary of State and initiated a series of conversations with Mr. Rusk, Mr. Sandifer and Mr. Blaisdell and other officials of the State Department, who with Mr. Rusk have the responsibility for United Nations affairs in the State Department.

We cleared quickly on the question of a nominee for the United Nations Mediator. The U.S. was prepared to present the name of Mr. van Zeeland and his name was forwarded to the U.S. delegation in New York.

Secondly, the Department was preparing a resolution declaring Arab action in Palestine a breach of the peace. It was cleared by the Secretary of State and the Secretary of State in turn cleared it with the White House. Mr. Rusk then outlined additional steps which top officials in the State Department were at the moment discussing and which the U.S. was prepared to take as a sequel to the resolution which was being submitted to the Security Council.

The first of these measures is the embargo on arms. It seemed clear from the conversation that the U.S. plan is to propose a universal embargo on arms to both sides and if the British do not cooperate in ending shipment of arms to the Arabs the U.S. would then lift the embargo on the shipment of arms.

The Department was also discussing the possibility, as a follow-up to an arms embargo, of the establishment of trade sanctions. It was understood, of course, that such sanctions would affect Great Britain more seriously than other countries and probably cause her to seek compensation which is her right under the Charter to offset losses sustained by her cooperation. The State Department is still distinctly in the discussion stage on this line of attack. . . .

They asked me to make sure that the strong initiative of the Secretary-

General over the weekend should not be interpreted to imply that the U.S. was inactive on the Palestine question. They recited the various moves, albeit some of the moves are inconsistent, that the U.S. had made in the Security Council, the Trusteeship Council and the General Assembly.

At the end of the day they humorously stated that the Secretary-General should not take too much credit for what happened that day but I facetiously retorted that in this kind of work it is rather dangerous for anyone to take credit lest later events fly back into our faces; and secondly that the time schedule suggested by Mr. Rusk on Saturday night was certainly a slower one than that indicated by the events of today. In any case I pointed out that all of us are in one big show together and we sink or swim together. The Secretary-General did not intend to make his current moves public, the letters were to be regarded as confidential and all of the steps that he proposed to take were in the one common interest of safeguarding the peace of the world, and of strengthening the United Nations for the urgent tasks that it had to confront both now and in the future.

Mr. Cordier's conversations in Washington took place on May 17, and they established that—at last—the United States was prepared to move resolutely in the Security Council. The big question was Britain's attitude, her general relations with the Arab states, and the position she would take in the United Nations. In the Security Council, Britain had again reverted to legalistic procedures, asking whether the invasion of Palestine was really aggression. Sir Alexander Cadogan himself, I had reason to know, disapproved of this approach. He was personally a stanch supporter of the United Nations and—I believed—shared my view that this was clear aggression, and that failure to meet it could easily lead to the ultimate downfall of the United Nations, just as the mishandling of the Manchurian and Ethiopian cases in the 1930's had led to the collapse of the League of Nations. However, he had his instructions from his Foreign Secretary and he loyally followed them.

On the battlefield, officers of British nationality were leading Jordan's Arab Legion, and British arms were used by the Arab armies. I was far from anxious that the United States and the United Kingdom should clash openly in the Security Council; what I sought was an Anglo-American agreement which would bring a United Nations peace with honor to Palestine. Accordingly, in order to make clear where the Secretary-General stood, and in order to do what I could to facilitate that understanding between Whitehall and Washington which was so crucial, I dispatched Commander Jackson to London. The United Nations had good friends and warm supporters within the British Government. The Prime Minister, Mr. Attlee, never missed an opportunity to put in a good word for the Organization; and Sir Stafford Cripps, I knew, was already leading a group of his colleagues into open attacks on Mr. Bevin's Palestine position. Here are the more vital paragraphs of Commander Jackson's report:

> In accordance with your instructions, I proceeded to London for discussions with the British Government.
>
> Leaving New York about midnight on Tuesday, 18 May, I arrived in London at 20.40 hours on 19 May. . . . As soon as I left the Chancellor [of the Exchequer, Sir Stafford Cripps], I telephoned the Office of the Permanent Under-Secretary of the Foreign Office, Sir Orme Sargent. I informed his Office of the purpose of my visit and arrangements were made to meet with him at 6 o'clock that evening, together with Mr. Gladwyn Jebb, who is in charge of United Nations affairs in the Foreign Office, and Mr. Michael Wright, who is responsible for the Middle Eastern Section. This meeting was held and I informed the officials concerned of your problem at the present time and stressed that if effective action could not be taken quickly to deal with the situation in the Middle East, then we feared a spread of armed intervention in the Middle Eastern area, possible repercussions in Kashmir, India and the Balkans following clear proof of the ineffectiveness of the Security Council, grave reactions on UK-US relations, *and the beginning of the end of the United Nations.* I discussed the situation in detail and it seemed evident that Jebb clearly appreciated our position and particularly *your own responsibilities under Article 99.*
>
> Sargent was very cautious during the meeting and enquired whether you were, in fact, issuing a "warning" to the British Government. . . . I quietly but emphatically denied that such was the case and Sargent then enquired whether it could be said that you were speaking both officially and as a friend of H.M.G. I said that this could be expected, having in mind the fact that your primary concern was the future of the United Nations.
>
> Sargent then asked if I would commit your views to paper. I said that I thought that this was unwise but eventually said I would have no objection to making a list of the headings of the various points with which you are concerned. . . .

I was left with the impression that Jebb alone appreciated the true position and that Sargent and Wright were seeking to find some extraneous reason for my intervention as your representative. I felt that the danger to the general relationship between the Great Powers was not fully appreciated, nor its real danger to the future of the United Nations.

It was then agreed that a meeting would be arranged with the Foreign Secretary. . . .

I saw the Foreign Secretary at 10.45 A.M. on Saturday, 22 May, and the following points emerged. Jebb and Wright were present.

The Foreign Secretary expressed displeasure that the Chancellor of the Exchequer, Sir Stafford Cripps, had been seen before discussions had taken place with him. I explained to him how his own movements and that of the Chancellor and myself had made such a sequence inevitable and reassured him that everybody concerned realised that the political aspects of your difficulties were matters for him and the Foreign Office. He appeared to accept this explanation. The Foreign Secretary then asked why I had come to London. I told him of your concern over the United Nations and enquired if he had read the general headings which I had prepared at Sargent's request. He informed me that he had read this paper. I said my main responsibility was to make clear the Secretary-General's position and to seek guidance as to what future action could most usefully be taken by the Secretary-General in the discharge of his official responsibilities.

The Foreign Secretary then informed me of the reasons behind his own policy, what the British Government had done in its efforts to solve the Palestine problem and then went on, reverting to his usual routine of itemizing the mistakes made by the United States Government in handling this problem. He laid great emphasis on the difficulties caused by the President's recognition of Israel, etc. However, I said that the Secretary-General was primarily concerned with the possible effect of the present situation on the future of the United Nations, and wished governments to know exactly what he felt. A situation existed, which, in his judgment, threatened the future of the Organization and wanted to help in any way possible in assisting governments (*preferably behind the scenes*) to obtain agreement on future action.

At that point [it was] suggested that the Secretary-General was "reading a lecture on Anglo-American relations" and that the place for doing that was Washington not London.

I told [them] that as the general headings prepared at Sargent's request indicated, and as I had said several times, the Secretary-General was not allocating responsibility to any government for the present situation or suggesting to any government that its policies should be modified. The Secretary-General had already made clear his position to the United States Government in Washington. The position of the Secretary-General was simple. In his judgment the present situation threatened the future of the United Nations and he desired that his views about this should be clearly appreciated by governments chiefly concerned. . . .

The Foreign Secretary then said that if the Secretary-General would read the latest British resolution, he should feel that it would produce satisfactory results. I enquired whether he thought that such a "cease-fire" order (similar to one already a month old) could hold back the Jews and Arabs. He said that if Washington and New York could control the Jews, he thought the Arabs could be restrained.

I then asked if there were any further guidance he could give the Secretary-General and he said "no."

These discussions indicated:

The uncertainty about the reason for our intervention, although I had painstakingly made clear your objective official and friendly interest in this matter.

No real recognition on the Foreign Secretary's part of your responsibilities and difficulties at the present time, and as a result of this:

No effective guidance was given to me on your behalf. . . . [Later I was told about the discussions in the Cabinet that morning, in which clearly two different opinions had been presented], the one from the Foreign Secretary; the other from other ministers concerned. From this I had reasonable confidence that your own position was now well understood, but that we were still lacking any clear-cut understanding of possible future developments. It seems to me that we must be guided by developments over the next day or two in deciding what our next approach to this problem should be.

Meanwhile, there was enough to do in New York. Washington had suggested that Paul van Zeeland, the Belgian statesman, be designated as United Nations Mediator for Palestine. I cabled and telephoned to him; but, after some hesitation, he found himself forced to decline. I then suggested Count Folke Bernadotte, a member of the Swedish royal family and the President of the Swedish Red Cross. The representatives of the Big Five agreed, and I telephoned to him. He had led a life of devotion to other peoples' well-being, and, in spite of the obvious dangers, he agreed to undertake the Palestine mission. The Permanent Members of the Security Council accordingly unanimously designated Count Bernadotte as Mediator on

May 20—after full-scale fighting had seesawed in Palestine for five days. He at once left for Palestine, stopping briefly in Paris to meet Ralph Bunche with a few members of the Secretariat. From that time on, Bernadotte's airplane, which I placed at his disposal, painted white and with "U.N." in capital letters on the fuselage and the wings, together with the Red Cross insignia denoting Bernadotte's status as President of the Swedish Red Cross, was a familiar sight in the Near East.

Aside from this appointment, the spectacle in the Security Council so far had been a sad one. The United States carried out its new pledges to press for action with teeth in it, but Britain did not go along. Certain other members of the Security Council, for reasons of their own, sided with Britain for inaction. The Council fell two votes short of responding to Warren Austin's eloquent appeal to reply forcefully to the international aggression which had violated Palestine's borders. By May 27 the Arabs had rejected four toothless Security Council appeals for an end of hostilities in Palestine. Without a change in British policy, the outlook for stopping the carnage was poor. London, while suggesting in effect that it would withdraw its support from the Arab Legion (the best of the aggressor armies) only if the United Nations condemned the action of the Arab states, gave no support to such a measure in the Security Council. Public criticism mounted. Reports from the British capital made it increasingly clear that Foreign Secretary Bevin was the main roadblock to a more constructive approach. The pressure—from Washington, from within Great Britain, from United Nations Headquarters, and from Israeli successes in the field—finally convinced the British Cabinet that a change of policy was necessary. On May 27 Sir Alexander Cadogan at last received instructions to agree to a truce order which threatened to bring United Nations sanctions against the party refusing to comply. This was what I had wanted two weeks before.

As amended, the resolution called for a four weeks' truce, and empowered the United Nations Mediator to negotiate its terms and supervise its implementation. Both Arabs and Jews accepted the Council's resolution. Count Bernadotte energetically negotiated to fix the date on which the truce would come into effect. He flew tirelessly from capital to capital and finally secured Arab and Jewish acceptance of his interpretations of the terms of the Council's resolution on June 9. Two days later, the United Nations achieved its first major success on the road to peace in Palestine: The cease-fire went into effect. The guns were silenced, the bloodshed stopped—for a while.

The Mediator set up his headquarters on the Greek island of Rhodes. He had at his disposal a secretariat headed by my personal representative, Ralph J. Bunche. Dr. Bunche from the beginning played an important role in the Mediator's mission, assisted by able senior members of the United Nations Secretariat like Henri Vigier, John Reedman, Constantin A. Stavropoulos, Paul Mohn, William H. Stoneman, and Pablo de Azcarate. Count Bernadotte had requested me earlier to supply some military personnel to assist him in truce control functions, and I arranged with the three governments represented on the Security Council's Truce Commission—Belgium, France, and the United States—to assign officers from their armed forces for duty as United Nations military observers. During the second truce the number reached five hundred. They were stationed at strategic points along the cease-fire line and in the capitals of Israel and the Arab states. No story of the United Nations effort in Palestine would be complete without a tribute to these gallant men who, without any previous experience in international teamwork, welded themselves in a matter of days into an effective team of United Nations officials. Their only protection was the modest blue-and-white armband added to their national uniform to identify them as United Nations observers. There was no risk they refused to take in the service of peace. Seven of them gave their lives, some suffered injuries. Two fliers, recruited to operate the airplanes chartered for this mission, lost their lives in a crash. But no danger ever deflected United Nations observers from carrying out their duties with true United Nations impartiality.

Toward the end of the first truce Count Bernadotte also requested me to supply him with fifty guards to assist the military observers in their truce control functions. The request was received on a Thursday. I personally appealed to the United Nations guards and members of the Secretariat for volunteers. The response was magnificent. On the following Sunday fifty volunteers, fully uniformed, emplaned for Cairo. In Palestine they drove jeeps and escorted convoys. Unarmed and with the United Nations uniform as their only protection, they stood guard over premises occupied by the United Nations, did maintenance work on vehicles, and performed other essential chores. One of them, Ole Helge Bakke, a compatriot of mine, was the first to lose his life from a sniper's bullet.

With a cease-fire achieved, Bernadotte could start his broader task of mediation. On June 28 he submitted some working suggestions for a more lasting accord between the Arabs and the Israelis. Though he termed them highly tentative, he presented them formally and simultaneously to the Arabs and Jews, without having had the benefit of advance soundings with each party. His aim at this stage was no doubt to convince the Arabs that they ought to stop their aggression. The suggestions were rejected by Israel, which had stood up well to the military onslaught. The Mediator was still engaged in negotiating his suggestions with the Arabs and Jews when the period of the four-week truce began to run out. He appealed more than once to both sides to agree to an extension, and the Security Council, on July 7, added its appeal. The Israelis accepted; the Arab League refused. On July 9 the Arabs renewed their attacks, with even less success than before. This, combined with a firm order from the Security Council explicitly adding a threat of sanctions against the party refusing to comply, induced the Arabs to yield. The United Kingdom, it should be noted, now stood with the Council majority. The second truce, without a time limit, came into effect on July 18.

Count Bernadotte resumed his efforts to negotiate a more durable agreement, and I cooperated as I had done from the beginning of his mission. He had proposed in the third week of June that I fly out to Rhodes, with the idea, Ralph Bunche reported, that my presence and the opportunity for consultations would be "extremely helpful"; but I sensed that my appearance in Rhodes might be misinterpreted, and thought it best to decline. However, I advised Bernadotte to avoid making any proposals to the Arabs and Israelis which had but a slim chance of acceptance, and to concentrate on securing an extension of the truce. I further invited the Count to return to Lake Success to report in person to the Security Council, and to consult with the delegations; this he did in July when the first truce expired. With the imposition of the second truce Count Bernadotte and I proceeded to negotiate with the Arabs and Israelis jointly, he from

ARMISTICE ACHIEVED IN PALESTINE

Rhodes and I in Lake Success. We were in constant consultation by telephone and cable, and also later, when Dr. Bunche had succeeded the Count, the intervention from Lake Success seemed to be decisive in preventing the parties from breaking off negotiations on the spot. There was always a good response from the Israelis to my suggestions. I should also like to stress that within the limitation of the policy of their governments some individual Arab statesmen understood the position which, as Secretary-General, I had to take in support of United Nations decisions. After the failure to make any serious impression on the Israelis in the fighting between the two truces, Cairo tended to negotiate on a more realistic plane, though continuing to maintain a strong official line.

In the long period before the Egyptians agreed to send a delegation to Rhodes to sign an armistice with the Israelis, progress was slow. The Israelis offered through the Mediator to undertake direct peace negotiations with the Arabs. The Arabs refused. Count Bernadotte's position with the Israelis was somewhat affected by his earlier suggestions during his attempts to extend the first truce, and he was unjustly accused of favoring the Arabs. There was, moreover, considerable restiveness over the truce, especially in Jerusalem, both in Israeli and in Arab quarters. Each side accused the other of repeated violations. Bernadotte, if he were to have a chance as Mediator, understandably had to treat the Arab aggressor and the Israeli defender in Palestine equally. This was not popular in Jewish quarters, since they felt themselves to be in the right, under the United Nations terms. In this discouraging atmosphere, Count Bernadotte persevered with characteristic coolness and energy.

When the General Assembly was about to convene in Paris in September, 1948, Count Bernadotte was doggedly seeking to arrange the demilitarization of Jerusalem, and to ameliorate the pitiful situation of the hundreds of thousands of Arab refugees who had fled from their homes in the course of the fighting. He had prepared a report to the General Assembly on the work of his mission with his recommendations for settlement. Addressing a private covering letter to me, he sent them both to me in Paris by Mr. Stavropoulos and Mr. Reedman. The letter read, in part:

> Since I talked with you in Paris two weeks ago I have made another tour and have consulted at length with Arab and Jewish leaders. As I

indicated in my formal note to you presenting the report, I am more firmly convinced than ever, as a result of these recent consultations, that it is altogether indispensable that the Palestine question be placed on the agenda of the Third Session of the Assembly.

As I appraise the situation, there is no risk involved in putting the matter before the Assembly. If the Assembly should take up the question and fail to reach a decision, that would unquestionably be very bad and the truce could not be long maintained thereafter. That is true. But the results will be precisely the same if the Assembly ignores the question, for then both sides will be emboldened and the truce may well break down even sooner. There is no one out here with whom I have talked, including Arabs and Jews, who does not fully share my opinion on the matter.

I hope very much, therefore, because the stakes are so frighteningly high, that you will do everything possible to get the question placed on the agenda, even if there is no alternative but to place it before the General Committee yourself . . . I think that with appropriate Assembly action now the back of this problem can be broken. It will be a terrible tragedy if the opportunity is not seized.

I hope to see you in Paris within a very few days, I trust you enjoyed your visit to Norway.

Sincerely Yours,
FOLKE BERNADOTTE

The Count's letter was written from Rhodes on September 16. He was murdered in Jerusalem the next day.

The shock was inexpressible. Ralph Bunche cabled that Count Bernadotte had been "brutally assassinated by Jewish assailants of unknown identity in a planned, cold-blooded attack in the new city of Jerusalem at 14.05 GMT today, Friday 17th September." The terrorism which had stained the Zionist cause had taken its noblest victim. Moshe Shertok at once cabled me:

> Outraged by abominable assassination of United Nations Mediator Count Bernadotte and observer Colonel Serot, by desperadoes and outlaws who are execrated by entire people of Israel and Jewish community of Jerusalem. Government of Israel is adopting most vigorous and energetic measures to bring assassins to justice and eradicate evil.

"Execrated" was the right word—it conveyed the horror which gripped us all. The enormity, the barbarism, the primeval stupidity of the act, were engulfing. And our grief was still more bitter.

I knew the Count and his family personally, and this was enough to give a special edge to my sorrow. But my pain was refined by the reflection that the Count had died for the cause of the United Nations.

The bodies of Count Bernadotte and Colonel Serot were flown to Paris, and that of the Count on to Stockholm. There was a memorial service at Orly airport for him and Colonel Serot, and for six other United Nations personnel who had been killed in Palestine either by the Arabs or by the Israelis. I flew to Stockholm for the funeral. The ceremonies were deeply moving. Count Bernadotte's uncle, the ninety-year-old King, was in attendance. Countess Bernadotte bore the tragedy of her husband's death with a dignity and nobility which seemed to symbolize the dedications to public service so characteristic not only of Count Bernadotte himself, but of his whole family.

The problem of Palestine remained. I appointed Ralph Bunche Acting Mediator, and the Security Council ratified my action. Dr. Bunche endeavored to maintain the truce amid increasing violations by both sides, and he pursued Count Bernadotte's efforts to assist the Arab refugees. Fighting broke out in Galilee and in the Negev, where Israeli forces advanced rapidly south, after an initial Egyptian attack; Dr. Bunche flew to Paris to request the Security Council to reaffirm the truce. At his urging, the Council further adopted a resolution on November 15 calling upon the Arabs and Israelis to replace the truce arrangements with more durable armistice agreements. The Assembly, meanwhile, approved a substantial relief program for the Arab refugees, which my Executive Office took the lead in implementing.

At the same time, the Arabs and the Israelis could not agree on the proposals for a permanent settlement which Count Bernadotte had made, and the Assembly contented itself with establishing a Conciliation Commission to assist the parties in arriving at a settlement.

In January, Egypt cabled to Dr. Bunche that it was prepared to negotiate under United Nations chairmanship with the Israeli Government. Bunche acted quickly to bring the parties together at Rhodes. Forty-two days of continuous negotiations followed, Bunche pressing untiringly for agreement at Rhodes and I exerting complementary efforts upon the Egyptian and Israeli delegates in New York. It is obvious that there would not have been an armistice at this stage without the skill and dedication of Ralph Bunche, and we all were proud of him. The Israeli-Egyptian Armistice Agreement was signed on February 24, 1949. Even before this the other Arab states and Israel had begun additional negotiations which culminated in the Lebanon-Israeli Armistice Agreement on March 23, the Jordan-Israeli Agreement on April 3, and the Syrian-Israeli Agreement on July 20. "Conciliation, mediation, and compromise are slow work," I remarked at a press conference the next day, "but they are —in the long run—the only firm foundation of a peaceful world. The enforcement of peace has, of course, a place under the Charter. But lasting peace cannot be founded upon force. It has to be founded upon consent freely given and agreement voluntarily arrived at. I think all who believe in working for a peaceful settlement of the conflict between the great powers should take heart from what has been accomplished by mediation and conciliation on the island of Rhodes—first by the late Count Folke Bernadotte, and from September by Ralph J. Bunche."

The Nobel Committee, a body appointed by the Norwegian Parliament, awarded the Nobel Prize for Peace to Dr. Bunche. The award filled me with pride. It not only expressed the admiration which the entire world felt for an outstanding American, but also, as Ralph Bunche was the first to say, it represented a tribute to the United Nations and to its Secretariat for their role in the settlement of international disputes.

Here I should say a word about two positive by-products of the Palestine experience.

All through the first half of 1948 I was acutely conscious of how different things in Palestine could have been had the United Nations had an international force at its disposal.

Over the summer I undertook preliminary soundings, with the idea of a force of 5,000 to 10,000 men as a beginning. The assassination of Count Bernadotte in September spurred me to place a proposal for the creation of such a Guard on the agenda of the Third Session of the General Assembly. There, it ran into heavy opposition from the Soviet bloc, which stood rigidly on the position that the United Nations should either carry out Article 43 of the Charter as originally intended, or have no force at all; but others, too, had hesitations and doubts partly because of the cost and partly because of inertia—an internationally recruited police force was too radical an idea for many governments. However, in order to take advantage of every possibility of agreement to proceed, I proposed to the Assembly that it establish a special committee to study the proposal and report back to the following session. This the Assembly did; I presented to the committee a much modified version of the plan, which was designed to meet objections which had been voiced by various governments. Ultimately, the Assembly agreed on something useful, but not at all what I had originally intended. It came to be called the United Nations Field Service.

This little group is not in any sense an army or a United Nations guard. It is, however, a branch of the Secretariat which has its own uniform and is specially trained in operation and maintenance of communications and transportation equipment. It renders invaluable auxiliary service to United Nations missions in the field; and, although unarmed, it is capable of maintaining a modest guard over premises occupied by the United Nations and valuable buildings located in demilitarized areas, such as Government House in Jerusalem, which has no other protection than the twenty Field Service men together with a few United Nations military observers who are stationed there.

My colleagues and I felt that the Government of Israel, though not directly implicated in Count Bernadotte's death, should make reparation, because the assassination had occurred in Israeli-held territory, in circumstances under which the Israeli Government could be charged with negligence in not affording him proper protection. I placed the question of the Organization's seeking reparations on the Assembly's agenda and, in a memorandum which Mr. Feller drew up, maintained that the United Nations had the legal capacity as an Organization to present a claim under international law against a State. This was a position which would create a precedent in international law, and so the Assembly decided to ask the International Court of Justice for an advisory opinion on the question. Ivan Kerno, Assistant Secretary-General for Legal Affairs, and Abraham Feller went to the Hague and argued the case for the Organization. The United Nations, they maintained, had international juridical personality—international law did not in fact have states alone as its subjects. The Court upheld our point of view and, in a decision of the most fundamental importance, declared that the Organization was an "international person," with international rights and duties and the capacity to protect its rights by bringing international claims. In accordance with the opinion, negotiations were undertaken with Israel, and the Israeli Government promptly and fully made such reparations as a payment of money can provide.

Similar action was undertaken in respect of every one of the military observers and United Nations Secretariat members who lost their lives as a result of attacks by the nationals of any of the parties in the Palestine conflict.

Israel was admitted to membership in the United Nations on May 11, 1949—a decision which pleased me greatly. "The establishment of the State of Israel," I wrote in the introduction to my fourth annual report to the General Assembly, was "one of the epic events of history, coming at the end not merely of thirty years, but of two thousand years of accumulated sorrows, bitterness and conflict," and symbolized "historical forces beside which the present ideological conflict appears to be a transitory phenomenon."

I am proud of the United Nations' role in aiding the establishment of Israel, but I could be far prouder. The decision for partition, once taken by the United Nations, should have been resolutely upheld not only by some governments and the Secretary-General, but by all Members of the Organization. In the face of armed defiance, there was for a time a disheartening disposition on the part of some to bury their heads in the sand. But, ultimately, the Security Council did solid work to bring peace to Palestine. Let us hope the lesson was learned.

As Secretary-General, I stood by the early recommendation to partition Palestine, subsequently endorsed by the General Assembly, and I make no apologies for that. As it turned out, the Arabs chose to assault the decision which I was obliged to defend, and the Jews, by and large, chose to uphold it. Accordingly, I earned the appreciation of the Jews and the condemnation of the less objective of the Arabs. It took time for these feelings to subside—if they have ever subsided entirely.

Neither has it proved feasible yet to arrive at the final peace arrangements envisioned when the armistice was signed—a sign, perhaps, of the long time it may take to reach settlements of other world conflicts.

I traveled to the Middle East in April, 1951, and visited four of the Member states whose forces had been on the battlefields in 1948 and were still guarding the provisional borders day and night. In Egypt, Syria, and Lebanon the burning question remained that of the existence of Israel. There was hatred—bitter hatred. It was clear that the Arab states considered Israel as a threat to their integrity and independence. They seemed to be convinced that Israel would have to expand because of its mushrooming population. Prime Minister David Ben Gurion was said to have predicted a population of four million within five years. With the small size of the country—it was no more than a ninety-minute automobile trip from Tel Aviv on the coast to the demarcation line in Jerusalem—the Arabs feared a first step in the direction of Jordan. Here, they insisted, Israel would demand areas occupied by Jordan, amounting to more than a third of Palestine before partition. Inroads into territory held by Lebanon, Syria, Transjordan, and Egypt would certainly follow. Their arguments were obviously sincere.

Subsequent talks in Israel with President Chaim Weizmann, Prime Minister David Ben Gurion, and Foreign Minister Moshe Sharett were reassuring. I brought up the current Syrian-Israeli incident and found that they regretted Israeli action in retaliatory bombing; on the other hand, they had no intention of halting land reclamation in the Huleh Lake region, which they asserted would benefit both Syrians and Israelis.

Further complaints are before the Security Council as I write—regarding the construction by the Israelis of a canal from the Jordan to Lake Tiberias in connection with hydroelectric development in Israel. Such complaints are bound to recur so long as an armistice regime that was designed to be a short-term transition to peace continues to be maintained as though it were permanent. Yet unless both Arabs and Israelis reach a peace settlement on a basis of mutual give and take, there is no alternative to continuing the Armistice regime unimpaired.

In all countries I discussed the problem of the Arab refugees, which was of immediate concern to the United Nations. Of the

850,000 Arabs who had left Palestine since partition, 450,000 had sought haven in Jordan, 130,000 in Lebanon, 85,000 in Syria, and 130,000 in Egypt. In theory, there was every reason for their return; in practice, repatriation was impossible, and most of them would have to be settled where they were. But the Arab governments themselves hotly disputed this conclusion; at least they refused to move unless and until fantastic claims for compensation were met. Israel, on the other hand, felt unable to pay more than a fraction of what obviously would be a fair compensation, and still continued to freeze the bank accounts of absent Arabs. This, I felt, was a situation where the United Nations had strong obligations.

Our efforts to help had been well planned, but so far were not too successful. The United Nations Relief and Works Agency, an organ with regional headquarters in Beirut, had been trying to encourage the Arab states to launch development projects, as Israel was doing, and provide the refugees with permanent and constructive employment. Results had not been very promising. As matters stood, these hundreds of thousands had been quartered in huge camps for several years, and had been fed and clothed by the United Nations at a cost of over $50,000,000. Clearly this could not go on indefinitely. A final settlement in the Middle East hinged largely on the question of refugee reintegration on a large scale.

In Damascus, I was told that Syria had plans to provide homes and work for 40,000 refugees—a good beginning. In Beirut, contradictory statements were made, because—as I found out—an influx of essentially Moslem Arabs would alter the existing even balance of Christians and Moslems in Lebanon. While in Beirut I heard also that Egypt actually planned a reintegration program for 20,000 refugees but preferred not to confirm this.

These were mere piecemeal advances. Still, no more progress was in sight. I concluded that, mainly for political reasons, it would be unrealistic to expect the Arab states to agree to the principle of resettlement at this stage, and that *de facto* settlement of the bulk of the refugees was all that could reasonably be aimed at. Developments supported this line of reasoning.

Israel's approach to its problem of Jewish refugees was strikingly in contrast. Hundreds of Jews were arriving daily, especially now from the Arab lands. At the time of my visit, I was informed that

Israel had already received 20,000 Jews from Egypt, 50,000 from Yemen, 80,000 from Iraq, and others from North Africa, Bulgaria, Hungary, and Rumania on top of the previous immigration from Germany.

The organization for receiving immigrants was most impressive. Every step had been worked out according to a rigid system; otherwise the whole of Israel would have been chaos within a week. Standing at the airport one day, we saw plane after plane landing with refugees from Iraq. Upon arrival the newcomers were first settled in a tent camp. In the next stage, they received a sheet-metal prefabricated house, together with a small piece of land, tools, and such other equipment as nine hens, a rooster, and a goat. If they did well, they would expect to receive in good time a better house and a cow; the permanent house, either of wood or of concrete, was generally erected not far from the hut. The immigrants worked on the site, clearing the fields, or building a factory, or doing reforestation. At each stage of their progress the government held out a further inducement for additional effort.

I found the mixture of racial types particularly interesting. The Yemenite and other oriental Jews were very evident, and the problems of assimilation looked formidable—not least because of the religious complications; for the Jewish faith has sectarian divisions like other religions. Railway and bus travel on the Sabbath was still a political issue in Tel Aviv.

Apart from studies of the problems of Arab and Jewish refugees, I had an opportunity now to judge the wisdom of the United Nations' original resolution of November 29, 1947, against the background of practical results achieved in the various fields during the intervening years. I was impressed in Israel—both by the accomplishments and by the spirit behind them. Coming from a mountainous country, I was struck by the way in which expanses of barren stone hills were claimed for productive acreage. Marshes were drained, and new irrigation projects launched; there was an intensive reforestation program. Everyone seemed to be working—and talking—hard. Inflation, however, was evident; prices were very high, and the Israeli pound was selling at an enormous discount. From what I could gather, this whole arena of bustle and progress was kept in motion by assistance from abroad, and at least five or six more years of aid at a high rate would be needed before it could carry along on its own. Leaders with whom I spoke were convinced that Israel could be self-sufficient in time; but I felt they were getting too used to the idea of perpetual miracles. A slower pace in immigration would be helpful, it seemed.

In the neighboring Arab states, I also saw the need for outside assistance. Poverty on a scale hardly comprehensible to a Northern European held the peoples down in grim misery. Ignorance prevailed, and sickness; I recall the groups of eager small boys who surrounded our vehicles whenever we halted on a trip: so many of them already had trachoma-infected eyes, the scourge of the Middle East. Government leaders were keen to tell me about their reform plans, and there were obviously many farsighted men who pushed for the emancipation of their peoples from traditional bondage. Not least in Syria did I gain the impression that serious efforts were being made. Progressive demonstration projects had been launched in Egypt, too, but the great mass of the population on the land, the fellahin, still lived largely as serfs. I shall only recall what I reported to the Assistant Secretaries-General upon my return to Headquarters in May, 1951: that Egypt, with its enormous social and economic problems on top of its frustrating political tribulations, would undoubtedly be the scene of a revolution within a year.

The Armistice Agreements of 1949 still remain in force, but no true peace has resulted. Whether a more durable Arab-Jewish settlement will be substituted probably hinges upon whether or not Arab statesmen and leaders can come around to a more realistic approach to the facts of our time. Israel now exists as a sovereign state: a member of the United Nations, maintaining diplomatic relations with a majority of the countries of the world. Without the recognition of the Arab states, Palestine will remain a source of conflict. The majority of the world's population hopes for real peace, understanding, and cooperation among the nations of the Middle East.

CHAPTER XII

MEDIATION IN BERLIN

The Soviet blockade and its impact.—Conciliation in currency conflict attempted while airlift holds front.—Assembly's appeal to great powers carried further by President and Secretary-General.—Conversation at Lake Success leads to solution.

WHEN THE General Assembly decided in December, 1947, to hold its 1948 fall session in Europe it did not foresee that a new threat to world peace would dominate the deliberations: the blockade of Berlin.

The Soviet Union had begun early in 1948 to interfere with the free access of the United States, Britain, and France to Berlin. Despite the fact that Berlin was an international enclave, divided, as was the whole of Germany, into four zones of occupation, and despite the fact that the Western powers had rights in Berlin equal to those of the U.S.S.R., Moscow undertook to cut them off from their troops and the two and a half million Germans in Berlin who were subject to their authority. By July the Soviet policy of piecemeal strangulation of West Berlin was fully applied. Communication by road, rail, and barge between the Western zones of occupation in West Germany and the Western sectors in Berlin was effectively interrupted. The blockade would have been complete but for the consequent launching and maintenance of the spectacular airlift, which successfully supplied the Western troops in Berlin, and the two and a half million citizens as well, with the essentials of life.

Meanwhile the three Western powers had vigorously protested Moscow's action and sought, by every possible channel of negotiation with Soviet authorities in Berlin on up to Generalissimo Stalin, to have the blockade lifted. On August 30 the Western envoys in Moscow seemed to have broken the deadlock and to have made a start toward a settlement with the U.S.S.R. The settlement was linked with the complicated matter of currency reform, which Moscow now asserted was the cause of her restrictions after first pleading alleged "technical difficulties" like railroad repairs. Britain, France, and the United States had reformed the German currency of their zones, and as a result the prostrate economy had begun to revive rapidly in those zones. The Soviet zone in turn introduced its own currency reform—for the U.S.S.R. had been unable to agree with the Western powers on a single program of reform for all Germany—and this East Zone currency began circulating throughout the whole of Berlin. The Western powers then began to employ specially marked currency from West Germany in their sectors of Berlin. In return for the lifting of the Soviet blockade, the West agreed to replace West German currency in Berlin with that of the Soviet zone, provided that agreement could be reached on joint four-power control over currency, banking, and trade facilities in the city. This was the essence of the August 30 agreement, and the West, additionally, was to lift the retaliatory restrictions which it had imposed on movement between the Soviet and the Western zones of Germany. The Moscow directive of August 30 to the commandants of the four powers in Berlin instructed them to work out the arrangements for four-power control over Berlin finance and trade. As soon as these arrangements were made, the August 30 agreement would come into full operation, and the blockade would be lifted.

The arrangements never were made. Marshal Vasili Sokolovsky, the Soviet commandant, apparently had different instructions. Rather than moving toward the lifting of the blockade through agreement on Berlin finance and trade, he proposed that the West agree to the imposition of fresh restrictions—namely, on Western rights of access to Berlin by air.

After another try in Moscow, the United States, Britain, and France appealed to the Security Council of the United Nations on September 29, 1948, on the ground that the Soviet blockade of Berlin constituted a threat to the peace.

That the blockade was in fact a threat to the peace had been obvious for some time. First, the Soviet Union appeared to be seeking to smash the West's show window in Berlin—a show window into which East Germany, if not all Eastern Europe, could easily look. This, apparently, was Moscow's first purpose, for there was, from its point of view, too much to see: economic recovery in the areas of Germany under Western authority was startling, and that in the Soviet zone unimpressive. Moscow seemed to be trying to make the West's position in Berlin untenable; but in a wider sense it also seemed to wish to stall the creation of a West German government and use a Berlin settlement as a means of regaining a voice in the disposition of West Germany. At all events the whole Berlin intrigue had been launched as a test of Western strength and will to hold firm in the struggle for the future of Germany.

The combined Western airlift dramatically frustrated the Soviet design. Instead of accepting the humiliation of a withdrawal from Berlin, or capitulating to terms which would have had like effects, the Western democracies by their determination turned the blockade into a triumph of air power. The threat to peace remained, however, not simply in the use by the Soviet Union of force to gain political ends to which it had no legal right, but in the constant danger of "incidents." If by any chance it was looking for a pretext the moment had much to offer, for Europe then was quite shorn of defensive power and the danger of war was greater than at any time before or since.

During the tense summer weeks of 1948, I had concerned myself with the Berlin crisis day after day. In July, I had talked in New York with Dr. Philip C. Jessup, the United States Ambassador at large; and he was good enough to keep me as fully informed as possible of the summer's Berlin developments. When the question came before the Security Council in Paris, I accelerated my study of the crisis, drawing particularly upon the informed advice of Abraham Feller and William H. Stoneman, both of whom enjoyed superior contacts with American sources. For the Soviet side of the affair I relied upon Assistant Secretary-General Arkady Sobolev, who enjoyed a like entrée to Moscow. It was obvious to me that any United Nations contribution to resolving the Berlin crisis, beyond the airing of the West's grievances before international public opinion, would have to be through mediation, for the Security Council would certainly be unable to take action against Moscow in the face of a Soviet veto. The first question was whether both the Soviet Union and the West really wanted mediation. There would then remain the difficult matter of means.

Moscow, as a counterthrust to the West's raising Berlin in the United Nations, proposed on October 3 that the Council of Foreign Ministers convene to discuss four-power disputes over Germany, including Berlin. Nevertheless, on October 4, over Soviet objections, the Security Council placed the Berlin blockade on its agenda. The West seemed to be disposed to welcome mediation. As a sign of its good will in this respect, the United States yielded its alphabetical right to preside over the Security Council for the month of October to the Foreign Minister of Argentina, Dr. Juan A. Bramuglia; and he became the leader of the Council's six "neutrals" in the first attempt at reconciliation. After extended conversations with the Berlin disputants, the "neutrals" put forth their resolution. It called upon the four powers to avoid acts which might aggravate the Berlin situation, to lift immediately all restrictions on commerce, transportation, and communications between Berlin and the four zones of occupation, to convoke an immediate meeting of the four military governors in Berlin to arrange for unification of the city's currency by November 20, and to convene the Council of Foreign Ministers to consider the entire German question within ten days of the fulfillment of these measures. On October 25 the U.S.S.R. cut down this resolution with its veto.

Deliberately, I had kept out of the negotiatory efforts of Dr. Bramuglia and his associates up to this point thinking that, if his initiative did not succeed, I might come forth uncompromised with another. Early in October, Philip Jessup and Dean Rusk, chief of the United Nations Office of the Department of State, had come to me and asked if I were willing to do what I could to find a way out of the Berlin impasse. I had responded that I would of course do anything within my power, and began at that stage by asking Messrs. Sobolev, Stoneman, and Feller separately to work out suggestions for a settlement. On October 10 Mr. Sobolev presented me with a memorandum entitled, "The Possible Basis for Settlement of Berlin Issue." Mr. Feller and I discussed it with Benjamin V. Cohen, the former counselor of the State Department who then formed with

Dr. Jessup as brilliant a pair of General Assembly delegates as could be found. After the conversation, Mr. Feller drew up his suggestions, and we considered these and others while Dr. Bramuglia and the six "neutrals" were at work on an acceptable formula. After the Soviet veto of their effort Dr. Jessup again came to see me. The following account substantially reproduces the memoranda I made of this conversation and others in the following weeks of intensive efforts to break the Berlin blockade.

Professor Jessup came to my office, and we exchanged the usual amenities with unusual warmth. We had known each other from the war years, when he had taken a strong position in favor of the Norwegian Government, against the contention by some quarters that our existence in exile was not "legal." He is an extraordinarily likable person, with a sweetness of character not always found in men of his exceptional intelligence. When he was attacked later in the Senate of the United States as a Soviet dupe I marveled at the length to which malignant prejudice (or political self-seeking) could go. (Or is it the anti-intellectualism sometimes evident in American political life that leads to intolerance of such high ability in public office?)

We both were dejected by the fact that a solution in the Security Council had not been possible. "Is it a fact," I asked directly, "that the United States wants a settlement?" "Yes," Dr. Jessup promptly replied, and I did not doubt him. (The question had not been a rhetorical one, for the success of the airlift and the consequent supposed mortification of the Russians had given rise to the theory that Washington would just as soon wait the blockade out, exploiting Soviet discomfiture and the effects of the West's counterblockade against the Soviet zone.) I then suggested to Dr. Jessup that the way out of the Berlin impasse might lie in the independent formulation of a proposal for four-power control and use of Soviet zone currency in Berlin. I could employ Mr. Sobolev in dealing with the Russians and Mr. Feller in dealing with the Americans. Working quietly with Soviet and American experts, they could secure the requisite data and work out a short draft for a "statement" or communiqué to be issued by the four powers. Or, if it seemed desirable, they might try to draft a more detailed technical proposal on the currency question, which would leave less to the later and subsidiary negotiations of the commandants in Berlin. If I could submit such proposals to the powers involved, then possibly the lifting of the blockade and the issuance of Soviet zone currency throughout the four sectors of Berlin could take place simultaneously. At the moment, I recalled, the Americans refused to negotiate on the currency question before the blockade was lifted, and the Russians would not lift the blockade until an agreement was reached on the use of Soviet zone currency. The scheme suggested was highly uncertain, but I felt that even this possibility should be examined.

Dr. Jessup listened sympathetically. No possible means of reaching an agreement should go untested, he said; but he had no authority to commit the United States to any undertakings. "And," he added, "I am honestly afraid that the Russians do not want a settlement." I remarked that I had made plans to talk with Mr. Vyshinsky. "Decide in your own mind," Dr. Jessup advised, "if the Russians really want an agreement. I doubt it very much."

Without being optimistic about my chances to mediate, I thought that, even if these efforts should fail, the very fact that efforts were being made might at least influence the main parties concerned and help them find the most conciliatory approach possible.

That day and the day following, October 27, I had a series of talks with Messrs. Sobolev and Feller in the Palais de Chaillot. Mr. Feller had been in touch with authoritative American sources. Mr. Sobolev also had had contact with some person or persons in the Soviet camp, but with whom he did not say. Mr. Feller ejaculated, with his usual pungency, that there had rarely been so small a difficulty in so major an international dispute as now existed over the currency of Berlin: "To think that a difference of opinion over financial technicalities could be the ostensible occasion for bringing all the misfortunes of a new World War upon the world!" And he recalled the story of Jenkins' ear—that sliced-off ear which had threatened in 1738 to involve England and Spain in war. Not that the dispute in Berlin was really about the currency. But, given the fact that the Soviet attempt to force the Western powers out of Berlin had apparently failed, it was not inconceivable that Moscow would be willing to lift the blockade in return for some face-saving concessions. If the West would make them—this too was conjectural—then removal of the small differences over financial technicalities might lead to a Berlin settlement.

As usual, Mr. Sobolev was extremely reserved throughout our talks. He was very doubtful that anything would emerge from our consultations and proposals. At first, in fact, he said he thought the place for negotiations on the currency question was not Paris but Berlin. When Mr. Feller and I smiled and replied that Mr. Vyshinsky obviously could get as many experts from Berlin as he liked without it becoming public knowledge, Sobolev apparently gave up that argument.

At this point let me quote the memorandum which Feller submitted to me on October 27, because it lucidly sums up the Berlin situation as it was at that moment, and sheds light on his trend of thought and mine:

Despite the present stalemate which exists in the Berlin question, I feel that there is some reason to retain optimism on the possibility of a settlement. In certain respects the Security Council proceedings represented an improvement. On the one hand, the United States demonstrated that it was willing to accept action by the Security Council which did not amount to a condemnation of the U.S.S.R. On the other hand, the U.S.S.R. indicated, at least by implication, that it was willing to accept some resolution of the Security Council despite its previous stand with regard to Article 107.* Moreover it would appear that the Soviet Government has abandoned any previous position which it might have had with respect to limitation with regard to the lifting of restrictions, or with respect to new restrictions on the air lift.

The existing impasse may be summed up as follows: The only formula to which the Soviet Government will agree is a simultaneous lifting of the restrictions and the introduction of the Soviet Mark. The United States, on the other hand, does not believe that it is possible to introduce the Soviet Mark, without further clarification of the conditions relating to its

---

* Article 107 of the United Nations Charter provides: "Nothing in the present Charter shall invalidate or preclude action, in relation to any state which during the Second World War has been an enemy of any signatory to the present Charter, taken or authorized as a result of that war by the Governments having responsibility for such action." Relying on this article when the Western powers sought to have the Berlin case placed on the Security Council's agenda, the Soviet Union asserted that the Council was not competent to consider it, and threatened to refuse to participate in its consideration if it were put on the agenda; but Moscow did not "walk out" when it was. Alleging that the very consideration of the question was illegal, the U.S.S.R. none the less took the precaution of vetoing the adoption of the resolution which the six "neutral" members of the Council submitted on October 25.

introduction and circulation. Such clarification involves a meeting of the four Powers. The United States will not agree to participate in such a meeting so long as the blockade is retained since, it claims, this would be negotiation under duress. From the substantive standpoint, the sole point which remains at issue is a difference over the control of the currency in Berlin. The August 30 Directive * contains certain provisions relating to the currency change-over; provides for the regulation of currency circulation by the Bank of Emission of the Soviet Zone; also provides for a quadripartite Financial Commission to control the practical implementation of the financial arrangements involved in the introduction and continued circulation of a single currency in Berlin. Following the August 30 Directive, there took place the conversations in Berlin. The Anglo-American view of these conversations is that Marshal Sokolovsky refused to admit that the Financial Commission was to have any control whatsoever over the operations of the Bank of Emission. On the other hand, the Soviet Aide-Mémoire of September 18 indicates that the U.S.S.R. does agree to control over those operations of the Bank of Emission in Berlin which are specifically provided for in the enumerated paragraphs of the Directive. The American technicians have not indicated to me precisely what operations of the Bank of Emission with regard to the currency in Berlin would need to be controlled beyond those specifically provided for, except that they have pointed out the necessity of continuing control on such matters as provision of banking and credit facilities, and the provision of sufficient currency for budgetary purposes.

On the surface, therefore, the area of disagreement over the currency issue would appear to be quite small, and it is, to me, rather startling that the peace of the world should be placed in such danger over so small and technical a disagreement. I feel that some way must be sought to solve this relatively small problem. On the other hand, there is much to be said for the American position that it would not be technically possible to introduce the Soviet currency into Berlin without some further clarification of the technical problems involved.

Under these circumstances, I should like to suggest to you the following plan. The Governments concerned should be asked by an intermediary whether they would be willing to accept a proposal for the simultaneous lifting of the restrictions and the introduction of the Soviet Mark on the basis

    a) of the August 30 Directive, supplemented by

* The August 30 directive mentioned is the one which the three envoys of the Western powers and Generalissimo Stalin agreed should be dispatched to their respective commandants in Berlin.

b) a statement of the conditions under which the Soviet Mark would be introduced into Berlin.

The practical implementation of this plan would be as follows. You, as Secretary-General, would undertake to draw up the statement on the conditions regarding the introduction of the currency. This statement would be presented to each of the four powers individually. If the four powers accepted this statement by letter to you, a revision of the six power resolution would be introduced into the Security Council, the revision to consist of substituting for the meeting of the Military Governors a provision for the immediate introduction of the Soviet Mark as stipulated in the August 30 Directive and in the supplementary statement described above.

It is obvious that the entire plan would depend on your ability to draft a statement of the conditions regarding the introduction of the currency which would be satisfactory to the parties concerned. While this would be difficult, I believe that it would be worth a try, and may lead to success. I do not think that you should undertake to draft such a statement, however, until each of the parties has agreed that it would be proper for you to proceed with this effort.

If you think well of the foregoing, I would be prepared at short notice, to draft an appropriate Aide-Mémoire to each of the four Governments.

Mr. Sobolev arranged a talk with Mr. Vyshinsky for me the evening of Thursday October 28. I met the Deputy Minister for Foreign Affairs in the Russian Embassy, at seven o'clock. Mr. Pavlov, Moscow's premier interpreter, was present.

After conversations with the United States Delegation, I said, I was persuaded that the United States wished to reach agreement on Berlin. I further ventured the belief, after hearing Mr. Vyshinsky in the Security Council debate, that the Russians too wished a settlement. At this point, Mr. Vyshinsky interposed a "Yes." It was my duty as Secretary-General, I went on, to do my utmost to preserve the peace. If therefore I could be of assistance in some manner, I should be grateful for his advice. Mr. Vyshinsky restricted himself to responding quickly: "Obviously you have the right and duty to do what you can to preserve the peace."

I then set forth my idea of having Mr. Sobolev work with the Russians, and Mr. Feller with the Americans, toward formulating a mutually acceptable currency plan. Because of the technical character of the currency difficulties, we should need expert advice from both sides. Should it prove possible for Messrs. Sobolev and Feller and me to work out a short communiqué—or, if the parties preferred, a detailed technical proposal which appeared acceptable—it could be presented to the four powers in such a fashion that it would not be known that the Secretary-General and his aides had prepared it.

Mr. Vyshinsky digested this, and began to speak. He did not believe, he said, that the Americans and the British wanted a settlement—witness the press interview with Generalissimo Stalin, who said that they did not—and he lacked authority to comment upon my plan. Furthermore, he had no economic experts, though he conceded as an afterthought that he could procure them. No, he said, the idea of employing Messrs. Sobolev and Feller was unpromising because Washington and London did not want a solution. Nor, he added, did he like the idea that Mr. Sobolev, a Soviet citizen, should negotiate on my behalf with Soviet experts: it would place Sobolev in a difficult position, and people might find such use of a Russian member of the United Nations Secretariat incorrect. I replied that Mr. Sobolev, after all, was chief of the Department of Security Council Affairs, which had the prime responsibility in the Secretariat for handling a political dispute like that of Berlin. That he was a Russian was, to my mind, an advantage. Mr. Feller had a similar understanding of the point of view of the United States Delegation, with which he was likewise well acquainted; moreover, he had legal training and skill in drafting which were essential to this sort of negotiation. Furthermore, I declared, he and Mr. Sobolev were among the most intelligent people in the entire Secretariat. After this rebuttal, Mr. Vyshinsky made no further reference to my intention to employ their talents; but he reiterated the conviction that, as Generalissimo Stalin had said, the Americans and the British really did not want an understanding.

I took this calmly and remarked, in a tone of bringing the conversation to a close, that I hoped he would think over my suggestions. Mr. Vyshinsky murmured something courteous and left the room for a moment to give an order. Mr. Pavlov and I began to talk, and I declared that the international situation seemed such to me that the prospects for war or peace appeared to be even. He translated this for Mr. Vyshinsky on his return.

Although Mr. Vyshinsky was the polite and amiable diplomat

throughout the conversation contact between us was lacking. He clearly was not prepared to negotiate seriously; but whether this represented the fixed position of the U.S.S.R. or was due simply to a lack of instructions I could not be sure. In leaving I turned to say that the door of the Secretary-General would always be open to those who wanted to avoid war.

Messrs. Sobolev and Feller met with me the next day, and the day after that, for sober discussion of the next move. I asked them to push ahead with their studies of the currency problem, despite the discouraging outlook. Soon after Mr. Sobolev left me on Saturday morning October 30 he returned to say that Mr. Vyshinsky had telephoned to ask if we might meet; he was prepared to come to my office: would I not set the time and place for the meeting? I thought it best to meet at the Russian Embassy, and we came together late in the afternoon.

Seeing Mr. Vyshinsky, I knew immediately that things were looking up. He was smiling and bland. He said he had thought over my suggestion and was deeply interested in my plans for an eventual solution. What, precisely, did I have in mind? And what made me think the Americans also wanted a settlement? Before I could reply, he inquired what knowledge I had of Dr. Bramuglia's negotiations, and then went on to present his version of them. The thrust of his exposition was that the Soviet Union actually had wanted an accord, but had been provoked by the American and British attitudes into employing the veto.

I told as much as I could properly tell of the talks with Philip Jessup and Dean Rusk, and then declared that I had been thinking about two alternative solutions. Both would lead to a simultaneous lifting of the blockade and introduction of the Soviet mark into the Western sectors of Berlin. The first alternative was to isolate the essence of the Moscow directive of August 30, and apply it—that is, to lift the blockade and simultaneously introduce the Soviet mark, while leaving the arrangement of the details of four-power control of the Soviet mark in Berlin to subsequent consideration. A second approach would be to work out all these details in advance through the good offices of the Secretary-General.

"Both possibilities," Mr. Vyshinsky said, "are interesting; but the first would be easier to manage here in Paris. I am not sure that a technical accord can be arrived at without exhaustive negotiations in Berlin."

I recalled that Mr. Sobolev would need to consult with Soviet financial experts. To this, Mr. Vyshinsky replied: "I shall be your expert. Come to me, or send Sobolev, and I will give you my view and whatever information I can."

I expressed my satisfaction with our conversation, and said that I understood that, while Mr. Vyshinsky had not bound his government in any way, while he had not said yes or no, he had authorized Mr. Sobolev and me to proceed. "That," he agreed, "is an entirely correct understanding."

The change in the substance and manner of his attitude was so open that I concluded he had consulted with Moscow and received instructions to welcome my initiative. Later that evening, I called Messrs. Feller, Stoneman, and Sobolev. We had now, I said, to concentrate on the task which lay in our hands. Mr. Sobolev seemed very happy with these new developments, and Mr. Feller, sitting up, exclaimed that this was "nearly an historic moment." At the same time, I informed the United States Delegation that I wished to see Dr. Jessup as soon as he came back from his brief trip to Germany.

Professor Jessup came up to my apartment at 5 Square Lamartine on Tuesday November 2. He gave me his impressions of the German scene. The airlift was operating successfully; the transports were arriving "like pearls on a string." Berlin could be supplied, no matter how harsh the weather. As for the complications of the currency question, about which he had consulted with General Lucius Clay's experts, they were intricate indeed.

I told Dr. Jessup about my conversation with Vyshinsky, and he seemed to be pleased, though not so pleased, it seemed to me, as he might have been had I been able to give him such news before the trip to Germany. Perhaps the lack of anxiety for an immediate solution which characterized American circles in Germany, as reported by Messrs. Feller and Stoneman, whom I had dispatched earlier to Berlin, also had affected him. They had seen General Clay, Robert D. Murphy, and other key figures, and had brought back a valuable report indicating that the Americans in Berlin were not disinclined to carry the "show" through to a successful ending. It would be hard, Ambassador Jessup cautioned, to carry out my plan without publicity; and French and British experts should also take part in the work. I asked him to keep things secret for the time. If agreement could be reached, then I should have no objections to its becoming known. I summed up our talk as I had with Mr. Vyshinsky: he had not said either yes or no, or bound Washington in any way, but he would give Mr. Feller every assistance. "I want to emphasize the fact," I said, "that no negotiations are going on between the parties." As Secretary-General, I had asked my aides to study the problem of a Berlin settlement and to bring me their conclusions. "We are now engaged in fact-finding, Phil," I concluded. Professor Jessup agreed.

We met again that evening at a dinner which Ambassador and Mrs. Austin gave at the Crillon. Dr. Jessup seemed to be a trifle reserved. He had, he said, spoken with Secretary of State Marshall; the French and the British must be kept informed. If the Americans insisted, I replied, I personally would inform them. But it would perhaps diminish the chances of keeping my initiative secret, and publicity at this stage could only do damage.

The next day I spoke with Alexandre Parodi, and then with Sir Alexander Cadogan. As I had expected, Mr. Parodi expressed full agreement with my initiative: he would inform Foreign Minister Schuman at once, but was confident that he could assure me of the French Government's warm support. As I had feared, Sir Alexander reflected the Foreign Office's traditional coolness toward any independent United Nations initiative. My activity, he pointed out, could be said to constitute negotiation between Moscow and the West, and the United States and Britain had agreed that they would not engage in negotiations as long as the blockade of Berlin continued.

I responded that it was precisely direct negotiations which my mediation would avoid. I was reluctant to believe that Great Britain would refuse to submit information to the Secretary-General which would enable him to form an opinion about a dispute which Britain had joined in bringing before the United Nations. Sir Alexander said that he would not give me an answer, but would telegraph the Foreign Office for instructions.

That evening I spoke with Messrs. Feller and Sobolev and asked them to put down something on paper quickly.

While I was in the chamber of the General Assembly's First Committee in the Palais de Chaillot on Friday November 5, following its discussion of my refusal to permit the showing of the Yugoslav propaganda film "Greek Children in Yugoslavia" at the Palais, Sir Alexander came up and asked to speak to me. He took me aside and read out a long cable from the Foreign Office. Bevin's answer was "No." My first approach to a solution was inadequate, because the Russians could reimpose the blockade whenever they chose. (It was never explained to me how any other solution for lifting the blockade could effectively preclude this.) My second suggestion—which hinged upon a detailed agreement on the conditions under which the Soviet mark would be circulated throughout Berlin—could not be carried through without the advice of the four-power experts in Berlin, and to draw them into my efforts would amount to negotiations between the parties, to which Britain and the United States could not agree before the blockade was lifted. Furthermore, Bevin went on, any negotiations should be carried on by Dr. Bramuglia and the "neutrals," rather than by the Secretary-General.

"Thus Bevin's answer," I restated to Sir Alexander, "is tantamount to a refusal of my request that British advice be placed at my disposal." "Yes, definitely," Sir Alexander replied. But he added that he would appreciate my keeping the British position to myself during the next forty-eight hours. Feeling that perhaps the full ramifications of my initiative had not been understood, he would himself fly to London to take up the matter with Bevin again. His obvious desire to help pleased me greatly.

Saturday, Dr. Herbert V. Evatt of Australia, President of the General Assembly, came to see me, considerably aroused. He had received word of my Berlin talks via Canberra (apparently the Foreign Office had cabled to the Commonwealth what I told Cadogan in confidence), and reproached me now for not keeping him informed. Dr. Evatt definitely likes plain speech, and I therefore replied without hesitation that the Secretary-General had a right to do what he had done without telling anyone about it. As for the proprieties, the Berlin question was on the agenda of the Security Council, not of the Assembly, and so was not officially within the compass of Dr. Evatt's responsibilities.

On Monday November 8, the doughty Evatt—who is as vigorous a friend as the United Nations has—was in good spirits again. I gave him a complete review of my talks and of the progress of Messrs. Feller and Sobolev. He brightened more and more, and then ventured that my initiative might well be linked with a larger plan. On November 3 the General Assembly had unanimously adopted, on the motion of Dr. Luis Padilla Nervo of Mexico and with considerable backing from a number of small nations, an "Appeal to the Great Powers to Renew Efforts to Compose Differences and Establish Lasting Peace." Dr. Evatt suggested that I or he, or both of us, might bring this resolution directly to the attention of the chiefs of government of the great powers with the request that they personally meet in an attempt to settle the Berlin crisis and advance the drawing up of treaties of peace with the former Axis states. He hoped that Messrs. Truman, Stalin, Attlee, and Queuille (the French Premier) would accept such an appeal, and he did not see how Mr. Bevin could oppose it. I listened sympathetically, and asked him to put his ideas down on paper.

Sir Alexander Cadogan sought me out the following day to report that Mr. Bevin was unmoved. Any attempt to settle the Berlin question would have to be made by the "neutral" members of the Security Council. Dr. Jessup and Mr. Parodi were present when he told me this, and I told them of Dr. Evatt's thoughts. When I also mentioned that Dr. Evatt had been informed of my discussions in a cable from the Foreign Office, Sir Alexander looked deeply embarrassed. He apologized earnestly for the Foreign Office's having informed the Commonwealth, in violation of my request that the matter be treated confidentially and between the four great powers alone. Of course it was not Sir Alexander that was at fault. But, as I feared, the "leakage" went further. The same day, press reports began to recount more or less factually what I had been trying to do.

On November 10 I had a talk with Dr. Bramuglia. I gave him an account of all that had occurred. He seemed to appreciate my activity and asked that I continue my currency studies, for the results could assist him in his mediatory efforts, which gave signs of reviving. By invitation, he had gone to London to see Mr. Bevin, and the Foreign Secretary had asked that the "neutrals" carry on. Contending that it was the British that had torpedoed his endeavors the first time (this corresponded with what Mr. Vyshinsky had told me), Dr. Bramuglia thought perhaps things would go better now.

Dr. Jessup and I had met earlier and agreed that I should join efforts with Dr. Bramuglia. The United States, he said, had to take account of the British position; "the door is not closed, but it is not as wide open as it was before." He inclined to the second of my approaches, that which envisaged a detailed agreement on currency circulation in Berlin, and asked that Feller come to see him so that they could continue their consultations.

Dr. Bramuglia and I had a number of meetings in the days that followed. The other five "neutrals" and the Western powers agreed that he should take up his attempt anew, employing the currency studies my aides had advanced. Accordingly I placed the materials they had prepared at his disposal; and he found a questionnaire they planned to send to the four powers on currency matters especially helpful. There was unquestionably a need at this stage for a juncture of my expiring efforts with Dr. Bramuglia's reviving ones. There was the danger of "too many cooks"—to which Bevin, to do him justice, perhaps had been understandably sensitive—and this danger grew with Herbert Evatt's entrance onto the scene. The close collaboration that Dr. Bramuglia and I in fact enjoyed was pictured in the press as something else, tending toward rivalry. We both laughed at that. He did a good job in trying to mediate the Berlin dispute. He may have had a weakness for publicity, however, not unlike some other figures on the United Nations scene. If so, it served him ill, for Perón could not tolerate fame for another Argentinian and dismissed him from office soon after his return home.

I showed Dr. Bramuglia the draft of the letter to the chiefs of state of France, Britain, the United States, and the U.S.S.R. that Dr. Evatt and I were working over and inquired if he would like to join in signing it, as President of the Security Council, or would prefer that we sign it without him, giving our express support to his efforts to mediate the Berlin dispute. He felt the second procedure was the better and strongly advised that I join Dr. Evatt in signing the letter.

Dr. Evatt and I dispatched our letter on November 13. It recalled the Mexican-sponsored appeal to the great powers by the General Assembly, and noted that their representatives had spoken in unqualified support of the Mexican resolution and had voted for it:

They have accepted the recommendation, and the world rightly expects them to take active steps toward carrying it out without delay.

We believe that the first step is to resolve the Berlin question. . . . We believe the history of the Security Council's consideration of this case demonstrates that it can be solved. Every day that the deadlock over Berlin continues, the danger to the peace and security of all nations continues undiminished. . . . We therefore . . . urge the desirability of immediate conversations and of taking all other necessary steps toward the solution of the Berlin question, thus opening the way to a prompt resumption of negotiations for the conclusion of the remaining peace settlements for Germany, Austria and Japan.

We also believe that the Great Powers should lend their full and active support to the efforts at the mediation of the Berlin dispute by the President of the Security Council. For ourselves we stand ready to lend all further assistance, such as the currency study now being made by the Secretary-General, as may seem most helpful to the Great Powers in the solution of the problem.

Three days later Moscow answered, substantially accepting our call for "immediate conversations." About the "other necessary steps toward the solution of the Berlin question"—that is to say, the lifting of the blockade—Mr. Vyshinsky said nothing. The three Western powers responded with a restatement of their conviction that conversations could take place only after the blockade had been lifted. But they would support the efforts of the President of the Security Council to find a solution. None of the four agreed to a meeting of the heads of government. That proposal died, to be revived by Sir Winston Churchill in later years.

After receiving the four replies, Dr. Evatt and I in a joint statement renewed our appeal to all four powers to assist Dr. Bramuglia's endeavors. The most that our letter could be said to have achieved was a reaffirmation of the willingness of the parties to the Berlin dispute to accept Security Council mediation—it was a step forward that the Soviet reply lent itself to this construction. But the letter created a diplomatic furore out of proportion to its results. British and American newspapermen were highly critical, and they may be said to have been not out of tune with many of their countries' diplomats. One American correspondent close to such circles cabled home a story suggesting that Dr. Evatt and I had fallen victims to "the corridor efforts of Mr. Vyshinsky." But the aim of the letter had not been to create a furore. I did not anticipate that it would have earth-shaking results, but I did hope it would impress upon the leaders of the great powers that the world wished to have the Berlin dispute settled. The British suggested that Dr. Evatt and I should have addressed ourselves to Moscow alone; after all, there was no doubt as to who was fundamentally at fault. They were right up to a point—Evatt and I had no illusions about that. But I for one had genuine doubts in signing it that the Foreign Office and all elements in the State Department at that time cared for a compromise solution from which no party would emerge wholly victorious: the fight for prestige and "face," I felt, was always dangerous.

Dr. Bramuglia issued a public statement endorsing our letter, and came some days later to give me the text of his proposal for the establishment of a committee of six experts from the "neutral" members of the Security Council with a seventh to represent the Secretary-General. He reported that all parties concerned, including Moscow, were agreeable to this fresh effort to work out a detailed formula for the circulation and four-power control of the Soviet mark in Berlin. I of course promised to appoint a representative to the committee, and chose Gunnar Myrdal, the Swedish Executive Secretary of the United Nations Economic Commission for Europe in Geneva. Dr. N. Kaldor, of the Commission staff, ably acted as secretary to the committee. As is often the case, especially in technical questions, the secretary did much of the work. Salvador de Madariaga, the Spanish historian and diplomat who was a leading figure of the League of Nations Secretariat, has a story of the place of secretaries in such committees that is still germane. Two League habitués were discussing the matter in the old days at Geneva. "A League committee," one said, "to all intents and purposes consists simply of a president and a secretary." "Do you think," the other responded, "that the President is necessary?" There is more than a little truth in this story.

The committee of experts labored throughout the winter, and, by February, aside from having helped keep the great powers talking rather than shooting over Berlin, they had produced a highly constructive report. But this time Washington balked. The situation in Berlin had so deteriorated, the State Department felt, that an agreement on currency control was not enough; and, even on this restricted issue, differences on technical points remained.

However, I felt that the outlook was not hopeless. The Western democracies had carried on the airlift successfully throughout the winter; they had proved their point. Moscow must have concluded that they could not be forced out of Berlin, or forced to concede economic domination of Berlin in return for a lifting of the blockade; and perhaps it was becoming alive to other results of its aggressive policy, which was being answered by the great increase of air power in Western Europe which followed upon the Berlin blockade. Some time after our return to Lake Success, I accordingly mentioned to Yakov A. Malik, the Soviet Deputy Minister of Foreign Affairs and Permanent Delegate to the United Nations, that he might talk to Professor Jessup if the Soviet Union wanted a settlement.

Some three or four weeks later, word came to me that Professor Jessup had approached Mr. Malik. Generalissimo Stalin had declared, in answer to a news agency's questions at the end of January, that the Berlin dispute could be settled. His statement said not a word about the ostensible cause of the blockade: the tangle over Berlin currency.

The omission was noticed in Washington, and it prompted Professor Jessup to take his famous initiative. It is the custom of the delegates to the Security Council to gather in the delegates' lounge some minutes before the Council is called to order, conferring with their aides, chatting with their colleagues, and sometimes patronizing the bar. It was at this time—one of those moments of casual opportunity for fruitful diplomatic intercourse which the permanent diplomatic conference of the United Nations continually provides—that Professor Jessup spoke to Mr. Malik. He inquired—not, as the legend has it, over a glass of orange juice—if in fact Stalin's omission was purposeful. Had it any particular significance?

Mr. Malik said he would find out—apparently, if the omission had been a trial balloon, he had not been informed. He consulted with the Soviet Foreign Office, and a month later, on March 15, he informed Professor Jessup that Stalin's failure to mention the issue of Berlin's currency was "not accidental." Malik and Jessup conferred at shorter intervals thereafter, not casually in the delegates' lounge but intensively in the Soviet Delegation's Park Avenue headquarters. One of their less formal meetings in those weeks took place one evening in my Forest Hills home.

It emerged from their conversations that Moscow had decided to beat a retreat. The issue of Berlin currency control, toward resolving which so much time and energy had been directed, was deferred. Moscow, which had raised it, chose for the moment to drop it. Its artificiality was thus revealed: the issue had been a technicality at the beginning and was a technicality at the end, ultimately becoming one of a number of items on a post-blockade conference agenda.

Finally, on May 4, 1949, the representatives of France, the United Kingdom, and the United States asked me to bring to the attention of the Security Council the fact that their governments had reached agreement with the government of the U.S.S.R. on Berlin. The blockade would be lifted on May 12, as would the West's retaliatory restrictions, and the Deputies of the Council of Foreign Ministers would meet soon after at the Palais Rose in Paris to consider German problems, among them, that of currency in Berlin.

Why did Moscow retreat? No doubt largely because of the propaganda and prestige effects of the triumphant airlift—perhaps also the pressure of the counterblockade. There may have been other reasons, including the force of world public opinion brought to bear by the United Nations' consideration of the crisis.

Whatever the reasons, the role of the United Nations was not discreditable. The United Nations applied nearly all the devices at its disposal to a problem the solution of which, in any event, rested essentially with the party which had created it: the Kremlin. The Security Council, the General Assembly, the Secretariat; mediation, fact-finding, expertise; public airing and private negotiation—all these weapons of modern diplomatic method were enlisted. The electric tension that the Berlin blockade generated between two non-negotiating worlds was very great. Had there been no United Nations, it might have been so great that the electricity would have shot across the gap, setting both sides afire.

CHAPTER XIII

WHERE EAST MEETS WEST— MOSCOW, 1946—PRAGUE, 1948

Uncertainty confronts the border lands.—Soviet persuasion tactics at close hand.—My first conversation with Joseph Stalin.—Czechoslovakian tragedy, the last bridge burned.— Aftermath in Prague.

THE CLOSE military alliance and seeming political cordiality between the great powers were the foundation for our hopes during the dark war years; but I was never free of a certain uneasiness regarding their future relationship. Sometimes it appeared to me that the spokesmen of the great powers approached the problems too much on a "wholesale" basis, forgetting that the world is, after all, like a mosaic, where each piece counts in the whole. Perhaps this apprehension was more natural to a man from a small country than to the leaders of the great alliance, preoccupied as they were with the work for victory in a global war. In particular, there were the smaller states situated along the borders of the respective spheres of military responsibility and emerging zones of political interest. Even my own country was to some extent exposed in this regard. In a pessimistic mood I had often warned my friends that the course of postwar relations in the world would be forecast by the fate of the border lands.

As early as 1943 it became apparent that events were pushing the states of Europe into a tentative regrouping, and that the pressures might well become stronger once hostilities ceased; but it was not until 1945, the year of victory, that the first clear indications of the new patterns began to emerge.

Tremendous forces from two opposing poles met along a line from the Baltic in the north to Greece in the south. The states along this line had to choose among several political alternatives. Finland again had found its natural place in its common inheritance with the Scandinavian countries. Poland suffered from internal weaknesses and was torn between rival forces as so many times before. Germany, in chaos after its third unleashing of war upon neighboring states within three-quarters of a century, was a political vacuum under military occupation. Czechoslovakia, a model democracy from its rebirth under Thomas Masaryk and later the victim of Nazi aggression, was striving frantically to reestablish itself as a free country friendly to all. Austria, another Nazi victim, also was occupied. Yugoslavia had been liberated largely by its own heroic efforts, despite internal strife. Bulgaria, Hungary, and Rumania had never reached political stability under any regime. Finally, Greece was in a state of civil war, and Turkey had escaped unscathed from World War II.

The Yalta agreement had been partly concerned with the fate of this strip of border states. Here East and West had agreed in principle. The Soviet Union had concurred—had, in fact, promised—that each of the countries involved, through many of which the Red Army was then marching to Berlin, should have the right to choose its own form of government through free secret elections. The West in turn had recognized the validity of the Soviet desire that the states so constituted be on friendly terms with their powerful neighbor.

With these considerations in mind Western negotiators had returned from Yalta, glad for the Russian promise of free elections but doubtful about eventual Soviet formulas for insuring "friendly" governments. Their apprehensions proved to be only too well founded. The aftermath was to have most serious implications for world peace, and for the formative development of the United Nations.

During my term as Secretary-General four events—as far as this new organization for the preservation of world peace was concerned —were determinative in the political development, or retrogression, of postwar Europe. The first was the decision of the United States to aid Greece and Turkey—the Truman Doctrine—in which the United Nations, with the succession of commissions on the Balkans was intimately involved. The other three took place in the strip of border lands during the first seven months of 1948. There were the Communist coup in Czechoslovakia in February, Marshal Tito's break with the Cominform in June, and the Berlin Blockade, which came into full force in July.

The role of the United Nations in developments on the Berlin sector has been told in Chapter XII. Here, I shall describe some of my experiences in Czechoslovakia, as well as my first postwar visit to Moscow, one of the poles responsible for these momentous clashes in the border area. My experiences in Moscow in July of 1946, and my talk with Generalissimo Stalin, were in no small measure an attempt to establish in my own mind how much justification there was for the conclusions of Winston Churchill's Fulton, Missouri, speech. Similarly, my visit to Prague in January of 1948 was in part an attempt to evaluate at first hand the one bridge still linking East and West. Finally, my visits to Yugoslavia and Greece in 1951 were respectively to offer support and encouragement to a brave people that had defied its geographical liability and taken its fate into its own hands and to acquaint myself with a country which had managed to hold to its side of the line only through the prompt action of the West.

In each instance, millions of hard-working and innocent people had been, or were to become, the victims of forces beyond their control. It was my duty to acquaint myself with the leaders who controlled these forces. Western leaders and their line of reasoning were familiar—after all, my years in politics had been spent among them. On the other hand, my dealings with leaders of the East had been but fragmentary, and I felt myself at something of a disadvantage. It was therefore with some foreboding that I prepared for my first meeting with Generalissimo Joseph Stalin.

I had been Secretary-General only a few days when, at a London dinner party in February, 1946, Mr. Vyshinsky brought up the idea of a visit to Moscow almost casually. Members of the Russian Government would like to meet the new Secretary-General, he remarked, adding that "a personal visit might also be useful to you, as a means of getting in closer touch with Russian statesmen, as well as becoming better acquainted with conditions in the Soviet Union." At that time my immediate duties were too pressing, and I could only thank him; but when Mr. Gromyko touched on the same question a few months later in New York my schedule offered an opportunity. This was shortly before my departure for Norway, where I intended to celebrate my fiftieth birthday with friends and family. After that I planned to pay short visits to United Nations offices at Geneva, Paris, and The Hague; and a brief detour to Moscow could certainly be fitted in.

Therefore when a telephone call from the Soviet Ambassador at Oslo in the middle of July informed me that a special Russian plane would bring my family and me to Moscow on July 20, there was no little excitement in the Lie household. The Russian plane, a DC-3 with a five-man crew, arrived duly at Oslo's Fornebu Airport on the afternoon of the 19th—and quite an arrival it was. Defying all risks to life and limb, the Russian pilot landed at right angles to the regular runway. While it was a superb feat of piloting, which charmed the Norwegian ground personnel immensely, I could only hope that it was not a normal Russian landing.

We took off the following morning: Mrs. Lie, Guri and Mette, Mr. and Mrs. William H. Stoneman, Mr. Kristen Klaveness (my former secretary) and I. Our plane, it turned out, was quite new and our crew was excellent, though, I must confess that Russian landings and take-offs were obviously inhibited by few formalities. Gradual circling to gain or lose altitude was apparently considered as a waste of time. Our party was also struck by the treetop altitude which the pilot persisted in holding all the way down the Oslo Fjord, over the fortress of Oscarsborg and in over the Swedish border. It being a clear day, I had the feeling that the crew might be trying some aerial photography; and the suspicion was strengthened as we approached Bromma Airdrome near Stockholm. Not far from the field, our pilot chose to take a long and—in my opinion—unnecessary swing out over the fortifications along the Stockholm skerries. What this interesting procedure actually meant, however, I was never to know.

The hour in Stockholm was the only stop that day. We continued across the Baltic and landed at Moscow that evening. Whether or not the route over Russian territory had been chosen with an eye to impressing the new Secretary-General, it is difficult to say. I know, however, that the chaos of charred and twisted villages and cities seen that day remains in my mind the most complete exhibit of destruction I have ever witnessed.

At the airport a delegation from the Foreign Ministry headed by Vice Foreign Minister Vyshinsky with the Chief of Protocol in full uniform met us and escorted us to the old Hotel National. The hotel had changed little since my last visit to Moscow in 1944: massive plush furnishings—a bit more shabby than I remembered them—and heavy draperies and bric-a-brac. Obviously, the crying need for rebuilding a war-ravaged country had left the old Hotel National with a low priority indeed; but the food, drink, and service were good. As guests of the government we received the best of care; there were the usual excellent seats at the theater and ballet, and every evening was planned with obvious care and foresight. A limousine and chauffeur was at our disposal, making it possible to visit a number of museums and exhibits.

Mr. and Mrs. Molotov held a luncheon in our honor, on which occasion I managed at the outset to stiffen Molotov's smile of accord into a frigid line of disapproval. It happened during a little, spur-of-the-moment speech of thanks. I referred to the honor extended in this invitation to the Secretary-General to visit one of the mightiest member lands. I then described the Soviet Union as leading the world in certain respects (the Red Army and its accomplishments) and ranking second in others (wealth, economy, and industry) and third in still others (Britain's sea power and world-wide influence through the British Commonwealth of Nations). I should have stopped with first and second. Carefully following Klaveness' translation, Molotov and Vyshinsky smiled and nodded approvingly at my first observation, and even seemed willing to accept the possibility that Russia might be second in certain fields. But in intimating that the Soviet Union could rank third in any respect whatsoever, I obviously went too far. Smiles and approval disappeared in an instant, and I learned another lesson about the Soviet mind. This little intermezzo notwithstanding, the luncheon proceeded in typical Russian fashion, Molotov toasting each member of my little party, and I returning the compliments on our behalf.

That evening, I was able to make my first short-range appraisal of Soviet relations with one of its East European neighbors. It was not encouraging. We, it seemed, were not the only official guests of the Soviet Government then in the Russian capital. In fact, the first official visit of the United Nations Secretary-General was overshadowed by a series of festivities welcoming a Czechoslovakian delegation about to sign a new trade agreement between the two countries. On the evening in question, all official Moscow had turned out for a mammoth reception in its honor.

For pomp and sheer luxury it is difficult to match an official reception in Moscow. The Spiridonov Palace was not new to me, as I had been there in 1944 as Norwegian Foreign Minister; even during the war, these festivities had been no less grandiose. The attractive low-lying stone structure was filled with top-ranking Russian officials, guests, and diplomats—all carefully segregated in the Palace's three rooms according to rank. When entering, the guest must remain in the first room until led by one of the hosts into room number two. Room number three, evidently the "holy of holies," was reserved to the top-ranking figures present, and was entered only upon special invitation. As is normal with such Russian extravaganzas the choice of food defied description: caviar, roast suckling pigs, every conceivable meat and fowl; only the choice of liquid refreshments was limited—being confined to vodka and Russian cognac and wines.

In room number three I was presented to members of the Czech delegation: Premier Klement Gottwald, Vice Premier Zdenek Fierlinger, and a number of others, including my old and dear friend Foreign Minister Jan Masaryk. There was always something bright and "happy-go-lucky" about a meeting with Masaryk, and I welcomed it particularly on this occasion. We had been close friends for many years; had worked together during the war, had flown to San Francisco together and had just attended the first General Assembly in London. So I was not at all surprised when, in his typical Masaryk manner, he hunched up a shoulder, raised an eyebrow, and nodded toward a vacant corner some distance away. "Blah, blah, blah," he whispered—his familiar slang simile indicating gossip to come. "Great big secret, one hell of a big secret." Moving toward the corner, he looked over one shoulder, then the other, in a comedy on Russian caution—smiling and apparently enjoying himself immensely. "Trygve," he began, "you've heard of this big trade agreement. Well, it's not what it seems to be. Everything looks fine on paper, but I'll tell you the Russians have the whole thing fixed."

He then gave me a short account of the Czech-Russian trade talks —brilliant and bitter, employing choice American slang and epithets. Three feet away, anyone would have thought from Masaryk's smiling face that he was delivering one of his latest jokes. "The whole thing is humbug," he continued, "They control the rate of exchange: what they lose on one thing, they'll make on another, and with those prices they'll strip us clean." We stood there at least five minutes, Masaryk doing all the talking. In the end he hunched his shoulders. "But what can we do? We've got to play along with them. Gottwald looks to Molotov before he dares take a breath." He clenched both fists against his vest, thumbs up. "Molotov, 'Da,'" he mimicked, lifting the left fist, "Gottwald, 'Da, da,'" lifting the right. "Molotov, 'Niet,' Gottwald, 'Niet, niet.'" Seeming to feel that Fierlinger and many other Social Democrats had been taken in, he was disappointed with the outcome of the trade talks. "I'd like to spend an evening with you," he concluded, "but I can't risk it. We'll have to talk some other time."

On Sunday we attended a gigantic sports demonstration in Dynamo Stadium. Our limousine had no sooner drawn to a stop outside the stadium entrance than uniformed and plain-clothes policemen pressed in to peer suspiciously at our party. Kristen Klaveness, the first man out, had hardly left the car when he was taken by the arm and hustled away by a policeman. A small package he was carrying seemed to be the root of the trouble. His protests in fluent Russian and an attempted intervention by Bill Stoneman, who also speaks the language, were to no avail, and my young interpreter soon disappeared through a door surrounded by guards.

Our consternation was relieved a few minutes later when Mr. Klaveness reappeared, smiling, to explain the mystery. The police had opened his package and, upon discovering nothing more than a few oranges and apples purchased in Sweden, had remained suspicious until they had prodded and probed each one. "Since the show will probably last some hours," he had explained, "we thought it might be good to have something to eat?" Finally convinced that the bomb-sized fruit could hardly threaten the lives of the Soviet greats who would be seated near by, they had released him with a round of laughter.

I had heard of the Russian spectacles and had seen motion pictures of several earlier sports meets, but was hardly prepared for what took place that day. Hundreds of teams—tens of thousands of young men and women from every corner of that vast country—marched in, went through their performance before the Generalissimo, and then moved on in an apparently never-ending procession. Against a background of band music and thunderous applause, our attention was divided between the spectacle before us, and the Generalissimo and his entourage—Messrs. Molotov, Beria, Malenkov, Bulganin, and others—seated only a short distance from the diplomatic loge where our party had been placed.

Hardly had we taken our seats, however, when I was pleased to see Jan Masaryk approaching. With pleasure every bit as great, he hastened to join me; and we were soon deep in conversation. Our meeting was a short one. Within half an hour a Soviet Foreign Office man came to inform him that he with the other ranking members of the Czech delegation was asked to join Generalissimo Stalin. He seemed to be greatly perturbed by this and, in the confusion, left with my hat, which was at least three sizes too large for him.

Our attention soon returned to the display; but as one hour merged into the next, with the end nowhere in sight, I began to pry into the meaning of it all. The impact of numbers and newness wore off, and I had an unpleasant sense of thousands of brown, hard young bodies joined in a show that absorbed every trace of individuality—a strange and disquieting worship of conformity. Here was a hardness, an absence of gaiety and smiles, that turned the whole display into a mechanical demonstration of physical strength.

On the evening of July 23 I was driven to the Kremlin for my first conversation with Joseph Stalin. Shortly before ten o'clock a Russian limousine called at the National and took me in a few minutes to the first guard station under the Kremlin wall. We did not enter by the gate on Red Square, but by a more obscure entrance where the guard and checking system were the same as I remembered them from 1944. Little was said; the security routine seemed to be rapid and efficient. Once inside the wall, I was transferred to a special Kremlin car. After being challenged at two new guard posts, we pulled up before the building where I had met Mr. Molotov two years earlier.

Within a few minutes Generalissimo Stalin and I were shaking hands—each of us making a first split-second appraisal of the other. What I saw was a short, solidly built figure with a sunburned face. As we walked across the room to seat ourselves at the table, I noticed that his stride and movements were oddly deliberate. I have never seen a man place his feet so solidly and precisely without his gait appearing military. He was short—far shorter than either Mr. Molotov or Mr. Vyshinsky; beside me, the top of his head came no higher than my chin. His shoulders were broad and full, under a simple buttoned-to-chin stiff-collar jacket, but he was by no means overweight: he must have weighed 180 to 190 pounds. In shaking hands, I had been struck by his deep-set gray eyes—cold and unwavering except when he smiled. But the times I have seen Joseph Stalin smile can be counted on my fingers. Neither then nor later was there any doubt in my mind as to his opinion of Social Democrats in general. I could imagine him as far more pleasant and congenial when meeting with people from other parties. The curved black pipe, familiar from all his pictures, appeared to be a fixture under a gray moustache which drooped slightly at the corners of his mouth. Like all pipe smokers, he had a constant and automatic smoking routine: tamping and relighting intermittently, and every now and then knocking out and refilling his pipe from a sack of tobacco which he carried in his pocket.

The Generalissimo's introductory remarks concerned Norway and King Haakon, and I passed them on to His Majesty in a letter written from Paris a week later: "As I recall our conversation," I wrote, "the Generalissimo made a point of mentioning that 'Norway's struggle against the German Nazis made a deep impression upon me and upon the Russian people. Your King is a brave King who has won my greatest respect.'" He went on to praise the resistance of the Norwegian people during the recent war, and stated that the excellent record of the home front in Norway and that of the Norwegian Government in London were known to him. Further, he seemed to be impressed by the fact that so many Norwegian merchant vessels had taken part in the Murmansk convoys; he made a special point of mentioning the Norwegian ships that had brought arms and ammunition to Vladivostok, too. It was also clear that he was pleased by the participation of Russians in the liberation of

North Norway. He added that he had spoken with many Russian soldiers and officers who had been in Norway at that time, and they had had only the best to say of the Norwegian people and its reception of the Soviet forces.

Though generally well informed on Norway and its role in the war, the Generalissimo slipped on one point. "It is true that you in Norway build warships, armed cruisers, destroyers, and the like, is it not?" he questioned. I realized that he was confusing Norway and Sweden, and hastened to correct him. "Unfortunately, we're not able to build warships," I explained. "Though we are a seafaring nation, our warships—aside from a few small, old destroyers—are all built abroad; the same is the case with most of our merchant fleet."

I continued by referring to the terrifying expanse of destruction glimpsed on the flight from Norway: "The liberation of Stalingrad and the defense of Moscow and Leningrad are tremendous accomplishments and have won the respect of all the Allied peoples." When I went on to mention the overwhelming reconstruction problem which must have been facing Russia then, he admitted that Russia needed help for rebuilding and that the need was extreme. Several times in the conversation, he mentioned ten billion dollars as the amount of foreign aid Russia should have: "We need the money urgently, and it's no more than the Soviet Union deserves, considering its contribution to the Allied cause." I promised to keep this in mind and mention it to the appropriate American authorities. (This I did in the first talks with President Truman and Mr. Byrnes after my return to the United States.)

His statements opened the way for a few remarks which I had determined to put forth during this first meeting. I dispensed with preliminaries, and openly expressed concern over the way in which relations between the Western powers and the Soviet Union had deteriorated since the war: "This is most unfortunate, particularly in light of the obvious misunderstanding here. From what I've been able to see, men like President Truman and Secretary of State Byrnes have often shown far greater understanding of the Soviet Union and its problems than have many other Americans." This made it all the more discouraging to see each friendly advance met with distrust, and each welcoming hand refused. "I've spoken to many people," I added, "both in the United States and in other countries, who seem to doubt that the Soviet's great leader, Generalissimo Stalin, is at all well informed about what's taking place in Europe, the United States, and the world at large."

The Generalissimo interrupted the translation of the last remark with a sweeping gesture of the arms: "But I am very well informed! Here"—he turned to press a button—"let me show you the American newspapers I've read today." A guard appeared, received a short order in Russian, and departed to return again with a sheaf of newspapers at least three inches thick. All were American dailies, to which were clipped a number of tightly typewritten sheets in Russian—obviously translations. I could see some of the mastheads. The New York *Times* and *Herald Tribune* and the Chicago *Tribune* were among them. Placing his hand on this reflection of everyday America, he repeated, "And these are the American newspapers that I've read just today." There was obviously little to be gained by pursuing the subject, and this part of the conversation ended with the Generalissimo returning to the matter of aid. "I am sorry that the Soviet Union has not received the ten billion dollars we needed, and still need," he repeated. "I believe that I know the United States very well, and I have seen the United States shift its point of view before, in my lifetime. I have seen how it can change its mind overnight. The same can happen again."

There were of course a few more things I wanted to say about the United Nations and the Soviet Union. I tried to impress upon this mighty leader the importance of the United Nations and how, in my opinion, this organization could be used to promote peace and understanding among the Member states. He said little in answer. Recalling that the Soviet Union had been one of the founders of the United Nations, he remarked, "We will try to do everything we can to work along a course determined by our own and by the world's best interests." I did not feel that I should press for a more detailed discussion of the subject. At that time, the Russians were pushing for a meeting of the Big Four foreign ministers prior to the Peace Conference in Paris, and seemed to prefer a Four-Power settlement outside the Conference—or the United Nations, for that matter.

Even with the Soviet leader's reserve and my knowledge of Russia's policy line, I still could not let the opportunity pass. There was no telling when I might see him again. "You must have a great deal of personal satisfaction out of having been among the United Nations' founders," I ventured. "Think of the hope which the Charter extends to all oppressed peoples; think of the colonies, of the enslaved and all those who now, for the first time, can look forward with hope for freedom, independence, and a better life. Do you not feel, Generalissimo Stalin, that the United Nations Charter is a most reassuring document, full of promise for a world still partially in bondage?" The reply I received was short and laconic. "Yes," he remarked, "the United Nations Charter is a rather good document."

Before we parted I asked whether he could not send more Russians for the Secretariat: on the basis of the geographical distribution system there were far too few. He was quick to reply that there were few who were qualified, and that he wished to send only the best. I then said goodbye.

Flying back to Copenhagen the next day, my thoughts were in a turmoil as I tried to piece together the statements, fragments of conversation, and impressions from the eventful week. My earlier forebodings had been in no way lessened by this visit. There had been the grand show for the Czech leaders; Mr. Masaryk's whispered comment, "The whole thing's fixed. It's all humbug"; the Generalissimo's statement that Russia would "work along a course determined by our own and by the world's best interests"—whatever those were—and his laconic observation that the United Nations Charter was "a rather good document." The little I had seen and heard coupled with the events of the year, left very little doubt that the Soviet leader had his own plans for Eastern Europe—all determined by Russia's own "best interests" and obviously to be realized outside the United Nations. And the "Iron Curtain"? Whether one put it in resounding Churchillian metaphors or simply identified it as a bitter, cynical policy aimed at setting up a bastion of "friendly" satellites, the result was much the same.

In the next two years, Czechoslovakia remained the one area of hope in the chain of European border lands. Deteriorating East-West relations notwithstanding, there was still the chance as long as a democratic Czechoslovakia held its own that some sort of *modus vivendi* might emerge. I followed day-to-day developments in Czechoslovakia with great concern. Yet the end came with unexpected suddenness.

WHERE EAST MEETS WEST

I remember only too clearly that we were driving home on Washington's Birthday—February 22, 1948—from a few days' skiing in the Catskills. My friend, Tor Gjesdal, and I were deep in our perpetual condemnation of Alpine, as opposed to Norwegian, cross-country skiing when suddenly we were stopped short. A third voice had intervened. My chauffeur and faithful guardian Bill had switched on the radio just in time to catch a last-minute news bulletin from Prague. The words were like a death knell: Communists had taken over the Czechoslovakian police; armed workers had already formed into "militia" and were "safeguarding" law and order; approximately half the members of the government had resigned. In short, Czechoslovakia was in revolution. The dike had finally broken.

No more than a month before, Masaryk and I in his apartment in the Foreign Office at Prague had discussed this very possibility.

For me as for so many others, the submersion of Czechoslovakian democracy was a personal tragedy. Together with my countrymen generally, I had felt that we held a vital stake in its preservation and development. In many respects we had. There were few countries on the European mainland with which Norwegian democracy had closer ideological ties. In fact, Norway's national poet Björnstjerne Björnson had done much through his writing and influence before the First World War to mobilize world support for a future free and democratic Czechoslovakia. Therefore, almost all Norwegians had been interested in that country's development into a modern, democratic state and particularly in its postwar fate. The chief actors and victims were well known. After the Nazi defeat, the Czech coalition governments formed in 1945 and 1946 with Beneš and Masaryk and their democratic compatriots strove to stem the tide from the East. The previous summer, the Czech Government had voted unanimously to participate in the Marshall Plan Conference in Paris, only to retract in the face of Soviet displeasure. Czechoslovakia's democrats—heroic visionaries, many of them—had recognized in their geographic and economic position an obligation to hold the friendship of both East and West and thus preserve one bridge across the gap, contributing towards a model solution for common-sense East-West relations. Now, the Iron Curtain had apparently crashed down, closing this last doorway and crushing Czechoslovakia's democrats and the hopes they represented. In the months that followed, Czechoslovakia's modern democracy was buried beneath a welter of familiar Communist techniques and slogans; steadily and systematically, its defenders were weeded out and sent to the salt mines or to an even worse fate. But, what was equally important, the countries of Western Europe, shaken to their very foundations by this latest onslaught, and with all doubts removed, rallied in protest against Soviet expansion. This one political event in February, 1948, more than any other single step taken by the Communists, threw the Western world into a state of alarm. The alarm later received expression in a new agreement for mutual defense, in which Canada and the United States joined hands with Western Europe: the North Atlantic Treaty.

In the night following our drive home from the Catskills, and in many nights that followed, I brooded over my talks with President Beneš and with Foreign Minister Masaryk at Prague in the preceding month. Mr. Masaryk had tried to prepare himself for what was coming, that was clear; and he had been prepared to meet it in his own way. I recalled going over the political situation with him at Czernin Palace on January 26 and 27. He had been in good spirits and had seemed to be far more confident as to political prospects in Czechoslovakia than a few months before in New York.

The Communists, he maintained, could not win any more votes in the coming May elections than the 38 per cent they already held—probably no more than 32 to 33 per cent; but he said: "I hope the position remains about the same. If the Communists are given too much of a setback, they might risk staging a *coup d'état.*" While aware of the possibility of a coup, he obviously was not expecting it to come within a month—and before the elections. We talked over the prospects for such a move by the Communists and I asked him as an old and close friend whether it might not be best to arrange a business trip to France or England—just in case. But I should have known Jan Masaryk. He was determined to remain in Czechoslovakia, come what might, and spoke disparagingly of the Polish, Hungarian, and Rumanian non-Communists who had fled when the Communists seized power. I remember his typical comment: "I'm not the kind of guy who could be happy to go to the United States and write five articles for the *Saturday Evening Post* for $15,000.

No, sir, I'm staying put." Though he did not say whether he expected to continue as Foreign Minister, I got the impression that he was determined to stay—even though he saw the possibility of a most unpleasant time. His reference to the Polish, Hungarian, and Rumanian politicians who had fled, seemed to indicate his intention to risk the kind of treatment they had been unwilling to face—imprisonment or death.

Jan Masaryk that day gave his range of colorful invective full play when referring to Klement Gottwald, Vladimir Clementis, and other members of the Czech Communist party, and was most bitter about the way in which they had been forced to bow to the Russians. But he was equally bitter, if not more so, about what he called the United States' "defeatist" policy toward Czechoslovakia. He sought to penetrate America's reasoning, trying to understand how the State Department could demand that Czechoslovakia take a definite stand in favor of the Marshall Plan after Russia had ordered that it remain outside. "Washington and London have failed completely to understand my position," he repeated, "and they are making a serious mistake in not granting my request for funds or material assistance." He went on to point out how democratic forces in Czechoslovakia had profited from a good harvest and from UNRRA aid during the winter of 1946–1947. "Now, UNRRA aid is at an end, and the 1947 harvest has been catastrophic. With the end of UNRRA and America's insistence on refusing help except in connection with the Marshall Plan, Czechoslovakia has become completely dependent upon the 300,000 tons of grain which the Soviet Union has promised to Gottwald." He felt that London and Washington had more or less written Czechoslovakia off as early as 1946. "This policy," he emphasized, "has completely spoiled my chances for playing Gottwald on even terms." By advertising their feeling that his country had moved in behind the Iron Curtain in 1946, England and the United States had done his country a profound disservice, maintained Masaryk. "This simply indicates to the Russians and to the Czech Communists," he continued, "that the American and British Governments don't give a damn about anything the Communists might feel like doing in Czechoslovakia." He turned to me. "Trygve, as a personal friend, will you get in touch with the proper people in London and Washington and tell them how I feel about all this? Will you try and get them to put an end to their defeatism?" (I carried Jan Masaryk's appeal to both London and New York. But by then it was too late.)

President Beneš that same day lacked even the spark of desperate optimism that Jan Masaryk had shown. For the first time that I can remember, he spoke most bitterly about the Russians; and he was even more outspoken about the Czech Communists: "I don't see," he said, "how the Communist party will be able to hold its own in the May elections. They are losing ground all over the country, but we don't know what they will do when such a setback becomes apparent." I came away from the great statesman convinced that he was completely disillusioned. His air and his remarks were those of a voluntary prisoner. To this day, I regard that hour with President Beneš in Prague in January, 1948, as one of the most tragic I have ever spent. The man sat there seeing the product of a life's work and struggle slip through his fingers, helpless to salvage any of it. What was even worse, I was all but powerless to help.

Going back through my correspondence, I find a letter written to Norwegian Prime Minister Einar Gerhardsen on March 9, 1948, after my return from Czechoslovakia, and just about two weeks after the radio report announcing the Communist coup. Messrs. Masaryk and Beneš had chosen to remain—to hang on until the bitter end, in the hope that their names and prestige might still serve as a buffer between Communist totalitarianism and the Czechoslovakian people. "I have been thinking a lot," I wrote, "over certain aspects of these recent events in Czechoslovakia. Was it right of Beneš and Masaryk to continue? I have thought it through, and I can only feel that—all factors considered—they have done the right thing. By running away, they could have risked losing all real influence at once, or they could have touched off a civil war which—in light of the current situation in Europe—could have developed into something far more serious. Now, with the two of them still holding their posts, they can still exercise a certain amount of control, by refusing to participate in or by refusing to sign various decisions. . . . Critical as the situation is, I still believe that Beneš, and the others who have defended democracy in Czechoslovakia, have once more spared the world an armed revolt—if not an open war. We have only to hope that matters do not deteriorate still further—as they did last time—and that the limit has now been reached."

But the limit had not been reached. The very next day—March 10, 1948—Jan Masaryk, Foreign Minister of Czechoslovakia, was dead.

They called it suicide. He was supposed to have jumped from his bathroom window—a contention which I found difficult to accept. I had spoken for hours with Jan Masaryk only six weeks before; we had discussed in detail the very eventuality which had become a reality within a month. I am convinced that in his own mind he was prepared for what was to come—that he was ready to accept imprisonment and death in preference to flight. In my mind, Jan Masaryk was not the suicide kind.

Jan Masaryk was dead, and President Beneš was soon to die. With their removal the weeding-out process in Czechoslovakia was resumed with new vigor, extending, in time, through the Social Democrats and members of other parties to Communists who might have been tainted by their contact with democracy. Vladimir Clementis was one of these. When I last saw him at Lake Success in the winter of 1949–1950 he was worried, and I could sense the reason why. "Why don't you make arrangements to stay?" I suggested. "Why go back? I'll see what I can do to help you." Though he was obviously tempted, he refused, and told me that he would return to Prague and take his chances. One year later, in Paris, word came that he too had been arrested; his trial and execution were soon to follow.

For me, the Czechoslovakian tragedy had a bitter, personal aftermath when I visited Prague once again in 1950, penetrating an unmistakable "iron curtain" to enter a chill bleak land under complete Communist control. Gone was any semblance of a "bridge," and the last democratic defenders were either dead or in prison. I had come to speak with the Czech Minister for Foreign Affairs Viliam Siroky, hoping against hope that I could influence him to release the kidnaped Greek children held in his country.* I might just as well have stayed in New York. As a parting request I had asked Deputy Foreign Minister Mrs. Sekaninova-Cakrtova whether I might not be shown where my friends President Beneš and Jan Masaryk lay buried in order to place some flowers on their graves. "I have no idea where they are," she replied, "and neither does the Foreign Minister." For a whole day I used every means at my disposal to find

---

* See Chapter XVI, "My Peace Mission—Outward Bound," for a full account.

where they were buried. Telephone calls and visits were unavailing, and in the end Assistant Secretary-General Constantin Zinchenko, who accompanied me on that trip, revealed what I had suspected all along. "Please," he implored me, "please don't try and find their graves. It would be misunderstood both here and in Moscow."

By then it was too late to brood over what might have been. Whether it was already too late in 1946 when even a little support could have helped reduce the odds facing Czechoslovakia's democrats, or in 1947, when any kind of aid outside the Marshall Plan was denied to Foreign Minister Masaryk, it is impossible to say. We know it was too late by 1948. Though no one can say whether Czechoslovakia might have been saved, there are times when I wonder—in the light of hind sight—whether the West does not now and then suffer pangs of conscience when reviewing the fate of that country.

CHAPTER XIV

THE BALKAN DILEMMA—BELGRADE, ATHENS, AND ANKARA, 1951

Yugoslavia in the vise.—Belgrade: "something big and inspiring halted in mid-motion."—Tito describes the plight of an ex-Soviet satellite.—Greece: saved by Western arms; supported by Western taxpayers.—The "sick man of Europe" is now strong.

YUGOSLAVIA under Marshal Tito, after breaking with the Cominform in June, 1948, was temporarily isolated between East and West. A boycott by the Soviet Union and its satellites brought to a standstill trade with the East, which had taken three-quarters of the country's exports. It was further weakened by a disastrous crop failure, and channels of aid and trade between it and the West had not yet opened. The need to maintain the second largest standing army in Europe was no help to the country's economic situation. Border incidents occurred daily, and there were reliable reports that unfriendly satellite neighbors had begun to receive increasing numbers of tanks and heavy artillery from Russia. The Soviet Union was turning the handle of the vise on Yugoslavia, while the Western powers moved very slowly toward relieving the pressure on their side.

Under the circumstances, I decided to visit Yugoslavia and extend the trip to accept the long-standing invitations of my friends Alexis Kyron and Selim Sarper, Ambassadors from Greece and Turkey to the United Nations, to visit their countries also.

I left New York on April 6, 1951, stopping over at Paris and Zurich, and arrived at Belgrade six days later. Mrs. Lie, Georges Peissel, Director of the United Nations Bureau of Documents, Abraham H. Feller, and Wilder Foote, Director of the Press and Publications Bureau, accompanied me.

Advance reports left me still uncertain of what to expect in Belgrade, other than the welcoming delegation, the numerous uniforms, the many police, the formal greetings. Less expected—and therefore all the more pleasing—were the tremendous crowds of onlookers, and the evidence of intense public interest. Most impressive during the first hour in Belgrade was the appearance of the city and the people. It was as if something big and inspiring had suddenly been halted in mid-motion—witness the huge unfinished buildings near the airport, where it was plain that workmen had not moved a timber or laid a stone for years. The effect was drab and depressing: people were thin and poorly clothed, shops had little to sell, vehicles were few but pedestrians numerous. Great shortages were indicated by the long lines outside the food shops, and one of our group found it impossible to buy a pocket comb. However, the scene improved upon closer inspection. A considerable amount of housing was going up; the children, unlike the parents, seemed well fed; and if there was little enthusiasm, there did not appear to be any great discontent either.

In the course of the ensuing days there was no mistaking that my trip was regarded as an event. One incident remains in my memory. Our party passed through a tiny village some distance out in the country, and apparently the majority of the population had turned out to watch. When we halted momentarily several men stepped out of the crowd to ask one of our drivers: "Which of these men is Trygve Lie?"

In Yugoslavia the United Nations seemed to symbolize support and aid from the world outside the Iron Curtain, but with full independence in internal policy. After having heard the tones of reverence which Russians reserved for the name of Stalin, I was struck by the contrasting status of Tito in Yugoslavia. I often heard him criticized in official as well as unofficial circles—not bitterly, but as one of their own who had failed to handle one or another problem in the way the speaker would have done. It was equally interesting to note that few pictures of the Marshal were to be seen—and they were only in government offices, and were of moderate size.

On Friday April 13, our second day in Belgrade, an escort arrived shortly before noon to accompany my wife and me to the notably well guarded residence of Marshal Tito. The Executive Mansion was in good taste without being in any way palatial. The Marshal's greeting was most cordial, as were those of Dr. Joze Vilfan, Deputy Minister for Foreign Affairs, and Ales Bebler, permanent delegate and Ambassador to the United Nations in New York, who were the only persons present during the ensuing conversation. They alternated as interpreters. The Marshal, I observed, was not a tall man—at any rate, not many inches taller than Stalin—and, though he was thinner than I had supposed, he seemed to be in relatively good health. Commenting upon his pleasure at our meeting, the Marshal explained that he had postponed entering a hospital for a gallstone operation in order to meet and talk with the United Nations' Secretary-General. Though he had lost some thirty pounds, he seemed to be proud of having held to a rigid diet: "How could I do other than follow the doctor's order," he remarked half humorously, "when I demand discipline from every Yugoslav citizen?" That his health was not the best was shown by his tired and worn appearance when Mrs. Lie and I left him at 3:45.

There were no preliminaries. Like all Yugoslavs, Marshal Tito regarded relations with neighboring states as the most pressing problem of the moment and apparently welcomed my request for a survey of the situation. He explained that Yugoslavia received daily provocation; shootings occurred nightly, and already there were many dead. "Our patience is being put to a hard test," he admitted. "Several times we have thought of bringing this matter of our neighbors' conduct before the United Nations; and the possibility is still being discussed in the government." A complaint, in such event, would also protest the severance of trade as well as the acquisition by Rumania, Bulgaria, and Hungary of large numbers of heavy tanks, heavy artillery, and jet fighters. "About half of this country's entire income," he explained, "now goes toward maintaining our army and air force." This need for constant preparedness, I found, was requiring an armed force of 600,000 men: 400,000 in the standing army, 100,000 police, and 100,000 in the various quasi-military organizations.

The Eastern Bloc boycott which had brought three-quarters of Yugoslavia's foreign trade to a standstill, together with floods of 1951 and the droughts of 1950, had rendered the economic situation "very difficult," as he put it. All new construction had been halted at the time of the breach with the Cominform countries; food supplies were very limited—even potatoes being rationed. "It is a troublesome time," he admitted; "but no sacrifices are too great when the independence of Yugoslavia is at stake. That is why the present government has been able to maintain the administrative machinery, and at the same time retain public confidence. The whole of Yugoslavia," he emphasized, "supports my foreign policy regarding the Soviet Union and the Communist Bloc."

But there were other aspects. Marshal Tito pointed out how the blockade had been broken: there were rail connections again between Belgrade and Athens, and civilian air routes linked Belgrade with Athens, Zurich, and Frankfort. "Quite a few states have also been benevolent with their credits and trade treaties," he continued, "especially Great Britain." What was needed now, however, was capital in loans for reconstruction, for new industry, and for defense. "A couple of months ago, we turned to the United States, the United Kingdom, and France about this; but it was not long before our request for arms was made public in Washington, and I was forced to make a statement to Parliament on the matter." I gathered that he was a little irritated by the "leakage" of state secrets in the American capital. Yugoslavia had also applied for a loan from the International Bank, and Bank representatives had been sent to investigate. "Never has a country been checked more effectively," he recalled; "but we are still without the loan. . . . Perhaps insuperable political obstacles are preventing this—but I don't understand what these might be. Yugoslavia is a Communistic State and can, of course, accept no loans, credit, or weapons on political conditions. We cannot change our constitution and system of government. But if these are respected we guarantee that we will not use power in any attempt to force other countries to adopt our system of government or our constitution."

He thought Yugoslavia a good risk, and saw no reason why it

THE BALKAN DILEMMA

might not receive loans and aid like many other states. "But," he emphasized, "we will have to refuse assistance if it is to be tied in with political stipulations regarding Yugoslavia's domestic affairs. We want to live in peace with the Soviet Union and with our neighboring states. For us, the United Nations is the only organization that can offer us hope of security. We cannot join the North Atlantic Treaty—in fact, we cannot belong to any bloc. But there are still people who think that our breach with the Soviet Union was not an honest one. They are wrong." He explained that Yugoslavia had been offered no choice: that the Soviet had utilized and exploited it economically, and had attempted to force it into accepting political and economic programs which the Yugoslavs could not possibly stomach. "It was apparent," he concluded, "that the Soviet Union intended to exploit us as it had exploited other Eastern European states. This, we could not permit. Therefore, there is no way back for us. We will always be happy if we are respected by the Soviet Union as an equal, but we cannot permit Moscow to regard Yugoslavia as any second-rate nation."

I assured Marshal Tito that I was acquainted with Yugoslavia's problems, but that I represented no state and could come with no promises of material aid. "As Secretary-General, I have only my two empty hands—no army and no force with which to help Yugoslavia in event of an emergency. On the other hand I will not hesitate to apply Article 99 of the Charter should Yugoslavia be confronted with the same situation as faced South Korea." The Marshal appeared to be satisfied as he reiterated how much it meant for his country to have this assurance from an impartial Secretary-General, "who would do all he could to support the right of every member state to live its own life in freedom and independence."

I voiced real concern over the border provocations, but cautioned against retaliation in kind: "Events like these are always very trying, but I am counting on you and on your colleagues in the Government as being great enough statesmen to disregard this challenge and to resist the urge to repay the same coin." I advised waiting and exercising caution, this being no time to bring such a complaint before the Security Council. "The main thing for the moment is to win time and avoid publicity as much as possible. There may be a chance to consider Yugoslavia's complaints against the Eastern states when there is a better balance between Eastern and Western influence and power." Admitting that this was slim comfort, I thought it "far better to be honest than to give bad advice. To win time," I added, "we must often be patient and long-suffering." Yugoslavia took my advice, and did not bring its complaints before the United Nations until the Paris (1951) session of the General Assembly, and then with good results.

At this point a most interesting bit of information came to light. I had dared to ask the Marshal whether, in view of his country's unfavorable geographical position, eventual defense cooperation with Greece and Turkey—in event of a Communist attack—might not be facilitated by informal exchange of experience and information even now. His reaction was positive and immediate: "We have considered such a possibility. Should the Communists attack any one of us, it would be most useful to know the defense plans of the others, the disposition of their forces, their strength in the various branches, etc." Yugoslavia would be more than interested in entering into such an informal three-way exchange, and he let me understand that preliminary steps in this direction had already been taken.

"You may think it strange," I admitted, "that I, as the head of this organization for the promotion of world peace, should be discussing these steps to foster defence cooperation. But peace for the time being can, in my opinion, be maintained only by recognizing the other side's respect for force." We both laughed roundly as I recalled Stalin's remark at Teheran, when it was suggested that the Pope request Hitler to guarantee the humane treatment of prisoners: "The Pope? How many divisions does he have?"

There were two other matters which I was interested in bringing up. Both, if properly handled, could do much to improve the Western democracies' relations with Yugoslavia. "Bishop Aloysius Stepinac is still in prison," I began. "If anything could be done to effect his release, such a step would be highly regarded throughout the free world, and in America particularly." Marshal Tito's reply was immediate: "That matter could be settled shortly if only it could be left with the Yugoslav Government and myself. But nothing can be done under pressure or stipulations. The Government will not be pressed to release Stepinac, and it will not agree to accept aid or weapons on the condition that Stepinac be released." Here again I caught a glimpse if Yugoslavia's intense resentment against external interference in domestic affairs. "Stepinac," he continued, "is a traitor who has received his legal sentence and punishment according to prevailing Yugoslavian law and regulations." However, were this matter only to rest awhile, the Government had the right to pardon him, and his release could be effected.

A second matter I wished to bring up was the return of Greek children sent to Yugoslavia during the guerrilla war in Greece. While a number of these had been repatriated, I recalled that several hundreds were still being held in his country. "Few cases have attracted as much attention in the democratic world as that of the Greek children," I pointed out. Evidently Marshal Tito was not too well informed here—he turned to Deputy Foreign Minister Vilfan, asking him to look into the matter and report. We had received reports on legal difficulties surrounding interpretation of the General Assembly's resolution in this respect, I continued, but I made it clear that I regarded these as poorly founded. As a way out I suggested that all Greek children in Yugoslavia be turned over to the Swedish Red Cross, which was then working on the problem: "Let that body have full responsibility and authority to decide whether the children should stay in Yugoslavia or be sent back to Greece or to any other country. Nobody knows as much about this as the Swedes." He promised to consider this alternative. Next time the issue of the Greek children came up in the United Nations, the Greek representative expressed his satisfaction with Yugoslavia's cooperation.

The discussion then turned to Korea. I admitted my difficulty in understanding why the Yugoslavian Delegation to the United Nations continually abstained from voting on all matters relating to the Korean War. "An open and clear statement from Yugoslavia," I maintained, "would do much to clarify her attitude, and would be much appreciated from my point of view." Further, I found it difficult to understand Yugoslavian neutrality here. "What would have been the position had Yugoslavia been attacked instead of the Republic of Korea?" This line of reasoning was understood, as were my intimations that Yugoslav "volunteers" could well be sent to Korea. The Marshal, however, went no further than to note that the government was now discussing its stands: as far as Belgrade was concerned, an end to the entire conflict was preferred, though hopes for this eventuality were slim for the moment. "In my opinion," he observed, "the Soviet Union is not interested in seeing an early end to the fighting in Korea."

I asked whether there were any indications of Russian troop concentrations in Bulgaria or Albania, and whether a Communist attack was feared. Marshal Tito replied that Yugoslav intelligence could report only Russian instructors in those countries; but they had continually been receiving arms and now, with the Russian and National troops in Rumania and Hungary, were so strong as to constitute a threat to Yugoslavia. "However, I do not expect any direct attack from the Soviet Union. If the Kremlin wanted to attack us, it would follow much the same line as in South Korea. The neighboring states would try to invade, but the Soviet Union would not join in unless things went very, very badly." He did not believe that the situation in Eastern Europe indicated any war that year. And that ended our conversation for the time.

Luncheon was something of a revelation. There were ten at table, including Mrs. Lie, several leading members of the government, and their wives. The atmosphere was pleasant, and there was not a trace of the slavish discipline so familiar in Moscow. All the ministers spoke freely of Marshal Tito's illness, and—among other things—their salaries: obviously, a sore subject. The Marshal, upon hearing salaries mentioned, broke in to note that members of the government were already receiving three times the wage of the most highly skilled workers, so that there could be no further increase. As for himself, he insisted that he was being paid less than his ministers.

Afterward, an incident at the coffee table did much to shape my opinion of the man Tito. One of the waiters serving us stumbled, and a dozen glasses of plum brandy showered down over the Marshal, drenching him from head to foot. There was a gasp from the whole party, and the servant's face went white; but, with perfect composure and not the slightest trace of anger, Marshal Tito merely smiled, rose, and bowed to Mrs. Lie, who was sitting beside him: "If you'll please excuse me for a moment. I'll have to go out and dry off a bit." He left without even a glance at the distressed waiter.

His remarkably strong personality drew from the ministers and officers present many expressions of admiration and affection that had a ring of genuineness. There was none of the servile submission or the strong party-line discipline I had so often observed in Communist countries.

After Belgrade, where it rained almost every day, the first sight of Athens was exhilarating. The air was soft, the town clean and attractive and—apparently—extremely prosperous. Traffic was heavy, and there were many American cars, large numbers of attractive homes, and a great many well fed, well dressed people. The villages, too, looked pretty and neat, and the peasant families showed little evidence of poverty.

How long would this last, I wondered. There was no mistaking that Greek prosperity was a product of foreign aid. UNRRA, ECA, and various other foreign assistance programs had pumped more than two billion dollars into Greece by that time, and—according to my information—ECA was then supplying some 70 per cent of the current Greek budget. Because Greece was supported by the American taxpayer there were real grounds for concern as to what would happen when the aid was withdrawn. Many persons with whom I spoke seemed to expect it would go on for a very long time—otherwise the country would be left open to domestic turmoil and Communist expansion. Greece at that time was also most interested in gaining a place among the North Atlantic Treaty powers.

However, little of all this was touched upon in my talks with Prime Minister Sophocles Venizelos and other Greek statesmen. They were anxious to know what Marshal Tito had had to say. While there was little I could report, my review of the conversation so far as it touched on an exchange of defense plans, data, and other necessary information among Yugoslavia, Greece, and Turkey awakened immediate interest. It was my impression that the Greeks had been hoping for such an exchange.

I was also asked about Marshal Tito's attitude regarding repatriation of the Greek children. To this I could only reply that we had discussed the matter, and that I had informed him that more positive action would have to be taken prior to the next Assembly. The subject was discussed again during my luncheon with King Paul and Queen Frederika. The Queen was also concerned over the impending cessation of assistance from the United Nations International Children's Emergency Fund, which was helping to feed some 90,000 Greek children. Unfortunately, I could offer little reassurance, as resources were extremely limited and aid was even more urgently needed in other areas.

It was reassuring to find that, with the guerrilla war at an end, leading circles in Greece were making efforts at a rapprochement with the Yugoslavs. Prime Minister Venizelos mentioned several times Greece's desire to establish better relations with that country. I saw the reestablishment of air and rail communications between Athens and Belgrade as an important first step.

Although reports of serious infringements upon democratic freedoms in Greece had reached me in New York, my short stay in the country failed to uncover any very convincing evidence. On the contrary, open—and obviously effective—bus and telegraph strikes were on in Athens, and I attended one dinner where no fewer than four former Prime Ministers were seated at the same table, notwithstanding their normally hot public quarrels and mutual recriminations. In the course of my two-day visit I also received scores of letters and telegrams from leftists and political prisoners, and the writers certainly seemed to have no fear of reprisals.

Turkey was the last of the border countries which I visited that spring. In terms of security—the number one question in the Balkans—Yugoslavia, Greece, and Turkey faced similar problems and were more or less equally exposed. President Celal Bayar, Prime Minister Adnan Menderes, and Foreign Minister Fuad Köprülü revealed an immediate interest in the opinions of Marshal Tito concerning the exchange of defense plans and information. Here too the leaders favored conversations about this question among the three countries. The formalities of such an exchange, I was assured, would involve few practical difficulties.

Turkey, like Greece and Yugoslavia, was most taken up with security against Communist attack. For thirteen years, from 40 to 45 per cent of the Turkish budget had gone for national defense, and at the time of my visit Turkey's standing army was the third largest in Europe, next to those of the Soviet Union and Yugoslavia. The extent of American military aid was at once evident, and Turkish as well as Greek statesmen showed great interest in the North Atlantic Treaty or in a Mediterranean Pact.

However, Turkey was not so much worried as to the immediate future. The only unrest I could note was over Iran, which the Turks

THE ISSUE OF CHINESE REPRESENTATION 251

the Council, whereupon a special meeting would be called to discuss the matter.

This did not satisfy Mr. Malik, and he challenged the President's ruling at once. The issue was put to a vote; and the Soviet motion was overwhelmingly defeated. Ambassador Malik promptly repeated his earlier statements, stressing that five Council members, which had broken diplomatic relations with Nationalist China, were nevertheless still dealing in the Council with the "Formosa group," represented—as he termed it—by "the person in the chair." Were the Council to meet, he argued, it would be under the presidency of a person who, from the point of view of common sense as well as law, represented no one at all. "No real meeting, but a parody of a meeting would be the result." He ended by saying that he could not remain seated at such a conference table, and rose and demonstratively left the chamber.

This was the second Soviet walkout in the history of the United Nations, under circumstances far more tense than those marking the Iranian dispute.

Attempts to return the Council to order enjoyed only momentary success. A proposal by Ambassador Ales Bebler of Yugoslavia that the meeting be adjourned to investigate and discuss the Chinese representation issue in more detail at a later date, touched off a full-dress procedural debate. Several speakers were quick to cite Rule 17 in the Rules of Procedure, which stipulates that a member of the Security Council whose credentials have been met with objection "shall continue to sit with the same rights as other representatives until the Security Council has decided the matter." Not even Mr. Malik was ignorant of this ruling, or the fact that it was still binding upon all Council Members. This seemed to trouble him little, as long as he had his instructions. Sir Benegal Rau's suggestion that the Rules of Procedure be revised in light of the new situation, awakened not even a halfhearted response. In the end, it was agreed to call a new meeting to discuss Mr. Malik's and all related proposals.

When the Security Council met again on January 12 there was a good deal of anxiety as to whether Mr. Malik would appear at all; but when the meeting convened he was found at his appointed place. There were then no objections to Dr. Tsiang's suggestion that, in the interest of a calm and impartial discussion, Dr. Carlos S. Blanco of

Cuba assume the chair during debate on the Chinese question. But any hopes that this considerate action may have aroused were soon dashed: the new debate turned out to be as inconclusive as the previous one.

Mr. Bebler declared that Yugoslavia would vote for the Russian proposal. Sir Benegal Rau suggested that a new committee of experts be named to clarify Chapter III of the Rules of Procedure. Dr. Tsiang took pains to make it clear that the Security Council could rest assured, *"and the Secretary-General of the United Nations can also rest assured,* that in connection with the present controversy, my delegation will do everything in its power not to hamper or injure the proper institutional development of the United Nations." At that point he was apparently willing to take cognizance of my concern and anxiety as to what might happen were Mr. Malik to decide on a new walkout. Ambassador Ernest A. Gross, who was the United States' Deputy Representative, declared that his government regarded Dr. Tsiang's credentials as valid, but that it would *"accept the decision of the Security Council on this matter when made by an affirmative vote of seven members."*

The following day, the whole issue was brought to a head in the Security Council. The U.S.S.R.'s proposal mustered but three votes (India, U.S.S.R., and Yugoslavia); six states opposed, while the United Kingdom and Norway abstained. This evidently came as no surprise to Mr. Malik who, as many as three times in a short address, made it clear that the Soviet Delegation would not participate in the work of the Security Council until the representative of the Nationalist Government was removed. Before rising to leave the chamber—this time for an absence of some six and a half months—Mr. Malik declared that *the U.S.S.R. would not recognize as legal any decision of the Security Council, adopted with the participation of the representative of the Kuomintang group, and would not deem itself bound by such decisions.*

January 13 was a dark day for the United Nations. Pessimism among the ten remaining representatives was obvious. How, after all, was it possible to penetrate the motives and ultimate purposes of the U.S.S.R.? How far did the Soviet intend to go this time? In 1949, when Yugoslavia had been elected to replace the Ukrainian S.S.R. in the Security Council, over furious Soviet opposition, Mr. Vyshinsky had confined himself to vague and obscure threats. Now threats had been replaced by action, and over the next few weeks the Russians and other Communist delegates actually marched out of no fewer than twenty-one United Nations councils and committees, duplicating the spectacle in the Security Council. Did this mean they would leave the United Nations for good? There was no way of knowing.

We did know that the United Nations was being pushed to the wall at a time when its existence hinged on holding fast to every vestige of strength and authority. Its stature was shrinking in the public eye from day to day. Was this what Russia really wanted? Past experience should by now have taught the Soviet Union that threats and arbitrary action only reduced its chances of gaining support for its resolutions. Clearly, there were deeper-lying motives; but what these were, we could only guess.

Momentous negotiations between Communist China and the U.S.S.R. had been under way in Moscow since December. Had the Kremlin hit upon this action as a first step toward breaking up the United Nations and establishing a new, rival organization of "Peoples' Democracies"? If so, we should be left with a United Nations far different from that planned and foreseen under the United Nations Charter. Together, the Soviet Union, Communist China, and the other Communist-dominated countries controlled a population of some 800,000,000. On this base a very strong organization might be established—strong enough, at any rate, to compete effectively with the United Nations. Were this the Soviet goal, the world might soon see two groups of states in open competition with each other. Furthermore, such a development might well induce many Arab-Asian states and even some others to leave the United Nations because they would not care to ally themselves with either group.

If the Russians, meaning only to exploit division in the ranks of the West, had refrained from the boycott, they could hardly have hit upon a better issue; but of course such crude and unrestrained pressure aroused widespread resentment. Aside from the Communist bloc, the Member nations differed sharply on which government of China to recognize. Most of China's non-Communist neighbors had already recognized Peking, as had an impressive number of other Member states, including Great Britain, Sweden, Denmark, Norway, New Zealand, Yugoslavia, Israel, and the Netherlands.

I fully sympathized with this position, taken by so many Western European states, including Norway. Without being happy that the Communists had won the Civil War in China, I did not feel that approval or disapproval of a regime was in question: it was a matter of recognizing the facts of international life.

The "Republic of China" to which permanent membership in the United Nations was extended at San Francisco was not a government but a nation of some 475,000,000 people. It was *China*, not Chiang Kai-shek, that belonged to the United Nations. Now the Nationalist Government had been driven from the mainland and controlled only Formosa, an island that had belonged to Japan for half a century and had not yet been finally awarded to China by the peace treaty. How could Chiang Kai-shek speak for China in the United Nations in these circumstances?

Another consideration that influenced my judgment was historical. Once before, the world had seen a Communist state—the U.S.S.R.—isolated by the West after a successful revolution. I had always believed that this was a great mistake, and that the West, instead, should have sought every means to fuller intercourse with Russia in the 1920's. Such a policy might well have influenced the development of the Soviet state in a direction other than the one it took. Was the free world now going to cut itself off, in similar fashion, from China and its 475,000,000 people—one-fifth of the world's total population?

Finally, the nearest possible approach to universality was a principle that I always felt to be fundamental to the fulfillment of the purposes of a *world* organization. What chance would the United Nations have of reducing tensions and improving the prospects of peace if it were no longer to be the meeting ground between East and West?

I was not sure at first what the Secretary-General should try to do. Before taking any further steps, I decided to consult with the Permanent Members. Accordingly, on January 21 Byron Price and I went to Washington for a talk with Secretary of State Dean G. Acheson and several of his advisers. I expressed grave concern over the situation of the United Nations. "Earlier, as during the Berlin Blockade," I explained, "the main difficulties lay beyond our reach, but now we are confronted by a crisis within the organization itself." Noting that a special Assembly could be called to go into the Chinese issue, I questioned the wisdom of such a move. "Dr. Tsiang," I continued, "is reportedly prepared to withdraw either when Peking has been recognized by a majority of the Member Governments, or when the United States has recognized Communist China. Therefore, it is of extreme importance to us to know whether the United States—or any other Member Government you might know of—is contemplating steps toward eventual recognition."

To Mr. Acheson's query as to whether we had any definite indication that the Russians would *withdraw completely*, I replied that we had none yet. "But we cannot *exclude the possibility* that the present withdrawals may *lead to a final withdrawal* unless something intervenes." Once again, I asked the Secretary of State whether—despite recent developments—American recognition of Communist China would be considered in the foreseeable future.

Mr. Acheson's answer implied a firm "No." It was his opinion, he said, that the whole Peking regime was an improvisation that scarcely knew what it was doing, or what repercussions its acts had internationally. He went on to recall the recent seizure of American properties, the closing of the American consular offices and the kidnaping of American citizens. The United States would certainly not recognize Peking in such circumstances and was opposed to seating the Communist regime in the United Nations. He indicated that a special session of the Assembly to discuss the Chinese question would be most premature.

Nevertheless, I emerged from our amiable—though often outspoken—conversation, with a possible solution in mind: the issue might well adjust itself within the Security Council. Five members of the Council already recognized Peking—the U.S.S.R., Norway, Yugoslavia, the United Kingdom, and India. If two additional members, say France and Egypt, would vote to seat Peking, that would be the requisite majority of seven which the United States had agreed to accept.

Back in New York, I at once resumed discussions with my advisers as to what the Secretariat and Secretary-General might do toward easing the present impossible situation. My legal advisers had concluded that the veto did not apply here, as the question of who should represent China was of a "procedural nature," being, in the final instance, a matter of credentials. But *could we reasonably hope for the seven affirmative votes needed in the Security Council to decide the issue once for all?*

At my request, the Legal Department reviewed the juridical aspects of the question in a memorandum prepared by Dr. Ivan Kerno and Dr. A. H. Feller. It opened with the observation that the central difficulty stemmed from an unfortunate linkage of the matter of representation with that of recognition by Member governments—a linkage it termed fallacious from the standpoint of legal theory. On the basis of all the facts, juridical precedents and practice, both in the League of Nations and in the United Nations, the memorandum concluded that membership of a state in the United Nations and representation of a state in its organs were clearly determined by collective acts: membership, by vote of the General Assembly on recommendation of the Security Council; representation, by vote of each competent organ on the credentials of the purported representatives. Because recognition of either state or government was an *individual* act, and both admission to membership and acceptance of representation in the Organization were *collective* acts, it would be *legally inadmissible to condition the latter acts by a requirement that they be preceded by individual recognition.*

The memorandum enumerated instances in the League of Nations in which members stated expressly that the admission of another state to membership did not involve their recognizing the new member as a state (e.g., Great Britain in the case of Lithuania, Belgium and Switzerland in the case of the Soviet Union, and Colombia in the case of Panama). Examples in the United Nations were Yemen and Burma, which were admitted by a unanimous vote of the General Assembly when they had been recognized by only a small minority of members; and in the Security Council a number of members voting for the admission of Transjordan and Nepal had not recognized them as states. When the U.S.S.R. withheld its vote for the admission of Ireland, Portugal, and Transjordan because it had not established diplomatic relations with them, most other members attacked it vigorously; and this led to the request for an advisory opinion of the International Court of Justice. The Court was asked if a state was juridically entitled to make its consent to the admission dependent on conditions not expressly provided by §1 of Article 4 of the Charter. Its answer was "No."

THE ISSUE OF CHINESE REPRESENTATION

In two instances involving nonmembers, the Republic of Indonesia and Israel, it was questioned whether these were really states. Each was said to be just an entity and not a state. Both were admitted to membership.

The Chinese case, the memorandum continued, was unique in the history of the United Nations, not because it involved a revolutionary change of government, but because it was the first in which two rival governments existed. It was quite possible that such a situation would occur again, the jurists said, and it was highly desirable to see what principle could be followed in choosing between the rivals. It had been demonstrated that the principle of numerical preponderance of recognition was inappropriate and legally incorrect. Was any other principle possible?

The memorandum submitted that the proper principle could be derived by analogy from Article 4 of the Charter, requiring that an applicant be *able and willing to carry out the obligations for membership*—obligations that could be carried out only by governments which in fact had the power to do so; and from this it reasoned:

> Where a revolutionary government presents itself as representing a State, in rivalry to an existing government, the question at issue should be *which of these two governments in fact is in a position to employ the resources and direct the people of the State in fulfillment of the obligations of membership*. In essence, this means an inquiry as to whether the new government exercises effective authority within the territory of the State and is habitually obeyed by the bulk of the population. If so, it would seem to be appropriate for the United Nations organs, through their collective action, to accord it the right to represent the State in the Organization, even though individual members of the Organization refuse, and may continue to refuse, to accord it recognition as the lawful government, for reasons which are valid under their national policies.

On the basis of the above, the immediate and practical conclusion was that France, Egypt, Ecuador, and Cuba—Members of the Council who did not recognize the Communist regime in China—might vote for representation of the Peking government in the Security Council while still withholding recognition. This consideration, I reasoned, would have special weight for France: the Peking government, in all probability without evaluating the consequences, had recognized the Viet-Minh movement which opposed the French-supported government in Indochina. Though Egypt, Cuba, and Ecuador would also find it difficult to recognize the Peking government, at least one of them, in the interest of the United Nations, might vote for seating it in the Security Council.

Armed with this memorandum, I proceeded to discuss the matter with all members of the Council. The first approach was to Sir Alexander Cadogan, the oldest and most experienced of the permanent delegates. Behind him lay many years of activity in the League of Nations; he had taken part in all preparatory work preceding the founding of the United Nations, and had been the United Kingdom's permanent representative to the Organization ever since its inception. Certainly, he represented a school holding that the Secretary-General should take a far less active part in the political work of the United Nations than I had done. For him, Sir Eric Drummond as Secretary-General approached the ideal; but, despite this and other differences on political questions, he and his wife, Lady Theodosia, had become very close to Mrs. Lie and me. Our friendship surmounted these differing opinions.

Accompanied by David Owen, I sat down for a talk with Sir Alexander, putting the same questions and passing along the same information as to Dean Acheson and his aides in the State Department. Sir Alexander admitted sharing my concern over recent developments, adding that he was the more disturbed because he suspected the Soviet attitude was based on a calculated policy of discouraging rather than encouraging recognition of the new Chinese government by either the United States or France. China, he pointed out, could thereby be kept more effectively in isolation from the West and under Soviet domination. The policies of Peking itself, whether at Soviet prompting or not, seemed to be leading China into this trap. How else could one explain the seizure of United States property in China and recognition of the Viet-Minh movement? He was doubtful whether it was reasonable to expect any positive response from the Soviet Union or the new Chinese government to overtures toward recognition. However, he believed that his government might authorize him to vote for unseating Dr. Tsiang, were a properly accredited representative of the Peking government to appear at Lake Success. He also remarked that, according to his latest information, Egypt was expected shortly to recognize the new Chinese government.

To a query as to whether his government would exert its influence on France in this question, he replied that he was not sure. He advised, however, against calling a special Assembly: "Ideally, the solution should be sought in the Security Council." And he expressed the hope that Dr. Tsiang would withdraw, once a majority of the Council favored the new regime.

In the ensuing days, I had private conversations with Ambassadors Jean Chauvel (France), Sir Benegal Rau (India), Blanco (Cuba), Mahmoud Fawzi Bey (Egypt), Homero Viteri Lafronte (Ecuador), Bebler (Yugoslavia), Sunde (Norway), and Ambassador Gross and Minister John C. Ross of the United States. Each of them requested and received my memorandum, at the same time expressing sympathy with my efforts to resolve this controversy before serious damage was done.

Ambassador Chauvel, in particular, displayed great understanding. I have always admired his clear and reliable thinking, and his good juridical judgment. He was, he said, very grateful for the memorandum, and would immediately make contact with the Quai d'Orsay.

My own feelings were expressed in a letter written about that time to Norwegian Foreign Minister Halvard Lange:

> The situation is difficult, and I fear that the Russians must not be allowed to remain outside the active work of the United Nations for any length of time. . . . I have expressed my uneasiness in the matter to all members of the Security Council and have met with them in an effort to determine how seven votes can be obtained. . . .
>
> But it is impossible at the present time to reach a solution binding upon all United Nations organs, as this can only be achieved through a resolution by the General Assembly. However, none of the people with whom I have spoken until now seem to favor a special General Assembly this spring. . . .
>
> The whole thing is a mess—and I have no desire to be sitting here with sole responsibility, should the United Nations collapse. Still, it is quite remarkable that when I speak to the various members privately, practically all of them agree that the Mao Tse-tung Government actually repre-

sents the Republic of China which should be represented in the United Nations.

For the moment, I saw no reason for conferring with either Dr. Tsiang or Mr. Malik. The former was too involved in the dispute, while the latter had, in my opinion, so betrayed his obligation to remain seated in the Council that he deserved no approach from the Secretary-General. By now, however, news of my meetings with the various Council members had begun to filter out, and I was obliged to acquaint the press with certain of my efforts toward a solution. I was not surprised, therefore, when Dr. Tsiang asked me on February 9 for a meeting.

Oddly unlike his normally placid self, he seemed to be highly excited during most of the conversation, reiterating time and again that the Peking government would never survive the two to three months famine period. He had read press accounts of starvation in China, and stressed the importance of sabotage and domestic disturbances on the mainland. The life of the Mao government, he maintained, would assuredly be short; but I received the impression that his hopes for reconquering China were really based on a new world war, and I told him outright that it was my duty as Secretary-General to prevent world wars as well as local wars.

With this conversation, however, it became clear that the Nationalist Government had recovered from the first effects of its disastrous defeat and would fight to the end on the representation issue. Chiang Kai-shek had always had a powerful and well financed "lobby" in the United States, and this was mobilized in the belief that all was not yet lost for the Nationalists, granted American support on an increasing scale. In Dr. Tsiang the Nationalists had a representative whose considerable mental resources would be ably employed for this purpose.

Many people had been wondering just why the Chinese-Soviet negotiations in Moscow were moving so slowly: after all, they had been going on since December. Was China asking too much, or was Russia trying to draw it into so intimate a cooperation that the free world would soon be confronted by a genuine alliance of powers representing 800,000,000 people? The answer came in the announcement from Moscow on February 14: The Chinese and the Russians had signed a thirty-year treaty of alliance, friendship, and mutual assistance; the U.S.S.R. would place $300,000,000 in credits at the disposal of the Mao government; and the Changchun Railway and the ports of Port Arthur and Dairen were to be returned to China.

The Soviet Union had won a new and significant diplomatic victory. Anyone with eyes to see, ears to hear, and a head with which to reason would now have to take cognizance of the enormous potential with which the democratic countries were now confronted in Eurasia. Winston Churchill's speech in Edinburgh, expressing a desire for direct negotiations with Stalin in an effort to improve the international situation, struck me as timely and realistic. Anthony Eden's support of this line of thinking served further to indicate a healthy reaction in at least one of the Western capitals.

All the more reason now, I thought, for seating Communist China in the United Nations and bringing its government under the obligations of the Charter and into contact with the world community. However, the Security Council members refused to budge from their earlier stands. Though domestic political considerations ruled out any modifying by the United States of its position, I had at least hoped otherwise. I had expected that the United States would refrain from exerting pressure against the seating of Peking. I was wrong. The State Department proceeded to take off on an entirely different course, bringing its influence to bear (I was reliably informed) on one of the Latin-American lands which, in the light of my memorandum, had planned to support the seating of the Chinese Communists in the Security Council. Neither from France nor from Egypt was there any sign of a modified stand.

The press, by this time, had got wind of my memorandum on Chinese representation—then in the hands of Council members as a confidential aide-mémoire. I therefore submitted it formally as a document, together with a letter referring to my informal conversations on March 8.

Publication of this juridical memorandum brought a barrage of fiery attacks from Dr. Tsiang, Dr. V. K. Wellington Koo, the Chinese Ambassador to Washington, and from the isolationist press in the United States. I was accused of "surrender to the Soviet," of being an "appeaser," and, of course, of transgressing the limits of my authority as Secretary-General. In a short public statement at this time, I recalled how, as Secretary-General, I was obligated to seek a solution in the best interests of the Organization. I had held many conversations on the subject and intended to hold many more. I declined to comment on Dr. Tsiang's attack, not wishing to launch into a controversy with him, but added that he was doing his duty as he saw it and I was doing mine. "He called my memorandum 'bad law and bad politics,' " I observed. "As to the law, I am quite willing to leave that to the judgment of any representative group of jurists or to the opinion of the International Court of Justice should it be decided to bring the question before the Court. As to the 'politics,' I am quite content to leave that to the considered judgment of the Member Nations and history."

I further expressed surprise that some people were evidently not aware of my views on "boycotts and walkouts and other acts by Member Governments harmful to the development and influence of the United Nations." I reiterated that all members of the United Nations have the duty to participate fully in its work. This was especially true of the Security Council, and I stressed that refusal to participate in United Nations meetings did not contribute toward solving such problems as the question of China.

On March 13 Dr. Tsiang sent a letter which he wished me to distribute to the Member nations, and I did so. It was strongly worded, and as a result one newspaper called me "a stooge of the Reds." Other papers said that I was "aiding the Reds," and that "Lie appeases the Soviet." But such attacks in no way slowed my efforts toward new solutions.

By now I had come to the conclusion that other and new ways had to be found to resolve the crisis. *Was it possible to bring the parties together again on other issues than that of Chinese representation?* I felt that it was, and it was these reflections and discussions which eventually led to my ten-points proposal for a twenty-year peace plan.

On March 21 I utilized an invitation to address the triennial dinner of the B'nai B'rith organization in Washington, not only for explaining the basic issue in the China controversy, but for airing certain ideas about a broader approach to the East-West deadlock. I recalled:

This division among the nations of the world does not at all follow the so-called "usual lines." I have been trying to help the Member Govern-

THE ISSUE OF CHINESE REPRESENTATION 263

ments settle the question of who is to represent China in the United Nations. I am not doing this because the Soviet Union and its neighbors have refused to attend meetings at which China is represented by Nationalist delegates. I have never thought walking out of meetings and staying away from meetings was a good way to settle differences of opinion.

Enlarging upon this, I explained that while the Soviet boycott was serious enough, it was not the first consideration.

The 475,000,000 people of China are, collectively, original members of the United Nations by the terms of the Charter itself. They have a right to be represented in the United Nations by whatever government has the power to "employ the resources and direct the people of the state in fulfillment of the obligations of membership" in the United Nations. I repeat—whatever government is thus qualified, regardless of its ideology.

A good part of the speech was devoted to bringing home to my audience the need for a revival of faith in the universal United Nations approach to peace, coupled with a better understanding of the long years of struggle and reconstruction that lay ahead before peace could be made secure. I concluded, "What the world needs is a twenty-year program to win peace through the United Nations." This was the beginning of the ten-point peace program described in Chapter XVI.

The day after the B'nai B'rith dinner, I visited the State Department for a talk with Dean Rusk, John D. Hickerson and Philip C. Jessup. I expected little encouragement, and received less. Peking, I was told, was exhibiting an implacable behavior, having recently appropriated commodities belonging to the United States valued at $30,000,000. In response to my query, Mr. Rusk replied that no change was anticipated as far as his government's stand on the China issue was concerned. My apprehensions were thus confirmed: China seemed to be bent on a policy of irritation, with the inevitable results.

Returning to Lake Success, I went to work on my twenty-year program for achieving peace through the United Nations. With the China issue stalled, this approach now seemed to be the best opportunity for a revival of East-West negotiations in the United

Nations. On April 17 I was able to go through the draft memorandum with the Assistant Secretaries-General and several of the Principal Directors, and told them of my tentative plans to call at the four capitals: Washington, London, Paris and—if expedient—Moscow.

Only three days elapsed between this final conference with my aides and advisers, and the first in a series of conversations which ultimately took me halfway around the globe. The first visit was to Washington, where Byron Price and I were received by President Truman and Secretary of State Acheson on April 20.

The President and I knew each other's views on Chinese representation, and so I felt free to speak frankly—an approach which President Truman, at least, seemed to favor—expressing the belief that the preservation of the United Nations depended on finding a solution to this problem. I recalled what had happened in the case of the Soviet Union, and suggested that the worst possible policy would be to risk isolating China as the U.S.S.R. had been isolated.

The President interposed that the whole trouble was that nobody could trust the Communists: they would not keep their word; they would not tell the truth; and they would not permit their people to know the truth. There was proof of that every day in the pains they took to keep the facts away from the people.

Without debating this, I returned to my main point: The United Nations must be preserved as a meeting place of East and West. To do this the China issue had to be solved on a basis that recognized the realities. "While it would be a hard decision for the United States to take," I said, "nothing would really be lost. The Chinese people themselves have little confidence in the Nationalist leadership." I indicated a belief that if Tsiang were unseated, the Soviet representatives might return to the United Nations, even though the Chinese Communists were still excluded.

The conversation soon turned to Formosa, which had been causing me considerable concern. "This island's eight million inhabitants of Chinese descent," I began, "are far more advanced than the average mainland Chinese in matters of health, literacy, and industrial capacity. For this, they have an efficient, though ruthless Japanese administration to thank." Their advanced status strengthened doubts as to whether the great powers had dealt altogether justly with the islanders at the time they drew up surrender terms for Japan. "The people of Formosa should be allowed to express their own views as to their future. Perhaps they want independence." I went on that I was in doubt whether the island, as ruled by Chiang Kai-shek and his mainland forces, was not in much the same position as an occupied country.

I had not intended to go any further, but decided to recall, at least, the balance-of-power considerations involved. "If the present situation continues, there is a chance that the Chinese Communists will overrun Formosa. Thus occupied, the island would, for years to come, remain a military threat on the flank of the United States and other countries with interests in the South Pacific; becoming in time, a problem for the United Nations itself." It should be remembered that this was more than two months before President Truman ordered the 7th United States Fleet to protect Formosa from Communist attack. At the time Chiang was getting little United States aid and had no assurance of continued United States support. I suggested that Formosa might be put under United Nations trusteeship before it was too late, with a view to its people deciding their own fate, after perhaps five years. "I am only passing this idea on for what it is worth, and am not asking for your reaction here and now."

With each of us already clear as to where the other stood, I thought it unnecessary to pursue the subject of China any further. My main reason for combining it with the presentation of my peace-program draft, which consumed the remainder of our conversation, was once again to make this great power aware of the bearing of the representation issue upon chances for peace under any kind of program.

The next day I left for London by ship. There, the situation was much as before. Accompanied by David Owen, I spoke with Sir Gladwyn Jebb on April 28, explaining that while much of my peace program was not directly conditional upon a settlement of the Chinese problem, there could be little meaningful progress toward peace without the participation in the United Nations of the Soviet Union and the government which, in fact, controlled the Chinese mainland. Sir Gladwyn agreed, at the same time admitting that, though attempts had been made to persuade Egypt, Ecuador, Cuba, and France to a new stand no success had been achieved. Everything, he said, seemed to depend on the attitude of the United States, which was unwilling to give even informal encouragement to Member states considering supporting the admission of the new Chinese Government's representative.

Ernest Bevin was ill in the hospital at the time of my visit. Talks with Prime Minister Attlee and Minister of State Kenneth Younger, however, disclosed agreement with Sir Gladwyn Jebb's appraisal of the situation, as well as interest in the suggestion of trusteeship for Formosa.

We had no sooner arrived in Paris than President Vincent Auriol honored Assistant Secretary-General Henri Laugier and me with an invitation to dine. We talked for a long time about the China muddle, and the President and I agreed though he never let us forget that it was the Premier and the Cabinet that made policy. In a later conversation with Foreign Minister Robert Schuman and Alexandre Parodi, the former French permanent representative to the United Nations, I was pleased to find that both favored my approach. They repeated that they had been prepared to back the seating of the Peking representatives, and agreed that the matter would have to be settled in the Security Council. If it had not been for Peking's support of the Communists in Indochina, France would have voted long since to seat the Chinese Communists. French troops in Indochina had suffered considerable losses, and Peking's recognition of Ho Chi Minh had made it impossible for the French Government to take such a stand up to the present. However, they hoped the situation might change, and there might be a solution by May or early June.

I left the Quai d'Orsay hoping that the French would take a new stand soon—an impression supported by a subsequent talk with Premier Georges Bidault. "France was ready to recognize the Mao regime," he confirmed, "but when Mao and the U.S.S.R. recognized Ho Chi Minh recognition on our part was rendered impossible." He believed, nevertheless, that "on pourrait s'arranger" ("matters might be arranged"), as long as the new Chinese Government took no active steps to imperil French interests in Southeast Asia.

More hopeful now, I proceeded to Moscow. There would certainly be no difficulties in the Soviet capital—as far as China was concerned, at any rate.

My first conversation there was with Foreign Secretary Vyshinsky on May 12, when we exchanged information on the Security Council dilemma. I had long since resolved to make the most of this excellent opportunity to tell him just what I thought of Mr. Malik's walkout, as well as my opinion of the boycott as an instrument of policy in the United Nations. "This act," I emphasized, "was in violation of the Charter, and I am certain that the walkout of your representatives has in no way benefited the cause of China. In fact, China's position has suffered." I even indicated that the representation issue might have been solved long since, had it not been for China's mistakes and Soviet intransigence. "No country likes to act under pressure," I reminded Vyshinsky. He merely smiled and admitted the right of the Secretary-General "to argue along these lines."

During my talk with Generalissimo Stalin on May 15, however, the China question seemed to rate little more than a peripheral remark from Mr. Molotov. In connection with a point in the peace plan memorandum about periodic meetings of the Security Council, he asked why the memorandum failed to deal with the representation of the Chinese People's Republic in the United Nations. Did I think that the "present representatives from the capitalistic clique on Formosa" represented China? I broke in at once—and with some heat—to recall that the whole memorandum was based on the assumption that the Security Council had to resume *normal operations* before a single periodic meeting could be called. No more was said about China; Generalissimo Stalin had not uttered a word on the subject.

On the following day I had a chance to talk, for the first time, with an official representative of the Peking government. Wang Chia-hsiang, Chinese Ambassador to Moscow and Vice Foreign Minister, came to see me in the Hotel National.

My invitation was prompted, I told him, by a telegram received at Lake Success from the Foreign Minister at Peking referring to his government's representation in the World Health Organization, UNESCO, and the International Labor Organization. The telegram had demanded that the Specialized Agencies expel the representatives of the "reactionary Kuomintang clique on Formosa," because they did not represent the Republic of China. "Does this mean, then," I asked, "that the Peking government wants to maintain

China's membership in the Specialized Agencies and is willing to send credentials for its representatives?"

The Ambassador's reply was somewhat beside the point, conveying nothing more than that his government had sent the telegram to emphasize that the "Kuomintang" delegates did not represent the Chinese nation. "But no representative from the 'Kuomintang' government is actually attending the meetings of the Health Organization in Geneva," I interrupted. "When meetings opened on May 8, a telegram arrived from Formosa, stating that no Nationalist representative would attend. After all it is difficult to expel a delegate who is not even present." However, I suggested that in the light of the telegram the Peking Government might well send representatives to Geneva as a matter of course. "It would then be that much easier for the conference to make a decision as to new credentials."

The Ambassador seemed to have difficulty in grasping the situation—perhaps he did not want to grasp it. At any rate, I asked him to inform his government that no representatives from Formosa were then attending the WHO Conference in Geneva, but a duly accredited representative from Peking might obtain a seat if he were present. Further, I suggested the same procedure in the case of the UNESCO Conference opening in Florence on May 22. The Ambassador agreed to pass this information on to his government.

As might have been expected, Ambassador Wang Chia-hsiang's remarks were interspersed with the familiar Communist arguments and accusations. Though most of these called for no reply, one indicated that certain of my earlier fears were well founded. "The Democratic People's Government in Peking," he complained, "is supported only by the Soviet Union and its neighbors." I resolved to try to make it clear to him where a large part of the blame lay. "The Russian boycott and walkouts," I explained, "have not made it any easier to seat the Peking government in the various United Nations organs. Instead of helping, they have actually made things more difficult for you." But I might just as well have saved my breath. There was no trace of reaction in his impenetrable face.

Realizing that little had been achieved thus far, I saw a last recourse in directing an appeal to his government that those states which had extended recognition or were intending to extend it be met with at least a degree of understanding and good will. "The way in which some of the states already recognizing the Peking Government have been treated," I told him, "certainly does not lighten the task of bettering United-Nations–Chinese relations. Speaking on my own behalf, it is hardly encouraging to see how the Peking government has treated Great Britain. Neither has its treatment of the American government tended to improve matters. The closing of the consulates, the arrest of the Consul General, American military personnel, missionaries, and civilians, has swung American public opinion so strongly against the new China that the resulting damage will take a long time to repair." If attempts could be made to improve relations with these countries, I emphasized, the chance of an early decision on the representation issue would be appreciably improved.

"Of course it is not my duty to try and influence the Peking government to give up any of its political principles," I assured Ambassador Wang. "But there are many practical questions that could be settled to the satisfaction of both sides, and every agreement might help prompt a practical and reasonable settlement of the main issue. Until now, unfortunately, the Russian walkout and the Peking government's conduct toward the United Nations members have made a final settlement difficult, to say the least."

At this point he asked why Great Britain had abstained from voting in the Security Council after recognizing his government. "This probably reflects the conduct of the Peking government toward the British, especially as far as diplomatic relations between the two countries are concerned," I replied. When he asked about France, I explained that, in my opinion, Peking's recognition of Ho Chi Minh could do nothing other than force France to alter its views toward his government. "In fact, I know that France was almost ready to support the seating of your representatives in the Security Council, until Peking's recognition of the insurrectionists in Indochina so aroused French public opinion that the government simply had to take a new stand." Ambassador Wang had nothing to say to this.

Though the conversation had been rather one-sided, I was grateful for the opportunity to get my views conveyed to Peking. Still, there was no way of knowing how much he dared actually to report to

Mao Tse-tung and Chou En-lai. At all events, I was relieved when the interview with this unresponsive representative of the new China came to an end. I felt as if I had been talking to a monolith.

On May 18, just before leaving Moscow, I paid a farewell visit to Mr. Vyshinsky—as bearer of the bad news that Secretaries Bevin, Schuman, and Acheson, meeting in London, had agreed to postpone discussion on the Chinese question to the end of August or the beginning of September. I admitted being perturbed, adding that I would raise the issue anew on my return visits to Paris and London.

When I took the matter up with Mr. Schuman in Paris on May 20 there was no mistaking that France had been dragged along as a third party to the London decision. He assured me that, while he was not unreservedly bound to postponement of the Chinese question, he felt that the United States and Great Britain would have to be consulted before France allowed new developments to change its position. His own view was that we must have a decision before August. The Security Council must be operating normally not later than July: we could not let this go on any longer, he said. He then recapitulated the factors calling for the seating of representatives from the government which administered and controlled the Chinese mainland. This had been his opinion for many months, as well as that of his experts in the Ministry of Foreign Affairs.

Not once in all my conversations on the subject had I heard a statesman of the Western democracies express himself more clearly as to just who governed China and—consequently—who should represent that country in the United Nations.

I met Ernest Bevin on May 23. The long and somewhat surprising conversation finally swung around to China, with my remark that I hoped Great Britain would actively support representation of China in the United Nations by the Peking government. To my astonishment, Mr. Bevin seemed to take this as a left-handed criticism of the agreement earlier in the month between Schuman, Acheson, and himself; but he quickly recovered and asserted that Great Britain had tried to induce other countries to recognize the Peking government, and would persist in the attempt. Complaining of the barriers the Chinese Communists had placed in the way of normal diplomatic relations, he expressed the view—consonant with one stated earlier to me by Sir Alexander Cadogan—that the Soviet Union was not really interested in seeing Peking seated as a Member because an isolated China would be more susceptible to Soviet control.

On returning to New York I proceeded at once to Washington for yet another meeting with Secretary of State Acheson and Assistant Secretary Hickerson, on May 29.

The United States could not change its policy toward the Chinese Communist Government for the time being: that much was clear from Mr. Acheson's opening statements. When Assistant Secretary Hickerson asked my opinion of the true significance of the Russian walkout I replied that the Russians had miscalculated—"just as they did during the Berlin Blockade and in so many other instances where they were misled by one-sided information or acted out of sheer ignorance. They probably thought they could win their point within a few weeks and be back in full force after a short interlude." Mr. Acheson answered with the remark that, in the eyes of the United States, success of such a maneuver would be damaging. "If it worked this time, Moscow would feel free to indulge in similar blackmail whenever it failed to get its way in the future, and the entire machinery of the United Nations could be paralyzed."

This visit to Washington was my last attempt, as Secretary-General, to help resolve the issue of Chinese representation in the United Nations. Less than a month later the Korean War broke out and the Security Council's prompt and clear-cut response to the armed aggression brought the Soviet Union back to the Security Council in a vain effort to undermine the United Nations action.

A letter of July 27 from the Permanent Representative of the U.S.S.R. informed me that, with the next month, he was assuming the presidency of the Security Council in his turn, and he was calling a first meeting at three o'clock on August 1. Soon afterward, he asked me to notify all Council members that the Security Council would deal with the following provisional agenda: (a) approval of the agenda; (b) recognition of the representative of the Central People's Government of the People's Republic of China as the representative of China; (c) peaceful settlement of the Korean question.

Mr. Malik's return in August was as sensational as his walkout in January.

The Russians were back; but that is all that was "normal again" about what occurred in the Security Council during the month of

August. Mr. Malik's sabotage and splendid disregard for all rules and regulations bordered on the grotesque. However, with the Russian representative back in the Security Council with Dr. Tsiang, the question of Chinese representation automatically took second place to the more pressing issue to be settled.

In November General MacArthur reported to the Security Council that Chinese troops had launched an attack against the United Nations defenders of the Korean Republic. In short, troops of the People's Republic of China had gone to war against the United Nations. For the duration of the fighting, that ended my interest in seating the Peking government in the United Nations.

On several occasions before, and after, Communist China's appearance as a combatant in the Korean War I wondered whether I might not have overestimated the bearing of the Soviet walkout upon the future of the United Nations. Perhaps, on the basis of hindsight, I had done so. But during the spring of 1950 the United Nations was in danger; and my reasoning in the China issue was based, I believe, on unassailable political and constitutional considerations under the United Nations Charter. Subsequent events in no way improved the general situation or relaxed basic tensions. I am still convinced that had my efforts been allowed to bear fruit, and in time, we might have witnessed a Soviet return, coupled with an improvement on the international scene, rather than a return motivated by events bordering on international catastrophe.

I have also wondered whether there might have been any Korean War at all, had the Peking Government been permitted to represent China in the United Nations in the spring of 1950. Was this aggression launched with Russian connivance alone, without advance endorsement by a Chinese partner not yet recognized-in international society? Could the drive of the Soviet Union's North Korean satellite toward Pusan have been part of a plan to compensate for the promised Soviet relinquishment of Dairen and Port Arthur? Was there not at least a possibility that Soviet strategists were worrying not only about Japan and the American bases there—but also about this rising new power on the Chinese mainland as a future competitor for influence in the Far East? Finally, would the Peking government have dared to send its armies as "volunteers" into North Korea had it been represented at Lake Success, bound by the obligations of United Nations membership and forced to defend itself in the "Town Meeting of the World"?

Perhaps no one now can answer these questions; but other participants in the events have pondered their significance and ask the same questions. One of them is Sir Gladwyn Jebb, who, speaking at Baltimore, Maryland, January 13, 1954, went so far as to declare: "It could even be argued with some force that, had the government of Peking been represented in the United Nations at the beginning of 1950, the North Korean aggression might never have occurred at all." At all events I am still convinced that my efforts in the spring of 1950 to resolve the Chinese representation issue were right.

What now can the future bring with respect to China's representation? The Peking government had become the enemy of the United Nations. Its soldiers were used deliberately to kill the defenders of the United Nations Charter, and those who were carrying out the resolutions of that body. Furthermore, no one can attain membership or representation in the United Nations by menace. No nation can shoot its way into the Organization.

But with the Armistice? Can the representation issue possibly be solved unless the Peking government agrees to hold to the principles of the Charter? In my opinion, no Member—above all, no permanent Member—can continue to place itself beyond these precepts. The United Nations has been established to place it in the power of all countries of the world "to practice tolerance and live together in peace with one another as good neighbors, and to unite [their] strength to maintain international peace and security, and to ensure, by the acceptance of principles and the institution of methods, that armed force shall not be used.". . .

Not only has Peking transgressed these binding regulations, but has also violated the Charter's obligatory Article 1: "The purposes of the United Nations are: To maintain international peace and security, and to that end: to take effective collective measures for the prevention and removal of threats to the peace, and for the suppression of acts of aggression or other breaches of the peace, and to bring about by peaceful means, and in conformity with the principles of justice and international law, adjustment or settlement of international disputes or situations which might lead to a breach of the peace."

Permanent Members, just as much as new Members, are bound by the stipulation of Article 4: "Membership in the United Nations is open to all other peace-loving states which accept the obligations contained in the present Charter and, in the judgment of the Organization, are able and willing to carry out these obligations."

In fact, the Central People's Government of the People's Republic of China faces a difficult trial before it in faith and in truth can be accorded representation of "the Republic of China" in the United Nations.

CHAPTER XVI

MY PEACE MISSION—
OUTWARD BOUND

*My memorandum of points for a twenty-year peace program.
—Why I decided to attempt it.—Visits to Washington, London, Paris, and Prague.—Arrival in Moscow.*

THE EFFORTS to find a solution of the problem of Chinese representation were prompted by wider misgivings about the course of the cold war. The end of the Berlin blockade had been followed by the failure of the deputies at the Palais Rose in Paris to agree on the agenda for a new meeting of the Council of Foreign Ministers. For many months the Western powers and Moscow had not had any significant diplomatic contact with each other. The Soviet Union had concentrated on the new alliance with the People's Republic of China, with which it was closely linking its Eastern European system. The foreign offices in Washington, London, and Paris, on their side, were devoting themselves to the creation of a Western defense system through the North Atlantic Treaty. The United Nations—the one organization keeping the world together—was relegated to a back seat in all the great-power foreign offices as the cleavage between two great concentrations of armed power hardened and widened. On top of all this, the usefulness of the United Nations itself as a bridge across the chasm was at an end so long as the Soviet boycott continued.

Something must be attempted. I did not underestimate the difficulty of reopening negotiations with the Communist world. I favored the North Atlantic Treaty Organization and other measures to strengthen the West, but not at the cost of allowing the United Nations to wither on the vine. That, I was firmly convinced, would be a disastrous and probably irreparable blunder in a world where atomic stockpiles were growing month by month. The United Nations remained the best hope for peace in the long run and the most constructive force for understanding and cooperation in international life. The instincts of the people were in this direction, I was certain, but were not encouraged by their governments. All the resources of leadership and planning seemed to me to be devoted only to winning support for a short-term policy of alliances backed by increased armaments. The longer perspective was receiving less attention—the necessity to prepare in every possible way for an ultimate peaceful settlement of the cold war as the alternative to a Third World War, even though such a settlement might be years, or even decades away.

With these considerations in mind I cast about for some means to restore the United Nations as a meeting place, and at the same time give a timely reminder to both governments and peoples that the purposes and principles of San Francisco were as essential to ultimate peace in 1950 as they had been in 1945.

My B'nai B'rith speech in Washington on March 21, 1950, which was the forerunner, sought throughout to recall the lasting and central significance of the United Nations to the struggle for peace in all its manifestations—political, economic, and social. It emphasized the long-term nature of the task: "I do not believe in political miracles. It will take a long series of steps to reduce the tensions of the conflict and bring the great powers together." And it concluded with the following words:

I have been encouraged by the recent affirmations from the two leading great powers—the United States and the Soviet Union—about the possibilities of peaceful co-existence between them and between the different economic and political systems they represent. The United Nations was founded upon that belief, and the hope of world peace depends upon its validity.

What we need, what the world needs, is a twenty-year program to win peace through the United Nations.

I believe that most people everywhere in the world will join me in the desire and hope that the Member governments of the United Nations will make renewed efforts to get together on the first steps of such a United Nations peace program without delay.

This speech received wide publicity, and there was an immediate and positive response. The Vice President of the United States, Alben W. Barkley, seconded me on the spot. A few days later the unswerving supporters of the United Nations, Carlos P. Romulo (Philippines), Oswaldo Aranha (Brazil), Herbert Evatt (Australia), and Mahmoud Fawzi Bey (Egypt), issued strong supporting statements. Understanding articles appeared in leading American dailies as well as in Canada, France, the United Kingdom, the Nordic countries, India, Israel, and Latin America. Surprisingly enough, the comments of Moscow Radio and Pravda were almost conciliatory.

A flood of letters from all corners of the globe convinced me that public opinion was on my side. Most appreciated of all was the one signed by Albert Einstein, dean of all scientists:

I feel I must wish you luck and success with your great initiative. You are one of the very few who in the midst of the bewilderment and confusion of our time has succeeded in keeping his vision clear, and whose urge to help remains undeterred by obstacles and narrow allegiances. May your concrete proposals succeed in showing us a way out of the present tension, occasioned as it is more by emotional factors than by material causes, and in providing a solution advantageous to all concerned. Even relatively small successes in the direction of economic cooperation should soon improve and stabilize the political and emotional situation.

Soon afterward I completed a "Memorandum of Points for Consideration in the Development of a Twenty-Year Program for Achieving Peace Through the United Nations."

"Why a twenty-year program?" was asked at my press conference in New York on March 24. I was glad for the opportunity to answer: "I used that phrase because I wanted to let everyone know that the question of peace in the world is one which cannot be settled immediately, but which will take time. We should all be happy if it could be settled within five years, or ten years, or twenty years. But I think the differences have multiplied each year since 1945; so we should not be too optimistic about the chances of getting a real peace settlement."

The press did not know that I was then completing my ten-point memorandum, much less that I would carry it in person to Washington, London, Paris, and Moscow on a trip in April and May that would extend some fifteen thousand miles.

The memorandum itself, I decided to keep secret until I had talked with the heads of government and the foreign ministers of the United States, the United Kingdom, France, and the U.S.S.R. Though the text was purposely drawn up in general terms, it was essential to frank and private discussion that not even this be on record ahead of time.

The memorandum, as it was handed personally to President Truman, Prime Minister Attlee, Premier Bidault, and Generalissimo Stalin, is as follows:

As Secretary-General, it is my firm belief that a new and great effort must be attempted to end the so-called "cold war" and to set the world once more on a road that will offer greater hope of lasting peace.

The atmosphere of deepening international mistrust can be dissipated and the threat of the universal disaster of another war averted by employing to the full the resources for conciliation and constructive peace-building present in the United Nations Charter. The employment of these resources can secure eventual peace if we accept, believe and act upon the possibility of peaceful coexistence among all the Great Powers and the different economic and political systems they represent, and if the Great Powers evidence a readiness to undertake genuine negotiation—not in a spirit of appeasement, but with enlightened self-interest and common sense on all sides.

Measures for collective self-defence and regional remedies of other kinds are at best interim measures, and cannot alone bring any reliable security from the prospect of war. The one common undertaking and universal instrument of the great majority of the human race is the United Nations. A patient, constructive long-term use of its potentialities can bring a real and secure peace to the world. I am certain that such an effort will have the active interest and support of the smaller Member States, who have much to contribute in the conciliation of Big Power differences and in the development of constructive and mutually advantageous political and economic cooperation.

I therefore venture to suggest certain points for consideration in the formulation of a twenty-year United Nations Peace Program. Certain of these points call for urgent action. Others are of a long-range nature, requiring continued effort over the next twenty years. I shall not discuss the problems of the peace settlements for Austria, Germany and Japan—because the founders of the United Nations indicated that the peace settlements should be made separately from the United Nations. But I believe that the progress of a United Nations Peace Program such as is here suggested will help to bring these settlements far closer to attainment.

1. *Inauguration of periodic meetings of the Security Council, attended by foreign ministers, or heads or other members of governments, as provided by the United Nations Charter and the rules of procedure; together with further development and use of other United Nations machinery for negotiation, mediation and conciliation of international disputes.*

The periodic meetings of the Security Council provided for in Article 28 of the Charter have never been held. Such periodic meetings should be held semiannually, beginning with one in 1950. In my opinion, they should be used for a general review at a high level of outstanding issues in the United Nations, particularly those that divide the Great Powers. They should not be expected to produce great decisions every time; they should be used for consultation—much of it in private—for efforts to gain ground toward agreement on questions at issue, to clear up misunderstandings, to prepare for new initiatives that may improve the chances for definite agreement at later meetings. They should be held away from Headquarters as a general rule, in Geneva, the capitals of the Permanent Members and in other regions of the world.

Further development of the resources of the United Nations for mediation and conciliation should be undertaken, including reestablishment of the regular practice of private consultations by the representatives of the five Great Powers, and a renewed effort to secure agreement by all the Great Powers on limitations on the use of the veto power in the pacific settlement procedures of the Security Council.

2. *A new attempt to make progress toward establishing an international control system for atomic energy that will be effective in preventing its use for war and promoting its use for peaceful purposes.*

We cannot hope for any quick or easy solution of this most difficult problem of atomic energy control. The only way to find out what is possible is to resume negotiation in line with the directive of the General Assembly last fall "to explore all possible avenues and examine all concrete suggestions with a view to determining what might lead to an agreement." Various suggestions for finding a basis for a fresh approach have been put forward. One possibility would be for the Security Council to instruct the Secretary-General to call a conference of scientists whose discussions might provide a reservoir of new ideas on the control of weapons of mass destruction and the promotion of peaceful uses of atomic energy that could thereafter be explored in the United Nations Atomic Energy Commission. Or, it may be that an interim agreement could be worked out that would at least be some improvement on the present situation of an unlimited atomic arms race, even though it did not afford full security. There are other possibilities for providing the basis for a new start; every possibility should be explored.

3. *A new approach to the problem of bringing the armaments race under control, not only in the field of atomic weapons, but in other weapons of mass destruction and in conventional armaments.*

Here is another area where it is necessary to reactivate negotiation and to make new efforts at finding some area of common ground. It must be recognized that up to now there has been virtually a complete failure here and that the immediate prospects seem poor indeed. Clearly disarmament requires an atmosphere of confidence in which political disputes are brought nearer to solution. But it is also true that any progress at all towards agreement on the regulation of armaments of any kind would help to reduce cold war tensions and thus assist in the adjustment of political disputes. Negotiation on this problem should not be deferred until the other great political problems are solved, but should go hand in hand with any effort to reach political settlements.

4. *A renewal of serious efforts to reach agreement on the armed forces to be made available under the Charter to the Security Council for the enforcement of its decisions.*

A new approach should be made towards resolving existing differences on the size, location and composition of the forces to be pledged to the Security Council under Article 43 of the Charter. Basic political difficulties which may delay a final solution should not be permitted to stand in the way of some sort of interim accord for a small force sufficient to prevent or stop localized outbreaks threatening international peace. The mere existence of such a force would greatly enhance the ability of the Security Council to bring about peaceful settlements in most of the cases which are likely to come before it.

5. *Acceptance and application of the principle that it is wise and right to proceed as rapidly as possible towards universality of membership.*

Fourteen nations are now awaiting admission to the United Nations. In the interests of the people of these countries and of the United Nations, I believe they should all be admitted, as well as other countries which will attain their independence in the future. It should be made clear that Germany and Japan would also be admitted as soon as the peace treaties have been completed.

6. *A sound and active program of technical assistance for economic*

development and encouragement of broadscale capital investment, using all appropriate private, governmental and intergovernmental resources.

A technical assistance program is in its beginnings, assisted by the strong support of the President of the United States. Its fundamental purpose is to enable the people of the underdeveloped countries to raise their standard of living peacefully by specific and practicable measures. It should be a continuing and expanding program for the next twenty years and beyond, carried forward with the cooperation of all Member Governments, largely through the United Nations and the Specialized Agencies, with mutual beneficial programs planned and executed on a basis of equality rather than on a basis of charity. Through this means the opportunities can be opened up for capital investment on a large and expanding scale. Here lies one of our best hopes for combating the dangers and costs of the cold war.

7. *More vigorous use by all Member Governments of the Specialized Agencies of the United Nations to promote, in the words of the Charter, "higher standards of living, full employment, and conditions of economic and social progress."*

The great potentialities of the Specialized Agencies to partcipate in a long-range program aimed at drastically reducing the economic and social causes of war, can be realized by more active support from all Governments, including the membership of the Soviet Union in some or all of the Agencies to which it does not now belong. The expansion of world trade which is vital to any long-range effort for world betterment requires the early ratification of the Charter of the International Trade Organization.

8. *Vigorous and continued development of the work of the United Nations for wider observance and respect for human rights and fundamental freedoms throughout the world.*

It is becoming evident that the Universal Declaration of Human Rights, adopted by the General Assembly in 1948 without a dissenting vote, is destined to become one of the great documents of history. The United Nations is now engaged on a program that will extend over the next twenty years—and beyond—to secure the extension and wider observance of the political, economic and social rights there set down. Its success needs the active support of all Governments.

9. *Use of the United Nations to promote, by peaceful means instead of by force, the advancement of dependent, colonial or semicolonial peoples, towards a place of equality in the world.*

The great changes which have been taking place since the end of the war among the peoples of Asia and Africa must be kept within peaceful bounds by using the universal framework of the United Nations. The old relationship will have to be replaced with new ones of equality and fraternity. The United Nations is the instrument capable of bringing such a transition to pass without violent upheavals and with the best prospect of bringing long-run economic and political benefits to all nations of the world.

10. *Active and systematic use of all the powers of the Charter and all the machinery of the United Nations to speed up the development of international law towards an eventual enforceable world law for a universal world society.*

These three last points deal with programs already under way to carry out important principles of the United Nations Charter. They respond to basic human desires and aspirations, and coordinated efforts by all Governments to further these programs are indispensable to the eventual peaceful stabilization of international relations. There are many specific steps which need to be taken: for example, under Point 10, ratification of the Genocide Convention, greater use of the International Court of Justice, and systematic development and codification of international law. More important is that Governments should give high priority in their national policies to the continued support and development of these ideals which are at the foundation of all striving of the peoples for a better world.

What is here suggested is only an outline of preliminary proposals for a program; much more development will be needed. It is self-evident that every step mentioned, every proposal made, will require careful and detailed, even laborious preparation, negotiation and administration. It is equally self-evident that the necessary measure of agreement will be hard to realize most of the time, and even impossible some of the time. Yet the world can never accept the thesis of despair—the thesis of irrevocable and irreconcilable conflict.

My mission was to be in the cause not only of peace, but of reason. I started out with no illusions, because I felt that the mood of the great powers at the time was not receptive to the long view or to any attempt to break the ice jam blocking negotiation. On the other hand I was fortified by the belief that the people everywhere were with me, and that they knew I was right to try. That belief was to be borne out in full measure in the course of my trip and afterwards, when I published my ten-point program. Never, before or since, have I received so many thousands of letters from men and women all over the world, expressing their support for my initiative and wishing me success.

I resolved to plan the trip in such a way as to leave copies of my memorandum in Washington, London, and Paris on the way to Moscow without discussion of its substance until my return from talks with the Soviet leaders. This was to be an exploration, not a negotiation. I would also take the opportunity of the visits to the four capitals to discuss not only the problem of Chinese representation but other matters of concern to the United Nations.

The following account of the conversations is based on detailed notes made during or immediately after each meeting. It reveals for the first time what was said on behalf of the governments approached and by myself.[*]

IN WASHINGTON

I began with Washington, the capital closest to United Nations Headquarters, because it would have been highly illogical to travel across the Atlantic first—whatever attempts to misconstrue the purpose of the visit might later be made.

On April 20, shortly after twelve o'clock, I called on President Truman in his office at the White House. Present at the meeting that day were Secretary of State Dean Acheson and United Nations Assistant Secretary-General Byron Price.

Mr. Truman gave us a typically cordial reception. Then we settled ourselves, and I began to go over the current position of the United Nations, by way of introduction:

"My information is probably in no way as complete as that of the State Department, which has its representatives everywhere; but, on the basis of what information I have, I am encouraged to believe that the Soviet Government is not now planning any permanent withdrawal from the United Nations. In fact, I feel more optimistic on this point than I have for some time.

"Still," I continued, "the situation is most unsatisfactory. No formula has been developed—even after long discussions—for bringing Soviet representatives back to the United Nations meetings, and the trend of discussion on the part of those concerned generally seems to relate to means for *winning* the 'cold war' instead of *ending* it." Here, I was careful to make an exception of the President who, I noted, "instead of talking about winning the 'cold war' has always

[*] See Chapter XV for the part relating to China.

been more concerned about means to establish a lasting peace."

President Truman nodded concurringly: Yes, he had been talking about a secure and enduring peace, and working for it, and would keep on.

At this point, I drew from a dispatch case a copy of my Memorandum outlining the ten possibilities within the United Nations which might be regarded as steps toward a twenty-year program for peace, and handed it to the President. Mr. Acheson also received a copy. "You will understand," I remarked, "that this implies no request for immediate comment. But I do hope that my Memorandum will be examined carefully." The President assured me that it would be.

Further to emphasize the actual potentialities of the United Nations as an instrument for securing the peace, I recalled what United Nations representatives had been able to accomplish with no show of force, and with only the distinction of the United Nations armband in such places as Palestine, Indonesia, Kashmir, and Greece. "In Western Europe," I pointed out, "communism has been stopped through the Marshall Plan and other peaceful measures." I emphasized my belief in the importance of technical assistance in preserving freedom and peace in other parts of the world. "Economic development and international trade are certain to be tremendously important factors in building a lasting peace."

Here the President interjected that, in his view too, they were extremely important.

As the conversation ended I remarked that I well understood the reluctance of the United States to have any dealings with the Chinese Communists: "If I am able to speak with Stalin in the future, I will try to impress him with the seriousness of this situation."

The President volunteered then that he liked Stalin personally. He had gone to Potsdam, he said, with the friendliest possible feeling and was even ready to consider a six billion dollar reconstruction loan to Russia; but he had received a slap in the face. He repeated that things could never be settled on a rational basis as long as the Russians persisted in their attitude toward the outside world, blocking all helpful communication and exchange of information; but he was not going to despair. His own devotion to peace was exactly the same as mine, and we should simply have to go on working for peace as best we could.

Rising, he thanked me again for this visit and for the Memorandum. The discussion had been most helpful, he repeated.

IN LONDON

Accompanied by David Owen, my British Assistant Secretary-General, I had two meetings in London on April 28: respectively with Prime Minister Attlee, and with Minister of State Kenneth Younger. Foreign Secretary Ernest Bevin was ill and in a hospital.

Mr. Attlee was pleasant and attentive but had little to say. I told him of my deep concern about the present international situation and its effects on the work of the United Nations, and explained that my mission was to see whether some basis could be found for ending the "cold war," at any rate over a period of years. He replied that he appreciated my efforts and was glad that I had come to London to see him.

I went on to say: "What a tragedy it is that now, when we have a really efficient international machine, its work is being frustrated by political divisions, culminating in the 'cold war.'"

I then presented my Memorandum. Mr. Attlee said he would read it with great interest, and have it examined carefully. He would also be glad to know how the Soviet government received it.

I thanked the Prime Minister for the admirable speeches he had made in the last few years on the United Nations: "It has helped greatly to have such influential support at such a time." He was grateful, adding that the speeches had sincerely expressed his convictions. I went on to develop the view that Britain (together with France) should do more to act as a balancing force between the two great powers if peace was to be maintained. I had been a little disappointed in Britain's playing a less active role in the United Nations than in the League of Nations, though I fully understood the difficulties. "But does not the present political situation afford a great opportunity for the Labor government to mobilize the many forces in the country which look to the United Nations as the one place where all outstanding international questions can be dealt with by methods of conciliation? Arms pacts are still necessary, but ordinary people prefer more direct expressions of the wish for peace." Mr. Attlee nodded in agreement, or seeming agreement. He thought there might be much in what I said.

At the end of the interview I repeated that the United Nations must be made to work more effectively, and that it was the only place in which the issues which underlay the "cold war" could be discussed by all the parties concerned. The Prime Minister replied that I was right in this.

Kenneth Younger, when we met, was his usual forthright self. Commenting on my introductory remark that if war was to be avoided the moderating influence of a middle force might be a decisive factor, he voiced serious doubts as to what good this would do in the current situation: the difficulty was that one side in this "cold war" made absolutely no concessions and showed no response to efforts toward mediation and conciliation.

Then, with a directness which I appreciated, he asked what I thought it possible to accomplish in Moscow. Disclaiming optimism as to the outcome of the trip, I said I felt obligated to speak openly and frankly with Stalin and Molotov concerning the consequences of their present policy: "My main purpose is to get them back as cooperating participants in the United Nations, and to emphasize the way in which they are endangering themselves by hardening world opinion against them. Should they persist in boycotting the meetings, I shall have to try and find how far they are prepared to cooperate along the lines of the memorandum I have prepared."

Younger still had doubts. Persons coming away from high-policy discussions with Stalin, he commented, generally seemed to get the impression that they had achieved favorable results, only to be disappointed at the practical outcome. "Something seems to go wrong at the next level below Stalin," he observed. "It seems necessary to make an impression on Molotov and Vyshinsky, to say the least, and it may well be that there are even more influential elements today whose names are not familiar to us."

IN PARIS

In Paris I had a number of excellent discussions with leading French statesmen, including President Vincent Auriol, Prime Minister Georges Bidault, and Foreign Minister Robert Schuman.

During an intimate dinner, given on May 1, in the small dining room of the Elysée, President Auriol and I had a general discussion

MY PEACE MISSION—OUTWARD BOUND

on the world situation from the point of view of the United Nations and from the particular point of view of France. I informed him of my intention of going to Moscow, and of announcing that decision —which was still confidential—to the press as soon as I had met Messrs. Schuman and Bidault.

The President expressed his best wishes for the success of my mission to Moscow. He especially asked me to declare to the Soviet government that France would never be a party to any aggression against the U.S.S.R., but that the U.S.S.R. should stop Cominform action within the democracies and should show a willingness to cooperate and to reach a solution as regards the problems of disarmament, both for atomic and other weapons.

I also brought up the subject of Indo-China. I told Mr. Auriol that I had been informed in Washington that the United States would not send military forces to aid the French in their hard battle in Indo-China against the Communist Viet Minh. Under these circumstances, he agreed that the United Nations—granted the return of the Soviet representatives and the seating of the Chinese Communists—might be a most useful forum where pressure could be exerted to bring lasting peace to Indo-China. The sending of a commission, together with United Nations military observers, we agreed, would effectively serve the interests of peace as well as of France.

Mr. Bidault, too, was deeply concerned by the potential threat to Indo-China. In this connection I had certain suggestions to air— mainly for the purpose of showing what the United Nations would be able to do toward relieving the situation. "The first and essential step," I suggested, "is to get the U.S.S.R. to renew full cooperation in the United Nations. If the Security Council can resume normal operations again, France might bring this problem before it, claiming a threat to the integrity of Indo-China. The U.S.S.R. would veto any action. Thereupon, France could bring the matter before the General Assembly, which, by a majority vote, could adopt a formal resolution in her favor, and—as in the case of Greece—send a control mission to the area with military observers, to stand watch against foreign intervention from across the frontier." To his request for a little time to consider the matter, I replied that, in any event, I should see him again on my return from Moscow.

Mr. Bidault was glad to receive my memorandum. I told him

that, in Moscow, I would state my belief that the current division of the world in two blocs in a state of "cold war," if continued, might lead to a world conflict; that I firmly believed that by using the machinery of the United Nations and adhering to the conception of "one world" which it embodied, the nations could be set on the road to peace; and I would urge in Moscow, as I had urged in Washington, London, and Paris, that a great new effort be made to this end. He indicated his general approval of this approach and of the course of action which I had decided to take.

"In Moscow," I said, "I intend to be frank. I will clearly indicate the mistrust with which the Soviet government and its policies are regarded in the West and the effect on public opinion all over the world of its refusal to participate in joint action with international controls, to meet the terrible threat of atomic war." The most serious and tragic thing, Mr. Bidault commented, "is that one cannot talk to them. Say to them, if you can, that the key to the whole problem lies in supervision [*contrôle*] . . . it can be done either by having Russians in the United States and Americans in Russia, or by having Swiss everywhere."

Mr. Bidault wished me luck and told me that, even if my visit resulted only in some little step forward, he would consider it a most important success.

Mr. Schuman was friendly and pleasant as always. We spoke about Formosa and French Indo-China. I gave him my memorandum and stressed the importance of Great Britain and France together now playing a more active role in the United Nations. If France and Great Britain could exert a moderating influence, we should have a better chance of coming through the "cold war," which, if allowed to continue as at present, could very well lead to a real war. We both agreed on the last point. He emphasized that France as usual would be independent in the present situation despite internal difficulties.

IN PRAGUE

During a short stopover in Prague on Wednesday May 10, I had time for an interview at the Foreign Office with the newly appointed Minister of Foreign Affairs, Viliam Siroky. Deputy Foreign Minister

Sekaninova-Cakrtova acted as interpreter. The conversation did not concern the ten-point peace program. I include this account, however, because it throws light on the kind of people Moscow seems to depend on in the satellite governments behind the iron curtain.

We began with a somewhat general exchange of remarks on the current situation—on the issue of Chinese membership in the United Nations and the increasing seriousness of the "cold war." Mr. Siroky, as I had expected, lost little time in coming forward with the familiar Communist broadsides against the United States, Great Britain, and Messrs. Truman, Attlee, Acheson, and Bevin. I was used to this propaganda in United Nations debates, and I was not going to waste time listening to it now. I interrupted to tell him that what he was saying about the United States and Britain was similar to what was said in those countries about the Soviet Union and its neighbors. "If I had not believed that Truman, Acheson, Bevin, and Attlee—as well as Stalin and Vyshinsky—were all interested in peace," I continued, "I would never have decided to make this trip. And I have reason to trust that the Great Power leaders are trying to do their best for their respective countries. But at this stage, they have drawn so far apart that they are no longer able to talk together. And if the present 'cold war' continues, it will, sooner or later, slip over into a 'hot war.' Were it only possible for the leaders—the true leaders—to refrain from using abusive language against each other, and, instead, get down to solving the outstanding problems through patient discussion, then there might be some hope for avoiding a third war in our lifetime. But if it goes on as now," I concluded, "there is little chance for even a modified peace to last much longer."

This having been said—in exactly the way I had wanted to say it —I proceeded to the question of the Greek children, who had been abducted to Communist countries during the guerrilla war in Greece. I recalled the General Assembly resolutions of 1948 and 1949 and made it clear that something would have to be done toward carrying them out. Mr. Siroky assured me that these resolutions were, of course, binding for Czechoslovakia, but . . . And then came all the *but*'s and *if*'s. In the first place, he argued, it was not certain that the parents really wanted the children back. Secondly, the parents or other relatives were probably in prisons or concentration camps, and of course the children couldn't possibly be sent there. Thirdly, even if the parents or other relatives had expressed the wish that the children be returned, there was no way of knowing whether they really wanted them; they might have been forced to write the letters asking for their return.

At this point Madame Sekaninova joined the discussion, outdoing Siroky in abuse and distortion of the case. As calmly as I could, I repeated over and over again—between charges and accusations—that the children had to be sent home, and at once. "Nothing," I emphasized, "absolutely nothing, has harmed Czechoslovakia and other countries harboring Greek children more than has their present unwillingness to return them. Every normal father and mother, grandfather and grandmother, aunt and uncle, wherever they may be in the world, feel their best instincts offended by this lack of response. Although Czechoslovakia and the other countries concerned have promised to return these children, they are still being held without moral reason."

I recalled that the resolution of 1948 had requested the International Red Cross and the Red Cross organizations in the countries concerned to cooperate in assuring the children's return. These organizations, I maintained, could determine whether the children were really wanted by their parents or relatives. "Why," I asked, "did the Czech Red Cross fail to attend the meeting held by the International Red Cross in Geneva in March?" There was no answer.

Throughout most of this somewhat hectic exchange, Madame Sekaninova had kept up a near-constant babble to the effect that "the children are much happier here than they would be in Greece," or "we are not interested in returning them to concentration camps." I soon had enough. I was not interested in this kind of discussion, and therefore closed suddenly, thanked them in a few words for receiving me, and left. My parting statement, as I recall it, reminded them that "the future of the United Nations also depends upon Czechoslovakia's respecting the resolution of 1948 and acting in accordance therewith."

I was somewhat depressed when I boarded the special plane that the Soviet government had provided for the last lap of the journey to Moscow. There a different reception awaited me.

IN MOSCOW

On Saturday May 13, Assistant Secretary-General Constantin Zinchenko came to my room in the Hotel National in Moscow. Smiling broadly, and apparently highly satisfied, he informed me that a meeting with Generalissimo Stalin had been arranged for Monday May 15, at 10:00 P.M.

By Monday morning, the laryngitis I had developed en route from London and Paris was somewhat improved. Upon arrival in Moscow I had been compelled to ask for medical care. That day I was still under doctor's orders. The two Russian specialists, Professor Feldmann and Dr. Dimidoff, came for a final visit in the morning and administered a last nasal injection of penicillin. The cotton was removed from my ear, and I was told that, with reasonable care, there would be nothing to prevent my returning to Paris by plane within two or three days. At the time I thought little of it; but I have often recalled, since, that Professor Feldmann was never alone with me for a moment—it was almost as though Dr. Dimidoff had been sent along to keep an eye on him. Was the professor suspected even then —some two years before the Moscow physicians hoax, where he stood among the defendants?

I worked most of Monday on a plan for the evening's conversation, preparing and ordering the notes I would have ready at hand. I was informed that Molotov would be present at the interview—a development I had not anticipated when I had requested a separate meeting with him earlier. Vyshinsky would also be on hand—he was, after all, the Foreign Minister.

At eight o'clock that evening, my party and I were to have been the guests of the Foreign Ministry at a folk-dance ballet then playing at the Moiowitz Theatre. Besides Mr. Zinchenko, I had brought to Moscow only my Norwegian secretary, Mrs. Ingrid Berntzen, and another Norwegian, Olav Rytter, who headed the United Nations Information Office in Prague, and whose extensive knowledge of the Slavic languages might be useful. In view of the "command performance" I was about to attend at the Kremlin, I asked these associates to go to the ballet without me; but I requested Michael Vavilov, the acting head of the United Nations Information Center in Moscow, to return early, so that the car and all details could be in order by a quarter to ten. When they had gone Chargé d'Affaires Helge Akre from the Norwegian Embassy sat down with me for dinner, and we sampled the Hotel National's famed caviar, and talked about everything except the forthcoming meeting. By half past nine I was prepared to leave for the Kremlin. Vavilov saw me into the car, which took me to the same obscure side entrance through which I had entered on previous visits. Five minutes later, the well known interpreter Pavlov ushered me into Generalissimo Stalin's conference room.

CHAPTER XVII

MY PEACE MISSION— MOSCOW AND AFTER

At the Kremlin with Stalin.—Agreement to periodic meetings of Security Council.—Return visits to Paris, London, and Washington, and Publication of Peace Plan.—Korean aggression interrupts my efforts.—Progress after four years.

IT WAS long since Generalissimo Stalin had received any Western diplomat; and I had not seen him since 1946. He was already in the room, with Messrs. Molotov and Vyshinsky, when I was ushered in. As we shook hands I noted that the Soviet leader, then seventy, appeared to have aged a little in the four years; but he still gave the old impression of robust vigor.

Stalin was the first to speak. He welcomed me and said he took it for granted that I had no objection to the presence of Mr. Molotov as an expert in United Nations affairs. I replied that I was pleased to have him included, for I had previously expressed the wish to see him, and it suited me very well to be able to combine the two meetings.

With the formalities thus in order, I proceeded, admitting that it was with some emotion that I sat down to speak with the Generalissimo and with his closest associates: "Aside from being the leader of a nation of 200,000,000 you also enjoy an influence in countries with altogether more than 800,000,000 inhabitants, and you and your associates, through your common ideas, influence many millions more in other lands. I, for my part, am undertaking a one-man peace mission. I do not represent any special government, but am making this trip as Secretary-General of the United Nations."

The words spoken were translated without eliciting any comment, and I could discern no indication either of approval or of displeasure. I therefore continued according to plan, extending my congratulations on the progress I had witnessed in the U.S.S.R.:

"I have been in Moscow five times now, in 1921, 1934, 1944, 1946, and 1950. It has thus been twenty-nine years since I first visited the Soviet Union. This is a good portion of a lifetime, and much has taken place in the course of these years." When this was translated Molotov, for the first time, nodded approvingly to Stalin who also seemed interested. "I have never been a Communist, but I have always tried to take an objective stand where the Soviet Union is concerned. So it is as an objective observer that I am able to congratulate you on the progress made by the Russian people between my first visit and this present one—especially since the years 1944 and 1946. I have been struck by the way in which so many streets and houses have been repaired, and how others are building. A walk or drive through the streets is enough to show how much better dressed the people are now." I had been impressed by the number of new trams, cars, and busses now traversing Moscow's streets, and I could not remember ever having seen such quantities of meat, bread, and other commodities in the Moscow stores and shops. "Perhaps the time has come now," I suggested, "for an easing of entry restrictions so that visitors from other countries can see this progress with their own eyes. After all, a nation that has grown strong, thanks to its own initiative and its own hard work, does not lose prestige by resorting to a milder approach. Compromise can often reflect increased strength."

Pavlov translated these remarks without arousing any visible reaction on the other side of the table, and so I carried on into the first item on my agenda: a possible meeting of the heads of government.

I recalled that Dr. Evatt and I, during the Paris Assembly in 1948, had issued an appeal to the leaders of the great powers to meet and discuss all the differences separating them at the time. Here, I drew from among my papers a copy of the General Assembly's unanimous resolution of November 3, 1948, the title of which I read aloud: "Appeal to the Great Powers to Renew Efforts to Compose Their

Differences and Establish a Lasting Peace." Laying the paper aside, I went on to note that while our appeal had concerned the Berlin Blockade primarily, and while this question had since been settled, our plea as well as the Assembly's resolution referred to other outstanding questions as well. "When Dr. Evatt and I composed this paper," I added, "Generalissimo Stalin, among others, had declared that he was prepared to meet with the leaders of the other great powers. Now, however, it seems to me that a solution will be even more difficult than in 1948, considering the more than a hundred unresolved questions that have accumulated in the interval. Because of this I have arrived at the same conclusion every time I have gone into the matter. A meeting of the leaders of the great powers, while it could not settle many things, seems to represent the best way to get things started on a different course."

I had mentioned this possibility to President Truman on April 20, and I recalled that conversation now: "President Truman assured me that he would always welcome Generalissimo Stalin in Washington, and that he would be willing to do whatever he could to arrange his transportation both ways; the best American battleship would be placed at his disposal." I felt I betrayed no confidence in recalling the President's assertion that he liked Generalissimo Stalin personally, and that at Potsdam he had been prepared to offer six billion dollars for the rebuilding of the Soviet Union. On the other hand, I was equally bound to report that Mr. Truman had never forgotten the lack of response from the Soviet side. I quoted his saying that he had received a "slap in the face," and remarked that in 1945, someone—I knew not who—had so offended the President that he might never sit down for another meeting with the Soviet leaders unless they were willing to come to the United States first. "It would seem to me," I observed, "that Washington might not be the best place for such a meeting. There might be other places in the United States —Key West, for example—which could offer the security and privacy needed. Or there might be a meeting somewhere in the Atlantic or the Pacific," I continued, recalling the first Churchill-Roosevelt meeting of the last war; "or a neutral country like Sweden or Switzerland might be fitting, or some spot in England, or in France." I closed my remarks on this point by emphasizing that the people of the entire world were living today in fear of the future and the threat of war. "In my opinion, something has to be done to bring the present deadlock to an end and restore normal, friendly, and peaceful relations."

Stalin was the only man to speak. He had had the same question in mind many times, he began, but with the current situation, with all the questions and difficulties accumulated month after month and year after year, a single meeting of the leaders of these same powers could not bring a satisfactory solution to all the problems within a reasonable length of time. He went on to recall that the leaders were only human beings, after all, and that the difficulties and unsolved questions were so numerous as to require long and careful preparation through the normal diplomatic channels if such a meeting were to produce results. A meeting of the kind I suggested, he finished, was not the burning issue in the present situation. And the place for such a meeting was not important.

With the exchange of views on the first item completed, I moved on to the crux of my mission, explaining that I had completed a Memorandum of Points for Consideration in the Development of a Twenty-Year Program for Achieving Peace Through the United Nations. Reaching across the table to hand the Memorandum to the Generalissimo, and a copy to Molotov, I added that it was my intention to return to further discussions with the statesmen who had already received it, retracing the route which I had just followed.

"This Memorandum," I explained, "is based upon the statements previously made both by Generalissimo Stalin and President Truman regarding the possibility of peaceful coexistence among the great powers, with their different economic and political systems, and upon the assumption that they evidence a readiness to enter into genuine negotiation."

I placed stress on my view that special or periodic meetings of the Security Council, attended by foreign ministers as proposed in Point One of the memorandum, could be held away from Headquarters in New York, perhaps in rotation in the major capitals. "Geneva, in my opinion, would probably offer the best conditions for a first meeting. Here the Foreign Ministers could meet for luncheons, dinners, and private conversations in a quiet atmosphere. They would have a chance to exchange views and opinions outside the immediate searchlight of the press, which would always be disturbing them more in New York." I concluded by referring again to the document I had just delivered, recalling that Minister of Foreign Affairs Vyshinsky had received his copy—in the Russian language—on Friday the 12th, the first day I had seen him in Moscow. One of the first things I had noted upon sitting down was that both the Generalissimo and Mr. Molotov already had copies of the memorandum spread before them. And I had observed with considerable satisfaction that Stalin had penned remarks in the margin of every page. A long and thorough comment seemed to have been prepared for each paragraph.

I arranged my notes and my arguments as Mr. Pavlov's translation drew to a close. We were now entering into the subject which had brought me on this long journey, and I was resolved not to let a single opportunity pass unused. The Generalissimo was the first to speak. He suggested, however, that Mr. Molotov, being more experienced in United Nations affairs, might open the discussion from the Russian side with an evaluation of my proposals.

Mr. Molotov began in his usual way, in what I took to be rather stilted or bureaucratic language. First, he wanted to make it clear that he had studied the document with great interest. He understood that I was trying to mediate in the present situation. He used the term "mediator" repeatedly in his ensuing remarks. If it was a mediatory suggestion I presented, he said, then he was not satisfied with it; then the memorandum did not conform with its objective, as in his opinion it was "quite one-sided." He went on to remark that several points expressed what he called the "American" or "Anglo-American" point of view, and that views forwarded in connection with other questions were decidedly "Americanized." Furthermore, he continued in a critical tone, I had omitted proposals and opinions put forward by representatives of the U.S.S.R.

This opening criticism in such blunt terms did not sit well with me. "I am surprised," I rejoined, "that you find reason to accuse me of being one-sided or influenced by the American or Anglo-American point of view. As a non-Communist, I could not possibly have written a more objective memorandum aimed at resolving the present situation." I made no effort to conceal the fact that Mr. Molotov's remarks—not to say, accusations—had offended me, and I lost no time in defending my position. "Are not Generalissimo Stalin and

Vice Prime Minister Molotov aware of the criticism that has been showered on me by newspapers in America," I returned, "how they have labeled me a 'Stalin agent,' 'pro-Communist,' etc., and have demanded that I be 'summarily dismissed'?"

But Mr. Molotov was too wound up to stop for these protests. He went on to maintain that I had also tried to meet American demands by suggesting under Point One that "use of the veto" and "veto restrictions" be taken up for study and discussions. This suggestion, he asserted, was "against the interests of the U.S.S.R. and favors those of the United States." I rejoined that the "Little Assembly"—the committee of all Members meeting between sessions, from which the Russians absented themselves—was already dealing with the matter, and also that an article in the Charter stipulated consideration of its revision in 1955. "When writing this Memorandum," I continued, "I was of a mind that it would be better were discussions and studies on this question to take place privately, at first, among the great-power members of the Security Council. In my opinion, no organ would be better suited for such study and discussion than the Security Council itself." I made clear my opinion that this question of the veto and veto restrictions could not be omitted. "Sooner or later," I said, "in 1955 at the very latest, it will be coming up for action; and, as far as I can see, it would be preferable were discussions started now. This consideration was what prompted me to include the veto question in the Memorandum."

So far as the position of the U.S.S.R. was concerned, I hastened to remind the Russian leaders that the Soviet Union had already accepted in practice a very definite modification of the veto: "Russian abstention in the Security Council has not been regarded as a veto, despite the fact that the Charter stipulates that no decision is valid unless there are, among the necessary minimum majority of seven votes, the five concurring votes of the five great powers. You agreed to this modification of the veto, and there might be possibilities of other modifications as well." I further pointed out that the Memorandum did not contain the phrase "veto restrictions" but referred, rather, to "limitations on the use of the veto power in the pacific settlement procedure of the Security Council" by agreement of the five great powers.

Regardless of their feelings in the matter, I tried to make it clear

MY PEACE MISSION—MOSCOW AND AFTER

that the passages in the Memorandum on use of the veto referred not alone to the U.S.S.R.: "In fact, I do not believe that the United States and its Senate would ever consider relinquishing its veto right entirely." My own position, too, had to be clarified, because Mr. Molotov's stress on the term "mediator" tended to throw my whole mission into a false perspective. "You will understand," I repeated, "that I am not acting as a mediator, but as an explorer and as Secretary-General as well. As Secretary-General, I have to pay due respect to what a majority of the Member states think and feel as to the great powers' right of veto and its use. I am therefore disappointed —quite disappointed—by Mr. Molotov's remarks."

The Generalissimo broke in at this point to say that he agreed with Mr. Molotov, but that "a mediator will always be criticized by both sides." A Secretary-General of the United Nations, he maintained, would always be a mediator in part, and, whether as Secretary-General or as mediator, he would have to be prepared for criticism from both parties to a dispute. "But you know, Mr. Lie," he appended, with the trace of a rare smile, "the middle way in such situations will always win."

With that, the Generalissimo turned to atomic energy control, which was Point Two in the Memorandum. He criticized it for failing to take up prohibition of the atomic bomb. I replied that I agreed as to the need of prohibition, but that the problem on international control could not be avoided, and the difficulty here was finding a system of control which everyone could accept. But he was evidently determined that some mention of prohibition be made, for he repeated his criticism, stating among other things that I did not discuss this aspect of the problem at all. Criticism on this point had been anticipated, and so I was prepared to put forward a suggestion at once: "The International Red Cross has just adopted a resolution urging the great powers to do everything possible to agree on prohibition of the atomic bomb. What we could do would be to mention the Red Cross resolution in the Memorandum, and append it as a new item to be discussed by the Security Council." This indication that the document might be corrected or added to seemed to meet with approval, and I decided that the Russians might be satisfied by a reference in the Memorandum to the Red Cross resolution.

Mr. Molotov then brought up Point Three: controlling the armaments race and effecting a reduction of armed forces. His chief objection on this score was that I again failed to mention the U.S.S.R.'s proposals. Here I pointed out that the Memorandum proposed no special approach one way or the other, calling only for "new efforts at finding some area of common ground." If the Memorandum were to be used as a basic paper for future periodic meetings of the Security Council, there was nothing to prevent the Russians from taking up their suggestions anew. "Though I might prefer," I added with a smile, "that they be changed a bit, if they are to have any chance of being adopted. This Memorandum, you must remember, is only a list of suggestions which can be added to, amended, or changed by the various Governments, provided they agree to assemble in periodic meetings. It is this last point that is essential."

The Vice Prime Minister then commented on Point Four and its suggestion, as a first step to break the deadlock over armed forces to be at the disposal of the Security Council (Article 43 of the Charter), of an "interim accord for a small force sufficient to prevent or stop localized outbreaks threatening international peace." He charged that this also represented the Anglo-American point of view. I replied, "That is not correct," and appealed to Mr. Vyshinsky for confirmation. Confirmation, of course, was too much to expect; but he did smile and nod while I recalled for the benefit of Stalin and Molotov that the United States in the Military Staff Committee and the Security Council had always supported, not a small force, but the largest possible armed force. "The Americans advocated the biggest air, army, and naval units for the United Nations, while the other great powers favored smaller units." I tried to explain: "The purpose of the Memorandum, at this point, is to secure temporary agreement on a small force consisting, for example, of the lowest number of army, navy, and air forces proposed by any one of the great powers. This would be more than sufficient to prevent or stop localized outbreaks threatening international peace. Furthermore, I do not believe that such military forces need often be used. In my opinion, even the United Nations observers with their blue armbands are frequently far stronger and more influential than armed units, planes, and warships. The mere existence of a small force would, in itself, give decided power to the Security Council and to its decisions regarding peaceful settlement." In winding up I reiterated that my own views on Point Four did not represent those of the United States: "In fact, I am fully prepared to find the U.S.A. raising some of the selfsame objections I've heard here today." At this, another trace of smile was perceptible under the Generalissimo's mustache.

There was no reference to Point Five, calling for universality of membership, which I believed the U.S.S.R. to favor. Mr. Stalin now took up discussion of Point Six, on an active program of technical assistance and capital investment for economic development for the people of the underdeveloped countries. "I am much interested," he said, "in seeing this very important work continued and extended during the coming years." However, he was of the opinion that the work should not be carried on outside the United Nations, but exclusively within the Organization. Did I not agree? My answer expressed agreement in principle, that the best solution would be for technical and economic assistance to be extended through the United Nations and the *Specialized Agencies,* continuing: "However, I must call your attention to the fact that funds for financing technical assistance are not included in the regular United Nations budget, but are voluntary contributions and the money is now coming mainly from the United States. Therefore, it is hardly for the United Nations to set terms regarding technical assistance. It would neither be practical nor politically feasible for me as Secretary-General to tell the United State Senate that the millions it appropriates for technical assistance should go exclusively to the United Nations and to organizations joined to or cooperating with it. In my mind, politics is the art of attaining that which it is possible to attain." In the light of such facts the United Nations would have to take what it received, and be content. "But in principle," I repeated, "I agree with Generalissimo Stalin. If technical and economic assistance were given and administered through and by the United Nations and its associated organizations, criticism as to imperialism, capitalism, etc., would be reduced, or would disappear altogether." Then, knowing that the U.S.S.R. had so far contributed nothing to the technical assistance program, I ventured to add: "The time has perhaps come for the U.S.S.R., as well, to begin contributing to the great purpose dealt with under Point Six." This elicited no response.

Point Seven called for more support of the Specialized Agencies by all the Member governments and specifically for the Soviet Union to join them. It also called for ratification of the Charter of the International Trade Organization. The Generalissimo passed over the matter of membership in the Specialized Agencies. Emphasizing that the Soviet Union was most interested in international trade, or, as he put it, "trade with the whole world, trade across the small countries, and with the great and all other countries," he volunteered the opinion that the charter of the International Trade Organization was a good one, and that, with a few changes, it might well be ratified by a number of countries which had not yet done so, including the Soviet Union. But, he added, the basis of the charter must be coexistence between the differing economic and political systems. An international trade treaty which would harm the prospects of the economic and political system then in force in the U.S.S.R., for example, must not be adopted. For this reason, the charter would have to be amended. He made clear that the mere ratification of the ITO charter would not mean that Soviet trade objectives had thereby been attained. The "policy of discrimination" which the United States, among others, had brought to bear against the Soviet Union must also be taken up. The United States, he contended, followed "most discriminatory practices" in its foreign trade, "all of them directed against the U.S.S.R." This policy and the resulting limitations of international trade must be discussed in the interest of bringing about a change. Not until then would all the Member states be able to obtain the advantages resulting from expanded international trade, such as a higher living standard. He seemed to have a keen interest in the subject.

In this connection the Generalissimo referred to President Truman's remark to me about having been ready at Potsdam to suggest six billion dollars for aid to the U.S.S.R.: After the war the country had needed credit; but not any longer. "We had four terrible years during which all our brave Russians suffered, but now we want trade and not credit." Modifying the statement slightly with the admission that he would not refuse, "were somebody to come along and offer dollars or credit," he repeated that the Soviet Union did not ask for it any longer. In answer to these remarks, I suggested that the abolition of present policies of discrimination could possibly be included under the Memorandum's Point Seven: "In this way this question, as well, could be taken up for discussion at possible periodic meetings." With this, our exchange on Point Seven was ended. Generalissimo Stalin had been the only one to speak from the Soviet side for some time now.

The Soviet leaders had nothing to say on the remaining points in the Memorandum; and, with a number of matters still to bring up, I obtained permission—for the purpose of drawing up a résumé of my impressions on this part of our discussion—to put two questions:

"I understand that Generalissimo Stalin and the others present agree to holding periodic meetings according to Article 28 (2) of the Charter?" (The answer was Yes.)

"As I understand the terminated discussion, the Memorandum, with the changes and additions mentioned during the discussion, can be used as a working paper for discussions within the Security Council or one of its subcommittees in order to form a possible program for periodic meetings?" (Again the answer was Yes.)

I thereupon asked permission to raise certain other questions, now that I had the rare opportunity to see and speak with Generalissimo Stalin. The three Soviet officials agreed at once, and told me to take whatever time was needed.

Starting with the Specialized Agencies, I touched on the resolution adopted by the Directors-General of all the Specialized Agencies—with whom I had met in Paris on May 3 in the Administrative Committee on Coordination—and referred also to Points Six and Seven of the Memorandum. I noted my earlier discussion of Soviet membership in the Specialized Agencies with Vice Minister of Foreign Affairs Andrei Gromyko, and referred to the articles of the Charter on relations between the United Nations and the Specialized Agencies, continuing: "At present the Soviet Union is an active member of only the United Nations itself, apart from such purely technical Specialized Agencies as the Universal Postal Union and the International Telecommunication Union. If the work of the United Nations is to yield results, it will be necessary for the Member states to maintain membership or become members of the most important Specialized Agencies." I placed stress upon the World Health Organization, the United Nations Educational, Scientific, and Cultural Organization, the Food and Agriculture Organization and the International Labor Organization. "When I spoke with Mr. Gromyko a few days ago he characterized the Health Organization —of which the U.S.S.R. has been a member, but has since left—as being useless. In my opinion, such a characterization is not correct. As I see it, the establishment of the Specialized Agencies expresses a spirit of solidarity which must be the very basis for our various international undertakings. And I therefore appeal to the leaders of the U.S.S.R. to consider this question very thoroughly. It may be possible that the Health Organization, the Educational Organization, the Food Organization, and the others are of little interest to the corresponding technical departments in the Soviet Union. But, in my opinion, the time has now come for the U.S.S.R. to join actively, nevertheless, to help support the work of those organizations in Asia, Africa, South America, and other underdeveloped parts of the world. A country cannot choose membership purely on the basis of what is desirable and useful to itself."

When Mr. Pavlov had completed his translation, Generalissimo Stalin leaned forward, remarking that he had listened with great interest, and promised that the question I had raised would receive serious thought. However, he could not promise a quick answer: it was a rule in the Soviet Union that they took time for a thorough consideration before making any decision.

The next question had to do with the Greek children. I opened by referring to the resolutions unanimously adopted by the United Nations General Assemblies of 1948 and 1949: "All the Member states have agreed that the Greek children at present in Yugoslavia, Rumania, Bulgaria, Hungary, Poland, Czechoslovakia, as well as in the Eastern Zone of Germany, be returned to their parents or relatives in Greece. According to a proposal made by the Soviet Union, a decision was taken in 1948 that the practical work be carried out by the International Red Cross in cooperation with Red Cross organizations in the countries concerned. But until now the whole thing has been a disappointment. So far, not one Greek child has been sent home to its parents or relatives. In fact, the entire matter has been sabotaged for two years." I went on to recall how, when the International Red Cross had invited representatives from its national bodies in these countries to meet at Geneva in March, not a single representative appeared. "On my trip through Prague, I just had an interview with the Czech Foreign Minister on this matter." And I expressed my disappointment over the interview. "All over the world, resolutions have been adopted, and protests have been sent to me as Secretary-General. The manner in which the Soviet Union's neighboring countries have dealt with this matter has been used in the anti-Communist propaganda which has been mounting for some time now. In my opinion this is injurious to the Soviet Union as well as to its neighbors; and I must therefore appeal to you, Generalissimo Stalin, to use your influence in such a way that this unbearable situation be ended and the Greek children returned to Greece." I concluded by maintaining that there should certainly be a way of ensuring that parents and relatives were free and able to take care of the children who were returned. "Cooperation toward this end, between the International Red Cross and the Red Cross organizations in the countries concerned, could provide security." I also mentioned that Foreign Minister Max Petitpierre of Switzerland had informed me at Geneva, that the Swiss government was ready to set up camps or places of residence in Switzerland for all Greek children before they were returned to their homeland. In this way it would be possible to make certain that they were being returned to "free" parents and relatives.

These remarks, when they were translated, received the expected answer: there were no Greek children in the Soviet Union, and the subject, therefore, did not concern the U.S.S.R. "This may be correct from a technical point of view," I maintained, "but it is still the duty of every member of the United Nations to assist in carrying out the resolutions adopted by the General Assembly. I must therefore ask you once more, Generalissimo Stalin, to use your personal influence in an attempt to solve this problem." Here Minister of Foreign Affairs Vyshinsky, who had remained quiet the whole evening, intervened with some remarks in Russian that were not translated. The discussion was ended abruptly by the Generalissimo with a very serious remark that "children belong to their parents." What this implied in the light of the preceding exchange, I was never to know; but I noticed that both Molotov and Vyshinsky carefully noted down what he had said. He then turned to Mr. Vyshinsky, asking for all available information.

It was now quite late, as my watch proved; but they asked me to go on. There was one last point on my agenda, and I decided to bring it up now: it concerned the peace treaties. Mentioning first the peace treaty with Germany, I said I expressed a desire held in every corner of the world in wishing that the peace treaties could become a reality as soon as possible. To demonstrate to the Generalissimo how seriously interested the Western world was in a settlement, I referred to a plan that had been mentioned to me in Paris: "It has been proposed that Western and Eastern Germany join in setting up a constitution for a united Germany. In this constitution a paragraph would be included, whereby Germany pledges itself to remain neutral, toward East as well as West, for a period of, say, twenty-five years. In other words, Germany would not be permitted to enter into either the Atlantic Treaty or any agreement with the Soviet Union, Poland, Czechoslovakia or with any other state. Germany would be neutral. Its borders would be guaranteed by the neighboring countries, and its heavy industry would be controlled, to make sure that it did not rearm. Control would be charged to representatives of the neighboring countries, with possible military and police assistance from other states, if necessary. This would imply active participation on the part of Denmark, Holland, Belgium, Luxembourg, France, Czechoslovakia, and Poland. As far as I am concerned," I concluded, "I can take no stand on this plan; but I would like to mention it in any case, now that I am in Moscow."

The three Russians listened to the translation without comment. They did not seem inclined to reveal their thoughts.

But there was also the question of elections in Berlin, and so I continued: "I have learned from the newspapers that the Russians, as a condition for these elections, are demanding that the forces of the Western powers be withdrawn. This, I understand, has been refused by the United States, Great Britain, and France on the ground that there must be adequate supervision and control to ensure free elections." It had occurred to me after reading the press reports that the United Nations might possibly be of help in this situation. "Obviously," I observed, "the citizens of Berlin must be allowed to vote freely and independently without pressure from any quarter. Granted these conditions then, could not the United Nations be asked to nominate a commissioner who would guarantee that the elections took place in a free and democratic manner? The commissioner could have police and military forces at his disposal, if necessary, which could be supplied by the so-called neutral countries." I asked Generalissimo Stalin to consider this suggestion. "When the leader of the Soviet Union and the other influential Russian statesmen present are faced with similar problems in the future they should remember that the United Nations can possibly be in a position to help." Generalissimo Stalin said that he would consider the view presented.

Finally, I touched on the peace treaty with Austria, saying that the entire world would be pleased to get this treaty signed now. I understood from what I had read and heard that the treaty was practically ready for signature, but that a final settlement had been postponed time and again. "A peace treaty with Austria," I said, "should be a sign of improvement in the current situation. One place or another, the present 'deadlock' has to be broken. Personally, I hold to the opinion that a treaty with Austria should be the first step." Again, the Generalissimo said only that he would consider the views expressed.

It was now well after eleven-thirty. Feeling that our conversation had lasted long enough, I expressed my thanks for the opportunity to meet with them, said good night, and returned to my hotel—alone, as I had come.

On May 18 I left Moscow for Paris.

RETURN TO PARIS

The first of the European statesmen with whom I spoke after the conversation with Generalissimo Stalin was the French Minister of Foreign Affairs, Robert Schuman. We sat down for a talk in his office at Quai d'Orsay about five o'clock in the afternoon of May 20.

Mr. Schuman took from his drawer the Memorandum I had delivered to him earlier, stating that he had studied it carefully (I could see that he had penned a few comments in the margin). Generally speaking, he agreed that it represented a good program for efforts toward peace and understanding. Although the government had not yet dealt with it he and Prime Minister Bidault had discussed it at length. (Mr. Bidault confirmed this to me in conversation two days later: it was obvious that he, too, was well acquainted with the document and its contents.)

Recounting what had taken place in Moscow, I reported that the Soviet Union had accepted the idea of periodic meetings of the Security Council, assuming that the Chinese representation issue was settled.

Mr. Schuman expressed the belief that the differing economic and political systems could exist side by side. In fact, this represented the only possible solution in the current political situation. Every other alternative would lead sooner or later to World War and catastrophe. Personally, he also agreed to periodic meetings in the Security Council, and believed that if we took the time to arrange practical agendas for the meetings, proposals that could be accepted by both sides could be worked out with caution, understanding, and patience. But we had to be careful not to create any illusions as to such meetings, he continued. He was also afraid that the United States—and probably Britain as well—might hesitate. He had received that impression, he admitted, after his conversations during the Western Foreign Ministers' recent meeting in London.

Mr. Schuman also agreed that discussions should be launched on the question of veto rights. France had always been of the opinion that such rights should be limited as much as possible. But he did not think that agreement could be reached quickly. The matter should be studied through several periodic meetings, and, as the Charter would not be up for revision before 1955, yearly reports should be issued to record the progress made. France's views on the control of "mass murder" weapons and a limitation of the armaments race agreed with those voiced in the Memorandum.

"I have spoken on my own behalf," he concluded; "but I know the French people, and they would certainly agree with my point of view and my observations. You can take it for granted that France will back your various suggestions with a positive vote. France sees in the United Nations the only organization that can lead the world to a lasting and stable peace and we will therefore give positive support to any current efforts that can bring this 'cold war' to an end."

As we rose, Mr. Schuman thanked me for having taken all the time and trouble which a trip to Moscow involved, remarking that it had been both my right and my duty to visit the governments in the four capitals. He felt that there was no need to state that he rejected any criticism which might be leveled against my attempts to bring the great powers together. "France is grateful for what you are doing, and we will do whatever we can to help end the present untenable situation," were his last words.

IN LONDON AGAIN

It was difficult for Foreign Secretary Ernest Bevin to get up from his chair when I entered his office. He seemed to be very tired, closing his eyes time and again, and it was clear that he was suffering considerable pain. His first remarks, after we had shaken hands, indicated that he had undergone an operation and would soon have to return to the hospital. Under the circumstances I decided not to enter into any controversial discussion, and limited myself to a résumé of the conversations in Moscow and Paris, to which he listened somewhat absent-mindedly.

Only once did he interrupt: when—under Point Seven of my résumé—I mentioned the interest Generalissimo Stalin had expressed in international trade, and quoted his remarks to the effect that the Charter of the International Trade Organization was a good one, but that the Russians wanted some changes. The Russians did not really want international trade, Mr. Bevin interjected. When they negotiated trade treaties they did so with countries on which they could force their conditions. He seemed to be getting excited. "I really did what I could," he went on, "in trying to work out a general trade treaty with the Russians, and I even went so far as to send Harold Wilson [President of the Board of Trade] to Moscow. But it was impossible to get an agreement with them."

Mr. Bevin now picked up a blue document which lay on his desk and began reading—in any event, I had the impression that he was reading. Britain, he began, would not, without further consideration, agree to periodic meetings of the Security Council. The main and most important thing at present was the firm establishment of the North Atlantic Treaty Organization and a corresponding solidarity among the nations bordering the Atlantic. This meant power, which was the only thing the Russians seemed to respect.

In the last consideration, I could readily concur; but I was disturbed by the indication that the British government did not wish to go along with any specific United Nations initiative in the present situation. Mr. Bevin said that as long as he remained Foreign Secretary he would not take part in any new discussions or negotiations with the Russians until their actions proved that they had changed their minds and hearts. Through acts and concessions, they must prove that they were prepared to negotiate and were worthy of negotiating with. They must prove that they were willing to accept and bow to the rules. They could not be allowed to go on using pressure as they had until now, and continue their walkouts and boycotts of the United Nations. As a Labor organization man, he ended, he had participated in the expulsion of the Communists because they would never pay any attention to the rules. And as Foreign Secretary his opinion of the Russians and their behavior since the Second World War was the same.

Mr. Bevin then turned to the suggestion in my Memorandum of a conference of scientists to discuss atomic energy. The British government did not favor such a conference, he informed me. It might cause confusion. The scientists would meet, and their statements would only frighten the common people, which again would only help the Russians. Atomic energy and the control of atomic and mass-extermination weapons was, above all, a political question that had to be decided by the governments.

He went on with his blue document. Reaching Point Nine, he let me know that Great Britain had never been satisfied with the United Nations' handling of the colonial question and its misunderstanding of England, which had done more than any other nation to bring freedom to dependent peoples but, instead of receiving credit, had only met ill tempered criticism and unpleasant attacks in the United Nations. It would be better if all the questions regarding greater social and economic progress in the colonies were left to the countries that governed them. I broke in to ask whether he was not satisfied with the report recently prepared in Geneva by a United Nations committee after a visit to some of the trust territories in Africa. This report, I knew, had been praised by the English. He replied in the negative, however, and went on with his complaints. He had used "the best Englishman" to deal with these questions—namely, Arthur Creech Jones; but all his reports gave the impression that the United Nations had not been dealing with these important questions in the right way—at any rate as far as Great Britain was concerned.

Mr. Bevin was clearly displeased with Point Nine in the Memorandum; and in order to get off to a new start I said of the Western Foreign Ministers' meeting, recently held in London, that I was "almost satisfied" with the communiqué they had issued. His face brightened for a moment as he rang for a secretary to bring a copy of the communiqué. Finding a copy in my dispatch case, I read from Point Two—"a statement that really has given me a good deal of satisfaction"—the passage:

They reaffirmed the adherence of their governments to the principles which inspire the United Nations Charter and their conviction that common action under the Treaty is an integral part of the effort which all free nations are making to secure conditions of world peace and human welfare.

I then cited a passage from the fifth paragraph:

Conscious of the strength and of the will to peace of their countries, the Ministers remain ready to seize any opportunity for achieving a genuine and lasting settlement of international problems.

Very carefully, then, I called his attention to the contrast between what he had first said, about not being interested in periodic meetings if the Russians failed to evidence a change of heart, and the avowal by the Ministers that they remained "ready to seize any opportunity for achieving a genuine and lasting settlement of international problems."

"If there is no attempt to meet for new negotiations," I persisted, "and if we merely sit back waiting for the other party to give in at one point or another, time may run out on us, there will be the danger of new conflicts and a Third World War may result." But Mr. Bevin would not go along. The North Atlantic Treaty had a first and absolute priority. Everything else would have to wait. However, he would not set himself against negotiations within the United Nations, were time and conditions favorable.

As usual, we parted friends, and I took my leave after wishing him a speedy recovery.

I arrived at 10 Downing Street to see Prime Minister Attlee at six o'clock that day. The bobby outside, whom I remembered well from earlier visits, gave me a friendly welcome. "I hope you have good news for the Prime Minister, Mr. Lie," he said courteously as I passed him at the door. I hoped so too, and it cheered me to realize this new evidence of the yearning for peace on the part of the everyday, down-to-earth people. There had been the elevator man in the Goring Hotel at the end of April, as I began my peace mission. "We've been expecting you now, Mr. Lie," he observed as the elevator climbed to my floor. "Right now, there are so many foreign officers and military missions in London that we're asking ourselves when it will all start again. But we're glad you're here, because we know you're working for peace."

It was good to sit down for a talk with Mr. Attlee. He says little, listens well, and is easy to get along with. But he may have one fault: the appearance of agreeing without this seeming to produce the positive results the other person is led to expect. I could hardly help recalling my visit with him here in late April, when I had gone over the reasons for my mission, emphasizing the need for supporting the United Nations as the one place where all outstanding international questions could be dealt with by methods of conciliation. He had seemed to agree then. "That's right," he had concurred emphatically. "What you say is true."

I opened by referring to the interview with the Foreign Secretary, making no effort to hide my disappointment: "I received an answer which I had not been given reason to expect, following my conversation with the Prime Minister and Kenneth Younger in April." Everybody had the right to be "a doubting Thomas" and ask for evidence, I said; and Mr. Bevin certainly was one. But how could anyone come with absolute evidence that a party to a conflict would make compromises before negotiations had even been launched? I would certainly not say that I had any evidence of a Russian change of heart. They were only willing to meet. "After all, no one is going to give anything away before he even sits down to the round table." And the round table this time, I maintained, ought to be the periodic meetings of the Security Council with the Foreign Ministers attending. Mr. Attlee nodded understandingly.

"But am I still given to understand," I asked, "that Bevin's negative answer was the full answer of the government?" Mr. Attlee replied in the affirmative, but slowly, and added after a pause that he could telephone and ask for a new interview on the matter; the Cabinet might also discuss the question again. I advised against a new meeting: "Bevin is ill now, and I have a feeling that any new discussion between the two of you or in the Cabinet would have a bad effect upon his health." Mr. Attlee agreed, and appeared somewhat relieved. The relief was even more apparent when I told him that I would try to prepare a noncommittal communiqué to the press on my visit to Great Britain. "We can say, for example, that 'no door was closed in London for genuine negotiations.'" He agreed to this. "And if the situation matures quickly," I suggested, "and I find that I need British support and good will, I would appreciate it were I able to contact the Prime Minister directly." Mr. Attlee again agreed.

Then I gave a short account of what had happened since we had last spoken, and of the reactions I had received in Moscow, both to the proposal for periodic meetings of the Security Council, with Foreign Ministers present, and to a four-power meeting of heads of government. Mr. Attlee seemed to be most interested in Mr. Stalin's observations here, that the leaders could not solve everything themselves. This view was the same—he observed—as that expressed by Mr. Truman at press conferences during the winter of 1949–1950. We agreed that a meeting of heads of government could not be regarded as likely for the time being.

The understanding, sympathy, and support extended to my mission by responsible government leaders of Western Europe and by the public, I went on, had been a real source of encouragement: "I appreciate, especially, the resolution from the 145 Members in Parliament voicing approval and support for my trip." What I had seen and heard, however, had convinced me that the prevailing international political situation would be putting world statesmanship to a most trying test. "It remains to be seen whether it will be possible to combine work for defense, through the North Atlantic Treaty, with work for world peace through the United Nations. It was right, and perfectly understandable, that the peoples of the Western democracies felt a real satisfaction when the North Atlantic Treaty was signed in 1949. The fear of war and Russian aggression had been so strong, and the masses had felt so helpless, that they were glad indeed to be given a treaty guaranteeing them American support and cooperation. A better balance of military power was also necessary. But it is not sufficient," I emphasized, "merely to build up a strong defense. It is not enough merely to try to inspire a willingness to subscribe large military grants. The broad masses want to live in peace; they do not want war. They are dead-tired of this conflict between East and West, and what they fear more than anything else is becoming victims of a new and fatal conflict between these two power blocs."

With the Prime Minister's permission, I would venture to advise his country that now, more than ever before, it should support actively the work of the United Nations. "In the regular periodic meetings of the Security Council I can see the possibility of a beginning toward a better understanding between East and West. Of course, these meetings will have to be thoroughly prepared in advance, and no meeting should be called before we have worked out a temporary agenda giving reasonable prospects for results. The people must be given no illusions. If, despite our best efforts and intentions, these meetings do not produce the desired results, the blame would then be laid on the doorsteps of those responsible."

The Prime Minister, as at our earlier meeting, conveyed the impression that he agreed. I mentioned once again Great Britain's strategic political position in the present world situation. "Now, more than ever before," I stressed, "there is no doubt in my mind but that Great Britain *must* play a leading role."

As I rose to leave, the Prime Minister thanked me for our conversation, assuring me that my trip had not been in vain and expressing the hope that the international situation would take a more favorable turn.

RETURN TO WASHINGTON

At half past ten in the morning of Monday May 29, I arrived at the State Department in Washington for an appointment with Secretary Acheson and Assistant Secretary Hickerson, again accompanied by Assistant Secretary-General Byron Price. The Secretary of State had set the time for the meeting, which was to be his first appointment after his return from the London conference of Western Foreign Ministers. I had understood that he was interested in speaking with me before seeing the President, and before preparing the speech he was to make to Congress two days later.

The atmosphere was entirely friendly and—from the American side—somewhat eager. There was no doubt that Mr. Acheson was anxious to hear about my visits to London and Paris and especially Moscow. No American diplomat had talked with Stalin for many months.

I began with the usual brief résumé of the visits in London, Paris, and Prague, and concluded with a more detailed account of what had happened in Moscow. I recounted the manner in which Generalissimo Stalin and his associates had received the Memorandum, and their comments on other matters. Both Mr. Acheson and Mr. Hickerson asked my impression of the extent to which Vice Prime Minister Molotov was active in international affairs; and when told of the four officials handling American relations—Sobolev, Gromyko, Vyshinsky, and Molotov—the Secretary of State commented: "Those are just about the best brains they have."

From what followed, it was clear that the State Department had devoted a good deal of attention to my Memorandum. Secretary Acheson sat with the text and a number of other papers, presumably related to it, before him; but no detailed exposition of the American reaction was forthcoming that day. The United States, Mr. Hickerson observed, would be prepared to offer various suggestions at the appropriate time. "I am now arriving at the decisive stage of the discussions," I explained. "Until now, I have merely been exploring; but now I must decide whether to publish this Memorandum alone, or in the context of my Annual Report, or as a document to which I could attach the comments of the great powers." I expressed doubt as to the wisdom of the last alternative—a view with which the Secretary of State agreed.

"We are not going to give you a 'No,'" he assured me, "as we will be glad to regard your Memorandum as a basis for discussion. . . . I have found your statement regarding your 'explorations' most illuminating and helpful, and you can be certain that we will be ready, when called upon, to consider all these matters further."

At a quarter to one President Truman received me in his office at the White House. Mr. Acheson was with him, and Mr. Price accompanied me.

Aside from Chinese representation (covered in Chapter XV) my résumé for the President concentrated on the portions of the talk with Stalin in which he would be interested.

Mr. Truman nodded his head several times as I described the reception to the proposal of a meeting between the President and the Generalissimo at some future time, and Mr. Stalin's emphatic assertion that such a meeting must be carefully prepared diplomatically and must not be held without some prospects for agreement. There was a similar response at several other points, though he made comments on but three occasions.

When I mentioned telling the Generalissimo that the President liked him, Mr. Truman interjected: "I do, and I believe he likes me."

When I referred to the ITO Charter and the Havana Trade Agreement, and Mr. Stalin's charge that it discriminated against the Soviet trade system, Secretary Acheson interrupted to exclaim, "That is not true!" The President made the same observation.

The President made his third comment when Russia's relations with the other countries of Europe came up. The true state of affairs, he said, was shown by the fact that Turkey, Greece, Norway, and numerous other countries lived in fear of Russia, whereas no neighboring country feared the United States.

At the close of our interview, the President thanked me cordially. "I think you have done a lot of good," he concluded.

AFTERWARDS

On returning to Lake Success I decided that the time had come to give official notice to all the Member governments of what I had done, without yet revealing the preliminary views of the leaders of the four great powers on the points in my Peace Memorandum. I therefore sat down at once to prepare a letter of transmittal. After recounting the reason for my initiative and my visits to the heads of government and Foreign Ministers in the four capitals, I wrote:

While it would not be appropriate for me to state the views of any of the Governments on the points of the Memorandum, I can say that I have drawn from my conversations a firm conviction that the United Nations remains a primary factor in the foreign policy of each of these Governments and that the reopening of genuine negotiations on certain of the outstanding issues may be possible.

It is evident that no significant progress can be made while the Members of the United Nations remain sharply divided on the question of the representation of one of the permanent members of the Security Council —the Republic of China. It is necessary that this question be settled.

I requested the earnest attention of all the governments to my Memorandum on the development of a twenty-year peace program and informed them I might formally submit it to the Security Council at an appropriate time and also place it on the provisional agenda of the next session of the General Assembly.

My letter sought to meet two of the objections raised in the talk with Generalissimo Stalin. In relation to Point Two, on atomic energy, I referred to the appeal by the International Committee of the Red Cross to the governments "to do everything in their power to reach *agreements on the prohibition of the atomic bomb* and 'blind' weapons generally." This, I felt, met Stalin's insistence that prohibition of the bomb be one of the matters for discussion on atomic energy. In connection with Point Seven (on the work of the Specialized Agencies) I pointed out that the conversations of Gunnar Myrdal, Executive Secretary of the Economic Commission for Europe, with various European governments had emphasized the need for further efforts to *liberate international trade from the restrictions and discriminatory practices hampering the free flow of goods.* This was included in response to Generalissimo Stalin's complaints about restrictions and discriminations, but also because of my own opposition to these trade policies.

I was also careful to submit to Mr. Malik my draft for the covering letter on June 2, four days before the transmittal and publication of the Memorandum on June 6, and to request his comments.

He brought to me at Lake Success on Tuesday morning, June 6, a brief message written in Russian, which he translated as follows: "Your letter shows progress as compared to the Memorandum, but the progress is little and insignificant. The position in Soviet circles is known to you from your conversation in Moscow."

To this, I replied that I appreciated the affirmation that there was some progress, even though "little and insignificant." "I would also appreciate your telling Mr. Vyshinsky that my work would be greatly facilitated were the Russians now really to do something toward solving a few problems. In Great Britain and the U.S.A. they are saying that the U.S.S.R. will not yield an inch. There is little probability that anything can be done to end the cold war if there is not a more positive spirit of accommodation on the part of your government."

This was my last conversation with anyone representing the great powers before I published the Memorandum and letter.

Nineteen days later the North Koreans launched their invasion of the Republic of Korea. What the next steps might have been if this brutal and stupid act of armed aggression had not been committed, thus ending all my efforts to break the great-power deadlock, no one now can say. I had been moderately encouraged by the reactions of the leaders of the great powers to my mission, in spite of encountering the expected polite coolness to negotiation and evident preoccupation with the immediate struggle for power on both sides. Nevertheless, I was prepared to continue the efforts. In this resolve I was fortified more by the support of the "man in the street" than of the governments.

Everywhere on my journey I had met with manifestations of public interest and support, though it was known only that I was seeking to bring the great powers around the same table again. Letters, telegrams, resolutions, flowers poured into my hotel rooms in London, Paris, and Geneva, and the flood continued at Lake Success. The mail swamped the correspondence unit in my office, so that it was necessary to publish an open letter of appreciation in order to express my thanks. Nor was this in any way an organized letter campaign of the kind with which all politicians are familiar. I was well aware that some Western statesmen had been fearful that the Communist peace campaign then under way would "use" my mission to the disadvantage of genuine efforts for peace. But the great majority of the letters were clearly spontaneous, written from the hearts of individual men and women, and not produced by any spurious propaganda effort.

Delegations from the United Nations Associations and other citizen groups working seriously for better international relations met me everywhere. The war veterans' organization in France, with three million members, pledged its support. I have referred to the resolution signed by 145 members of the British House of Commons. And then there were the many individual expressions, like the remarks of the bobby outside Number 10 Downing Street and the lift man in my hotel in London, already quoted.

No less impressive was the support and solidarity shown by the leaders of the Specialized Agencies affiliated with the United Nations. Present at our May meeting in Paris at the semiannual conference of the Administrative Coordination Committee were some of the leading men in our international life: Jaime Torres Bodet of the United Nations Educational, Scientific and Cultural Organization, David A. Morse of the International Labor Organization, Norris E. Dodd of the Food and Agriculture Organization, Dr. Brock Chisholm of the World Health Organization, Edward Warner of the International Civil Aviation Organization, Eugene Black, Jr., of the International Bank, Andrew N. Overby of the International Monetary Fund, F. Blanchard of the International Refugee Organization, Gerald C. Gross of the International Telecommunication Union, Fulke R. Radice of the Universal Postal Union and E. Wyndham White, Interim Commission of the International Trade Organization. When I had reviewed the political situation and explained the ideas upon which I had based my visit to the four capitals, this distinguished group unanimously agreed on a strong and forthright statement, affirming the positive United Nations approach to peace, with its principle of universality in membership and programs. "We also believe that it is necessary for all governments to renew their efforts, to conciliate and negotiate the political differences that divide them and obstruct economic and social advancement," they said, and urged "that the present political deadlock in the United Nations be resolved at the earliest possible moment."

This statement was very helpful in my conversations with the statesmen, and I included it in the letter transmitting my peace program proposals to all the Member nations on June 6.

My mission received a degree of publicity surpassing anything I had expected or desired. Millions of men and women who had previously heard little or nothing of the United Nations now became aware of its vital significance in the struggle for peace, and immediately responded with demonstrations of support.

All this, I believe, has had its effect in one way or another upon later developments.

The leaders of the great powers had an unmistakable reminder that the people not only wanted peace, but demanded something more from their governments than a policy—necessary as that might be—of building up defensive alliances and armaments. They wanted something more than to be continually frightened into paying the taxes and voting the budgets for military security with no end in sight except an eventual world collision. They wanted constructive, positive action from their leaders in support of the United Nations and its Charter as a means of avoiding a Third World War.

Even the Korean aggression that immediately followed had its hopeful side in this respect. The previous acts of the United States to strengthen the West against the threat of aggression—the Truman Doctrine for Greece and Turkey, the Marshall Plan, and the North Atlantic Treaty Organization—had been largely outside the United Nations. Now President Truman turned to the United Nations itself, and United States leadership was largely responsible for the fact that the United Nations passed its greatest test, in its collective resistance to aggression in Korea. The Soviet Union had two alternatives once the battle was joined in Korea. One was to withdraw from the United Nations and set up a rival organization of Communist states. The other was to return to the United Nations and seek to extricate itself inside the Organization from the consequences of its colossal blunder. It chose the second course, and all the subsequent maneuvers and blustering of Mr. Vyshinsky and Mr. Malik could not hide the fact that it was compelled to bow to the judgment of mankind as expressed in and by the United Nations.

After June 25, 1950, it was clear that the original and main objective of my proposals for a twenty-year peace program would have to wait for the conclusion of the Korean War. Nevertheless, I decided that a General Assembly discussion of the Ten Points would be useful, even in the existing situation, for the long-range validity of this approach to peace had in no way been diminished. I therefore proposed the program for the Assembly's agenda, and a two-day debate upon it took place on November 18 and 20, 1950. The interest of the delegates in the ideas underlying my proposals proved to be strong and overwhelmingly on the positive side. Of course my stand on Korea drew a full measure of Soviet wrath. The speech of the Foreign Minister of the U.S.S.R., Andrei Vyshinsky, referred to my mission as follows: "It has been said here that Trygve Lie came back from Moscow with his Memorandum. No, he came to Moscow with his Memorandum, which had been already sanctioned by the State Department of the United States of America, subsequently visaed by the Foreign Office in London, and, later, countersigned by Schuman in Paris. In other words, it was approved by that whole company of plotters against peace, and finally it appeared before our eyes in Moscow." Nevertheless, while emphasizing that it was "essential that this Memorandum should be reworked" in line with amendments which he offered, Mr. Vyshinsky also declared that the Soviet Union was "prepared to cooperate in this task" and that it agreed with "the consideration set forth in the Secretary-General's Memorandum to the effect that it is possible successfully to take measures through the United Nations in order to put an end to the so-called cold war and to foster the strengthening of peace."

Notwithstanding the personal attack on me, I was well satisfied with the otherwise high level of discussion and with its outcome. Vyshinsky's amendments suffered a resounding defeat, obtaining but 5 votes. With an affirmative vote of more than 50 of the Members, the General Assembly thereupon passed a resolution commending the Secretary-General for his initiative and requesting the appropriate organs of the United Nations to give consideration to those portions of the Memorandum with which they were particularly concerned, and to report any progress achieved to the next Assembly session.

Such, then, was the immediate fate of the ten-point peace program. I say "immediate," because the further and main chapters of its history have yet to be written. Every one of its ten points holds good today as it did in 1950. In fact, rewriting it now, I would repeat it almost word by word. Steps toward a lasting peace will have to follow the broad outline set forth on June 6, 1950, whenever and wherever they can be taken.

Even as I conclude this chapter, I am encouraged by some things that have been happening. Great-power negotiation has been revived. After six years the Foreign Ministers have met again, though not yet in the special periodic meetings of the Security Council which I am sure will come in time. Within the United Nations, the General Assembly has called upon the great powers to meet in private on atomic energy, and President Eisenhower has come forward with his great and constructive proposal. When I heard his speech, emphasizing a new approach to the old deadlock, I could not help recalling words from Point Two of my peace proposals: "One possibility would be . . . to call a conference of scientists whose discussions might provide a reservoir of new ideas on . . . the promotion of peaceful uses of atomic energy that could thereafter be explored in the United Nations Atomic Energy Commission. . . . There are other possibilities for providing the basis for a new start; every possibility should be explored."

In Korea an improvised United Nations army has been forged in battle and now guards the armistice under the United Nations flag, not yet organized as my peace program envisaged, but still the first army in history to serve an international organization in defense of collective security.

The United Nations expanded program of technical assistance has made great strides since 1950, and the Soviet Union, three years after my appeal to Stalin in Moscow to contribute, has come forth with its first pledge.

These, I hope, are straws in the wind. Immense problems and dangers are still on every hand, but *if* the world will only persist on this path I am sure we shall find that the prospects for lasting peace will improve steadily as time passes.

CHAPTER XVIII

KOREA

The fate of an Asian borderland people.—I invoke Article 99 of the Charter.—Problem of participation.—The "Acheson Plan" is born.

THE GREAT POWERS had originally agreed that the Korean people were to win complete freedom in 1950. They reaped tragedy instead. The aggression in Korea might also have doomed the United Nations; but here in continental Asia the United Nations passed the test and set a first precedent for armed international police action in the field. And though its Secretary-General was severely criticized by those who sided with the aggressor I consider my stand on Korea the best justified act of seven years in the service of peace.

In August, 1945, the Japanese, who had ruled Korea since 1910, surrendered to the forces of the United States and the Soviet Union. Japanese troops north of the 38th parallel surrendered to Soviet commanders; those south of it, to American. The 38th parallel was selected as the temporary demarcation line, not between a "North Korea" and a "South Korea"—entities that were unknown—but between the Soviet and American occupying forces; it was simply a convenient geographical bisecting device. At the Moscow meeting of the Foreign Ministers in December, 1945, it was decided to recommend as a part of the peace settlement that a trusteeship government for Korea be established for a period of five years. A joint commission of the United States and the U.S.S.R. was set up to arrange for this system of government, and for the gradual transfer of power to organs freely elected by the Korean people, whose sovereignty would be complete at the end of that period. But the commission soon reached an impasse: in Korea, as elsewhere, Moscow and Washington failed to see eye to eye. Two separate administrations emerged. Soon the 38th parallel became a border. The unification of the two territories into one independent state was blocked.

This was a most serious trend in the light of earlier Korean history. As a link between the mainland and the Japanese islands, the Korean peninsula had been fought over and divided before. In fact, through four thousand years Korea had been a constant bone of contention between the changing "land power" and "sea power," with border lines and respective "zones of influence" moving up and down the peninsula according to the relative strengths of those powers. In fact, a truly independent Korean state had existed only when the neighboring great powers were in a state of exhaustion. Few nations had suffered so much from foreign rule as Korea. Was its fate once more to be that of the unhappy borderland, squeezed into partition by conflicting great-power interests?

This would certainly not be in conformity with today's concepts of the sovereign rights of a people and a nation as expressed in the United Nations Charter. Clearly, here was a case where the world organization would have to exercise its responsibilities if the powers most directly concerned could not reach an agreement. Accordingly, the United States submitted the problem of the independence of Korea to the United Nations General Assembly.

Thus, the Korean people became a United Nations ward as early as 1947. The General Assembly that autumn did not shirk its responsibility. It decided—against strong Soviet opposition—that at the earliest possible date a national government of Korea should be established through nation-wide elections, which a United Nations Temporary Commission on Korea, composed of the representatives of nine Member states, would supervise. The government so formed would constitute its own national security forces, take over the functions of government from the military command and civilian authorities of North and South Korea, and arrange with the occupying powers for the prompt withdrawal of their troops.

This was the plan, and it would have given to the proud Korean people all the political and other sovereign rights which were clearly their due. The Soviet bloc contended, however, that the General Assembly decision was "illegal." The Soviet government and its repre-

KOREA

sentatives in North Korea would not cooperate. The Ukrainian Soviet Socialist Republic, elected with eight other states to the Temporary Commission, refused to serve. Such attempted intimidation, though complicating matters, could in no way change the General Assembly's resolution. The Commission had been elected and instructed to fulfill its task; the decision had to be carried out. And so it was—within the limits forced by the Soviet noncooperation.

The Temporary Commission was a thoroughly international one, drawn from five continents, including members from India, the Philippines, Australia, and Syria. I designated Assistant Secretary-General Victor Chi-tsai Hoo as my personal representative to get work started in Korea, and a very competent Dutchman, Petrus J. Schmidt, as Principal Secretary. They accompanied the Commission to Korea, and kept me closely informed on Korean affairs from the beginning. Let me quote from one of Dr. Hoo's dispatches to me, for a sense of the atmosphere in Korea at that stage and, incidentally, an impression of Dr. Hoo's wry wit.

All political parties and individuals, except the Communist party, welcomed us most sincerely. Many Koreans say that we are their last hope. . . . [In Seoul] 100,000–250,000 people stood along the streets waiting for our arrival for several hours in the cold. . . . Of course individually they did not all come spontaneously. . . . The Korean radio broadcasts from North Korea are hurling invectives at the Commission. They say that the members of the Commission are hirelings of American imperialism which wants to colonize Korea, and that even I and Schmidt are Americans, and that the Commission will not be allowed to go to North Korea. There were even some rumors that there is a Communist plot to assassinate me, and I was offered, by the American authorities, a bodyguard; but I refused because it would have made a bad impression. I expect that, since we now have a Chairman, he might be assassinated in my stead.

The Chairman, who fortunately, like Victor Hoo, escaped whatever danger of assassination there may have been—was the representative of India, K. P. S. Menon. In a speech to the Korean nation broadcast from Seoul on January 28, 1948, Ambassador Menon set the tone of serious purpose which characterized the Commission's substantially successful attempt to insure that the Korean elections would be genuinely free. "The Commission has established three committees," he reported, "one to study ways and means for securing a free atmosphere for the ensuing elections; another to study Korean opinion; and still another to study the electoral system. . . . The committee which has been appointed to sound Korean opinion will shortly issue a statement regarding the procedure it proposes to adopt. The committee which is to consider the mechanism for the elections will scrutinize the existing electoral laws in North and South Korea and examine how far they are compatible with the General Assembly's recommendations, generally accepted democratic practices, and local requirements. But more important than the mechanism is the spirit. Hence the creation of a separate subcommittee with the object of ensuring a free atmosphere for the ensuing elections. If the elections are to be of any value at all, they must be free and unfettered. They must faithfully reflect the will of the people. Not only must the electors be free to vote as they please at the time of the elections, but there must be freedom for the candidates of all parties—parties of the extreme right, right, middle, left, and extreme left—to put their views before the electorate on a free and equal basis. The Commission will insist upon the observance of this elementary principle, not only at the time of, but before the elections. We would rather pack up and go home than be idle spectators of a faked election."

The authorities of North Korea remained unmoved in the determination not to allow the United Nations to supervise elections in the area they controlled. It was decided that elections would accordingly take place south of the 38th parallel, where about two-thirds of all Koreans lived. The Commission, through extensive field investigation, ascertained that the atmosphere in South Korea was free enough for a free election, and then proceeded to supervise carefully the registration of voters, the campaigning, the voting, and the counting of ballots. It concluded that the elections of May 10, 1948, were a valid expression of the free will of the electorate, and this conclusion was confirmed by a vote of the General Assembly. The Government of the Republic of Korea was formed, as a result of the elections in South Korea, and Syngman Rhee was elected President. The General Assembly during its Paris session in 1948, and again in 1949, declared this government to be the only freely elected and lawful government in Korea. It further established a United Nations

Commission on Korea which was charged with facilitating the peaceful unification of all Korea.

In the meantime, a "Government of the People's Democratic Republic of Korea" had been established in the North, where elections had also taken place. "International" supervision, if any, must have been under Russian auspices. Soon after, the Soviet government announced its withdrawal of all occupation troops. A few months later, the United States government did the same. In each case, it was announced officially that groups of military instructors were left behind, to assist with the organization of national security forces. It has since been disclosed that, at a very early stage, the North Korean Army began to form around a core of two battle-trained divisions comprising Korean exiles and refugees who had served in the Soviet forces, some of them at Stalingrad. It has also been revealed that modern Soviet equipment particularly suited for a "blitz" assault, was freely provided—or "sold," as Mr. Vyshinsky said—to North Korea during this period. But the outside world heard next to nothing of the sinister preparations. In Korea, the United Nations Commission was becoming uneasy as tension and the number of border incidents increased. Finally, in May, 1950, it suggested that careful diplomatic explorations be made with the Soviet authorities to determine the intentions of the North Koreans. Such an attempt was made, but brought no results. Not until early June, when the North Korean Communist party congress at Pyongyang began to talk loudly about unity of the Korean people and even the liberation of the South, was there any real foreboding of imminent danger. The Commission therefore quietly expanded its observation teams in the area of the 38th parallel, where South Korean troops were deployed in defensive positions. Even then it was felt that some demonstration of force was all that might be expected, as part of an anticipated political offensive.

That was all—before the avalanche came.

On June 24, 1950, shortly before midnight, I received an urgent telephone call from Washington at my home in Forest Hills. John D. Hickerson, Assistant Secretary of State for United Nations Affairs, told me that the American Ambassador in Seoul had reported that the North Korean forces had suddenly attacked the Republic of Korea at daybreak (June 25, Korean time). Such details of the assault as he was able to give me indicated that it was much more than a border skirmish. I replied that this sounded like a major violation of the Charter's ban on military aggression, and that I felt the Security Council would have to take immediate action. In fact, I feared it might lead to a Third World War. I took the initiative in assuring Secretary Hickerson that I was prepared to bring the Security Council together at once, and requested that the American authorities insure our communications with the United Nations Commission in Korea. He of course understood that any action I, as Secretary-General, might take to summon the Council on my own initiative or to call the Korean attack to the Council's attention in invocation of my rights under Article 99, should be in response to data furnished by an impartial United Nations source rather than an interested state. I then telephoned to my Executive Assistant, Andrew W. Cordier, conveying to him the news received, and instructed him to cable to the United Nations Commission which was based at Seoul but had its observers well deployed along the 38th parallel, a request for an immediate report on the situation. I furthermore asked Dragon Protitch, the Principal Director of the Department of Security Council Affairs, to locate and inform the President of the Security Council, Sir Benegal Rau of India, and to make preparations for an emergency meeting. At this point, Ambassador Ernest A. Gross telephoned, and we reviewed the situation. We talked over the various possibilities of Security Council action, and he promised to call back when he received his instructions. I had then done everything I could for the moment, and went back to sleep. I was awakened at three o'clock by another call from Mr. Gross, who formally requested me on behalf of his government to convene the Council as soon as possible. I set the session for two o'clock that afternoon and then slept on, between further telephone calls from Mr. Gross, until morning.

Messrs. Feller and Cordier met me at Lake Success at noon, when the cabled report from the Commission had arrived. It confirmed the fact of the North Korean aggression, gave details of its launching, stressed the seriousness of the situation, and suggested that I consider employing my powers under the Charter to bring the situation to the Security Council's attention. I resolved to take up the Commission's suggestion, not only because the United Nations organ most immediately involved so advised, but because this to me was clear-cut aggression—apparently well calculated, meticulously planned, and with all the elements of surprise which reminded me of the Nazi invasion of Norway—because this was aggression against a "creation" of the United Nations, and because the response of the Security Council would be more certain and more in the spirit of the Organization as a whole were the Secretary-General to take the lead. My determination to speak out was hardened by the feeling that Moscow, in its public show of warmly welcoming my peace mission a month before, had been building up a peaceful atmosphere well suited to the surprise attack in Korea. The three of us accordingly settled down to drafting.

In the few hours before the Council's meeting, I exchanged views with the delegates who were assembling at Lake Success. I discussed the situation with three delegations which lacked instructions or seemed doubtful—those of India, Egypt, and Norway. Sir Benegal Rau had been delayed, but I spoke with him over the telephone. I believe I may say without risking any offense that my views probably influenced the Indian delegation, as well as the delegate of Egypt, Mahmoud Fawzi Bey, to vote in favor of the resolution which was adopted that Sunday afternoon. When they later had time to receive instructions from home, Egypt, and then India, retreated to a policy of abstaining on votes of support for the United Nations action in Korea. Equally, my exchange of views that day with Arne Sunde of Norway served to clarify the issue, and Norway was to remain a resolute supporter of the United Nations police action throughout.

When the meeting opened, the President by previous arrangement called upon me to speak first. With emphasis, I declared:

"At midnight yesterday I was informed that a conflict appeared to have broken out in Korea. I immediately dispatched telegrams to the United Nations Commission in Korea asking for a report. This morning the reply of the Commission was received, and it has been circulated as a document of this Council.

"Since November, 1947, the problem of Korea has been a concern of the United Nations. In its Resolution 293 of 21 October, 1949, the General Assembly recalled its previous declaration that there has been established a lawful government (the Government of the Republic of Korea) having effective control and jurisdiction over that part of Korea where the United Nations Temporary Commission on Korea was able to observe and consult and in which the great majority of the people of Korea reside. The General Assembly directed the United Nations Commission to observe and report any developments which might lead to or otherwise involve military conflict in Korea, and among other things to render such interim reports as it may deem appropriate to the Secretary-General for transmission to the members. The General Assembly also called upon Member States, the Government of the Republic of Korea, and all Koreans to afford every assistance and facility to the Commission in fulfillment of its responsibility and to refrain from any acts derogatory to the purposes of the Assembly's resolution.

"The report received by me from the Commission, as well as reports from other sources in Korea, make it plain that military actions have been undertaken by Northern Korean forces.

"These actions are a direct violation of the Resolution of the General Assembly, which has been adopted by a vote of 48 to 6 with 3 abstentions, as well as a violation of the Principles of the Charter.

"The present situation is a serious one and is a threat to international peace. The Security Council is, in my opinion, the competent organ to deal with it.

"I consider it the clear duty of the Security Council to take steps necessary to reestablish peace in that area."

My statement, if a bit technical in wording, contained in essence everything I wanted to say. With it, I labeled the North Koreans as the aggressors, anticipating similar action by the Council. I drew attention to the dangerous international ramifications of an outbreak which the Soviet bloc would attempt to portray as civil war; and I offered the legal opinion that the Security Council was "the competent organ" to deal with the Korean invasion, a view which I advanced in spite of and in opposition to the Soviet contention that the Security Council was not competent to act because of the presence of the "Kuomintang clique" and the absence of representatives of the U.S.S.R. and the Chinese Communist government. Lastly, I called upon the Security Council to fulfill its "clear duty" to meet the aggressor's challenge. I accordingly anticipated and associated my office and myself with the most determined effort to give reality to the principles of collective security.

The Council proceeded to a grim discussion, which grew especially tense when the floor was granted to the representative of the Republic of Korea for an appeal to the Security Council to direct the invaders to cease fire and withdraw. A draft resolution submitted by the United States was adopted, after some revision, by a vote of 9–0, with Yugoslavia abstaining. The Soviet Union, which could have vetoed the resolution had it not been boycotting the Council over Chinese representation, had outmaneuvered itself. The resolution noted "with grave concern the armed attack upon the Republic of Korea by forces from North Korea" and determined that this action constituted a breach of the peace. It called for the "immediate cessation of hostilities" and directed the authorities of North Korea "to withdraw forthwith their armed forces to the thirty-eighth parallel." It further instructed the United Nations Commission on Korea to report on developments, and called upon "all Members to render every assistance to the United Nations in the execution of this resolution and to refrain from giving assistance to the North Korean authorities."

The Commission's cabled reports the next day from Seoul continued to be disturbing. The North Koreans were pressing on in defiance of the Security Council's injunction, and their advances had created a dangerous situation. The critical operations in progress, the Commission warned, might end in a matter of days, and the question of a cease-fire and withdrawal prove "academic." The direct observations of its military observers along the 38th parallel led it to conclude that the Northern regime was carrying out "a well-planned, concerted and full-scale invasion. South Korean forces were employed on a wholly defensive basis in all sectors of the parallel. They were taken completely by surprise.". . .

That night reporters of the United Nations Correspondents Association interviewed me on the radio program "United, or Not?" asking if the Security Council could properly use armed force in Korea. I replied that "it could . . . if the order to cease fire were not obeyed by the Northern Korean troops."

On June 27 the Security Council met to consider that eventuality; for, far from obeying the Council, the North Koreans had raced ahead, while calling upon the government of the Republic of Korea to surrender. The Council met in the afternoon; it would have met earlier in the day, but the representatives of India and Egypt had asked for a postponement pending receipt of their instructions. Hours began to count; the South Korean retreat was turning into a rout. The Americans had given the South Koreans only light defensive armaments, and their troops were terrorized by the large tanks which the Soviet Union had furnished to the aggressor. "The Security Council," President Truman proclaimed, "called upon all Members of the United Nations to render every assistance to the United Nations in execution of this resolution [of June 25]. In these circumstances, I have ordered United States air and sea forces to give the Korean Government troops cover and support." The President further ordered the Seventh Fleet to prevent any attack on Formosa—a move required for protection of the flank of the defenders in Korea—and the acceleration of military assistance to the Philippines and Indo-China as well. This was to warn the aggressors, I surmised, of the United States attitude in case a wider aggression were contemplated.

Because of the delay in the Security Council meeting, the President thus ordered American forces into action before the Council adopted, that same evening, a resolution which recommended that "the Members of the United Nations furnish such assistance to the Republic of Korea as may be necessary to repel the armed attack and to restore international peace and security in the area"; but the order was fully within the spirit of the Council's resolution of June 25 and did not anticipate its resolution of June 27 so much as it seemed to do, for diplomatic consultations before the issuance of the order had made it clear that there were seven votes—the required majority—in the Council for authorizing armed assistance to the Republic of Korea. While the Council waited in the hope that instructions from New Delhi and Cairo would increase those seven votes to nine, the North Korean aggressors went ahead; and I, for one, welcomed the United States' initiative. As it turned out, the Indian and Egyptian delegates still were awaiting their instructions when the Council voted though Sir Benegal Rau reported at the meeting of June 30 that India accepted the resolution of June 27, while Fawzi Bey declared that, had he received his instructions in time, he would have abstained.

The afternoon of June 27, I had attended a luncheon which the Soviet Assistant Secretary-General for Security Council Affairs,

Constantin Zinchenko, gave in the Stockholm Restaurant on Long Island. I was seated between Ernest Gross and the Soviet delegate, Yakov Malik, whose boycott of the Council was then in its fifth month. As we came to dessert and coffee, I recalled to Mr. Malik that the rest of us were about to set off to the meeting of the Security Council. "Won't you join us? The interests of your country would seem to me to call for your presence." He shook his head, and replied: "No, I will not go there."

Ernest Gross and I walked out together and got into my car. His relief that Mr. Malik had not come was unconcealed. "Think," he said with considerable feeling, "what would have happened if he had accepted your invitation." I responded: "Yes, it would have been difficult. We would have had to fight it out, and move on to the General Assembly."

The Secretary-General very frequently is the executive for the decisions by the legislative organs of the United Nations, and this was my role in the Korean conflict. Upon the passage of the resolution of June 27 which Mr. Malik through his absence had made possible, I cabled to all Member governments drawing attention to the call for assistance to the Republic of Korea and suggesting that, if the governments were in a position to assist, early information on the type of help they could furnish would facilitate the carrying out of the resolution. Numerous replies quickly began to come in, and it was soon apparent that some coordinating mechanism for the United Nations effort in Korea was imperative. My advisers and I prepared a draft resolution and circulated it on July 3 to the United States, British, and French delegations, and to the President of the Security Council for the month of July, Arne Sunde of Norway. It would have requested the government of the United States to assume responsibility for directing such armed forces of Members as might be furnished in pursuance of the resolution of June 27, and recommended to the government of Korea that it place its armed forces under American command. It would further have authorized armed forces acting in accordance with that resolution to fly the United Nations flag and—a key point—would have established a "Committee on Coordination of Assistance for Korea." This committee, I suggested, could be composed of Australia, France, India, New Zealand, Norway, the United Kingdom, and the United States; it might add to its membership states furnishing assistance; it would have a representative of the Republic of Korea; and the Secretary-General would serve as Rapporteur. The explicit purpose of the committee was to stimulate and coordinate offers of assistance. Its deeper purpose was to keep the United Nations "in the picture," to promote continuing United Nations participation in and supervision of the military security action in Korea of a more intimate and undistracted character than the Security Council could be expected to provide. The delegates of the United Kingdom, France, and Norway liked the idea of such a committee; the United States Mission promptly turned thumbs down. The Pentagon was much opposed to such United Nations activity. Later it even proved a bit difficult to arrange that the reports of the United Nations Commander in Korea should be officially transmitted to the Security Council before being released to the press by American attachés in Tokyo. As the Korean War developed, Washington complained, and had reason to complain, that the United States was carrying too much of the burden; but its unwillingness, in those early days when the pattern of the police action was being set, to accord the United Nations a larger measure of direction and thereby participation no doubt contributed to the tendency of the Members to let Washington assume most of the responsibility for the fighting. As it was, the Security Council met on July 7 and adopted the essence of the draft I had circulated on July 3, less the provision for the Committee on Coordination. Thus the Unified Command came into being, and President Truman announced the next day that he had designated General of the Army Douglas MacArthur as United Nations Commander. A week later the Chief of Staff of the United States Army presented to General MacArthur a United Nations flag which I had given to Warren Austin earlier for forwarding. It was the flag which the United Nations Mediator in Palestine had flown.

I felt the need for closer contact with General MacArthur and with the situation in Korea, and accordingly appointed a personal representative to the United Nations Commission, the Unified Command, and the Republic of Korea: Colonel Alfred G. Katzin of the Union of South Africa, an energetic officer who had been a senior official of UNRRA and had served in Allied intelligence during the war. He proved to be a liaison officer of capacity and imagination.

His relations with General MacArthur were excellent, as indeed were mine, and he was particularly useful in coping with the tragic problem of the Korean refugees.

The powerful propaganda apparatus of international Communism by this time was chanting that the action of the Security Council in Korea was "illegal." The Americans, Andrei Gromyko asserted on July 4, were the real aggressors in Korea. The resolution of June 27 was not actually adopted for there were but six votes, the seventh being that of "Kuomintangite Tsiang Ting-fu, who unlawfully occupies China's seat in the Security Council." Besides, the U.S.S.R. and (Peking) China were absent when the decision was taken, and the resolution was the more illegal because it constituted "interference in the domestic affairs" of Korea. If the Council had "valued the cause of peace," Mr. Gromyko suggested, "it should have attempted to reconcile the fighting sides in Korea before it adopted such a scandalous resolution. Only the Security Council and the United Nations Secretary-General could have done this. However, they did not make such an attempt, evidently knowing that such peaceful action contradicts the aggressor's plans." Trygve Lie, Mr. Gromyko charged, had played "an unseemly role," having "obsequiously helped a gross violation of the Charter on the part of the United States Government and other members of the Security Council."

Some of this it was not my place to answer, at least at that time; but, in response to the purportedly legalistic objections which the Soviet Union thus officially raised, I reiterated my view that the Council's actions were wholly legal. The Legal Department, at my request, prepared a memorandum on "Legal Aspects of Security Council Action on Korea" which I circulated privately among key delegations and persons. Mr. Zinchenko no doubt passed it on to the Soviet Delegation, as was my intention. It set forth the solid legal basis for the Council's resolutions, and then examined the charges against the Council's competence to adopt them. The lawful occupant of China's seat, it maintained, was to be determined by the Council. The absence of the U.S.S.R., in accordance with United Nations practice, did not constitute an automatic veto of substantive resolutions then adopted; rather it was equivalent to an abstention. As for the argument that the Korean War was a domestic affair, the memorandum pointed out that Korea had been an international and a United Nations concern for years, and that, moreover, the clause of the Charter which forbade United Nations interference in matters "essentially within the domestic jurisdiction of any state" expressly did not prejudice enforcement measures by the Organization. Communist propaganda made much of this theme of domestic jurisdiction—Mr. Gromyko said that the Koreans had the same right to arrange their internal unification as the North and the South had had in the American Civil War. In the world today, legally bound by the new factor of the United Nations Charter, such an argument seemed to me to be transparent nonsense; for the United Nations clearly was empowered to deal with any threat to international peace, whether its origins were in an international dispute or in a civil one.

Without the slightest doubt about the legality—and the imperative wisdom—of the Security Council's resolutions, I was concerned with the "solo" role which at once was left to and assumed by the United States. It was obvious that the United States would have to make the major contribution to the United Nations effort in Korea —military exigencies compelled this; but I wanted our response to aggression to be as genuinely international as possible and was determined that other Members should assume a meaningful proportion of the burden, and that the contributions of many countries should be effectively coordinated. I accordingly called a meeting on July 10 of the President of the Security Council, Arne Sunde, and of representatives of the United States Mission to the United Nations and of the Republic of Korea. Ambassadors Austin and Gross and John Ross of the United States Mission participated, as well as Mr. Cordier. Many delegations, I noted, had been approaching me for advice about possible offers of assistance. I was, I said, less interested in votes than in tangible evidence of support; but the governments would find it easier to offer help to the United Nations rather than to one state. I emphasized the importance of moral and political, as well as military, support and, together with the Korean Ambassador, stressed the short-term relief and long-term rehabilitation needs of Korea. This meeting was one of an exchange of views; I wanted to stimulate the Americans, who had responsibility for the Unified Command, into thinking about how to broaden and equally unify that command.

Three days later Warren Austin and I met again, and he submitted a rough draft of the substance of cables to be dispatched to all Members which had favored the Security Council's resolutions. Its essence was to request the individual country to consider without delay what it could contribute in effective assistance, including wherever possible combat forces, particularly ground forces. The draft suggested, with an eye on military security, "Offers of military assistance should be communicated to the United Nations Secretary-General in general terms, leaving detailed arrangements for subsequent agreement between the offering country and the Unified Command." We discussed the suggestion thoroughly, and I agreed to it, but pointed out that the Security Council had entrusted this task to the Unified Command (the United States Government) and not to the Secretary-General. It would therefore have to be made clear to the Members before they received my cables that I was acting with the full agreement of the Unified Command—that is, of the United States. I accordingly requested him to have Washington immediately instruct its ambassadors in fifty-three capitals to see the respective foreign ministers at once with the assurance that the Secretary-General and the Unified Command were acting in unison, and equally to instruct the United States Mission to inform the permanent representatives at headquarters. Mr. Austin agreed, but, I regret to say, our understanding was not carried out as it should have been. Some confusion resulted, while I was publicly criticized for sending cables without "adequate consultation."

I, for my part, lost no time. In consultation with the United States Mission and the President of the Security Council, I worked out the texts of the fifty-three cables. They varied somewhat according to the Korean response of the government concerned up to that date, and were dispatched on July 14. Let me quote the text of the one to Sir Gladwyn Jebb:

> I have the honour to acknowledge your reply of 28 June 1950 regarding the Security Council resolution of 27 June 1950 and wish to express my appreciation for the decision of the United Kingdom government under the terms of the resolution of immediately placing His Majesty's naval forces in Japanese waters at the disposal of United States authorities to operate on behalf of the Security Council in support of South Korea. Your reply has been transmitted to the Security Council, the gov-

ernment of the Republic of Korea and to the Unified Command (USG). I have been informed the government of the United States which under the resolution of 7 July 1950 has been given responsibility for the Unified Command is now prepared to engage in direct consultations with your government with regard to the coordination of all assistance in a general plan for the attainment of the objectives set forth in the Security Council resolutions. In this connection I have been advised that there is an urgent need for additional effective assistance. I should be grateful therefore if your government would examine its capacity to provide an increased volume of combat forces, particularly ground forces. Offers of military assistance should be communicated to the Secretary General in general terms leaving detailed arrangements for subsequent agreement between your government and the Unified Command (USG).

The day of the dispatch of the cables, I sent Messrs. Cordier and Feller to the United States Mission. They stressed the importance of not leaving the Security Council's role to the Secretary-General, and also advanced the suggestion, which various delegations had made to me, that officers of governments which were furnishing substantial assistance in Korea be appointed to high posts in the United Nations command. A variety of important problems, from strengthening the personnel of the United Nations Commission on Korea to the formation of an international brigade, were informally discussed.

Replies from the fifty-three Governments began to come in quickly, but not adequately; the disposition to provide the Unified Command with substantial armed assistance was disappointing. At my press conference on July 14 it was asked whether the Members could content themselves with contributing token forces. "No," I replied, "I think they should give effective assistance; that is my personal opinion." Meeting with John Hickerson, Livingston T. Merchant, Ambassadors Austin and Gross, and others of the United States Mission a week later, I reviewed the replies: too many were of a token nature. I could not agree to the French statement of inability to supply ground forces, I told them, and noted that I was sending an emissary to Paris with the request that France send at least 2,000 troops. My negotiations with the United Kingdom, Australia, Canada, and New Zealand were promising. It would be unfortunate, I said, for nations which were parties to the North Atlantic Treaty, like Belgium, to plead treaty commitments as a reason for not supplying ground forces: we were aware of the charges that such treaties were considered as superseding the United Nations Charter. I was, I stated, sending personal messages to the prime ministers of the Scandinavian states, urging that they add to their present offers of assistance, and saw no reason why Brazil and Argentina could not furnish troops. Mr. Hickerson made it clear that the United States was in full agreement with me on the political and military importance of wide contributions of forces. "The political battle, presently taking place," I suggested, "is even more important than the military battle."

A new method might be necessary, I stated, in order to secure the maximum effective military forces. The Unified Command should find a way of using all capable volunteers from foreign countries. An international brigade which would be organized by the United States, but at the disposal of the Security Council, might be the device. I suggested that such a brigade would bear the United Nations name and wear United Nations uniforms and be enlisted for a term of two to three years. I anticipated that the number of volunteers would be large, but felt that the only practical way of organizing the brigade was to entrust the responsibility—and the expense—to the United States.

The American representatives gave my idea a mixed reception. It would, they acknowledged, facilitate the participation of small countries in the United Nations effort. But special United States legislation would be required; perhaps the job might better be left to Canada. They wondered what might be done with the troops if the Korean fighting ended in 1950, and I responded that they could be used for police duties there. To this they agreed; but they doubted whether volunteer forces could be molded into combat units in time for the Korean fighting. The idea, though not put into practice—some other governments, like the Yugoslav, were opposed for reasons of their own—was, I think, a good one; the idea of an international brigade still merits consideration.

By August 7 I was able to announce that forty-one Member countries had replied to my cable, most of them offering concrete assistance. In the end, fifteen states, besides the United States and the Republic of Korea, had combat forces in Korea: Australia, Belgium, Canada, Colombia, Ethiopia, France, Greece, Luxembourg, the

Netherlands, New Zealand, the Philippines, Thailand, Turkey, the Union of South Africa and the United Kingdom. A British Commonwealth division was formed which, like all the United States contingents, fought with great distinction. The morale of this first international army to fight for collective security was extremely high. The nonmilitary contributions which many Members made—like the Norwegian and the Swedish field hospitals, the Danish hospital ship, the Indian ambulance team—were also of considerable value. Though too much was left to the extraordinary self-sacrifice of the United States, the United Nations effort in Korea was, in a significant measure, truly international.

Early in the fighting, deeply disturbing reports of shooting of prisoners and other atrocities began to come in. On July 11 I sent identical cables to the governments of North Korea and the Republic of Korea, strongly urging them to accept the proffered services of the International Red Cross, and to follow strictly the principles of the Geneva Conventions on the law of war, as the best means of avoiding such incidents. Two days later the Republic of Korea informed me that it had declared its adherence to the Geneva Conventions, that its armed forces were acting in their spirit, and that it had arranged to accept the services of the International Red Cross. The same day, I received a cable from the North Korean authorities that its army was acting in accordance with the Conventions in respect to prisoners of war. "I am hopeful," I declared, "that these strong official affirmations of support for the Geneva Conventions—which are now on record for all the world to see—will help in preventing atrocities on either side of the fighting, and that representatives of the International Red Cross will be able to work on both sides of the fighting lines." As it turned out, however, the North Korean authorities refused to permit the International Red Cross access to the territory they controlled until the signing of the armistice in the summer of 1953.

My executive office, and Colonel Katzin in Tokyo and Korea, took the lead in making arrangements for relief assistance and medical aid, in cooperation with the government of the Korean Republic, the Unified Command, and the Tokyo office of the United States Economic Cooperation Administration (ECA). The Security Council on July 31 asked the Unified Command to determine relief requirements and requested the Secretary-General to coordinate and help provide assistance.

Early in July, Henry A. Wallace, the former Vice President of the United States, whom I had known during World War II, came to see me. The candidate of the Progressive Party for the Presidency in 1948, he had, these last years, been left-wing in his public pronouncements, and there was considerable interest in his reaction to the Communist aggression in Korea. But he had put off a public statement on the ground that he did not yet have all the facts, and he came now to secure them. We had an earnest talk for two to three hours that Saturday afternoon. He asked my advice, and I gave it: his obligation as a believer in the United Nations was to support its effort to repel aggression. He took all the relevant documentation I could give, and returned some days later for a second talk. Soon after, he announced his stand: he favored the action of the United Nations and of his country in Korea. This led to his break with the Communists and with the Progressive party, and, I am sure, helped many other good people around the world to make up their minds about the United Nations action.

Support for this action did not, of course, include Moscow. The Soviet Union turned down the request of Washington, a few days after the North Korean attack, that it use its good offices to bring about a cease-fire, and made clear from the beginning its support of the aggressor. I was accordingly most interested when Mr. Zinchenko advised me on July 26 not to leave headquarters for Norway on the brief home leave planned, and, therefore I was not wholly surprised when Yakov Malik informed me on July 27 that he would assume the presidency of the Security Council and called a meeting for August 1, thus ending the U.S.S.R.'s six-month boycott. On that day—in spite of all the Soviet Union had said time and again about not sitting at the table with the representatives of the "Kuomintang clique"—Mr. Malik indeed returned, and launched a month of misuse of his powers, in an attempt to bog down the Council's Korean action; but the debate which raged in the Security Council left its Korean resolutions unshaken, and, from the point of view of "propaganda," the wit of Sir Gladwyn Jebb and the indignation of Warren Austin did not permit Malik to get the best of things.

My relations with the Soviet Union were in remarkable contrast to those which had existed just two months before. "I have been received in a most friendly way," was my report after the trip to Moscow in May, 1950; and, as far as the superficial cordialities went, this was very much the case. Of that visit, a Soviet spokesman wrote not many weeks later:

> Only recently, after he donned the mask of objective arbitrator, Trygve Lie traveled about European capitals on a "peace mission." Newspapers wrote much about his "valuable initiative." What is such a "mission of peace" worth after Trygve Lie's openly coming forth against peace and in defense of an aggressive war?
> Evidently, this "valuable initiative" was no more than a maneuver designed to distract attention from the war venture being prepared by the Americans in the Far East.

In Moscow's eyes I had thus become "the abettor of American aggression . . . humbly aiding Truman and Acheson to wreck the United Nations." The "availability" I had enjoyed as a bridge between East and West seemed to be destroyed. Because the Secretary-General had the opportunity and obligation, as spokesman for the interests of the United Nations as a whole, to avoid partisan identification with any particular power or group of powers, some quarters questioned my Korean stand. They said I should have attempted to mediate the war (thus allowing the aggressor to press his attack while I was talking to him and, quite possibly, to occupy all of Korea) rather than directing all my energies toward mobilizing a United Nations army to throw back the aggressor. I rejected this point of view then, and I reject it now. The Secretary-General is not to be "neutral" above all else, "for neutrality implies political abstinence, not political action," and in certain circumstances might well keep him from conscientious fulfillment of his Charter obligations. There is, for example, an "unneutral" predisposition about the Secretary-General's calling the Security Council's attention, under Article 99, to a matter threatening the peace, since it is unlikely that it can ever be in the equal interests of the parties to a dispute, in an exact, precisely neutral degree, that a situation in which they are involved be brought before the Council.* Rather, the duty of the Secretary-

---

* Stephen M. Schwebel, *The Secretary-General of the United Nations: His Political Powers and Practice* (Cambridge, Mass., 1952), p. 111.

General is to uphold the principles of the Charter and the decisions of the Organization as objectively as he can. This is what I did in Korea.

The position of Mr. Zinchenko was of course difficult, and so was mine. The spectacle of a Soviet national reading out to the Security Council the condemnations of Communist aggression in Korea cabled by the United Nations Commission and Command had in it something of unreality. I also realized that, for other reasons, the position of members of the Security Council Affairs Department under Zinchenko might be equally difficult. No military secrets whatsoever were in fact involved, but the layman outside the United Nations—and even people in high political office in Member states—did not always understand the precise functions of the Secretariat. I therefore placed Korean affairs in the hands of a specially constituted unit attached directly to my own office.

Colonel Katzin was doing a highly competent job in Korea. His August 29 report on developments was remarkable for the prescience of its intelligence estimates and the keenness of its reasoning. It was sent at a time when the United Nations forces had retreated to a small defense perimeter—almost a bridgehead—in the southeast corner of Korea. Let me quote a few passages:

> There is no doubt . . . that much of [the North Koreans'] impetus is lost and that their viciousness and determination in attack is as much due to the practice of their own side in liquidating their troops who fail to meet their objectives as it is to enthusiasm for the cause for which they are fighting.
>
> My own estimate of the present situation, based not only on estimates and reports given me but also from personal observations which I have made of the front-line situation, is that when the United Nations has concentrated enough forces for attack, the North Koreans *could* fold up very rapidly indeed. There are many who disagree with this estimate. . . .
>
> I lean towards the belief that the North Korean has not shown himself to be unrealistic or unintelligent either in his war tactics, which from a military point of view have been almost flawlessly conducted, or in his political thinking as exemplified by the "timing" and conduct of his first act of aggression which, but for UN intervention, would undoubtedly have achieved its objective within two or three weeks. My thinking is that he is as likely as not to be equally realistic when faced with the possible destruction of his forces. Should he then not be materially assisted

with men or supplies from Chinese or Russian sources, I believe that there will be every possibility that he will withdraw behind the 38th parallel. . . .

If we reach the 38th parallel and are there required to stop even for a relatively short time there can be little doubt at all that, even though the enemy might have been badly battered and have lost most of his equipment in his retreat, it will be a matter of weeks only before he can re-form his forces and equipment with outside assistance. This will constitute a continuing military threat not only to our own United Nations forces, but to South Korean freedom.

Some of the eventualities with which Colonel Katzin dealt were realized with exhilarating rapidity. The brilliant Inchon landings of September 15 turned the tide of battle almost overnight; the aggressor, in danger of being cut off, ran for the north. The question was no longer, "Can we hold the Korean bridgehead?" but "Should the United Nations forces pursue the aggressor into North Korea?"

On September 30 my advisers and I prepared a draft working paper, "Suggested Terms of Settlement of the Korean Question," which I circulated among the American, British, French, Canadian, Indian, and Norwegian delegations, and discussed with Mr. Zinchenko. It suggested that the General Assembly, then in session, demand that the North Korean authorities agree to a cease-fire and withdrawal to the 38th parallel; demilitarization of their forces; entry of the United Nations Commission into North Korea with the opportunity to fulfill its functions; entry of United Nations relief personnel as well; a general amnesty for persons who had taken up arms for the Republic of Korea and were now in North Korean territory; and agreement for a free election to be held in all Korea within a year, at a date and under regulations to be promulgated by the United Nations Commission. If the North Korean authorities accepted these conditions, I suggested, their *de facto* jurisdiction in the area north of the parallel would be preserved until after the election. United Nations troops would not cross the parallel until then. At that point, authority would be handed over to the new all-Korean government chosen in the elections. The Republic of Korea, for its part, would be asked to agree to accept the elections and their results, and to grant a general amnesty for all persons who had taken up arms against it. "In the event of refusal by North Korean authorities, the General Assembly will recommend to the Members that United Nations troops proceed to conduct military operations north of the parallel, with the objective of eliminating the North Korean authorities. Upon the achievement of this objective North Korea will be placed under the jurisdiction of the United Nations occupation authorities . . . until such time as the Assembly or the Security Council decides that an election for all Korea should be held."

The suggestions met with considerable interest, but they were apparently outdistanced by American negotiations with various delegations. The United States advanced a resolution which recommended that "all necessary steps be taken to ensure conditions of peace throughout the whole of Korea," and that elections be held under United Nations auspices to complete the establishment of a unified, independent, and democratic government of all Korea. "United Nations forces entering North Korea" (this would constitute their authorization to enter) should not remain otherwise "than so far as necessary for achieving objectives," already stated. The General Assembly resolution of October 7, incorporating the essence of this American draft with various revisions, established a United Nations Commission for the Unification and Rehabilitation of Korea. The dominant feeling in the Assembly, which I shared, was that the North Korean failure to heed the Security Council's call to cease fire and withdraw, and continued broadcasting that the retreat was temporary and "strategic," indicated that they would soon strike south again, giving the United Nations forces no alternative to an advance north of the 38th parallel. Without a readiness in the aggressor to cease his aggression, it would be militarily untenable for the United Nations army to halt on an imaginary line and permit him to pull himself together for a fresh assault. Nevertheless, I was unhappy in the abandonment of my own plan—particularly after the Communist side, through Czechoslovakian Foreign Minister Siroky, showed some interest in similar ideas.

There was at this fateful hour a feeling of elation and of high and successful purpose which the United Nations experienced only rarely —at San Francisco, at the end of the Berlin blockade, and at the conclusion of the Armistice Agreements in Palestine. The feeling had mounted with the prompt and decisive action of the Security Council in June; it reached its crescendo in these brief weeks when the

Organization seemed to have put aggression to flight. This was Korea, not Manchuria; this was the United Nations, not the League of Nations.

With the thought that in the case of another Korea the Soviet Union might be present in the Security Council from the outset, able to veto action, the Assembly in these weeks adopted the "Acheson Plan" for "United Action for Peace." The plan provided for emergency special sessions of the Assembly to be called on twenty-four hours' notice after the veto-less vote of any seven members of the Security Council or by a majority of the Members of the Organization. If the Security Council were blocked, then the Assembly could take action. It could recommend, in the case of a second Korea, what the Security Council had recommended on June 25 and June 27, 1950 —for, though the Council has the power to command, it is important to note that its resolutions simply recommended assisting the Republic of Korea; and the General Assembly equally might adopt such recommendations, of equal effectiveness. The "United Action for Peace" resolution further established a Peace Observation Commission, composed of the representatives of fourteen Members, including the Big Five, to observe and report the situation in an area of international tension, and established a Collective Measures Committee to study, "in consultation with the Secretary-General and with such Member States as the Committee finds appropriate," methods of maintaining and strengthening international peace and security. The Collective Measures Committee was, in a sense, designed to extract and apply the lessons of the Korean experience. There was a further recommendation that Member states maintain elements within their national armed forces for prompt availability as United Nations units; and the resolution requested "the Secretary-General to appoint, with the approval of the Committee, . . . a panel of military experts who could be made available on request to Member States wishing to obtain technical advice regarding the organization, training and equipment for prompt service as United Nations units of the elements referred to."

This last provision particularly excited Mr. Vyshinsky's sarcastic ire:

"This provision," he informed the Political and Security Committee of the Assembly, "is basically and fundamentally incompatible

KOREA 347

with the Charter. It short-circuits the Military Staff Committee and the Security Council. . . . It is even more bizarre than that: it speaks of military experts and advisers who it suggests . . . will be under the orders of the Secretary-General.

"Apparently, the military experts will be at the beck and call of the Secretary-General. He is to be commander-in-chief of the armed forces of the General Assembly . . . riding on a white horse. . . .

"However, under the Charter the Secretary-General can only command his workers in the Secretariat. . . . He does not have military experts with or without special panels. He has mimeograph machines. . . . One does not need military experts to run mimeograph machines. . . .

"The weakness and illegality of this proposal are patent."

The Assembly was not deterred, and, by adopting the Acheson Plan, engineered a profoundly important shift of emergency power from the veto-ridden Security Council to the veto-less General Assembly—a shift the full potentialities of which have still to be realized. I publicly indicated my support of the plan while it was being debated, and, once it was adopted, I appointed a special coordinating committee of senior Secretariat members, to advance the implementing of the resolution.

A letter from General MacArthur in this same flushed period illustrates the feelings of the hour, and I wish to quote from it for the suggestion from the great general which it contains. He wrote from Tokyo on November 5:

> In further reference our exchange of messages through Colonel Katzin, I am delighted that the United Nations has now extended your term of office and taken measures to unshackle its freedom to act in emergency situations and provide the physical means to enforce its orders. All this has strengthened the organization immeasurably. For your private information, it is my personal view confirmed by many thoughtful men who have conferred with me that you should now proceed vigorously to provide within the structure of the United Nations a permanent supreme military command adequately staffed to develop and maintain current, on a global basis, strategic and logistical plans designed to effect the immediate deployment of the available military force to meet any emergency situation and to keep the United Nations constantly informed on the military aspects concerning any area of actual or threatened trouble.

Stand-by forces earmarked for United Nations service within the political boundaries of member nations will do no good unless through detailed prior planning their deployment in time of need is strategically sound and immediate. Only thereby may the risks inherent in the initial stages of the Korean campaign be eliminated and the threat of resort to war by recalcitrant elements minimized.

I am looking forward to Colonel Katzin's early return, and to the arrival of the United Nations commission. Both may be assured of my hearty support.

With all good wishes for your continued success in the great work in which you have already rendered such distinguished service, I am

Most faithfully,
DOUGLAS MACARTHUR

A later letter from General MacArthur while still chief of the United Nations command in Korea demonstrated his faith in the United Nations by offering his services as chief of such a permanent supreme military command; and presumably he wished to retire both from his Far East command and from the United States Army for that purpose.

But events now changed the character of the Korean War decisively.

CHAPTER XIX

PEKING FAILS TO UNDERSTAND

*The Yalu River is reached.—A new aggression unfolds.—
Fruitless discussions with Peking representatives.—Nehru on
"Asia first."—Status quo rejected by Communists
but finally achieved.*

ON THE day that General MacArthur wrote the letter just quoted, he reported to the Security Council that "forces other than Korean are resisting our efforts to carry out the resolutions of the United Nations. . . . The United Nations forces in Korea are continuing their drive to the north, and their efforts to destroy further the effectiveness of the enemy as a fighting force are proving successful. However, presently in certain areas of Korea, the United Nations forces are meeting a new foe. It is apparent to our fighting forces, and our intelligence agencies have confirmed the fact, that the United Nations are presently in hostile contact with Chinese communist military units deployed for action against the forces of the United Nations Command."

Strong fears had already been felt for some time that the Peking government might come to the rescue of the North Koreans before their rout was complete. The Soviet Union, perhaps because of its Membership in the United Nations, did not seem particularly anxious to do so; but Peking had no similar obligations. There was also the possibility that the young Chinese Communist regime, suspicious of the outside world, would "advance its line of defense" into Korean territory, at least beyond the watershed, to protect the reservoirs of their huge electric power plants in Manchuria. Were that their intention, there might be room for negotiation or persuasion. Now, with General MacArthur's report, it was time to act.

Six powers submitted a draft resolution to the Security Council on November 10 which, in diplomatic terminology, called upon Peking to withdraw its national forces from Korea, and affirmed "that it is the policy of the United Nations to hold the Chinese frontier with Korea inviolate and fully protect legitimate Chinese and Korean interests in the frontier zone." If the Chinese were fearful of their border, the Security Council could thus reassure them; if they were fearful about the power plants, the United Nations was offering the further assurance that "legitimate Chinese and Korean interests in the frontier zone" would be protected. The British also proposed that the Peking government be invited to take part in the Council's discussion of General MacArthur's report on their intervention. But the Chinese Communists refused the invitation, while their Soviet allies vetoed the six-power draft resolution.

Our original fears proved to be well founded, and on November 29 disaster struck. The obscure "presence" of the Chinese Communists was suddenly revealed to be a counterattack of massive force; across the river from Manchuria, a new aggressor poured in. The United Nations troops had penetrated to the Yalu, which marked the boundary with Manchuria; victory was in sight, and it looked as if the war would end within weeks. But General MacArthur, miscalculating Chinese strength and Chinese intentions, had overextended his forces. In what had seemed to be the moment of fulfillment, hideous defeat for the United Nations army suddenly loomed.

The confusion stemming from this overnight reversal prompted me to send the following telegram to General MacArthur on December 1, in order to leave no room for doubt as to my own position vis-à-vis the United Nations Commander:

Whether in the days of victorious advance or in the difficult days of the beachhead or in the midst of the present temporary crisis you have assurances of my warm personal support. I am confident that the United Nations forces under your able leadership will succeed in bringing peace and stability to Korea. I am grateful to you for your letter. There is a slight possibility that if time and circumstances permit I shall be able to come to Japan and Korea in the near future and in that event will of course wish to visit you and UNCURK.* I also have invitation from the government of Korea. I shall be happy to discuss the substance of your letter in connection with the eventual visit. If I am unable to come I shall transmit a reply to your letter with Colonel Katzin. Warmest regards.

The confidence which I affirmed at this black hour was not shared in all United Nations quarters. Some—though not all—members of the United Nations Commission, then in Seoul, wanted to evacuate to Tokyo with all dispatch: a move which would have been disheartening for the United Nations effort. Angered, I cabled an injunction not to leave Korea; and, though this caused resentment among certain delegations, the Commission did not in fact evacuate for Japan. The Commission carried on as well as it could in the unexpected circumstances, buoyed by stanch delegates like James Plimsoll of Australia and Manuel Trucco of Chile, and by its Principal Secretary, Constantin Stavropoulos.

My advisers and I were in constant consultation to evolve a formula which *might* halt what then appeared to be a precipitous rush toward an extension of the conflict. "For all of us who have shared the labor and the dreams of the past five years," I declared in a speech on December 5, "this is a moment when we are sick at heart. The peace of the world is in the gravest danger only five years after the end of the Second World War and the establishment of the United Nations."

An opportunity for diplomatic action now presented itself, and I decided to use it. Peking, while rejecting the Security Council's invitation to take part in its consideration of her intervention in Korea, had accepted the invitation to send a delegation to Lake Success to participate in the Council's discussion of Peking's complaint against the United States of "armed invasion of Taiwan" (Formosa). Under the chairmanship of General Wu Hsiu-chuan, the delegation arrived at the end of November. On December 1, we had our first talk.

Ambassador Wu opened the conversation by thanking me for the assistance which his group had received from the United Nations Secretariat in visas, tickets, and the like at Prague and London. We discussed a number of administrative matters, such as facilities for their dispatch of code telegrams. I remarked that the Secretariat

* That is, United Nations Commission for the Unification and Rehabilitation of Korea.

would be happy to give the delegation any administrative assistance it could, and added that perhaps I might, on the basis of mutual confidence between us, be of some eventual political assistance.

The next day, Ambassador Ales Bebler of Yugoslavia, President of the Security Council, asked me to arrange a meeting for him with the Chinese, and I did. We met them together. I was highly interested to see how Chinese Communists would receive a Titoist. They were correct, polite, and they rebuffed all his advances. As President of the Security Council, Bebler suggested, he was prepared to play the part of mediator. Thank you, the Chinese replied; they had their instructions for the debate on Formosa and were not in need of assistance.

I received Ambassador Wu and his colleagues for the third time in the new headquarters building in Manhattan, explaining that I had arranged the meeting in order to take up the matter of the United Nations Information Center in Shanghai, which was under the direction of a Belgian, Henri Fast. He had left China on home leave and was now in Hong Kong awaiting a visa from the Communist authorities so that he might return. I asked Ambassador Wu to have this matter taken care of as soon as possible.

We talked about a few other questions before I raised the point which was my main reason for proposing the conversation. I wanted to take some soundings on their approach to a cease-fire in Korea.

I pointed out that, if the Chinese "volunteers" and North Koreans would agree to a cease-fire now, the Peking government's chances of obtaining what it believed to be its international rights would be far better than they were. But if, as conditions of a cease-fire, they continued to demand immediate admission to the United Nations and possession of Formosa, their prospects for success were slender. In reply, General Wu and his colleagues repeated that they had their instructions about their Formosa complaints, and would follow them. I concluded that he lacked the power to engage in serious negotiations, and did not then press them further. We had been talking more than an hour, and so I took them on a tour of the new building and on the roof. They were pleased with what they saw, and returned to the Waldorf-Astoria in high spirits.

That evening I gave a dinner for the Chinese at my home in Forest Hills, inviting the chief delegates from a number of key countries

PEKING FAILS TO UNDERSTAND

which had recognized the Peking government: Sir Gladwyn Jebb of the United Kingdom, Sir Benegal Rau of India, Sir Muhammad Zafrulla Khan of Pakistan, Moshe Sharett of Israel, and Sven Grafstrom of Sweden. My purpose was to bring the Chinese into amiable contact with the United Nations world. At this dinner Mr. Sharett broached the principles of the cease-fire resolution which the General Assembly later adopted.

On the same day, December 4, I had a talk with the Foreign Minister of Czechoslovakia, Viliam Siroky, and asked his opinion about the possibilities of obtaining peace. He asked what I meant by "peace." Naturally, I was talking about the Korean conflict. That, he unhesitatingly responded, was an easy matter. The conflict could be settled by establishing a line of demarcation between the opposing forces at, for example, the 38th parallel. Foreign troops would have to be removed, and then the Koreans themselves could decide the future of Korea without interference. It was, he said, a matter of reestablishing the status quo ante, that is, conditions as they had been in Korea before June 25.

I became most interested: peace on such terms would mean that the aggressor had been pushed back to the line from which he had started. The status quo ante further would involve the presence of a United Nations Commission in the Republic of Korea. "When you say 'foreign' troops," I inquired, "I presume you include the Chinese 'volunteers'?" Mr. Siroky answered affirmatively. "May I ask," I pursued, "if your opinions are shared by Mr. Vyshinsky?" He looked somewhat confused: had he taken this for granted? He would find out, he said.

I spoke with Ambassadors Austin and Gross, with Sir Gladwyn Jebb, and with Ambassador Jean Chauvel. Mr. Austin appeared to discount the importance of the Czech Foreign Minister's statement, while Chauvel ventured some doubt about the American tactical considerations at the time.

The Chinese asked to see me on Saturday December 9, in order to talk in more detail about the situation in Asia. Mr. Wu stated that his government was for peace, and wanted a cease-fire. He said nothing of Chinese conditions therefor; not a word about representation, or Formosa. "What are the United Nations conditions?" he asked. I responded by inquiring if he had not discussed them with

Sir Benegal Rau that morning. "The Indian views don't count for much," he answered, "since, among other things, they have no soldiers in Korea." His delegation would be grateful if I could help them in learning the cease-fire conditions of the United Nations and of the United States.

This was a direct challenge to me to assist them—my preparations seemed to be bearing some fruit, after all. I replied that I would consider how I might help (wishing first to learn from Sir Benegal Rau what the Chinese had told him). We parted cordially.

When Ernest Gross came to my home that evening, I told him what had occurred, and he in turn told about Sir Benegal Rau's talk with the Chinese: Ambassador Wu had expressed a desire for a cease-fire, and Sir Benegal had taken this as supporting the Arab-Asian bloc's approach to the problem. Mr. Gross was in touch with Washington, and would advise me further. We agreed that care was required lest Sir Benegal's efforts and my separate talks confuse things.

I met with the Chinese a few days later to ask if their government would assist in insuring that United Nations prisoners in Korea received treatment according to the Geneva Convention on prisoners of war, and if, particularly, they would permit a representative of the International Red Cross to enter North Korean territory. Ambassador Wu brusquely replied that that was no concern of his government; his government had no interest in the volunteer forces fighting in Korea. I remarked that the United Nations held a number of Chinese prisoners, but he maintained that this was the concern of the People's Government of Korea. He did reveal, however, that no United Nations prisoners were held on Chinese territory. When I asked if he or Peking could help put me in touch with North Korean authorities, he said no—that he did not know where the North Korean authorities were. All this did not augur well for agreement on wider questions; a sudden change seemed to have come over the Chinese delegation. I suspected that they had been talking to Mr. Vyshinsky or had received a rebuke from Moscow by way of Peking.

The General Assembly, to which the Chinese intervention in Korea had been referred when Moscow blocked action in the Security Council, had now designated a three-man Cease-Fire Committee. I met with this committee on December 15, and it presented

PEKING FAILS TO UNDERSTAND

the cease-fire terms of the Unified Command. Ambassador Wu, it said, had lately turned cool toward Sir Benegal Rau, but it would attempt to establish contact with him through Sir Benegal none the less (this being the more appropriate because he was one of the committee members, the others being Nasrollah Entezam, the Assembly President, and Lester Pearson). All three seemed to be depressed. When I reported that General Wu had telephoned for an appointment with me that evening Sir Benegal took pains to make certain whether he had actually telephoned me, or whether I had telephoned him.

In the afternoon I saw the British Minister of State, Kenneth Younger. General Wu had come to him that morning, bringing as interpreter an Englishman who knew Chinese perfectly; and he stated that he had never before heard a Chinese use such language as that used by Ambassador Wu. Mr. Younger thought there was no basis for negotiations with the Chinese.

Ambassador Wu and three of his associates appeared at six o'clock. He began by thanking me for the Secretariat's administrative help—he was "deeply moved" by the friendly attitude he had met. But his delegation had been in New York without "real work" for several weeks, and accordingly had decided to depart in a few days. They would like to hold a press conference before their departure. Would I arrange it at Lake Success for Saturday?

I responded forcefully with a barrage of reasons why the delegation should not leave so soon. At the very least, they should postpone the press conference until Monday, and see what happened then, for on that day the Political and Security Committee of the General Assembly would set its agenda. The very Formosa question which they had traveled so far to discuss might come up. But General Wu was absolutely unmanageable: they had, he said, received instructions from Peking to return. Look here, I said, you have told me you want a cease-fire. We are prepared to present to you the terms of the Unified Command. If you have a press conference and say that Peking will not negotiate, and then go off, the world will draw the obvious conclusions. The Assembly's Cease-Fire Committee has not even been able to obtain official contact with you, and now you propose to leave.

It was useless. They were going December 19: would we kindly secure them air reservations via BOAC (that is, not by an American air line)? I had to agree. General Wu added that he had told Sir Benegal Rau that he could not negotiate with the Cease-Fire Committee. Peking would only consult on the terms suggested by Mr. Malik, which involved simultaneous negotiations for a cease-fire, Peking's admission to the United Nations, and settlement of the Formosa affair.

As soon as the Chinese left I rang up Mr. Entezam, Mr. Pearson, and Sir Benegal, reported that my talk with Wu had been far from encouraging, and said we ought to meet that evening. When they came to Forest Hills I reported the disheartening news in detail, and we discussed a variety of moves designed to do whatever might be possible to change the Chinese mind.

I met with General Wu before his Saturday press conference, and asked him not to commit himself publicly to departing. He agreed; but he told me after the conference that his delegation still was determined to leave on the 19th. I suggested that they break journey in London for some days, and they said they would consider this. I then inquired if he would be willing to be introduced to the three-man Cease-Fire Committee. He conferred with his deputy Chiao Kuan-hua, and said no; but he would see Mr. Entezam in his capacity as President of the General Assembly. I excused myself, and went to the committee in the next room. I brought back Mr. Entezam, introduced him, and then left him alone with the Chinese. I returned after a half-hour with a copy of a cable which the Cease-Fire Committee had addressed that very day to General Wu and to Chou En-lai, Peking's Minister for Foreign Affairs. The message was, in essence, a plea to the Chinese simply to discuss a cease-fire through the good offices of the committee. Could they, I asked, still leave on the 19th, before further instructions arrived from Peking in response to the cable? Yes, Mr. Chiao—who now had taken charge of the discussion—replied, a delay was out of the question. He insisted that their travel plans be released to the press after our conversation. Time and again I tried to change their minds, and finally they stated that, if their request was not complied with, they would issue a press release themselves. I then said that the information officer attached to the Cease-Fire Committee would make the matter public. General

Wu declared himself satisfied, and requested that I come to see the delegation at the Waldorf-Astoria before it departed.

When I did so, they thanked me for the Secretariat's courtesies, and before leaving, I expressed regret that I could not have done more political mediating. I would, however, I added, always be at their disposal if they wished my assistance.

This was the last direct political contact the United Nations had with the Peking regime for a long time. I have often wondered which, if any, change in the course of events might have occurred, had some degree of direct liaison been maintained, so as to avoid the sifting of all communications through indirect channels.

The Cease-Fire Committee made further efforts, but at this time it seemed that Peking—or was it Moscow?—did not find it advantageous to stop the bloodshed. The basis for negotiations advanced by the Unified Command, which we had attempted to convey to General Wu and had cabled to Peking, called for a cease-fire and the establishment of a demilitarized zone with its southern border on the 38th parallel. In accordance with a draft resolution advanced by the Arab-Asian bloc in the General Assembly, it was anticipated that negotiations among the major Pacific powers on the primary Far Eastern problems would follow. In reply, Chou En-lai charged: "The reason why the hostilities in Korea have not yet been put to an end is precisely because of the fact that the United States Government has dispatched troops to invade Korea and is continuing and extending its policies of aggression and war . . . Therefore, the Chinese people, who, impelled by righteous indignation, have risen to volunteer in resisting the United States and helping Korea, and thus protect their homes . . . are fighting for their own existence . . . as well as the peace of the whole world . . . We firmly insist that, as a basis for negotiating a peaceful settlement of the Korean problem, all foreign troops must be withdrawn from Korea. . . . The American aggression forces must be withdrawn from Taiwan. And the representatives of the People's Republic of China must obtain a legitimate status in the United Nations."

The Chinese pressed their assault throughout December and January, and this, together with their uncompromising stand on negotiations, made the outlook depressingly grim. I gave a Christmas talk over the Scandinavian broadcasting networks at the end of 1950 which expressed the United Nations determination to repel the aggression; but at the same time I emphasized the United Nations' desire to reassure the Chinese about any genuine doubts they may have had concerning United Nations intentions.

"The United Nations' starting point," I declared, ". . . is that the North Korean aggression which began on June 25, 1950, must be repelled, sooner or later, and that peaceful conditions must be re-established . . . This basic position . . . the United Nations cannot go back on. We cannot agree to having any particular system of government—be it a nazi, fascist, communist, socialist, or capitalist system—forced upon any people by the use of arms from outside.

"If the United Nations should lose in Korea, we would have reason to ask ourselves: Which country may become the next victim?

"The collective military defense against aggression and invasion which the United Nations undertook in Korea was the first action of its kind in history. It was not without risk. . . .

"The first victory for the United Nations' principles, the purely military one, was . . . within sight until four to five weeks ago. It was then that half a million Chinese soldiers were suddenly thrown into the battle. The government of the People's Republic of China openly called upon its young people to participate as so-called 'volunteers' in the war in Korea. The political and material backing which two great powers had previously given to the aggressors now became a direct military intervention as far as one of them is concerned . . .

"This created a new situation . . . If the United Nations should arrive at the stage where it found itself, directly or indirectly, involved in a state of war with the 475,000,000 people of China, then the danger of a new world war would have been brought closer.

"The blame for such a development could not be placed upon the United Nations. The purposes and goals of the United Nations have been and are clear enough. The full responsibility would rest with those who have been pulling the strings—who perhaps may hope for selfish advantages through aggression—and who do not seem to hesitate from taking such steps which *might* lead to another world war.

"The United Nations does not wish to get into a state of war with the new China . . . There, a revolution has taken place, which, whatever one's own opinion may be, is now proceeding to transform the conditions under which almost half a billion people are living. China is faced with enormous problems, and one can only hope that the new central government in Peking will fully comprehend the importance of peaceful international cooperation when it comes to the future of the Chinese people.

"The world has sympathy for China and wishes the best for the Chinese people. It is not correct that history always repeats itself, and that there *has* to be, or *must* come, revolutionary or interventionist wars as we had them after the French and Russian revolutions, as the new rulers in China perhaps believe.

"The world would wish to cooperate with China and to help China if there should be an opportunity to do so."

The word "opportunity," I did not equate with appeasement. The opportunity I asked for was one built on the United Nations principles of abandonment of aggression and establishment of mutual good will thereafter, not necessarily before.

I did not feel that all attempts to stop the war were founded on equally sound principles. The latest proposal of the Indian government, for instance, was that a cease-fire be established in Korea on condition that Peking first be admitted to the United Nations, and that a committee consisting of the United States, the United Kingdom, Peking China, the Soviet Union, India, and Egypt begin negotiations on Formosa and other Far Eastern questions. The Indians did not conceal that they favored handing Formosa over to Peking—a proposition which seemed to me to be entirely beyond political reality and might even be considered as a reward to the aggressor.

I accordingly welcomed a conversation with Prime Minister Pandit Jawaharlal Nehru in Paris on January 18, 1951, as an opportunity to impress the facts of international life as I saw them upon the gifted Indian leader. After all, he might give some consideration to my viewpoint, because he knew my record as a Social Democrat, an opponent of colonialism, and a Secretary-General who had pressed strongly for East-West conciliation and, until the Korean aggression by Peking, had favored admitting it to the United Nations. I looked forward to a mutually useful exchange of views. Madame Vijaya Lakshmi Pandit, his sister, was the only other person present.

Prime Minister Nehru looked very tired, as if he had had little sleep for a long time. He had just come from the Commonwealth Conference in London, where things had not gone too well, and recent American press comment also was troubling him. That very morning, the papers had been most severe in their criticism. His highly strung, sensitive nature was clear at a glance. It was perhaps not a good occasion for a realistic political talk. The result may have been disheartening for both of us.

I began by thanking him for his friendly support of my endeavor to find a solution to the Soviet boycott and my Twenty-Year Program for Achieving Peace through the United Nations, in the spring of 1950. Notwithstanding his good will and, in fact, that of the whole free world, Moscow's stand had stopped any further progress. I had therefore concluded that negotiation with Stalin, unless accompanied by a show of strength, was essentially hopeless for the time being. The Program I had submitted in Moscow was certainly not unfair to Soviet interests. Yet I had found that I could not elicit a trace of desire or interest in reaching a meaningful compromise on any substantial point. Admittedly, they had said that they would agree to extraordinary periodic meetings of the Security Council, to be held away from headquarters, at which the foreign ministers or the prime ministers could meet, and they said they agreed to adopt my Twenty-Year Program as a basis for discussion. But—aside from half challenging my good faith—Stalin was not willing to go an inch further. No matter what concrete question I raised, in the hope of obtaining a concession which would be evidence of their desire to come to an agreement, Stalin and Molotov had limited themselves to stating that they would consider this or that point more closely. They refrained from positive commitments, allowing the Soviet Union full freedom of action. Such had been the Communist procedure in all political negotiations until now, I said, and there was no particular reason to expect a different attitude in the present situation.

My approach did not seem to please the Prime Minister of India. His starting point was a different one: Asia first. The peoples of Asia themselves would have to decide the future of Asia, he repeated. He was not moved by references either to the global aims of world Communism, or to the interdependence of all continents and the United Nations' equal concern for them all. His mind seemed to be imprisoned by the concept of Asia as a special entity. When I followed this narrow trend of thought and mentioned the overwhelming military superiority of Communist China and the Soviet Union on the Asian continent, he still maintained that he was not concerned about the security of his country: he was interested in making peace in Korea and settling the differences between the United States and the Communist powers, and the immediate objective was to persuade Peking to withdraw from Korea. Then Formosa should be given to Peking.

I replied that any settlement compromising fundamental principles would be a defeat for the United Nations. Aggression had to be stopped, not rewarded. Of course, Asia should be ruled by Asians—even the Chinese Communists said so. But which Asians did they mean? And who ruled Soviet Asia? It would be a tragedy for the whole world were India's newly won political freedom ever to be threatened, compromised—or lost. Nehru made no reply to this—just smiled wryly.

Obviously, there was no meeting of minds. We discussed the United States as a Member of the United Nations and as a world power. Our opinions continued to differ. There was no reason to pursue the discussion in this direction.

I have often recalled that meeting with Nehru in Paris. From the early 1920's I had followed his tireless work, admiring his decisive contributions toward the liberation of India and often enraged by the sufferings forced upon him. Now, as the undisputed leader of 375,000,000 people, a statesman of world stature, he (perhaps because of his steadfastness in his original struggle) appeared to me to suffer from a narrowness in approach toward world affairs which might easily interfere with the magnificent contributions toward the solution of global problems of which he was otherwise capable.

Luckily, at the end of our talk I received a clue to his feelings. I turned the conversation to economic and social matters, where it was easier to find common ground, and I concluded that his most immediate concern was the enormous poverty of India and what he considered lack of understanding on the part of the "wealthy" nations. We did not differ on the vital promise and importance of the United Nations Technical Assistance Program. We agreed on the need for more money from all sources for world-wide economic development. When I asked his opinion of the Commonwealth Technical Assistance Scheme, known as the Colombo Plan, he replied that it was excellent, except that there was not enough money to carry it out. Otherwise, he wanted grain at once.

Jawaharlal Nehru was understandably tired; and his preoccupation with the welfare of his own people prevented him from reviewing or evaluating the world situation in its broadest perspectives. But outside help, with increased understanding of India's internal problems, should make it easier for him to do this later—if it comes.

In the meantime, however, the war in Korea went on.

While efforts to find a formula for a cease-fire continued in New York through the winter, the initiative in Korea passed to the United Nations forces. The Korean aggressors and the Chinese "volunteers" were thrown back to the 38th parallel. The time seemed to be ripe for a realistic agreement which would mark the United Nations' success in driving aggression back to its starting point and would return the unifying of all Korea under a free government to political methods. On June 1 in a speech at Ottawa, I expressed the belief "that the time has come for a new effort to end the fighting in Korea. The United Nations forces there—as things stand today—have repelled the aggression and thrown the aggressor back across the 38th parallel. If a cease-fire could be arranged along the 38th parallel, then the main purpose of the Security Council resolutions of June 25 and 27 and July 7, 1950, will be fulfilled, provided that the cease-fire is followed by the restoration of peace and security in the area."

Early in the spring I had put forth suggestions for a direct approach to the North Korean authorities; and in the middle of June I circulated privately among the delegations a memorandum, "Ideas Concerning Attainment of a Cease-Fire in Korea," suggesting that the most suitable approach might be an attempt to arrange cease-fire negotiations between the *military commanders in the field*, the United Nations Commander being authorized to deal only with military matters related to the cease-fire; he would have no authority to discuss questions of a political character, Korean or otherwise. Although this assumed that Peking was prepared to abandon its stand for discussion of political matters like Chinese representation and Formosa until a cease-fire was effected, the fresh United Nations military success made it an assumption worth testing. To clear the way for purely military negotiations in the field, the memorandum suggested that the General Assembly adjourn, automatically removing its three-man Cease-Fire Committee from the scene; for Peking still refused to recognize the committee, and it had the further disability of being linked with political questions.

Mr. Zinchenko conveyed my memorandum to Moscow, I am sure. It met with considerable interest in Western quarters (if with some skepticism in Washington). The Soviet reply may, in a sense, be said to have come in a broadcast by Mr. Malik on June 23. The Secretariat's Department of Public Information had arranged a series of radio talks on "The Price of Peace," and it was in one of these that Mr. Malik made his unexpected offer:

"The Soviet peoples," he declared, "further believe that the most acute problem of the present day—the problem of the armed conflict in Korea—could also be settled. . . . The Soviet peoples believe that, as a first step, discussions should be started between the belligerents for a cease-fire and an armistice providing for mutual withdrawal from the thirty-eighth parallel.

"Can such a step be taken?

"I think it can, provided there is a sincere desire to put an end to the bloody fighting in Korea.

"I think that, surely, it is not too great a price to pay in order to achieve peace in Korea."

I had just arrived in Norway for a brief holiday, and had hardly entered my summer house on the Oslo Fjord when a cable informed me that Mr. Malik's talk scheduled for that evening included the passage here quoted. I at once telephoned United Nations headquarters, authorizing comments in which I urged that "negotiations for a military cease-fire now be entered into at the earliest possible date," and then made plans for an immediate return. At London Airport en route to New York, I conferred with Lester Pearson, Canadian Minister of External Affairs, and Kenneth Younger, the British

Minister of State, and told the press that Mr. Malik's suggestion for negotiations looked to me like "a sincere statement which has to be taken seriously."

Arriving in New York on June 27, I entered into a round of consultations. The American Ambassador to the U.S.S.R. saw Mr. Gromyko, and on June 29 General Matthew B. Ridgway, who had succeeded General MacArthur as Commander-in-Chief of the United Nations Command, invited enemy leaders to discuss a cease-fire on board a hospital ship in Wonsan harbor. On July 4 the Communist military leaders broadcast their reply, agreeing to begin talks on July 10. Their slowness in sitting down to negotiations aroused my hardly latent suspicions, but we did not then imagine that negotiations would extend over more than two years.

The last days of June, I circulated a memorandum from the Legal Department supporting the authority of the Unified Command to negotiate a cease-fire in Korea. An aide-mémoire that I wrote on July 2 reflects my uneasiness:

"While the agreement on behalf of the North Korean and Chinese authorities to discuss a cease-fire represents substantial progress, no guarantee exists, as yet, that the proposed cease-fire negotiations will, actually, lead to the cessation of hostilities and, thereafter, to appropriate armistice arrangements.

"Already the dates proposed in the North Korean and Chinese reply indicate that now and/or later, delays may occur, which the aggressors might try to utilize for sowing dissension between the United Nations Members, or other purposes.*

"In order to strengthen the hand of the United Nations Commander in his negotiations, as well as the unity of purpose of the fifty-three nations backing the principles of the Charter, the Secretary-General urges, therefore, that Member Governments should, at an early stage, declare themselves satisfied that a Korean cease-fire now seems feasible, but at the same time take the opportunity to stress their readiness to furnish ground troops—or additional forces —for Korea, *in the event* that a cease-fire, with a satisfactory armistice arrangement to follow, is not now obtained."

I gave a copy of this aide-mémoire to Ambassadors Austin and Gross and discussed it with Tage Erlander, the Prime Minister of

* In place of "other purposes," the first draft of my aide-mémoire read explicitly, "for a build-up of forces in North Korea."

Sweden, who was then on a good-will visit to the United States. I further expressed willingness to travel to key countries in South America and elsewhere from which it might be desirable to obtain the pledge of fresh ground forces. The Americans warmly favored the suggestion and brought it forth among the sixteen countries which had forces with the United Nations in Korea; but it was decided that a general call for pledges of additional support at this stage might not bring all the results desired.

While advocating planning for the contingency of continued fighting, I also advanced a plan which might be put into effect were a cease-fire achieved. In a note of July 3, which I submitted to the delegates of the United States, Britain, and France and to Mr. Entezam, the Assembly President, I suggested that consideration be given to dissolving the United Nations Commission for the Unification and Rehabilitation of Korea and appointing in its stead a United Nations Mediator or Representative with a broad mandate to control truce supervision and negotiate political questions, such as the unification of Korea. Among those I had in mind for such a job were Erik Boheman, the Swedish Ambassador to Washington, Gustav Rasmussen, the former Foreign Minister of Denmark, J. H. van Roijen, the Dutch Ambassador to Washington, and Sir Ramaswami Mudaliar of India. But my fears about the intentions of the Communists proved to be more in point.

No one was more disappointed than I—despite my fears—when negotiations dragged on. I even asked myself what the real purpose was, when the discussions were embittered by grotesque Communist fabrications that charged the Americans in Korea with carrying on germ warfare. In that connection, it was sad to see how human beings could degrade themselves so as to become tools of a propaganda built entirely on falsehoods. But the attempt to sow dissension within the United Nations was doomed to failure. I expressed my feelings in the introduction to my Seventh Annual Report (1952): "The United Nations has sought and should continue to seek in all ways to reach a reasonable and fair armistice agreement without sacrifice of moral principle. . . . Until there is an armistice, it is the part of wisdom and of duty under the Charter, for Members to carry on the fight . . . and to do so with a more equitable sharing of the burdens."

Equally, no one was more relieved when an armistice was finally signed on July 27, 1953. From my lodge in the Norwegian mountains I issued the following statement on that occasion:

"I am deeply gratified to learn that a truce in Korea at last has been achieved. It is an historic achievement, and a profoundly welcome one. The grievous loss of life in Korea is finally at an end. The suffering which aggression has inflicted upon the Korean people will be greatly eased. The work of United Nations reconstruction can begin. Let us hope that this agreement on a truce in Korea will pave the way for wider agreement upon other issues which threaten world peace.

"As much as any man, I have been gripped by the tragedy of the Korean War. But I am also conscious of the nobility and surpassing significance of the United Nations police action in Korea, in which sixteen Member nations actively have taken part. It has been the first determined stand against international lawlessness and aggression which the peace-loving governments of the world have taken. It has been a successful stand. Collective security has been enforced for the first time in the whole of human history.

"Korea proves that aggression does not pay. If the aggressor can learn a lesson, Korea should have taught it to him. Certainly, after Korea, the world can never again permit any clear case of international armed attack to pass unchallenged."

Though the price was high and the waiting long, Korea was not permitted to become another Manchuria.

CHAPTER XX

MY TERM IS EXTENDED

Early decision to "quit while quitting is good."—Western powers' call to continue.—Soviet maneuverings and charges of "illegality."—Threat of an American veto.—My stand on Korea upheld.

AS MY five-year term as Secretary-General neared its close I was brought into a highly uncomfortable personal situation. At no time has greater controversy raged about the person of the Secretary-General than in October and early November, 1950. Conflicting assertions as to my real attitude toward continuing in office—either by reelection or by an extension of my term—have painted me as everything from a "hard-to-get" to a ruthless office seeker. Did I honestly oppose any plan for continuing me in office? Did I secretly change my position under pressure while continuing in public to say no? Or did I actively work for a new lease on the Secretary-General's chair?

The fact is that I did all three—in succession and in that order—the final action being forced upon me in defense of the integrity of my office and my own honor. During 1950 events brought my views around in a full circle: from those of a tired public official genuinely grateful for the chance to "quit while the quitting is good," to the ultimate conviction that I could not permit myself to be pushed out of office in punishment for having done my duty. In the end, events over which I had no control made the decision for me.

One of the first in the long series of events culminating in the extension of my term as Secretary-General, took place October 1, 1949, at 680 Park Avenue, Soviet Delegation quarters in New York. The occasion was a dinner for a number of delegates given by Andrei Vyshinsky—who, when he wishes, can be a most charming host, with an easy smile and a ready fund of stories. He intermingled freely that evening and made careful efforts to persuade his guests that to elect Yugoslavia to the Security Council over Soviet opposition would be a breach of the London "agreement" to accord an Eastern European seat to a Soviet ally. At the dinner table, in the midst of a sprightly conversation with General Romulo, Padilla Nervo, Dr. José Arce, and me, he swung abruptly to the election of a Secretary-General which was to occur a year later. In the hearing of these gentlemen—and to my embarrassment—he forthwith announced that I was the only candidate he could imagine the U.S.S.R. supporting. My embarrassment was in no way diminished when this piece of news leaked to the press the following day.

The following January I was privately informed that the Norwegian Foreign Minister had received a memorandum from Norway's Ambassador to the U.S.S.R. reporting a conversation with Arkady Sobolev, head of the Soviet Foreign Ministry American Division and former Assistant Secretary-General of the United Nations. When asked which candidate the U.S.S.R. would back for Secretary-General at the 1950 Assembly, Sobolev had replied that only one name was considered in Moscow, and that was my own. On May 15, I was at Moscow in the course of my peace mission to the four world capitals, attending a luncheon at which Messrs. Gromyko, Zinchenko, Sobolev, and Helge Akre, the Norwegian Chargé d'Affaires, were present; and here again Mr. Vyshinsky announced the U.S.S.R. intention—despite Soviet criticism of my support for the Marshall program and the North Atlantic Treaty.

There was similar activity in other quarters. At a dinner given by the American Deputy Representative to the Security Council, Ambassador Ernest Gross, on June 14, shortly after my return from Moscow, I received a hint of the trend of thinking in the State Department. Assistant Secretary of State John Hickerson took me aside before the dinner and opened with a few questions about my trip. Suddenly he asked, "Do you trust the Russians?" My answer was: "Whether we trust them or not, we have to go on playing the game without compromising the principles." Finally he got around to what was obviously on his mind, and informed me confidentially that the

State Department, "with approval from the highest authority," had settled on me as the United States candidate for Secretary-General for a new term. When asked if I would accept the nomination, I replied that I had already decided to quit. Only if events made it clear that the interests of the United Nations really required it might I consider an extra year or two: "Five more years," I stated, "is out of the question in any event." Later, I heard from Norway's Ambassador to the United Nations, Arne Sunde, that Ernest Gross and John Ross, deputy and alternate on the American Delegation, had also been probing to determine whether I could be persuaded to continue in office.

This was all very flattering, but it merely served to bolster my earlier decision that now was the time to leave: my public statement of December 16, 1949, "I am not a candidate for reappointment," was right and should stand. As Secretary-General, my overriding objective had been to establish a record of complete fairness and impartiality, and now I had evidence of backing by both the opposing camps. An active Secretary-General could not hope for a better voucher for personal integrity after five years in such an international maelstrom. It was time to go home. As I put it in a letter to my daughter and son-in-law in Norway on December 13, 1949, "It seems to me that I've done my duty, and I'll be completely satisfied if only I can get through this final year with my whole skin." I would be "finishing the race in good form" as the United Nations' first Secretary-General on February 1, 1951. The Permanent Headquarters, my special pride, would be near completion; in spite of the intensifying "cold war" the Organization would have held together and preserved the hope of peace; the record was an honorable one in spite of all the disappointments and difficulties, and I could withdraw with support from both sides intact.

Then came June 25 and my stand against aggression in Korea. As early as July 8 the Soviet writer Lev Oshanin was out with a scathing criticism in *Literaturnaya Gazeta* under the title "The 'Greatness' and Decline of Trygve Lie." A single sentence from it will suffice to set the now familiar tone: "When he supported the illegal resolution of the United Nations Security Council on the Korean question, Trygve Lie, whose mission it is to protect the peace, took on the role of an accessory to the American aggressors." This first blast was followed by a *Pravda* article on July 13, "The Peoples of the World Are Keeping the Aggressors in Check," which contained an early version of what was to be the standard Soviet appraisal of my role in this affair: "Dropping his mask, Mr. Trygve Lie . . . became one of the direct and active accomplices of United States armed intervention in Korea."

It was not entirely unexpected from *Pravda*, for nearly two years before, in September, 1948, my statements favoring the Marshall Plan had incurred the wrath of that publication—an intended warning, perhaps. Although Mr. Malik was silent about my position when he returned to the Security Council in August, there were other attacks from Moscow; and it was evident that, without a radical change in the situation, the Soviet Union would no longer support me for reelection. My first reaction was gratification that my statement a full eight months before had taken me out of the race.

Then came second thoughts. Although naturally angered by the unjust personal attacks in the Soviet press, I could live with them, knowing that my stand on Korea was right. However, there was another and more disturbing aspect for the United Nations. Because of my intervention in the Korean issue I, as Secretary-General, had obviously become a thorn in the side of the Soviet Union. If I left office, either by my own choice or by that of the Member nations, would the Soviet Union interpret it as a victory and, correspondingly, as a defeat for the stand I had come to represent? I did not care to be used as a political football in a struggle between the Great Powers. On the other hand I did not wish to leave office as a man defeated and punished by the Soviet Union for my stand on Korea.

By early September it was hard to know just what to think. Who would be the next Secretary-General had long been challenging the speculations of editors, especially in view of the recent anti-Lie trend in Moscow. However, most papers agreed that I should probably be forced to continue, despite the apparent opposition of the Soviet Union—and Nationalist China. I concluded that were I to be drafted by the United States, France, and Great Britain to run in defense of United Nations policy, I might have to accept one or two years more as a means of blocking a Soviet political victory, although under no circumstances would I accept a full term.

At that stage it began to be rumored that the Russians might after all abstain, were it proposed to extend my term; and there was some indirect support for the rumors. In mid-September, Foreign Minister Vyshinsky arrived at New York—amazingly enough, all smiles and cordiality; but he volunteered no indication of the stand the Soviet Union would take on the next Secretary-General. I asked my Russian Assistant Secretary-General, Constantin Zinchenko, to sound out the Soviet Delegation on the point, so that I could make up my own mind, once for all; but Messrs. Malik and Vyshinsky kept him at arm's length. The fifth session of the General Assembly opened at Flushing Meadow on Tuesday September 19, and a few days later I heard reports that Messrs. Bevin, Schuman, and Acheson, then in New York, had met and agreed that I be asked to continue as Secretary-General another two years.

The first supporting evidence came during a dinner my wife and I gave at Granston Tower on September 22, with Messrs. Acheson and Vyshinsky among the guests. Mr. Acheson, who stayed with Ambassador Gross a few minutes after the others had left, appeared to be in high spirits. There was small talk on various subjects until he suddenly broke out, almost gleefully: "Well, the problem is solved. There'll be no home leave for you: you'll have to continue." And that was all. Very "un-Acheson," I thought, for the normally cool and collected Secretary of State.

Three days later I met Foreign Secretary Bevin at another evening affair, and told him how much I had appreciated his encouraging speech in the General Assembly that same week. I was just a little surprised by the good humor in this quarter as well. "Yes," he remarked, "the United Nations has developed into something now. I've not always liked it, and I believe that you've exaggerated a good bit on many occasions. But perhaps that was necessary to hold the whole thing together. Now the United Nations has become an organization which can work for peace with power backing words. . . . I hope I can see you continuing in the job, now that we're on the right course." These words from Ernest Bevin pleased me.

Only a few days were to pass before French Foreign Minister Robert Schuman, calling at my office to say goodbye, observed that he was leaving for home with a better impression of the United Nations than before. "I hope," he concluded, "that I can see you in your office when I return next year." Shortly afterward, André Ganem met me in one of the corridors at Flushing and put the following question, in his quiet manner, without even the pretext of prelude: "What can I do for you as regards your position and your new term? If there is anything you want, just let me know. Now is the time to arrange your affairs to your satisfaction." I was somewhat taken aback. André Ganem was then a member of the Advisory Committee on Administrative and Budgetary Questions, with an influential position in the French Ministry of Foreign Affairs, and was very close to all French governments—known in diplomatic circles as "His Excellency the Gray Eminence." His approach could mean but one thing: I was the French candidate, and the Delegation had, without doubt, received instructions to that effect.

As far as I could determine, then, three of the great powers had agreed that I should be asked to continue. Under these circumstances, and after a long consideration of all the pros and cons, I decided that I should have to accept an extension. But I did not like coming out with a formal acceptance just then. Only three of the great powers had indicated their support, informally; and the Soviet Union had yet to be heard from.

Time soon began to press. The Assembly had now been in session more than a week, but had maintained a conspicuous silence as to the election of a Secretary-General. I began to find my position most embarrassing. It was difficult to handle the normal flow of business requiring daily decisions, not knowing whether I or someone else would have to carry them out after January. In committee meetings and talks with delegates I was continually confronted by statements and opinions about the course "Mr. Lie" should take on various matters in the coming year. Silence was becoming increasingly difficult, despite an attempt on my part to keep the press "at least twenty paces" distant.

I decided that a talk with Sir Gladwyn Jebb was essential. He was president of the Security Council for September and could probably help bring the issue into the open and give me peace of mind. At a dinner which he gave at Oyster Bay during the last week of September, he was surprisingly reserved. All he had to say was that there was "time enough"; and when I suggested that I take a fortnight's leave he remarked that a few days' absence might be "a good idea."

MY TERM IS EXTENDED

This conversation with a man whom I had always regarded as a personal friend was most disappointing: here had been an opportunity for a frank word of advice or encouragement. I recalled an earlier impression received from the American delegation, that the French and British camps had some hesitation about extending my term—an impression later erased by Schuman's and Bevin's forthright statements. Now, however, I began to wonder again. I wondered even more when I heard that Sir Gladwyn had approached Mr. Malik, suggesting that the five great powers get together for a conference on the matter, and that Mr. Malik too had brushed off the suggestion. At one time he assured him that there was "no great hurry"; later he said he had not yet received instructions. Something odd was taking place. My position was already far extended, and it seemed as though the ground I stood on was beginning to give way.

I could wait no longer. With Tor Gjesdal, my Principal Director for Public Information, I sat down and drafted an ending to the speech I was to deliver in the Assembly the following day—September 28. There, before the Assembly, I would reiterate my determination to retire; I would thank them for the five years past, and that would be the end. If they wished to accept my statement they could do so; if not it would smoke out what might be going on beneath the surface. When we showed this draft to Andrew Cordier, Abe Feller, and Wilder Foote there was immediate protest. They strongly advised against the statement, and recommended as an alternative that I send identical letters to Sir Gladwyn Jebb, President of the Security Council, and to Nasrollah Entezam, President of the Assembly. As drafted, the letters called attention to the expiration of my term, and to the inclusion of the appointment of the Secretary-General as Item 17 on the General Assembly's agenda. "I stated on December 16, 1949," I wrote, "that I was not a candidate for reappointment. I wish to inform you that my position in this regard has not changed." I gave an unsigned copy of the letter to Sir Gladwyn and also showed it to Ernest Gross of the American Delegation and to Assembly President Entezam. The Americans advised strongly against mailing it. "If you send it, and if you give that speech as intended," declared Ernest Gross, "it will make our work much more difficult." Mr. Entezam too seemed to favor waiting. I therefore followed the advice from three different quarters, and when Sir Gladwyn asked a few days later whether I had decided to send the letter officially I said, "No—not for the time being."

In light of events to come, I have often regretted this decision: the speech should have been made, and the letter sent. Such a step, I am certain, would have helped clear the air, and would have given us far more solid ground on which to operate. A letter home to the family on October 3 described the situation as I saw it at the moment: "As yet, the Security Council has held no meeting where the post of Secretary-General has been mentioned. But at the same time I've heard no other name—although candidates can emerge at any time, once negotiations get underway. My position remains the same—that I'm still not a candidate. But we'll have to wait and see how the whole affair works out."

On Monday October 9 the Security Council in secret session took up the matter of a new Secretary-General. It was the turn of Ambassador Warren Austin of the United States to assume the President's chair. Aside from the four other permanent members, Cuba, Ecuador, Egypt, India, Norway, and Yugoslavia were represented.

The meeting was no more than a few minutes old when the core of the issue emerged: Ambassador Bebler of Yugoslavia rose to invite an exchange of views on prolonging my service another five years—a challenge which Ambassador Malik accepted with alacrity. Referring to the resolution "On the Conditions of the Appointment of the Secretary-General," adopted by the First General Assembly on January 24, 1946, he maintained that the incumbent had been appointed for five years, and that any change in the term of office must be made by the Security Council and the General Assembly acting together. Article 97 of the Charter, he continued, demanded concurrence of the Security Council for the appointment of the Secretary-General; unilateral action by the General Assembly would be in violation of the charter, and a Secretary-General thus elected would be holding office illegally. "In view of the above consideration, I cannot accept the view that the term of the first Secretary-General can be prolonged. . . . The proposal to prolong Mr. Lie's appointment is unacceptable to my delegation." This was his opening statement, and comprised the essence of the Soviet Union's juridical stand on the extension question during the weeks to come.

With the Soviet now on record as opposing extension—and presumably reelection as well—Sir Gladwyn Jebb saw no use in pursuing the Yugoslavian proposal; and he added that the Council would be forced to consider another proposal or another candidate. Equally interesting was the viewpoint of Mr. Chauvel, the French representative, who agreed that the first thing was to see whether the Council might be in a position to make a recommendation, and that it would be desirable to know whether there were any other objections to the only name put forward thus far. The French Delegation had "no strong feelings in the matter" but was concerned over the ability of the Organization to function.

With reports of that first meeting, all my earlier forebodings were confirmed. Now the chips were down. The U.S.S.R. was determined to throw me out of office, and the United States equally determined to retain me; Britain merely acknowledged the Soviet stand and proposed a search for new candidates, and France had "no strong feelings in the matter." The Western Big Three were less firmly together on extending my term than information from the highest sources had led me to believe. Against my own inclinations, I had allowed myself to be led far out on a limb. Soviet strategy was now clear, but intentions in other quarters had been confused by this first meeting. Clearly, I was about to become a political football—a role which I had been determined to avoid, and which could not but damage me personally. I was angry with myself for having been led on, and angry at others for having led me on, despite my appreciation for the broader and far more serious political issue at stake; but it was too late to turn back.

Some weeks later I wrote to a friend in Norway: "When [the Russians] finally revealed their intentions, (1) to punish a Secretary-General who had done what he thought was right in accordance with Article 99 of the Charter, and (2) to administer the United States a resounding political defeat, I was left no choice. Had I said 'No,' I would have given the Russians the smoothest sailing they had ever enjoyed in a political conflict—which was precisely what the struggle over the Secretary-Generalship had been turned into."

On October 10 I had a chance to corner Sir Gladwyn Jebb at a dinner given by Cyro Freitas-Valle of Brazil at the Metropolitan Club. In what I fear were somewhat unvarnished terms I made my personal sentiments known to the British Ambassador. Once for all, I had to know the United Kingdom's position. I no longer wished to be an expandable commodity held in readiness for use now as a threat, now as a bargaining item, in whatever maneuvers were going on. I recalled Mr. Bevin's words at Granston Tower and made it clear that I wished to be informed within forty-eight hours of London's position. There was a limit to my patience, and no human being could be expected to sacrifice himself for a cause as questionable as this one now seemed to be. Sir Gladwyn only responded that he would cable to London for instructions.

Never have I longed more than on that evening for circumstances and surroundings that could inspire free and forthright speech. Sir Gladwyn and I had put in a good deal of hunting together, and we had always enjoyed the opportunity these shooting trips afforded for speaking frankly. I wished ardently that we could be at that moment in my hunting lodge in Norway, instead of at New York's Metropolitan Club. That same night I wrote to my daughter in Oslo: "I'm certain that my happiest day will be when I can take Mama in one hand and my suitcase in the other and leave for home. This is like living in a madhouse."

The next day I spoke with Ambassador Austin, who was distressed by the sudden wavering of the British and French governments. I requested the same definite answer from the American government and warned that, were not the situation clarified, I was prepared to abandon ship. However, the British Delegation's instructions arrived the following morning, and—according to my sources —reaffirmed that I was Britain's candidate for reelection, as well as for extension.

Security Council proceedings that day confirmed the worst. In accordance with his renewed instructions, Sir Gladwyn supported the proposal to continue me in office. Mr. Malik rose to reaffirm my inacceptability to the Soviet Delegation, and proposed the nomination of Zygmunt Modzelewski, Foreign Minister of Poland. With the candidacies of Mr. Modzelewski and myself before it, the Council rejected the former by a vote of four (China, Cuba, Ecuador, Yugo-) slavia) to one (U.S.S.R.), with six abstentions. The Yugoslavian proposal that I be reappointed Secretary-General received nine affirmative votes and one negative (the U.S.S.R. using its veto), with one abstention (China). The Soviet Union had thus taken the full step, casting its forty-sixth veto, and offering little explanation other than Mr. Malik's bitter characterization of me as Secretary-General following the outbreak of the Korean War. China, by abstaining, had chosen to take a neutral stand in light of the forthcoming Soviet veto and the risk of offending the United States. It being apparent that the issue was deadlocked, the Council voted ten to one (U.S.S.R.) in favor of informing the General Assembly that it had been unable to agree on a recommendation.

Far from being stopped there, however, the Soviet Delegation had now "just begun to fight." To forestall a plenary session of the General Assembly planned for October 19, when a fifteen-nation joint resolution extending my term would be placed before it, Mr. Malik requested the President of the Security Council to call another meeting. This was the first of four meetings which resulted in the postponement of Assembly action until October 31. During these ten days, the Soviet Union tried every ruse on record to find a new man at any price—any man, it seemed, upon whom the Council could agree, other than the incumbent.

At the Council meeting on October 18 Mr. Malik assumed a soothing line. He cautioned against undue haste and stressed that it might be possible to find an acceptable candidate among the Permanent Delegates of the middle and smaller powers, particularly among those from Latin America and Asia—perhaps even among those present in the Security Council. Sir Benegal Rau of India, sincerely interested in exploring all possibilities in the hope of making a positive recommendation, came forth with what he termed a "possible procedure." According to his proposal, the eleven Members of the Council might each write the names of two candidates and deposit them in the ballot box. The Secretary of the Council would then prepare a list of all the names submitted, which could not exceed twenty-two, and would probably be much less. This list might then be turned over to the five Permanent Members, who would eliminate all names to whom there was objection. The list of names still remaining could then be circulated to the Nonpermanent Members, with another three days allowed to permit withdrawal by those candidates who so desired. Such a list would avoid the contingency of a veto.

Sir Gladwyn Jebb asked for twenty-four hours in which to consult his government regarding what he called an "ingenious suggestion." China, Egypt, and—not unexpectedly—the U.S.S.R. lent immediate support to the Indian plan. Mr. Chauvel of France agreed that the Indian suggestion was "ingenious"; but Ambassador Austin, while agreeing to circulate the Indian plan as President of the Council, lost little time in speaking out as representative of the United States, warning members to consider what this plan would mean. "The first effect," he cautioned, "would be that Mr. Lie would be removed as a candidate." Pointing out that the great majority of the Council had supported me earlier, he now asked whether they wished to reverse their stand.

At this point Ambassador Sunde of Norway came forth with the most outspoken statement yet made in connection with the immediate struggle. Describing the Indian plan as fair under normal circumstances, he emphasized that it would be eminently unfair to the present Secretary-General. As the first speaker to admit openly and honestly the political significance of the deadlock, he abandoned all pretense of overlooking Soviet and Chinese motives, and justified his departure by the need for "bearing the background in mind."

"It might be properly asked," he stated, "whether the U.S.S.R. intends to retaliate against Mr. Lie because of his stand with regard to Korea. Is the U.S.S.R.'s attitude an attempt to punish Mr. Lie for his stand under Article 99 of the Charter?" He concluded: "Nine members of the Council have voted in favor of Mr. Lie. His elimination would therefore be tantamount to victory for the North Koreans."

At the Security Council meeting on October 29, it soon became apparent that the Indian plan was losing ground. Mr. Chauvel stated that the French Delegation was ready to confirm its previous vote for me, although it had not intended to abandon the right to consider any candidate who might be acceptable to the five Permanent Members. The failure to approve one candidate did not necessarily end the consideration of the question as far as France was concerned. Yugoslavia, which turned out to be almost as stanch a supporter as the United States of the position of the Secretary-General, came out flatly against the Indian plan and affirmed that the Council had already expressed its opinion on the matter. Sir Gladwyn

Jebb had also consulted his government, which "after much consideration" had instructed him to oppose the Indian plan. The United States, of course, also opposed it.

In Mr. Malik's view the Security Council could adopt or reject the Indian proposal, but did not have the right to put an end to discussion; and he seized forthwith a Cuban suggestion that the Permanent Members meet for consultations. India withdrew its voting plan, and the members—in a sort of "hands-in-the-air" gesture—voted by seven, against four abstentions, to permit the Permanent Members to meet in the hope of finding a possible candidate. That prospects for the success of this procedure were not good was indicated by the fact that the United States and Britain were among the four abstaining. The Permanent Members were to report back to the Security Council not later than October 24.

On October 24 Mr. Chauvel telephoned to me that I was now France's only candidate. On that same day President Truman came to town with Secretary of State Acheson on the occasion of United Nations' Day. For convenience to Flushing Meadow he had chosen to continue by train direct to Belmont Park, Long Island, without stopping in Manhattan. Ambassador Austin, Assembly President Entezam, and I welcomed him, and he invited us into his private car, where Mr. Entezam and I shared a table with Mr. Acheson. Just across the aisle the President and Warren Austin entered immediately upon a discussion of the Secretary-Generalship, and it was then that the President was heard to authorize Austin to use the veto, if necessary, to uphold the United States' position.

Later that day, after President Truman, Mr. Entezam, and I had addressed the Assembly, and Mr. Truman had met the Delegates, the official party and other guests arrived for a luncheon at my home which Mr. Entezam and I were giving in honor of the President and Mrs. Truman. After this luncheon, and just before leaving, President Truman took me aside for a moment. "You must go on," he said, and confirmed what he had told Ambassador Austin earlier in the day.

Secretary of State Acheson, before he left my home, reaffirmed the President's remarks—but in more detail. He told me that Ambassador Austin had been instructed to use the veto on behalf of the United States, should such a measure prove necessary, to assure my reappointment. To this I replied: "The choice is, of course, up to you. But, if it is decided to use the veto, please give me word in advance." This, I was informed, would be done.

The following day, however, I learned that the day before the President's visit—as best I can reconstruct the sequence—Ambassador Austin had already raised the possibility of using the veto against any other candidate, in the course of a private consultation of the Permanent Members of the Security Council—the first time in the history of the United Nations that the United States had reached for this weapon.

The Security Council reconvened on October 25 to hear Ambassador Austin as President report that the Permanent Members, after two meetings, had failed to agree on a candidate. In addition to myself, they had considered Luis Padilla Nervo, Sir Benegal Rau, and Charles Malik (of Lebanon)—all proposed by the U.S.S.R.—as well as General Romulo, nominated by China. Yakov Malik, however, was not satisfied with the President's version of events, and hastened to make a purposive revelation. Referring, apparently, to the Permanent Members' consultation on Monday the 23rd, he related that three members had supported me, one had opposed, and one abstained. Sir Benegal Rau, among the Soviet candidates, had been supported by one member, one had opposed him categorically, one had stated that he would oppose if necessary, and the other two had abstained. Of the two remaining Soviet candidates, Mr. Padilla Nervo and Charles Malik, and China's nominee, General Romulo, each had received the support of two Members, two had abstained —though one indicated he would support any one of the three upon which the other Permanent Members might agree—and a final Member had opposed all three candidates, with an indication that the veto would be used if necessary. Yakov Malik insisted that the Council vote on all five candidates.

This was the first indication to the other Council Members that Warren Austin had threatened to use the veto—and Yakov Malik brought it to light. In the ensuing debate that day, he lost no opportunity to recall this fact, noting at one point: "The United States, as a permanent member of the Security Council, has abandoned its widely advertised position of giving up its right of veto. The United States representative has stated that he would veto any candidate other than Mr. Lie, and thus apparently intends to promote Mr. Lie's candidacy, even though the latter is illegal, by resort to the veto." There was no mistaking the almost gleeful persistence with which Mr. Malik sought to draw Warren Austin into reaffirming in a Council meeting what he had hinted in an informal gathering. It would serve Soviet interests to get this point on record. I can imagine that Ambassador Austin was able to resist this needling only so long, and finally—fortified by a clear-cut go-ahead received only the day before from the President and the Secretary of State—he resolved to come straight out with it. Warren Austin is one of the most thoroughly honest men I have met, and I am convinced that it would have been physically impossible for him to remain silent. Conscience and honesty demanded that he speak for what he felt was right; but I am sure he also decided that it was time to settle the matter once for all. There had been enough maneuvering, and he knew that this unprecedented threat by the United States to use the veto, if necessary, against any other candidate would end all that for good.

Following a detailed review of the way in which the selection of a Secretary-General had become a main issue in the broader struggle embodied in the United Nations' Korean action, Mr. Austin affirmed: "The case is not one in which a United States veto would conflict with the interests of its friends. The Council is face to face with an attack on a moral principle, and the question is whether the unity of the free peoples will be maintained or broken up. Shall that strong weapon be used, or shall it be left unused to rust? It must be used in defense of the general security."

As it turned out in the Council meeting, the veto was not necessary. Mr. Chauvel had previously reported that Mr. Padilla Nervo did not wish his name to be considered, and Sir Benegal Rau also formally withdrew—as I knew he had always wanted to do. Yakov Malik continued to insist on a vote on the remaining two. The U.S.S.R.'s proposal to recommend the appointment of Charles Malik of Lebanon was thereupon rejected with four votes in favor (China, Egypt, India, and the U.S.S.R.) and seven abstentions. The proposal to recommend General Romulo was rejected by an identical vote. Over the protests of the Soviet Delegate, a second letter was finally drafted for transmission to the General Assembly, noting that the

Security Council "remains unable to agree on a recommendation to the General Assembly regarding the appointment of a Secretary-General."

With that, the issue had, in fact, moved out of the hands of the Security Council, despite a last-ditch delaying action by the Soviet Union the following day, when it requested that the Council be called into session once again. This meeting, on October 30, was largely a Soviet rehash of its position, coupled with a warning that the forthcoming action by the General Assembly would be considered as illegal by the U.S.S.R. Earlier, Yakov Malik's proposal to postpone considering the appointment of a Secretary-General was rejected by a vote of seven to three. He thereupon concluded with the threat that "if the appointment of Mr. Lie is imposed, the U.S.S.R. will not take Mr. Lie into account and will not consider him as Secretary-General of the United Nations."

Item 17 on the agenda of the General Assembly was a joint draft resolution, sponsored by fifteen nations, recommending that I be continued in office for three years. Reference was made to the two communications from the Security Council, verifying its inability to agree on a recommendation, and "the necessity to ensure the uninterrupted exercise of the functions vested by the Charter in the office of the Secretary-General." The Assembly, according to the resolution, would be basing its action on the fact that I had already been recommended by the Security Council in 1946, that the Assembly had set my term of office at five years, and that it would now, within its constitutional rights, extend this term for an additional three years.

The resolution was scheduled for the agenda of the General Assembly, meeting in plenary session on October 31. Following Mr. Malik's unsuccessful delaying maneuvers in the Council meeting on October 30, Foreign Minister Vyshinsky decided to hold one of his rare press conferences that afternoon. Mr. Vyshinsky was in fine form that day, and had a great deal to say. I heard it all, for he met the overflow crowd of newspapermen in the Security Council chamber, which had loud-speaker connections with my office. At the end of a fiery sixty-three minutes I had learned a good deal about Trygve Lie, as seen through Soviet eyes: I was violating the Charter already by not withdrawing formally, in light of the Soviet veto.

MY TERM IS EXTENDED

"Nevertheless," Mr. Vyshinsky rolled on, "Mr. Lie does not say: 'I have not received the appropriate recommendation under the Charter; I therefore withdraw my candidacy.' On the contrary, he has done everything possible to cling to his job. Well, $25,000 is quite a bit of money—in addition to everything else, of course." From all indications, that press conference was much to his liking; he seemed to relish the chance to play "prosecutor" as in the Moscow purge trials. And he suited the part well. As the vilification and abuse went on and on I could see that my position was not destined to be a happy one, should the General Assembly vote to extend my term the following day.

What took place in the General Assembly on October 31 and November 1 is a matter of record. The actual battle had already been fought and won in the Security Council, and the main question now was how decisive the majority in the Assembly would be. Without the support of at least forty-five Member states, I was still prepared to refuse an extension of my term—regardless of how the refusal might appear in the face of Mr. Vyshinsky's "scare" tactics. The opposition of the Soviet bloc, as a form of political retaliation, was one thing: though its wrath would make the next three years difficult, they would probably not be impossible. On the other hand, if more states came out against me there would be insufficient justification for my continuing, for I was, in fact, facing a vote of confidence on my interpretation of the Secretary-General's duties.

Of the many speakers that day, there was one who managed to bind the salient factors of this controversy into an argument so keen and cutting that even Mr. Vyshinsky must have winced. That was Lester B. Pearson of Canada. Only a few hours earlier the Soviet Delegation, in a last desperate maneuver, had approached the man who—in my estimation—should have been the new Secretary-General of the United Nations. Had the Soviet Union started with Lester B. Pearson instead of ending with him, I would have assembled my family and my baggage and left for Norway, a happy man: the future of the United Nations would have been as certain in his hands as it could be in those of any human being. But his reasons for saying No were precisely the same as mine for saying Yes.

Shortly after the midday recess, Mr. Pearson arose to declare flatly, "Whether we like it or not, we are confronted with a situation where the General Assembly must do something." His commonsense approach was simply: "No article of the Charter, and far less any General Assembly resolution, can possibly be interpreted in such a way as to render inoperative the whole structure of the United Nations as established by the Charter." In refuting the charges of illegality hurled at this "expedient to meet the situation created by the deadlock in the Security Council," he maintained that this latest Soviet charge of illegality was really a means of settling scores with me personally:

Mr. Vyshinsky declared that during the last five years his delegation and his government had acquired gradually some doubts as to Mr. Lie's fitness for the post. I suspect, however, that it was not during five years, but during five days in June, 1950, that they began to realize that Mr. Lie was possibly not their kind of Secretary-General.

What is the basis of the attacks being made now by those who, not long ago, were praising Mr. Lie to the skies and trying to harness him to their own particular brand of peace campaign? Indeed, so highly praised was he by these people that extremists on the other side attacked him as a "red." If a Secretary-General of the United Nations is attacked from both sides, he is either a cipher or a sincere, honest, impartial servant of the United Nations. Mr. Lie is no cipher. It is, of course, quite unnecessary to defend him from the adjectives now being thrown at him by those who desired his appointment in 1946, supported it during 1947, 1948, and 1949, and insist on dismissing him now.

The five members of the Soviet bloc fought back with a veritable hailstorm of invectives and accusations. Juliusz Katz-Suchy of Poland referred to the "army of United States 'arm-twisters.'" Anatoli M. Baranovsky of the Ukraine spoke of "Trygve Lie's two-faced, double-dealing attitude." Vyshinsky included his usual light touch, maintaining that I should be recognized if I "entered through the right door," and then riding his simile: "Why should we make him come through the window or through the back door? He is big enough to enter through the door and perhaps too big to enter through the window."

After two days of such proceedings, which I followed on the television set at home, the fifteen-nation joint resolution was put to a vote. My request to the Assembly President that the vote be by secret ballot was opposed by the representative of Chile—for what reason, I have not been able to determine—and so it was taken by a simple show of hands. Forty-six nations voted to continue me in office; five—the Soviet bloc—opposed, and eight states abstained. Among the abstainers, Nationalist China's reason was clear enough. Australia, while favoring me personally, admitted "genuine doubts" about the legality of the proceedings. The Arab bloc, too, explained its abstention on "legal grounds"; but this took on a different tinge, once the Delegate from Iraq slipped off into a review of the "Palestine tragedy since 1947," where "Mr. Lie has not been entirely impartial."

Though a nine-to-one majority, the result of the Assembly vote was not completely satisfactory. Although I had had serious differences with the Arab bloc and with Nationalist China, I had dared to hope that the decision at which others had arrived on my behalf would win the support of fifty nations. Australia hurt even more. The narrow margin over the minimum vote on which I had set my mind, did not make it any easier to return to three hard years.

Events between 1951 and 1953—the purgatory of the personnel investigations, the interminable Korean struggle, and the persistent Soviet boycott—made me doubt seriously that I had been right in accepting three more years as Secretary-General. With the Assembly's vote returning me to office, the immediate political objectives had been won: United Nations action in Korea had been reaffirmed, the continuity of United Nations administration had been assured, and the independent position of the Secretary-General had been preserved against the threats and pressures of a great power. But the winning of these objectives—vital as they were—was at a heavy cost to me and to my office. The immediate advantages to the Organization have to be weighed against the serious impairment in the usefulness of my office that followed. The Soviet boycott limited my activities to a small part of the political role intended for the Secretary-General by the Charter.

It was not a happy state of affairs, and I sincerely hope that future Secretaries-General of the United Nations will be spared such tribulations.

CHAPTER XXI

THE COMMUNIST ISSUE IN THE SECRETARIAT

> "In an international organization that in most respects faithfully reflects the world as it is—a world of sovereign nations, the Secretariat has exclusively international responsibilities. The Secretary-General and his staff have in some respects been placed by the Charter in an advanced—and correspondingly exposed—position."

DURING THE last six months of my term as Secretary-General the "exposed" position of the Secretariat was all too forcibly demonstrated when it was caught squarely in the middle of the furor over internal security that gripped the United States. It was a cruel turn of fate that the Secretariat, the Delegations, and I should have been battered by all the turmoil of highly charged emotions, mutual misunderstandings, and even recriminations in those months. Being human, I of course made mistakes; but both blame and praise came to me then for positions I did not take and beliefs I did not share. The following pages attempt to set the record straight, clearly and honestly, so that considered judgment may be based on fact.

To understand the events of the period from the fall of 1952 to the spring of 1953 it is necessary to go back as far as 1946. In the first year of the United Nations we had had to recruit members of the Secretariat rapidly—twenty-nine hundred between March and December, 1946, and several hundred more in 1947. The rapidity of recruitment made me uneasy, though it was necessary. Of course we checked references and previous employers and went through all the normal personnel procedures of a careful business firm; but we did not have the investigative resources of a national government, nor had we yet perfected the elaborate system for international recruitment that later went into effect. I was especially concerned about American recruitment. To be sure, the Americans appointed gave a most satisfactory performance, by and large. The trouble was that so great a proportion of the staff were of United States nationality, and the United States government gave so little help in choosing among the applicants.

It was my practice to ask Member governments to propose candidates for the Secretariat and to check with them often on proposed appointments. Of course I always reserved the final decision in accordance with the constitutional authority of the Secretary-General under Article 100, and the international recruitment procedures were conducted on an independent basis. Nevertheless, help from governments in getting the best people was obviously necessary, and advisable, so long as my independence of judgment and decision was respected.

The United States, however, leaned over backward from the beginning. Not a single nomination of an American for employment in the Secretariat was received from the State Department except for the Assistant Secretary-General for Administrative and Financial Services and my legal Counsel, Abraham H. Feller. Nor could I get any help, for years, from the United States in checking on the records of either applicants or employees. The motivation of the United States was honorable. Secretary of State James F. Byrnes told me that his government did not wish to appear in any way to influence my selection of personnel or to invade the exclusive responsibilities of the Secretary-General under the Charter. While I appreciated his motives I was, as a result, deprived of assistance which the vast machinery of the United States government enabled it to render, far better than the very limited resources of the United Nations, in re-screening all these temporary appointments when the question of their staying on came up. So far as ability and devotion to duty are concerned experience was to prove that the overwhelming majority of these hasty appointments were, in fact, very fortunate; but one matter caused me increasing concern as the months passed and the "cold war" between the West and the Communist world developed into the dominating political fact of international life: the suspicion that a few members of the American Communist party might be in the Secretariat.

Nothing in the Charter or in the Staff Regulations bars a Communist from being a member of the United Nations Secretariat; nor could there be in an Organization that embraces both Communist and non-Communist Members. Furthermore every Secretariat member has full freedom and privacy for his personal political and religious convictions so long as he lives up to the oath of office of an international civil servant. Nevertheless I would never knowingly have employed a member of the American Communist party in the Secretariat. First of all, an American Communist is not a representative American citizen. Although the Communist party had not been directly outlawed in the United States, many laws and regulations, in effect, labeled it as a subversive organization dedicated to the overthrow of the government of the United States by force and violence. With the Permanent Headquarters in the United States, it was plain common sense not to want any American Communists in the Secretariat.

I had no fear of espionage or sabotage or other threat to the security of the United States by reason of activities of such Communists within the United Nations. There was nothing to spy on in the United Nations. Governments did not give it secret information they wished to withhold. Its meetings and documentation were public property. The work of the Secretariat was under constant scrutiny of the Member governments, who were quick to protest any imagined deviation from objectivity—and such protests were rare indeed. No, the United Nations was about as barren a field for spies as could be imagined. The only Secretariat official who was ever accused in court of espionage was a Russian, Valentin Gubitchev. He was convicted and deported to the U.S.S.R., not for spying in the United Nations, but for allegedly receiving documents which Judith Coplon brought him from Washington.

My reasons were the common-sense and practical reasons of policy I have given. If there was even one American Communist in the Secretariat I wished to get rid of him. I would do it quietly and in accordance with the Staff Regulations, in the ways to which I had been accustomed in Norway. Western European governments do not make a public row, nor destroy a man's future chance to make a living, when they find a Communist in a position they feel it is bad policy for him to occupy. They transfer him to a nonsensitive post or quietly replace him. That was my intention toward any American Communists I might find in the Secretariat.

I did not know there were any—I only had the uneasy feeling there might be a few. I tried to find out. In 1946 and 1947 I informally asked the United States government for personnel data about American nationals in the Secretariat. In August, 1948, before the first Assembly session in Paris, I submitted a list of 377 American officials in the Secretariat with the request that the usual passport inquiries be made, hoping to be notified of any case where a barrier to issuance of a passport existed. Such an indication would not, of course, be ground for dismissal, but might furnish a basis for investigation. In June, 1949, Byron Price inquired, at my request, of a senior official of the United States Federal Bureau of Investigation whether it would be possible for the FBI to give us any "derogatory information" it had on American applicants of Secretariat positions. The reply was "No"—I suppose, because of existing laws and regulations. Finally, in the fall of 1949, the State Department agreed to examine available records in United States government files regarding American applicants for posts; and this was later extended to cover American personnel already in the Secretariat.

I was grateful for this much cooperation, but the arrangement did not prove satisfactory. Reports were very slow in coming back: a few in 1950, more in 1951 and 1952. Nor was I provided with information upon which I could base a judgment. I received instead evaluations by the State Department of whatever information was in the files; and the few evaluations that were negative were transmitted orally, usually in a single word such as "Reject," "Questionable" or "Incomplete." I could not and would not act against any staff member on the basis of such comments. They were helpful only in the sense that they put me on my guard and were cause for such independent inquiry and investigation as the limited facilities of the Secretariat permitted it to make.

All this took time. Then a further complication ensued. In 1950 I dismissed several staff members with temporary contracts, against whom I felt I had convincing evidence of improper activity. Appeals were taken to the Administrative Tribunal, which had been erected by the General Assembly to consider charges of breach of employment contracts. The Tribunal held that, even in the case of temporary employees, specific reasons for termination must be given. This I could not do in many instances without revealing information that was highly confidential. In the 1951 General Assembly I sought and obtained an amendment to the Staff Regulations permitting the Secretary-General to terminate temporary members without giving any other reason than the opinion that "such action would be in the interest of the United Nations," which became effective on March 1, 1952. Under it, in the ensuing months, I dismissed a few more temporary staff members about whom I had obtained convincing information of the undesirability of their remaining in the Secretariat.

At the beginning of the summer of 1952 there were perhaps a score of American staff members (out of eighteen hundred) about whom I had received such warnings as the State Department evaluations of "Reject," "Questionable," and "Incomplete." Some of these held permanent contracts and were subject to dismissal only on a showing of abolition of post, unsatisfactory service, physical incapacity, or as discipline for misconduct. About none of these staff members did I then have any solid evidence of Communist party membership, or improper conduct. I was making the customary careful and confidential inquiries in these doubtful cases when the storm clouds that had been gathering on the American scene burst in all their fury.

It is now necessary to survey briefly the causes and nature of the American climate of opinion on the issues of Communism and internal security as it had developed over the preceding years.

My friends in Norway find it almost impossible to understand the passion for "security" which seems to have gripped the United States. They know that Norway, with a population of three million, has a Communist party as large—thirty thousand members—as the Communist party of the United States, with a population of one hundred sixty million. They know that Norway shares a common border with the U.S.S.R. At the same time Norway is a resolutely anti-Communist member of the North Atlantic Treaty Organization; the country is rearming; and Norwegians are the last people in the world who are going to permit a new Quisling to subvert their free democracy. Yet no hysteria racks Norway. Why then is America today so tortured? When she was a younger, weaker nation, she dared to be tolerant in an intolerant world. Now, when she is the most powerful country on earth, she suddenly insists that she is beset with an internal disease which is an imminent threat to her very life. The very real outside threat to Western democracy from aggressive and totalitarian Communist power is one thing, my European friends say. But it is impossible for them to conceive that the United States —the greatest, richest, and most solidly stable society in the world today—is threatened from within by the weakest Communist party in existence in the West. The common European belief is that America is in the throes of a deception of immense proportions.

To a considerable extent I sympathized with this reaction. I had fought the Communists all my life in the Norwegian trade unions and labor movement and fought them successfully, but never in an atmosphere even remotely resembling the hysteria that gripped America. In dealing with the few American Communists found in the Secretariat, I had been employing the same quiet, steady common-sense approach. I did not want them there for good policy reasons; but I was not afraid that any who remained would overthrow the United States government and subvert its constitution. Nor did I expect to find spies in so open and easily watched a place as the "glass house" on the East River. I was dismayed and horrified as I saw the American concern for security go far beyond the reasonable precautions against subversion that any government should take. The dividing lines between subversion and dissent, between present activity and past association, were blurred and lost. The hunt by headline-seeking Congressional committees invaded every profession: government workers, professors, teachers, scientists, writers, artists, and actors. Reputations were indiscriminately blackened while a scattering of past or present Communist party members were here and there disclosed or surmised when witnesses refused to answer questions about Communist activity, under their Constitutional right not to answer questions that might incriminate them. All this ran so strongly against the finest traditions of American history as I had read them, that I gave much thought to the causes for such unreasoning fear and intolerance in "the land of the free and the home of the brave."

To European friends who fear they are witnessing the beginnings of Fascism in the United States, I have tried to explain that America's new position in the world is the underlying cause. For generations Americans had felt isolated and safe behind the Atlantic and Pacific oceans. Wars were fought thousands of miles away, and it never occurred to the average American that any enemy could visit destruction upon his own country. Even when after two world wars the United States emerged as a great power, whose fortunes were henceforth inextricably bound up with the rest of the world, the American continent itself remained unscarred. But then came a sudden awakening. The age of jet propulsion and the atomic bomb stripped away at one stroke the century-old security from physical attack. At the same moment the cold war involved the United States as the principal protagonist against the new imperialism of Soviet Russia, which used the Communist parties everywhere as instruments of its designs. So the American people were placed almost without warning in a position to which they were not accustomed, exposed to changes that most Europeans had long ago learned to accept as facts of life. Now almost any American city would be exposed to enemy attack in another war, almost any home to enemy destruction.

To Americans in this new and unaccustomed mood of insecurity, even the weak and futile Communist party assumed a new aspect. Small as it was, they looked upon its members as potential or actual agents of a hostile power that they knew was capable of inflicting terrible damage on the country if war should come. This is a state of mind that should be better understood by Europeans and Asians who are so shocked by what has happened. The obsession with internal security, and the accompanying hysteria, mark in a sense a last convulsive transition from the youthful, carefree America of the endless frontier and the happy isolation from "other people's wars" to the full maturity of a great world power with all its cares and burdens.

Furthermore the situation lent itself to demagogic exploitation by politicians and publicists not encumbered with principles or a sense of responsibility. That Communist spies for Russia were capable of doing great damage to the country, the atomic spy cases fully demonstrated. If so trusted and respected a government official as Alger

Hiss could be convicted for perjury in denying he had spied for
Russia, was any government official above suspicion, especially if he
had been associated with the New Deal and the wartime alliance
with Russia under Roosevelt? If there was one Hiss, might there not
be a hundred more who had cunningly wormed their way into positions of influence and authority? Therefore many otherwise sensible
people thought Senator McCarthy might be right when he launched
his red-hunting by charging there were twice that number.

Then came the Korean War, which added much new emotional
fuel to the fires that had been kindled. A million young Americans
were taken from their homes to fight in that war. The casualty lists
mounted and mounted to make it the third most costly war in American history, next to the Civil War and the Second World War. Such
an experience cuts deep. And Americans rarely thought of the war,
in the terms of United Nations resolutions, as a collective international action to repel armed aggression by "the North Korean authorities" and the "so-called Volunteers from the People's Republic
of China." It was, quite simply, a war against Communists. They
thought of the enemy, killing and wounding more than 130,000
Americans, as Communists far more than as North Koreans and Chinese. The emotions thus aroused were an irresistible temptation to
men who did not hesitate to exploit sorrow, hate, and fear in order
to advance themselves; and such as these were in full cry in the
summer and fall of 1952 when the United Nations Secretariat became involved in a situation that was beyond the control of reasonable and responsible men.

Before this, I had had a few isolated encounters with "red hunters"
in America and "capitalist-hunters" from behind the Iron Curtain.
As far back as 1947 a brief flurry stirred by rumors reflecting on the
objectivity of some members of the Secretariat I had assigned to the
staff of the Balkan Commission, which the Security Council dispatched to Greece to investigate border incidents with Greece's
Communist neighbors. No government submitted an official complaint or supporting facts, though the rumors appeared to be promoted by Greek sources which were not disinterested. The climax
came with the allegation in the column of a leading American
journalist that a Pole on the Commission's staff had been caught
trying to steal into the room of the British member of the Commis-

sion. I was consequently accused of attempting to undermine President Truman's program of aid to Greece and Turkey, or at least of having "packed" the Commission's staff in the Communists' favor. That the allegation and others that followed were altogether false did not silence my critics. I sent William H. Stoneman to Europe to investigate the work of the staff of the Commission, which was under the direction of a Norwegian, Colonel Roscher Lund. He found that, while some of the staff might have been more tactful toward Greek authorities, the sinister charges against them were nonsense.

Soon afterward, I was belabored from the other side. Mr. Gromyko came to protest against the White Russians—émigrés and children of émigrés—who were employed in the Secretariat as interpreters, translators, and document officers. He submitted no facts which indicated that these people had done anything amiss, and so I declined to discharge them. The next year, the coup in Czechoslovakia brought a similar experience when Vladimir Houdek, representing the new Communist regime, demanded that I dismiss all Czechs and Slovaks in the Secretariat who were regarded with disfavor in Prague, and handed me a list of names. Responding that this was not his government's affair, I refused to consider such action. He pursued the conversation with a letter, to which I replied in the same vein, and that was the last I heard of that.

In 1948 two junior security officials of the State Department charged in widely publicized testimony before a Senate Judiciary subcommittee that "hundreds" of foreign agents were using United Nations employment or accreditation to the delegations as a cover for subversive activities. Secretary of State Marshall responded that the United States did not have knowledge of a single individual associated with the United Nations who was engaged in activity against American security. A year later, again before a Senate Judiciary subcommittee, an unidentified witness, called "Witness Number 8," alleged that the Secretariat was under Communist domination, and that I myself was a Communist tool—among other things, that Commander Jackson's post had been abolished because he had stood up to my alleged pro-Communist doings. I was in Europe at the time, and Byron Price, as Acting Secretary-General, protested the "unfounded and irresponsible" attacks. But, though the relevant authorities of the United States government publicly affirmed their confidence in me, it is doubtful that the repudiation ever caught up with the charge—as is so frequently the case.

All these were mere skirmishes in comparison to what happened next. A federal grand jury, impaneled to investigate Communist activities in the New York area, turned to the American staff of the United Nations Secretariat. Such a jury is supposed to conduct its inquiries in complete secrecy; but there came a succession of "leaks" to the press, especially to newspapers which had consistently attacked the United Nations, with the general purport that the Secretariat was full of subversives who were endangering American security. Soon statements began to come out of certain Congressional committee offices in Washington that the United Nations harbored "a nest of Communist spies" and an immediate housecleaning was demanded. Meanwhile, hearsay reports reached me that some United States members of the Secretariat were refusing to answer questions before the grand jury about Communist affiliations and possible subversive activities, invoking for that purpose the Fifth Amendment to the United States Constitution, which provides, "nor shall any person . . . be compelled in any criminal case to be a witness against himself."

If the distorted and exaggerated stories from New York and Washington had disturbed me in one direction, the reports of United Nations Fifth Amendment cases disturbed me in another. United Nations immunity extended only to acts of Secretariat members in their official capacity. It did not extend to their outside activities or private lives. I felt strongly that a United Nations official should cooperate fully with investigations conducted by an official agency of his own government, at least in those countries where Western democratic traditions protected him from the exercise of arbitrary power. After becoming Secretary-General I had myself returned to Norway in 1946 to answer fully to exhaustive questioning during a parliamentary inquiry into the conduct of the Norwegian government in London during the war. Furthermore by virtue of the very fact that a United Nations official was an international civil servant, special obligations were imposed upon him to conduct himself vis-à-vis the Member governments at all times in a manner above just reproach. This latter opinion was fully shared by the General Assembly when it adopted Article 1.4 of the Staff Regulations, which read:

Members of the Secretariat shall conduct themselves at all times in a manner of befitting their status as international civil servants. They shall not engage in any activity that is incompatible with the proper discharge of their duties with the United Nations. They shall avoid any action and in particular any kind of public pronouncement which may adversely reflect on their status. While they are not expected to give up their national sentiments or their political and religious convictions, they shall at all times bear in mind the reserve and tact incumbent upon them by reason of their international status.

I believed that to plead a privilege against self-incrimination, though it was a constitutional right, would be clearly in violation of Article 1.4, except in extraordinary circumstances. This was not the only constitutional right that United Nations officials had to waive in becoming international civil servants. Under the staff rules that implemented the Regulations they could not, for instance, campaign for political office or take public part in partisan political campaigns.

For these reasons I immediately sought official information on the grand-jury proceedings upon which I might base further action. This was denied to me on the ground that grand-jury proceedings were secret, although the vague leaks to favored newspaper and radio columnists continued.

Then, in October, 1952, the Internal Security Subcommittee of the United States Senate Judiciary Committee moved to New York and held a series of public hearings. In these a total of eighteen United Nations staff members pleaded the Fifth Amendment. As I read the transcript of the testimony in each case I was more and more convinced that these staff members had gravely and irresponsibly transgressed the Staff Regulations. Furthermore, I knew that the exercise of the constitutional privilege under American law does not imply any similar constitutional right to continued public employment by the one who exercises it. On the contrary, the practice for federal, state, and municipal employment alike in the United States is the opposite—the invocation of the privilege in such circumstances normally leads to dismissal. The United Nations, of course, was not bound to follow this or any other national legal practice. Its rules cannot incorporate those of any single state. But the precedent strengthened my conviction. Furthermore, the attitude of these witnesses tended under the circumstances to discredit the Secretariat as a whole, to cast suspicion on all the staff—and, still more serious, it imperiled the position of the Organization in the host country. The impression that the Secretariat harbored those subversive of American institutions was heightened by the practice of the Internal Security Subcommittee in generally calling only those staff members to testify in *open* session who earlier had refused in closed session to answer questions about Communist party membership, or who had admitted past membership. Although these witnesses were about one in a hundred of the Americans employed by the United Nations, the impression conveyed to the public was that of a parade of Americans working for the United Nations who were Communists, former Communists, or at least had something to hide.

The public outcry in the United States, whipped up by elements of the press which had never been friendly to the United Nations, grew to appalling proportions, while the morale of the Secretariat slumped badly. Mr. Feller and I had been following developments carefully—with Byron Price, we had carried the main load of the "subversive" issue—and we were seriously alarmed. On the one hand, the sweeping attacks upon the standing and integrity of the Secretariat were vicious and distorted and out of all proportion to the facts. On the other hand, there was no question in my mind that the cases involving the Fifth Amendment ought to go, as a matter of sound policy entirely divorced from the public hue and cry. They had not conducted themselves as international civil servants should. Those holding temporary contracts, I dismissed; but I was not certain that I had the legal right under the Staff Regulations to discharge those with permanent contracts. For the time being, therefore, I put them on compulsory leave. It occurred to Mr. Feller and me that a sound procedure would be to seek the advice of an international commission of eminent jurists as to what further action I could and should take. Discussing this idea with my advisers and the Assistant Secretaries-General and a number of the delegations, I met approval on all sides. The delegations, particularly, supported the proposal, even though some of them later criticized me for acting on the basis of one of the commission's recommendations. In the meantime I was left virtually alone to deal with the American authorities and American public opinion as best I could. In the autumn of 1952 the other governments had little disposition for getting involved in the defense of the good name of the Secretariat though in the next spring, after it was all over, certain delegations were not slow to suggest how things might have been done in a different way.

Deciding to appoint a commission was one thing; finding prominent jurists to take on such an assignment was another. It seemed to be necessary to have an American member, with an intimate knowledge of American law; we felt an English jurist would provide both the legal capacity and the detachment desirable; and, for a third, we sought a representative of a small power and a legal system other than the Anglo-Saxon. The Legal Department searched ceaselessly for a panel. Leading jurists of the United States, Great Britain, and Belgium were canvassed or suggested, either directly or through their governments. Men like Judge Learned Hand of the United States, Sir Hartley Shawcross of Great Britain, who had been Attorney General in the Labor Government, and Henri Rolin of Belgium, who was later to criticize the Jurists' Report with great severity, were among those we sought. Many of the most illustrious legal minds of the Western world declined the invitation for one reason or another, or the governments advised against our original proposals. Finally, we constituted a panel of three distinguished lawyers: Sir Edwin Herbert of the United Kingdom, a prominent solicitor; William D. Mitchell, who had been Attorney General of the United States under President Hoover; and Paul Veldekens, professor of civil law at the Catholic University of Louvain. It was part and parcel of the atmosphere of Greek tragedy that pervaded the whole affair that I was later accused of "packing" the Commission of Jurists, whereas in fact my effort from beginning to end was to obtain for it men especially qualified to pass on the issues.

The Commission came together on November 14.

On the day before, the United Nations—and I personally—suffered an incalculable loss. I was at lunch in the Metropolitan Club as the guest of the Foreign Minister of Brazil, with Secretary of State Acheson, Ambassador Gross, and several other ranking delegates among those present, when an urgent summons came to go to the telephone. The call was from Andrew Cordier, with the news that

THE COMMUNIST ISSUE IN THE SECRETARIAT

Abe Feller had died in a jump from the window of his twelfth-floor apartment.

Shock and grief engulfed me. Abe Feller had been nearer to me than anyone else outside the circle of my immediate family. He had been a close adviser for seven years, and hardly a day passed at Headquarters when he did not come to see me—most days he would come several times. Whenever something was up, Abe was there, alert, discreet, full of energy and ideas. I had a deep admiration for his intelligence, and an affection for him which was strengthened by his own loyalty and personal regard.

No doubt Abe Feller was a victim of the witch hunt, of the awful pressure of the hysterical assault upon the United Nations that reactionaries were promoting and using for their own ends. He was a liberal in politics, and a conservative in his lawyerlike respect for due process. He knew that no American in the Secretariat had ever been indicted for espionage or any other subversive activity against his country. Although he felt as strongly as I that the United Nations officials who had pleaded the Fifth Amendment had betrayed their obligation and should be removed, he had a genuine sympathy for the victims of the headline-hunting investigations and resented deeply the "smear" against the whole of the Secretariat which was so assiduously advanced. Day after day, he followed the Senate hearings and saw the tragedy unfold. He saw the hysteria invade high places and sweep his country in violation of fundamental principles of fair play and orderly justice by which he had lived all his life. The strain finally grew too strong, and he broke.

At Abe Feller's funeral I was too much under the sway of emotion to speak; but eleven months later I had the honor of dedicating the Abraham Feller Memorial Room in the United Nations Library to the memory of a great and loyal international civil servant and a great and loyal American.

On November 29 the Commission of Jurists submitted its opinion. Like many legal interpretations, it was controversial. While disagreeing with it in some respects, I appreciated the devotion, good will, and high intelligence they had shown in carrying out so delicate a task.

The main conclusion of the jurists, which I accepted and upon which I acted, was that refusal by the American staff members on grounds of possible self-incrimination to answer questions about Communist party membership, or any subversive activity, constituted a fundamental breach of Article 1.4 of the Staff Regulations. This confirmed the view I later expressed in my report of January 30, 1953, to the General Assembly on Personnel Policy; "Especially in a time of serious political tension and concern over national security, the United Nations staff member has a positive obligation to refrain from conduct which will draw upon himself grave suspicion of being a danger to the security of a particular State. When he has refused to answer official interrogations relating to crimes involving subversive activities, he has by his own free choice violated that obligation; he has thereby contributed substantially to undermining the confidence which the international official is required to maintain."

The jurists found that I had the power to dismiss the nine staff members with permanent contracts who had used the Fifth Amendment in this manner and recommended that I do so. First, however, I decided to give them a second chance. After announcing to the whole staff my acceptance of the jurists' recommendation I notified the suspended staff members that I should have to dismiss them for a fundamental breach of the obligations laid down in Staff Regulation 1.4 unless, within three days, they informed me that they had notified the appropriate United States authorities of their intention to withdraw the plea of privilege and answer the pertinent questions put to them. This they all refused to do. The refusal created, in my opinion, a clear case for summary dismissal for serious misconduct under Article 10 of the Staff Regulations. I decided, however, to give them the normal indemnities and severance pay to which summary dismissal did not entitle them, in order to help them over the difficult time they faced in finding other employment, after all the publicity.

A few days after the Commission of Jurists had presented its report to me, the federal grand jury in New York, which had been seeking evidence of subversive activity by American members of the Secretariat, came to the end of its term. Had there been meaningful evidence of illegal subversive activity against any member of the Secretariat, it would have returned indictments in accordance with its duty. It did not return even one; but its "presentment" made a blanket and indiscriminate finding of "Guilty," charging that there was "infiltration into the United Nations of an overwhelmingly large group of disloyal United States citizens," and that this situation constituted "a menace" to the United States Government. The presentment not only named no names but gave no figures to support the words "an overwhelmingly large group of disloyal United States citizens." This strange use of the judicial process received wide publicity. My formal request for a copy of the records of the grand jury or, if these could not be supplied, an official statement of the specific evidence on which its conclusions might have been based was denied.

Senator McCarran, chairman of the Internal Security Subcommittee, soon introduced a bill "to prevent citizens of the United States of questionable loyalty to the United States Government from accepting any office or employment in or under the United Nations." It provided that any American citizen taking a position with the United Nations would first have to receive a security clearance from the Attorney General of the United States, and citizens who were already in the employ of the United Nations would have to obtain a similar clearance. "Whoever, being a citizen of the United States . . . shall willfully fail to comply . . . shall be fined not more than $10,000, or imprisoned for not more than five years."

To my dismay the only precedent I could discover for such a law was the edict promulgated by Fascist Italy in 1927 to prevent Italians opposed to Mussolini from being members of the League of Nations Secretariat. It too provided for governmental clearance, though the penalties for violation were less severe than those Senator McCarran found appropriate, being only a fine of not more than 5,000 lire and a prison term of not more than one year.

The executive branch of the United States government now moved rapidly into the breach. President Truman's executive order of January 9, two days after Senator McCarran introduced his bill, prescribed "procedures for making available to the Secretary-General of the United Nations certain information concerning United States citizens employed or being considered for employment on the Secretariat of the United Nations," including a full field investigation by the FBI of American members of, or candidates for, the

Secretariat's internationally recruited staff, and a less extensive investigation by the Civil Service Commission of other Americans employed in the locally recruited lower echelons of the Secretariat. If a resultant report contained derogatory information the staff member had the right to hearings before United States loyalty review boards. After the investigations were completed, information "in such detail as security considerations permit" would be transmitted to the Secretary-General for use "in exercising the responsibility with respect to the integrity of the personnel employed by the United Nations imposed upon him by the Charter." The investigations, the hearings, if any, and the findings and evidence transmitted to the Secretary-General, all would be conducted without any publicity whatsoever. There would be no circus, no hysteria, no blackening of reputations. The United States government, by the terms of the order, did not undertake to instruct the Secretary-General as to whom he should or should not employ, nor to imprison any American citizens he might employ contrary to the Attorney General's judgment. The evidence gathered by United States agencies would be submitted to the Secretary-General, and the Secretary-General would make his own decision.

While the executive order was not promulgated as a result of any agreement with me, I welcomed it as giving help I had sought for years. A great many American members of the Secretariat likewise welcomed it, believing it would enable them to clear themselves of indiscriminate suspicions, and were as anxious as I to get the investigation started quickly. Fingerprinting and the filling out of forms were the first steps, and the question arose as to whether I should allow these procedures to be carried out by United States authorities in the Headquarters building, which was international territory. There were vehement protests, mainly from European staff members and delegations, against my decision to permit them; but the Americans with whom I talked—they, not the Europeans, were the "victims"—took the decision as a sensible and convenient way of getting past the preliminaries quickly. Americans during the war, in government service or the armed services, had come to take fingerprinting as a matter of course, without the humiliating connotations of suspected criminality that it still has for so many people. I also permitted interviewing by the United States FBI and Civil

Service agents of American staff members in their offices, if they chose. This also caused protests, again mainly from European staff members who were not involved. Most Americans preferred their offices to their homes for such interviews. As for legal precedents, this was not the first time national police had been admitted to United Nations premises. At the first session of the General Assembly in London, British security police had been admitted to Church House for the purpose of protection; and, at the third and sixth sessions in Paris, French security police had been admitted to the Palais de Chaillot both for security and for investigative reasons. The Secretary-General has, and should exercise, a certain latitude of discretion in admitting national officials on United Nations "soil" when he believes that the interests of the United Nations require it.

President Truman's executive order and the events preceding it now clearly demanded a full report from me to the General Assembly, and a discussion by that body. I accordingly proposed an item on personnel policy for its formal consideration and, with a few advisers, set about preparing a comprehensive report. It was distributed at the end of January, and the Assembly came to consider the item in March. I introduced it in a speech to the plenary session of March 10.

I began by placing the problem in context—pointing out that the advanced position of the international secretariat is correspondingly exposed. "This position, while an honorable one, would have been difficult enough if the first seven years of the United Nations had been lived in a period of comparative world stability and good feeling. . . . We know that the circumstances have, in fact, been quite the reverse. . . . The great conflict of policy and ideology between the Western world and its supporters on the one hand, and the Soviet Union and its associates on the other hand, clearly creates a supreme difficulty for a Secretariat serving an Organization in which both sides are represented."

I noted that locating the headquarters within the borders of one of the most powerful protagonists created a special problem for the Secretariat, for the host country, and for the Organization as a whole. I recognized that there were nationalistic pressures from various quarters against the provisions of Article 100 of the Charter, that the responsibilities of the Secretariat must be exclusively international.

But, I recalled, the pressures were of more than one kind. "In every case but one . . . the Member Governments have respected my right as Secretary-General to speak and act as I did, while exercising their own right to support or oppose me either privately or publicly. The one exception has been the Soviet Union, together with the four Member Governments allied with it." Their three years' boycott had been the crudest form of pressure against the independence of the Secretary-General, and the most flagrant violation of Article 100 of the Charter; and there had been continuous vilification and abuse of me and my staff by the Soviet press since 1950. The central theme of it all had been that the Secretariat was dominated by Americans, and that they and I were in all respects tools of Wall Street and Washington. In the light of such charges, it was indeed ironic that the Secretariat should have been subjected at the same time to attacks in the United States for exactly opposite reasons. As for the American attitude, I declared:

"I am hopeful that, with the completion of the current executive investigation by the United States Government, the situation will improve. I have referred to the political climate in which the United Nations Secretariat has had to carry on its work here over the past months. It is not for me to express my opinion of some of the things that have been said and some of the things that have occurred.* These are matters the government and people of the United States must work out for themselves.

"I cannot, however, in all fairness, refrain from recalling the main impression I have received of the record of the Government and people of the United States over the past seven years in support of the Charter and institutions of the United Nations. This support, in my opinion, is a far more solid and enduring expression of the basic purposes of the United States towards the United Nations than the temporary difficulties to which I have referred."

The body of the speech was an exposition of the events, and the policies which I had pursued; and I concluded:

"Let us be clear about this matter. I have not yielded one inch on the essential principles I have sought to uphold and defend throughout this time of trial. Some of you may not agree with all the practical steps I have taken to meet the political realities. But there

* Out of office, I am free to do so at last.

should be no misunderstanding of my intention in taking each of these practical steps to uphold and defend the international character of the Secretariat and its ability to function in the manner laid down for it in the United Nations Charter. . . .

"Mr. President and Delegates, permit me to say simply that I have done the best I could in political circumstances that were not of my doing."

The speech was well received, and I may even say that it answered the doubts of many. The Assembly debated the question for a week, and, on the whole, it lent support to my stand. There was of course criticism, especially of the jurists' report, some of which I attempted to answer in a brief "rebuttal" on April 1, pointing out that, while "grateful to the three jurists who agreed to help me, when I was left alone by the Member Governments to deal with a situation which all delegations have since come to recognize as an extremely difficult one," I had not accepted all of their recommendations.

The Assembly concluded its debate by adopting a resolution which, in effect, expressed confidence in the policies pursued.

I left office a few days later, and my official responsibilities came to an end. The difficult situation of the Secretariat, as an island of internationalism in a nationalistic world, did not; and it remains true that the world struggle to sustain freedom, which America has led abroad, still has its home front. Although the Secretariat of the United Nations cannot fight the battle which is properly to be left to the American liberal tradition, it must stand guard against the assaults which continue to be made against its international integrity and ideal.

CHAPTER XXII

RESIGNATION

*Best kept secret.—Reasons for my decision.—Soviet boycott.
—My hands are tied as dangerous cold war deadlock continues.—Lester Pearson nearly becomes my successor.—
New Secretary-General takes over.—Home again at last!*

ON MONDAY afternoon November 10, 1952, I spoke to the General Assembly from my accustomed chair at the President's right hand, disclosing to the delegates and to the public what was, I think, the best kept secret in the United Nations history.

The delegates' seats and the public galleries alike were filled. Everyone was waiting to hear the French Foreign Minister, Robert Schuman, and others who were scheduled to make the customary statements of foreign policy in the general debate with which the General Assembly begins its annual sessions. Only a few days earlier this great Assembly hall in the Permanent Headquarters had been inaugurated in a moving ceremony that had meant for me the culmination of long years of effort to provide the United Nations with a home worthy of its place in the world.

I had been deeply moved then. I was even more so now. I began by reading the text of a letter I had handed to the Assembly President, Lester B. Pearson that morning: "I wish to refer to our personal and confidential conversation on the 11th of September, in which I informed you that I had decided, after lengthy consideration over many months, to submit my resignation as Secretary-General of the United Nations." I went on to explain that I had delayed the announcement until the Foreign Ministers of the five Permanent

Members were gathered in the Assembly, hoping that this would facilitate a quick agreement on a successor, and requested that the item "Appointment of the Secretary-General" be added to the current agenda. I reminded the Assembly of my desire to retire in 1950: "I agreed to continue only because the aggression in Korea created circumstances that put me under an obligation to carry on. Now I feel that the situation is somewhat different. Should there be an armistice, a new Secretary-General, who is the unanimous choice of the five great powers, the Security Council, and the General Assembly, may be more helpful than I can be. On the other hand, if, the world situation should go from bad to worse, at least I would not want the position of Secretary-General to hinder in the slightest degree any hope of reaching a new understanding that could prevent world disaster."

Among other reasons making it appropriate for me to retire, I mentioned the completion of the Permanent Headquarters Building and my administrative reorganization program, which I felt deserved the appraisal of a new Secretary-General prior to Assembly action.

"I would like the Members to know," I concluded, "that I am stepping aside now because I hope this may help the United Nations to save the peace and to serve better the cause of freedom and progress for all mankind."

As I left to go to my private office behind the rostrum, there was absolute stillness in the Assembly hall. The surprise, complete for all but the very few who were in on the secret, combined with the import of the announcement, and the deep feeling I was unable to conceal, to bring one of those rare moments in a public gathering when shared emotion is best expressed by a uniting silence. Soon other, equally human but less charitable reactions set in. The corridors were filled with the usual speculation and rumors running off in all directions: I did not really mean what I said; it was a maneuver; I was a captain who left his sinking ship and was only adding one more problem to the difficulties of the delegates. It was even rumored that I was leaving to accept a business offer involving gigantic sums. While my decision was communicated suddenly and without warning to the Assembly and to the world, it had been reached not in haste, but only after many months of consideration.

From the very beginning of my extended term on February 2,

1951, the Soviet Union and its four satellites had refused to recognize me as Secretary-General. The boycott was complete and was carried to absurd lengths. The rules of procedure of the General Assembly, for example, require that the credentials of the delegates "be submitted to the Secretary-General." Those of the Security Council require that the credentials "be communicated to the Secretary-General" and "be examined by the Secretary-General who shall submit a report to the Security Council for approval." From February 2, 1951, however, I received no credentials, no proposals, and no communications regarding any of the United Nations organs from a single one of the five Communist Member states. These now were addressed only to the Secretariat.

I might easily have made an issue of the matter and rejected the credentials as improperly addressed; but the split between the Member states was wide and deep enough already without adding another problem. Therfore I let the boycott pass without the protest it deserved. It was extended to social life as well. The opportunity to talk informally with one's colleagues at social functions is a long established element of international diplomatic work, and the obligations of the Secretary-General of the United Nations in this respect are heavy. During our years in New York, Mrs. Lie and I had often entertained the Russians as well as representatives of the other East European countries. We in turn were often the guests of the various Communist delegations. On February 2, 1951, however, this social exchange came to an abrupt end, not of our choosing. As was proper, we continued to send out invitations to representatives of the boycotting countries; but there was never a reply: not one declining note or even a telephone message expressing a polite refusal. Nor was there ever an invitation to a function arranged by any of the Communist delegations. The Russians, in giving their yearly dinner for members of the Security Council and for my subordinates in the Secretariat, made a point of notifying the press that neither the Secretary-General nor his wife had been invited. The Communist "freeze-out" prevailed in all quarters. I did not mind missing a few receptions and dinners, for international relations would be far better were there fewer of them; but I resented such uncivil behavior toward a man and his family. I shall not soon forget the solid support shown by a stanch group of friends in the Secretariat who refused every invitation from the Soviet and satellite delegations during these two years. Delegates and others made no protest against this total political and social boycott—overlooking its implications for the prestige of the office of Secretary-General, which is after all one of the six principal organs of the United Nations, and forgetting entirely, as far as I could tell, the human side.

While such surface irritations could be accepted, the matter had for me a more serious aspect: it was no longer possible to exercise the political role of the Secretary-General as the Charter had intended, and as I had sought to develop it over the preceding five years. In a world organization where all sides were represented, my hands were tied with respect to governments which controlled or influenced one-third of the population of the world. The series of precedents with which I had carefully sought, stage by stage, to build up the influence and prestige of the Secretary-General, not for myself, but in the interests of effective world organization and of peace, could not be carried forward, in the circumstances.

At the same time the fighting in Korea had continued, and my hopes for an early armistice had been disappointed. There was no break in the cold war, and the danger of a Third World War remained undiminished throughout 1951 and 1952. Could I, I asked in family discussion during my home leave in Norway in the summer of 1952, permit this situation to go on any longer? The influence of the United Nations for peace was weakened when its Secretary-General could not exercise the full influence of his office as the universally recognized spokesman of the whole Organization. Above all, I desired that my continued presence in the office of Secretary-General should not reduce even by the smallest margin the chance of preventing war and preserving peace.

These were the decisive factors in my decision to resign when the General Assembly reconvened in the fall. I indicated them in my speech of resignation on November 10, but explained them more fully in the following paragraphs of my address on personnel policy in March, 1953:

"So far as political matters are concerned, I think most of the Delegates here know very well that I have, over the past seven years, exercised and firmly defended the political responsibilities that the Charter and Organs of the United Nations conferred upon my office. I have sought to do so with caution and with full recognition of the political realities of the times.

"But I need only recall the Iranian case, the question of the representation of China, my Ten-Point Peace Program, Korea, and my annual reports on the world situation as evidence of my desire to uphold and strengthen the constitutional position of the office of Secretary-General in this respect. There have also been the innumerable private discussions and negotiations on issues before the United Nations in which I have participated and frequently taken the initiative.

"I know that a number of Member governments on occasion have wished I would remain silent when I felt the situation demanded that I speak out for what I believed to be the interests of the United Nations as a whole. In every case but one, however, the Member governments have respected my right as Secretary-General to speak and act as I did, while exercising their own right to support or oppose me either privately or publicly. The one exception has been the Soviet Union, together with the four Member governments allied with it.

"Because of the stand I took in support of United Nations action against armed aggression in Korea, these five Member governments have refused since 1950 even to recognize me as Secretary-General. For almost three years I have borne with this situation in silence, overlooking the many violations of established procedure that followed.

"Now, however, I believe the time is appropriate for me to say that this action, in my opinion, is by far the most serious violation of Article 100 of the Charter that has occurred. The policy of the Soviet government and its allies has been, and continues to be, a policy of the crudest form of pressure, not only against me but against any future Secretary-General who may incur the displeasure of the Soviet Union for doing his duty as he sees it under the Charter.

"It is to a large extent because of this Soviet attitude that I have offered my resignation and requested the General Assembly to appoint my successor during this present session. Do not misunderstand me. I would have been quite willing to stay to the end of my term if it were simply a question of continuing to bear with the many attacks upon me of the Soviet Union and its supporters. I have been used to them for a long time, and I have at other stages of my career had to stand up to similar attacks under different circumstances.

"But there is a larger consideration. I want the office of the Secretary-General to be in a position to wield its constitutional powers with the greatest possible degree of influence and prestige. When the Secretary-General speaks or acts for peace and freedom in some future crisis, he should have behind him not only the weight of his constitutional authority, but the weight of political influence conferred upon him by the fact that he is in office by the affirmative votes of all five Permanent Members of the Security Council and is recognized as Secretary-General by all the Member states.

"Thus, although some may say that my resignation constitutes in one respect a yielding to Soviet pressure upon me personally, I regard it as an act to strengthen for the critical times ahead the office of the Secretary-General in the framework of the United Nations and to enhance its influence for peace in the world. That, my friends, has always been my first consideration in everything—not for myself personally, but for my office and my staff."

There were also other considerations. The Permanent Headquarters, in which I took so much pride and joy, would be completed except for landscaping before the end of 1952. The General Assembly would meet for the first time in that great building to which so much effort had been given over the years of my service. Then there were the human elements. All who know me are aware that I have my full share of these and am quite open about them—the frailties along with the virtues. I was, to use a good American expression, "fed up." I knew the signs—my irritation at the Soviet needling, my feeling that the Permanent Delegates generally were losing stature, my growing impatience with the Fifth (Administrative and Budgetary) Committee of the General Assembly. I had no doubt there were reciprocal feelings about me from some who had lived too long with my shortcomings. No, the signs were unmistakable. My political experience had taught me that no single person is indispensable. I was dispensable, and should be replaced by a new Secretary-General who could enter the work fresh and with fewer fixed ideas about persons and issues than I. In short, it was time for a change.

All this may seem to some readers to form a rather surprising mixture of reasons of high policy and very personal considerations; but I can assure them that people in high places are not different from other human beings. People are people in all walks of life, the public image notwithstanding.

After we had agreed as a family during that summer in our mountain lodge that I should resign, I communicated my decision to only a very few. Tor Gjesdal and Andrew Cordier in the Secretariat knew about it. On a visit to London in September I told Anthony Eden, who advised me that the British government would be unable to recommend my retiring at that time. In London I also saw Lester Pearson. Sure that he would be elected President of the Assembly that fall, and well aware of his firm loyalty to the United Nations during my seven years in office, I acquainted him with my plans. His sympathetic acceptance of my decision implied immediate recognition that my mind was made up. The same impression was apparently conveyed to Mr. Schuman and Mr. Parodi in France, though I discovered later that both understood me to say that I intended to resign as of February 1, 1954, instead of immediately.

On returning to New York, I asked Norwegian Prime Minister Oscar Torp—then on a visit—to inform His Majesty King Haakon of Norway that I intended to announce my resignation in November. Dean Acheson, with whom I spoke on November 5 (the day following the presidential election), regretted my stand but understood that the decision was made. In fact, there was no mistaking that I had his full sympathy—for understandable reasons. He himself was probably the happiest man in America when he was relieved of office—the defeat of his party notwithstanding.

On Sunday November 9, Wilder Foote came to my home and helped draft my letter to the President as well as the next day's address to the General Assembly. His surprised arguments against my retiring were of no avail, and before the evening was over, Andrew Cordier, Abe Feller, Dragon Protitch and Tor Gjesdal had convened at Granston Tower. To most of them, the news came as a shock; and by the time we had worked out the two papers in the early hours of the morning, I was moved and disturbed to see how my most immediate staff was taking it. But their best arguments had won no ground.

At half past two on November 10, all the Assistant Secretaries-General were called in. Normally, I have little trouble in getting matters "off my chest"; but that day the words would hardly come. The expressions on the faces of the people seated about me did not help; some sat numb and shocked, others looked almost desperate. The effort to explain what the Assembly would be hearing from me within a half-hour, brought home to me how difficult it would be to place a final period at the end of these seven years. I tried to pull myself together.

A little after three o'clock the General Assembly was seated, and I made my speech. The job was done!

I had hoped to vacate my office by the end of November—at any rate before Christmas; but it became clear that a successor would not be agreed upon so soon. The various appeals to reconsider began the next day, in the general debate, from some of my closest friends in international life. Foreign Secretary Anthony Eden was, as I recall, the first to protest my decision: "It would indeed be a misfortune if, at this critical time in our affairs, we were to lose the devoted services of our Secretary-General. I hope that Mr. Lie can yet be persuaded to reconsider his decision." Brazilian Foreign Minister João Neves da Fontoura, Sir Muhammad Zafrulla Khan of Pakistan, and Ambassador Kyron of Greece reaffirmed this hope. Other Chief Delegates, who must have numbered between twenty and thirty, came in private to ask me to reconsider, and express the hope that some means for changing my mind might yet be found. And there was Mrs. Helen Rogers Reid of the New York *Herald Tribune*—an eminently loyal person, and a stanch friend and defender of the United Nations for the past seven years. She, I believe, was the first to telephone to me. After explaining my reasons, which she understood, I assured her that I would not leave the United Nations until a qualified successor had been appointed.

These statements, visits, and messages reflected one side of the picture: the side composed of a mixture of perplexity, a feeling of defeat and sadness, and the query put by so many, "Where does the United Nations go from here?" The Soviet side, however, showed no such uncertainties. A jubilant Moscow radio was soon out with a "victory" version which I felt I could have written in advance: "Trygve Lie's resignation was a revelation of his complete political bankruptcy. His efforts to help the United States to hide, with the United Nations' flag, the American aggression in Korea gave rise to waves of indignation throughout the world."

But this time no appeal or attack could force me to continue. Though I assured persons who feared my announcement would bring the Organization into a state of crisis that I would carry on until a successor had been chosen, I would go no further, and made it clear that I would appreciate this choice being made before the Assembly recessed for Christmas vacation. "While there's no changing my decision," I told them, "you must take the time necessary to select the best qualified successor."

My family's reaction was one of profound relief; there were indeed happy and cheerful days at home. The step had been taken, and we could begin to anticipate a far more peaceful future. To my daughter Sissel in Norway, about a week after my Assembly speech, I wrote: "With this decision and announcement, my job in the United Nations is done." But I should not return to Norway until a successor had been found. "This is no desertion of the colors, and it doesn't mean that I'm leaving a sinking ship. I believe in the United Nations. But the Organization doesn't need me in order to continue its work for peace and security."

A few hours after my statement to the Assembly, possible successors were already being weighed by the press. First, was Lester B. Pearson of Canada—obviously the candidate of the British Commonwealth, of Western Europe, and of a number of the South American states, and incidentally the man I myself preferred as a successor. Brigadier General Carlos P. Romulo of the Philippines was rumored to be America's favorite, while the quiet intelligent Nasrollah Entezam of Iran was termed the choice of France and the Middle East. Other names often heard were Dr. Padilla Nervo, the able Foreign Minister of Mexico and an old and stanch friend of the United Nations, Dr. Charles Malik of Lebanon, Sir Benegal Rau and Madame Vijaya Lakshmi Pandit of India, Dr. Dirk Stikker of the Netherlands, Henri Spaak of Belgium, and Erik Boheman of Sweden. This list of "potentials" mounted by the day to a total at one time of seventeen.

It was soon clear that accepting a resignation was one thing, but finding a successor was another. December passed, and January and

February, with no action by the Security Council. I counted the days, for it was increasingly difficult to work "half in and half out" of my chair. The day-to-day problems were heavy. The budget had to be passed before the Assembly recessed for Christmas, and the ceaseless interrogation of personnel by overlapping United States authorities gave us at the Secretariat some of our worst days. But even then, for the first time in years, I could walk into my office with a feeling of well-being—as though an immense weight had been thrown off my shoulders.

On March 11, the day after the speech on personnel policy, the Security Council finally sat down to choose a new Secretary-General. Ambassador Henry Cabot Lodge of the United States proposed that the Council recommend Brigadier General Carlos Romulo; Ambassador Valerian Alexandrovitch Zorin of the Soviet Union proposed the Polish Foreign Minister, Stanislaw Skrzeszewski, while Ambassador William Borberg of Denmark came out for Lester B. Pearson, Canadian Secretary of State for External Affairs. The Council met two days later to turn down all three candidates: General Romulo received five ayes, two nays, and four abstentions; Mr. Skrzeszewski received one affirmative vote, three negatives, and seven abstentions; Mr. Pearson won nine affirmative votes and one abstention, but was stopped by the Soviet veto. I hoped it would be of some comfort to "Mike" Pearson that he and I had shared an identical fate at the hands of the Soviet Union—he in 1953 and I in 1950—but felt it was a mistake for the Western delegates to force a vote that day. The Soviet Union had wanted to delay, and I still think that it might have accepted him in the long run if the Western powers had stood firm for another week or two.

The Permanent Members thereupon entered on a series of private consultations, and could report on March 19 that a number of new candidates were discussed. There were those earlier mentioned and still in the running, as well as Prince Wan Waithayakon of Thailand, Dr. Eduardo Zuleta Angel of Colombia, Dr. Ahmed S. Bokhari of Pakistan, and Mr. Boheman of Sweden. The Pakistan and Swedish candidates, however, soon withdrew from the race. When Security Council meetings on March 24 and 27 brought no nominations, further meetings were postponed until the big powers could hold new consultations.

On March 31 came the big surprise. Meeting in secret, the five great powers agreed on a Swedish candidate, Dag Hammarskjöld, "Director General of the Swedish Foreign Ministry," as the announcement read. Events had probably moved with such speed that the announcement—while right about the man—was wrong about the title. At that time he was a Minister without Portfolio in the Swedish government. The nomination had been unanimous, and even Mr. Vyshinsky was happy "to replace the person currently fulfilling the functions of Secretary-General." Probably the most surprised person was Dag Hammarskjöld himself. Having heard a report the day before that he was being considered, a member of the Swedish Delegation had cabled to Stockholm to break the news. He refused to take the report seriously. "Amused, but uninterested," was his first reply to what he no doubt thought was pure speculation. But twenty-four hours later it was a fact.

In the General Assembly debate on personnel policy on April 1, I was the last to speak, and grasped the opportunity to say: "I had hoped that my successor would occupy my chair when you came to the consideration of the problem now before you. It is to the future, and not to the past, that the attention of all of us should be directed." This, too, was my last chance to prod Mr. Vyshinsky. Turning toward him and catching his eye, I added: "I was not surprised that charges of illegality should emanate from Soviet delegates during this debate, but I am truly grateful to them for refraining, at least, from declaring illegal and a gross violation of the Charter, my resignation as Secretary-General." It was the first time during the whole debate that he smiled.

The nomination of Dag Hammarskjöld as Secretary-General was confirmed by the General Assembly on April 7. There were speeches by the retiring Secretary-General, by his successor, by the Assembly President and many others. My last speech as Secretary-General to the General Assembly began:

"The seven years and two months I have served you have been the hardest and at the same time the most challenging of my life. To be the first Secretary-General during the formative years of the United Nations has been indeed a rare opportunity to be given any man for service in the cause of peace and for his fellow human beings. I thank the Member governments for giving me this opportunity. . . .

"By your election of Dag Hammarskjöld, you have fulfilled the main hope that moved me to submit my resignation last November. The strains and stresses of the age in which we live, the power of the destructive forces that threaten peace and civilization, are so immense that it is our duty to leave no door unopened to fuller use of every resource for strengthening the prospects of peace that can be found in the Charter and institutions of the United Nations.

"It was to provide an opportunity for you to open one door that had been closed since 1950 that I submitted my resignation four months ago. By your election today of a Secretary-General, recognized as such by all five Permanent Members of the Security Council, you have reopened the door of the office of the Secretary-General.

"I hope with all my heart that this is a good augury of an intention to lessen tensions in the present situation."

That farewell speech ended with a personal declaration:

"The Delegates know very well that I am no utopian. I see in the United Nations a practical approach to peace and progress—not by any quick and easy formulas, but by a wise, loyal, and persistent use of its institutions by the Member governments over many years —not just for seven years, but for seven times seven.

"I see the judgment of history that, in this present day and for all the future, world peace is necessary to the survival of mankind, and the United Nations, in turn, is necessary to the attainment of a world peace that will endure.

"This is the cause I have sought to serve as Secretary-General of the United Nations. This is also the cause that will continue to command loyalty in the years to come."

So now I was Mr. Lie—no longer Secretary-General Lie. With the depth of feeling and sincerity which only a former Secretary-General can know, I was able to wish Dag Hammarskjöld the utmost in luck and happiness; but I had warned him upon our meeting at Idlewild Airport, "The task of the Secretary-General is the most impossible job on earth." Any Secretary-General will find it so if he tries to be the kind of officer that I think the San Francisco Charter envisaged. Should his conception be the same as mine, he will find it impossible to avoid the displeasure of one or more of the greater or smaller states during the years to come. He will be the target of criticism from right, left, and center.

I had tried to face those seven successive years in complete honesty with myself. My eyes were open as I pushed my way into each of the many problems that arose. I did not try to avoid them. I felt it was my duty to enter into them; it was a part of my interpretation of the United Nations Charter and its laws, as well as of the resolutions passed by the General Assemblies. Just as the Secretary-General is the servant of the United Nations and not of any single nation, so he is obligated to risk himself in the interest of a just solution.

And so, the last days were at hand. I took farewell of the Secretariat on May 1—an occasion which Secretary-General Dag Hammarskjöld had arranged. I had had staff problems, and difficult ones —particularly during the last two years. But these differences were forgotten as my eyes moved along the rows of loyal, familiar faces, and I recalled all the good and bad days we had shared since starting together. Whether in London, Geneva, Paris, or New York, regardless of time, the pressure of work, or personal problems, these men and women had always been willing to give just a little more. They had joined into a solid, well integrated force, working for the United Nations and its objectives.

"They say the first seven years are the hardest," I recalled, "and I hope for your sake, Mr. Secretary-General, and for your sake, members of the staff, that this saying is true. I do not mind admitting that the past seven years have been hard for me, and I know they have not been easy for you. So before I leave, I shall do one thing which I have wanted to do for a long time: I am going to take all the troubles of the past, all the disappointments, all the headaches, and pack them in a bag and throw them into the East River. I shall carry away with me the memory of all the good things, all the happy things which have made this job I leave one of the most satisfying experiences of my life. And I hope that you too will remember only the best about our associations together."

But it would be hard to leave New York, and especially Granston Tower. For seven eventful years it had been our home in Forest Hills, as comfortable a residence in as congenial a neighborhood as anyone could desire. There we had entertained distinguished guests from every corner of the world, statesmen, royalty, and celebrities whose comings and goings have helped shape history during our decade. Though our seven years at Granston Tower may at times have intruded somewhat upon the tranquillity of the neighborhood —for there had often been police escorts, guards, and streets closed for security reasons—our good neighbors were exemplary. They appreciated the extent of our duties, and understood why we had so little opportunity to become better acquainted with them. There was no fence surrounding our property, nor was there need for one. Not once was there any trespassing, nor was even a single flower ever missing from our front yard or garden. Recollections of the quiet and correct neighborliness of Forest Hills did not make our departure any less difficult.

And there was the West Side Tennis Club and all that it represented. What those hours of exercise and complete relaxation could mean in the course of a hectic week, I owe to such good friends as Julian Myrick, Alrick H. Man, Jr., Renville McMann, George Koch, and Lloyd Larson. No matter where we might be, I intended to see to it that the former Secretary-General remained on the list of the Club's members.

Now, only the last steps remained. The hectic last days in New York, prior to our sailing on May 8; the parties and presents culminating seven years of living in, and becoming a part of a great city and its people; New York's farewell program, with Grover Whalen driving us from United Nations Headquarters to the City Hall behind the city's traditional police escort—much as he had done seven years before. Our farewell to New York and its authorities could hardly have been more fitting, in my eyes. No single group of persons more deserved the thanks of my family and me than those who had shared their city with us during these eventful years.

And so, home to Norway!

CHAPTER XXIII

REFLECTIONS

What is the United Nations?—The rule of unanimity.—The veto privileges and Soviet abuses.—Need for a general conference to review Charter in perspective.—Revision now, or better application first?

HERE AT "LIESET," my hunting lodge on the Röros Plateau, more than a year after my resignation, it is possible to reflect in peace and quiet. Here in the solitude of the Norwegian mountains, far from the hectic life of Headquarters and New York, there is opportunity to think over all the problems with which I was confronted nearly every day as the United Nations' Secretary-General.

After eleven years in the Norwegian government and more than seven in the United Nations—in all, eighteen years of uninterrupted public service—it is wonderful to be alone for a change; alone with my reflections on problems and difficulties met; removed from any and all attempts to influence my thinking or my decisions.

What first come to mind—and this is probably true, regardless of politics or profession, for everyone who quits a job at a relatively early age—are the persistent memories of defeats and disappointments. As far as my own experience is concerned, and from what I have heard and read of others in the same situation, this is probably the natural human reaction. But, once the trials of this first period of adjustment are successfully surmounted, the bright points—which are seen as measurable advances toward the goal—begin to dominate his reflections.

May I therefore establish at once that that which stands for me as the greatest and best—and as something of a victory—is the fact that world peace *was* preserved during my service as Secretary-General. The outlook had been dark more than once—so dark, in fact, that even the most optimistic gave up hope for the world organization and world peace, and awaited a catastrophe within weeks or days. I recall a statement reported reliably to me in one of the European capitals. The remark had been made by a Norwegian representative abroad, an aging diplomat who, like many others, was disappointed in the outcome of the Security Council meetings at London in 1946 and exclaimed in a dark moment: "No, this is not going too well. But I hope that the United Nations can last through the year so that Trygve Lie won't be appointed my successor."

In 1948, just after the Communist coup in Czechoslovakia and about the time when the Berlin Blockade was in full force, an English friend and his wife visited me at Lake Success. Bill Stoneman and I took them around, and then I suggested that Bill take the two of them to the bar for a drink. They were enthusiastic over what they had seen, and over the United Nations generally—as long as I was with them. Bill told me later that after I had gone this calm and collected British banker took him aside and asked in a distressed whisper: "But how long is all this going to last?"

Probably many people nurtured similar thoughts. I had heard such remarks often. But let us remind ourselves that "all this" did last—that a world war, the most dreaded threat of all, was avoided. Not that the credit was due to the United Nations—a matter that must be established beyond all doubt. So many factors, known and unknown, too numerous to recount here, combined toward the achievement. But one of them—by no means the least important—was the United Nations.

I probably made many errors as Secretary-General. As the skipper said who suddenly found his ship fast aground: "We all make mistakes." My position was not made more comfortable by my regarding myself as "part" of the United Nations. I felt morally and legally compelled to take what I saw as the "United Nations view," particularly when I felt that the Member states were not living up to their Charter obligations. I did everything in my power to keep the United Nations from sinking or running aground. Had this occurred I am certain that we should have been far closer to a world war today. There were many times when I believed that the United Nations was the last barrier between peace and war; and for that reason—here in the peaceful mountains of Norway—I am grateful that it was possible for us to keep the peace, even though the cold war raged through all my years in the United Nations. This thought dominates my recollections, brushing all other factors aside.

Upon going more into detail, however, and analyzing what has taken place from 1946 on, I shall be first to recognize the weaknesses of the United Nations' organization, and the defeats and the disappointments it has represented. For many of them I see myself in part to blame; and for many, responsible. But before we can take an objective view of the United Nations and what goes on in it, it will be necessary to know just what the United Nations *is* and what it *is not*.

The United Nations is a voluntary association of nations committed to common goals. It is dedicated to encouraging and facilitating effective cooperation in matters of mutual interest and to the peaceful adjustment of international differences; but it does not, in general, have the power to impose its will upon any Member government. The veto in the Security Council and the clause in the Charter forbidding the United Nations from interfering in the domestic affairs of any Member state, are only two of many evidences of this principle of free association which leaves the final power of decision to the individual Member governments. When the Assembly or Councils of the United Nations come to a vote and reach "decisions," they have not passed laws binding on the governments in the ordinary legislative sense. They have adopted "recommendations." These resolutions represent the consensus of the Member governments on the best course of action to follow. As such, they have great moral weight; but no government is compelled to follow that course.

There is one major exception to this general rule. That is when the Security Council orders action against armed aggression, or against threats to or breaches of the peace. This it can only do when none of the five Permanent Members employs its veto—and among the five, of course, are the Soviet Union and the United States. The Security Council has taken such action just once, when it ordered the belligerents in Palestine to cease fire. Even in the case of Korea the Security Council only recommended to the Member governments that they assist the Republic of Korea in resisting aggression.

Thus the United Nations is not a supranational authority. It depends almost entirely upon the willingness and capacity of the Member governments to carry out its recommendations. The power to act continues to reside almost exclusively with the respective governments. The role of the United Nations is to enable them to act in concert, effectively and in the common interest.

But this does not mean that the United Nations need be either weak or ineffective.

It means simply that the United Nations relies in the first instance upon the recognition the governments have given, by their membership in the organization, to the principle that their national interest and the survival of their respective countries depend upon its success.

Beyond that, the effectiveness of the United Nations is determined by the wisdom and skill with which the governments apply this principle of higher national interest to each of the questions with which they deal in the United Nations.

The United Nations therefore is what the Member governments want it to be—neither better nor worse.

I believe that this is a sound and sensible approach to the dilemma of our times.

It is inconceivable that societies so diverse as those living under the Western democratic tradition on the one hand, and under Communist dictatorship on the other, would agree in present circumstances to give up any significant segment of their national independence to a supranational authority. This also holds true when we consider the vast differences between the societies of the West and those of the greater part of Asia.

When on September 23, 1953, President Eisenhower welcomed members of the United States Committee for United Nations Day to the White House, he included the following observations on the United Nations:

"With all its defects, with all the failures that we can check up against it, it still represents man's best organized hope to substitute the conference table for the battlefield.

"It has had its failures, but it has had its successes. Who knows what could have happened in these past years of strain and struggle if we hadn't had the United Nations? I think it is far more than merely a desirable organization in these days. Where every new invention of the scientist seems to make it more nearly possible for man to insure his own elimination from this globe, I think the United Nations has become sheer necessity."

A better evaluation of the United Nations' present status and stature has, in my opinion, probably never been expressed. There are probably a good many who agree. Were one to ask the average man —outside the dictatorships, that is—just what he thinks of the United Nations, he would in all likelihood reply that the United Nations is a good and useful organization, but . . . Then would follow the reservation concerning the great powers' right of veto and their use of it: an aspect most difficult for him to understand.

Let us look for a moment, then, at this veto right. As discussions surrounding this point are now a part of any evaluation of chances for a revision of the United Nations Charter, it is only reasonable that these two basic problems should be treated as one. And I think we shall hear a great deal of talk in the next two years about amending this international constitution and especially about modifying or abolishing the veto.

We must not make the mistake, however, of exaggerating the importance of changes in voting procedure or in any other articles of the Charter, desirable as they might be. In this connection a sentence from Napoleon as quoted by Sir Winston Churchill in *Their Finest Hour* (page 15) is worth noting: "A constitution should be short and obscure." Here I believe Sir Winston is reminding us that it is not only the words in a constitution that count, but the popular will to accept the constitution's spirit. This certainly applies to the United Nations, which has done a great deal through constructive interpretation of the Charter. The impact of the veto, for example, has been significantly lessened by the practice of regarding an abstention by a great power in a Security Council vote as not constituting a veto; and there has been a healthy shift in power from the Council to the veto-free General Assembly. Thus progress by no means alone depends upon textual revision of the Charter. A continuing liberal construction of the Charter we now have holds out great promise, and perhaps is the more practical way to strengthen the bonds of the world community.

With respect to the veto, let us remember that the peaceful settlement of the great political issues requires the free consent and agreement of all sides concerned, regardless of the kind of voting procedure observed in the Security Council or the General Assembly.

Let us also remember that the veto exists only in the Security Council, and that the Member governments have already found ways and means under the present Charter of building up a system of collective security against armed aggression that incorporates regional and self-defense pacts, and action by the General Assembly whenever the Security Council is paralyzed by the veto. Neither this system nor any other that could be devised will work effectively unless Member governments are prepared to carry their fair share of the burden.

Thus we come back to the policies and conduct of the Member governments. Upon them rests the final responsibility—for war or peace; and there is no escape from that fact in any amendments to the United Nations Charter that might be proposed or adopted.

On the other hand, there is no denying that the right of veto has been misused. Almost threescore full-fledged vetoes have been cast, nearly all by the Soviet Union—to be exact, 58. That is not use—that is a series of flagrant misuses. Clearly, such practices must impede the efficient application of the United Nations Charter for the settlement of practically any dispute brought before the Security Council. Clearly, such procedures will reduce the confidence of the peoples of the world in the United Nations' ability to act at all.

The abuse of the veto privilege in the United Nations is the one that has aroused the greatest dissatisfaction and even suspicion among average men and women. Without the understanding and support of such men and women all over the world, the United Nations will never become what it was intended to be. Nor will there be any guarantee for world peace until the majority of the world's population chooses to back the principles set forth in the Charter and to demand that they be correctly applied. In time to come, it will therefore be the duty of one and all to study and form opinions on the complicated questions which a possible review of the United Nations Charter can involve.

In a sense, the United Nations Charter is an international constitution, at the same time that it is a convention or agreement, ratified by the United Nations' sixty Member states.

At one vital point the writers of the Charter were most farsighted, and fortunately so. They were aware that the Charter might require review after ten years of experience, if not before. This would presuppose that a majority of the Member states and seven of the Security Council's members voted to hold a conference of the type described in Article 109 of the Charter. At that time, there was also agreement on Article 108 and 109—both a part of the United Nation's constitution and thus binding upon the signatory states, including the Soviet Union and its allies.

Let us take a look at the two articles:

ARTICLE 108

Amendments to the present Charter shall come into force for all Members of the United Nations when they have been adopted by a vote of two-thirds of the members of the General Assembly and ratified in accordance with their respective constitutional processes by two-thirds of the Members of the United Nations, including all the permanent members of the Security Council.

ARTICLE 109

1. A General Conference of the Members of the United Nations for the purpose of reviewing the present Charter may be held at a date and place to be fixed by a two-thirds vote of the members of the General Assembly and by a vote of any seven members of the Security Council. Each Member of the United Nations shall have one vote in the Conference.

2. Any alteration of the present Charter recommended by a two-thirds vote of the Conference shall take effect when ratified in accordance with their respective constitutional processes by two-thirds of the Members of the United Nations including all the permanent members of the Security Council.

3. If such a conference has not been held before the tenth annual session of the General Assembly, following the coming into force of the present Charter, the proposal to call such a conference shall be placed on the agenda of that session of the General Assembly, and the conference shall be held if so decided by a majority vote of the members of the General Assembly and by a vote of any seven members of the Security Council.

There is no doubt that the United Nations Charter is open for review. That was, in fact, decided at San Francisco in June, 1945.

No other interpretation of the articles quoted above, and particularly of Article 109, is possible.

I am all for holding a General Conference of the United Nations Members to review the present Charter as soon as possible after 1955, and reached this position several years ago as evidenced by the last sentence in Point 1 of my Ten-Point Peace Program Through the United Nations, which reads as follows: ". . . and a renewed effort to secure agreement by all the Great Powers on limitation on the use of the veto power in the pacific settlement procedures of the Security Council."

I may also recall the discussion between Mr. Molotov and myself in the presence of Generalissimo Stalin at Moscow on May 15, 1950.* My present views on the veto question do not result from hindsight. I was convinced then, and am convinced now, that a General Conference must be held when the other conditions set forth in Article 109 have been met. Furthermore, it is both desirable and correct that the Charter be reviewed.

A measure may appear to one person or one government to be wholly right and desirable. It is a far different matter to know what, in the end, the various Member states can be persuaded to accept. As noted above, the right of veto is limited to the Security Council, and when this body receives the authority to "enforce peace" a majority of seven votes is required, among them the "concurring votes" of the five great powers. This, of course, gives every one of them an influence in matters of life and death for the whole world, on the assumption that it would mainly be the great powers that would have to contribute the armed forces needed to repel aggression. Because none of them wished to be voted into war or warlike actions against their own will by any majority of other nations, they agreed among themselves on the veto formula. Originally, the Soviet Union held out for a more far-reaching version of the veto power than the other great powers were inclined to accept. At Yalta, President Roosevelt won agreement upon a compromise formula, which the great powers advanced at San Francisco.

The representatives of the smaller nations at San Francisco contested the veto rights the great powers wished to reserve to them-

* See p. 298, preceding.

selves—sweeping, even under the terms of the Yalta formula—and submitted as many as seventeen amendments; and twenty-three separate written questions, many of them intricate, were sent to the great-power delegations with requests for clarification. Finally, some satisfaction in the form of interpretations was achieved, mainly concerning the right of any Member state to have its complaint placed on the Security Council's agenda for debate; but when the existing veto provisions eventually came to a vote in the Technical Committee of the San Francisco Conference the result was significant: they were endorsed by a vote of 30 to 2, while 15 countries preferred to abstain in silent protest.

Such is the history of the veto rights in the Charter.

There are certain fundamental steps which, as I see it, must be taken if the United Nations is to endure and gradually attain the central role in international relations which world developments demand. To take these steps may not necessarily require formal amendment of the Charter—much can be accomplished by a constructive reading of the present text.

First, the range of the veto must be sharply reduced. In my opinion, the requirement of the veto for the five "concurring votes" of the Permanent Members of the Security Council is unjustified in cases of pacific settlement of disputes. In such cases, there is no immediate question of the Council ordering its Members to take armed action; and, accordingly, I see no convincing reason why a single great power should be able to block the Council's investigatory and conciliatory efforts. If full acceptance cannot be assured for this concept, then at least some changes of substantial importance should be made. The unanimity rule—that is to say, the veto—should not apply to the admission of new Members to the Organization. Throughout my term of office, I consistently and publicly advocated liberality in admitting new Members. I still believe that universality of membership should be an essential of the Organization. Furthermore, I may be forgiven for stating that election of the Secretary-General of the United Nations should also be a matter not requiring five "concurring votes"; in fact, the General Assembly should have the main responsibility for selecting the Secretary-General, on the recommendation of any seven members of the Security Council.

And the double veto[1] a farce in itself, the intricacies of which are too discouraging to be discussed here—should be abolished. There might be other examples, as well, and they are certain to be brought before the General Conference in well prepared proposals.

What then, are our chances of improvement? As a practical person, and on the basis of political experience, I am of the opinion that a General Conference cannot be avoided. In the course of many years there has been nearly endless discussion in most United Nations organs of the Charter and the interpretation of many of its articles. Numerous suggestions for changes and improvements have already been advanced. The active and interested United Nations supporters should now have an opportunity to air their many opinions and ideas. Any attempt to restrain them would be poor politics indeed. A broad and well integrated agenda with ample opportunity for discussion would tend to benefit the Organization, and would bring all the various conceptions and proposals into the light of international public opinion. Furthermore, a debate on the problems involved in an improvement or revision of the Charter would, in my opinion, contribute directly to the preservation of peace. Whatever the decisions reached as a result of such a conference, they would carry considerable weight, especially if passed by a solid majority. Opinions of the Member states must be allowed to come forth freely at such a conference, without pressure from any quarter. It is therefore most unfortunate that the Soviet Union and its allies have already declared (1953) that they are unwilling to accept any changes. They have even objected to the collecting of documentary evidence and the presentation of a study of the Charter's history. If that entirely negative position is maintained to the end, the world will have sad proof that the original adherence of these countries to the United Nations Organization was a matter of political expediency alone, without any continuing sense of responsibility to the needs of a growing world community.

The kind of ultimatum delivered by the Communist countries dur-

[1] The casting of a negative vote by a permanent member of the Security Council when seven or more affirmative votes have been cast on the question whether a proposed resolution of the Council is procedural. Rule 30 of the Security Council Rules of Procedure, in the light of the Czechoslovak Case (1948), provides a means of preventing a double veto.

ing the 1953 General Assembly has no place in a democratic world, and its effects are precisely the opposite of those they are trying to achieve. No free nation, and no independent, free-minded individual, will bow to such an ultimatum. Sound arguments, tried and tested through reasonable discussions, must be allowed to come to the fore. And this is precisely what an eventual General Conference must seek to promote. The leaders of the Soviet Union know perfectly well that friends and supporters of the United Nations—both Member states and individuals—are not going to do anything which will damage its chances of survival and thereby impair chances for preserving world peace. I therefore hope that the achievements of such a General Conference will be of such obvious significance that they will carry weight even for the Communist leaders. Disregard by the Soviet leaders, in the next round, of what world opinion outside the "iron curtain" regards as reasonable and desirable would be unfortunate indeed; but I still have sufficient confidence in Communist political acumen to dare hope that they will not risk isolating themselves from the workers, the middle class, the intelligentsia and all positively inclined persons—regardless of calling or politics—in what the Communists call the "capitalistic world." Should these Communist leaders make such a mistake, the future of the United Nations and the chances for peace will not be bright.

All factors considered, then, I see good reason to expect that such a conference will produce results which can constitute a decided advance.

But what then? Eventual Charter amendment proposals from a General Conference must be approved and ratified by the Member states. Here the matter of the veto emerges again, and precisely at this point the great powers will have to help, in the first instance. At one time I hoped that it would be found possible to bring the great powers together to begin discussions on the various means of making the United Nations Charter more effective. I made such an attempt as early as in 1950, but the results were negative. On the other hand, we are all aware that the great powers held many long conferences—well before the 1945 meeting in San Francisco—and there is still time for similar meetings before an eventual General Conference in 1956. Without agreement among the great powers before or, possibly, after the Conference, there can be little hope for progress in textual revision or in interpretation of the Charter and the rules of procedure of the various organs (though such interpretation is not equally dependent upon Big Five agreement). At these great-power meetings, the participants can take up a number of questions in connection with the United Nations Charter, and with the Organization's activities, which, in event of agreement, can represent decided improvements. I am convinced that the other fifty-five Member states will accept almost any proposal upon which the Big Five agree.

Among the questions which should be discussed at such a General Conference and at eventual great-power meetings, perhaps the most important concern the obtaining of loyal compliance with the Charter we already have. I should like to ask in this connection: Why has there not yet been held one single meeting under Article 28 of the Charter, providing: "The Security Council shall hold periodic meetings at which each of its members may . . . be represented by a member of the government . . ."

It is to be regretted that no Member state, great or small, has even taken definite steps to demand that Article 28 be respected. Let us hope that there can be agreement on the practical utilization of this vital provision which has lain unused ever since 1945.

Another question is equally important. What has been done toward applying Chapter VII of the Charter: "Action with Respect to Threats to the Peace, Breaches of the Peace, and Acts of Aggression"? It would be of the greatest interest and importance to reach agreement on military forces, and so on, as set forth in Articles 43 and 45; but here, again, agreement among the great powers is a prerequisite. The Military Staff Committee, covered under Article 47, so far has been a stillborn. Chances for reviving it depend upon the outcome of discussions on the establishment of military forces. A renewed discussion of these matters could be most useful, though a practical political solution would hinge upon the prevailing international situation. Differences are still far too pronounced, and it has been impossible to achieve any results; but we must try yet again. The faith of the common people in the great powers, as well as in the United Nations, will be undermined as long as the Charter we have is not respected. At the same time, my reference to these two provisions and the fate they have suffered can be taken as a warning to all those who now believe that world peace will be so much better secured, and that all else will proceed so much more smoothly, if only we can get the Charter revised in 1956. Many good idealists are inclined to pin far too much faith on the text and wording of the United Nations constitution. However, these idealists and United Nations sympathizers should in no way give up: I only hope that they will not be disappointed once the results of these efforts are established.

As already mentioned, one important improvement concerning the veto practice was in fact attained at an early stage in United Nations history. In 1947, when the Soviet Union disagreed with a proposal to refer the British-Yugoslav conflict over mines in the Corfu Straits to the International Court of Justice, the Soviet delegate did not cast a negative vote in the final instance: he "abstained." Despite the fact that the Security Council decision in this way was taken by a majority with only four "concurring votes" from the great powers, all Member States, including the Soviet Union, accepted it as legal and fully binding. The practice of "abstention" has since been considered legitimate, and no one has ever contested it.

By skillful diplomatic discussion, similar agreements may be reached now. Faced with the possibility of far-reaching revisions of the Charter, and the heightened political isolation which might result from its identifying itself so graphically as the barrier to international progress, the Soviet Union may find it wise to go along with even important modifications. Its government may already have learned a lesson from the "Uniting for Peace" resolution of the 1950 Assembly, which transferred a not inconsiderable part of the Security Council's recommendative authority to the General Assembly.

There are many agreements or understandings which, in my opinion, are politically feasible—provided they are not only entered into, but loyally carried out.

Another matter requiring particular attention is the consistent practice by the Soviet Union over a period of years of declaring any and all resolutions it dislikes "illegal": there have been no fewer than forty-seven cases. It is always fully permissible for the General Assembly or the Security Council to ask the International Court of Justice for advice or opinion on any such matters. But this practice has not yet been followed to any extent. Full application would require the declared agreement by all Member states that when they have such contentions in the first instance they will eventually accept and consider as binding the opinion given by the International Court whenever such matters have been referred to it.

Also to be considered is whether or not it might be possible to agree on an arrangement whereby both the majority and minority, as well as the Secretary-General, receives the right to request an advisory opinion from a special organ—in instances where a decision passed by a legal majority is still branded illegal. The judicial body might be a panel of the International Court of Justice, or it might be a body set up for the purpose—preferably not elective, but constituted jointly, for example by the President of the International Court of Justice and the Secretary-General. It has been the case that those failing to agree with a decision keep on coming with charges of "illegality" until far too many begin to believe them. Here, the propaganda apparatus of the Member governments can be particularly effective, especially where a great power is concerned. Propaganda thus applied generally relies on the "stock phrase" coupled with endless repetition. For the United Nations, such tactics are damaging—not to say intolerable—in the long run; and a way out of this dilemma has to be found.

Another problem worthy of consideration concerns the number of Permanent Members in the Security Council. Suggestions have already been forwarded that the number of Permanent Members be increased to six, with total membership set at thirteen. I am inclined to doubt whether this is practical policy in the prevailing international situation. My experience is that there is much to support the view that, *if* the number of members is increased, Asia should have a priority in the form of a stronger representation than that which it now enjoys. In such event India's candidacy for Permanent Membership should be seriously considered. With the present world situation, there should be no need to detail my reasoning on this point. The grounds are self-explanatory, in the size of population compared with that of the six other continents, and in the political importance of linking Asia's hundreds of millions into an influential and responsible cooperation with the rest of the world.

Many, many other ideas can be expected to emerge during the coming years, worthy of the most serious evaluation and discussion.

No constitution can be taken as final. Without changes—either in the form of amendments to the present Charter, or in agreement on interpretation which can resolve these problems—the United Nations would find itself in a state of stagnation. And in the present difficult—not to say critical—international situation, stagnation would be tantamount to retrogression. Every forward step toward increased clarity regarding the United Nations Charter and its practical day-to-day application will serve the interests of peace.

CHAPTER XXIV

THE FUTURE—FOR PEACE WITH FREEDOM

A survey of conflicts threatening the peace.—Why have we chosen to risk the "cold war"?—No idea can be killed with arms alone.—The "have-nots": a threat and an opportunity.—Time now mobilized as an ally for peace.—Peace without freedom, a hollow shell.—Of what value is the threat of self-destruction?—"Somewhere between past and future."

"MORE THAN five years have elapsed since the end of the last World War, but we have yet failed to attain a genuine peace. The popular hope for an understanding among the States has been turned into disappointment. At the same time, fear of a new war continues to mount. Vast sums are being spent for military purposes, while millions still lack what for us would seem the essentials for a life worthy of human beings.

"The reason why the Scandinavian countries and the other free nations of the West are today increasing their military preparedness as a guarantee for security, is that international Communism has shown such aggressive tendencies during recent years as to provoke fear of a Third World War.

"Whether or not humanity is going to survive depends upon putting a stop to this development and creating an atmosphere which can render possible the peaceful solution of all unsolved problems. The determination of the Democracies to defend their freedom is no threat to the peace."

The paragraphs cited—part of a proclamation on January 27, 1951, by the Federations of Trade Unions and the Labor parties of Denmark, Norway, Sweden, and Iceland—express in my opinion the point of view generally held by all democratic political parties in the Western world, and put forth in concise form what was my own line of reasoning at the time.

But has the situation changed appreciably in the interval? As I see it, not so very much has taken place since 1951 to alter the general international scene. On the other hand, a book like this cannot be concluded without a few thoughts of the writer as to the future and the prospects for peace. That the thoughts will have to stand on their own feet, as just another man's opinions, goes without saying. On this subject no one can speak with certainty. There are so many uncertainties and incalculables that can enter in; and many are the prophets who have been proved false.

In order to form any opinion of the prospects for peace, however, one must first evaluate the problems which, since 1945, have led to disturbance of the peace or to the actual threat of war. Not all can be enumerated here; but they can be grouped under specific headings, and all the most important can find a place in one of three categories:

(A) Problems arising as a result of East-West conflicts—more precisely the conflict between international Communism and the democracies, or, as it is now known, the "cold war."

(B) The economically underdeveloped lands and areas, and their demand for improved living conditions plus a more just distribution of the world's economic wealth.

(C) The struggle of presently or recently subjugated people for fuller freedom and national independence. Under this heading would come such sources of discord as racial problems and religious differences, as well as "colonialism." One conflict of particular immediacy stems from the hostility that still divides the Arabs and the Jews.

Let us begin with a discussion of the first two categories.

Today, the greatest threat to world peace is in the ideologic tug of war between Communism and democracy—the latter in its many forms and variations. Evidence in support of this contention is hardly necessary. The Korean conflict is sufficient to bear out the point, not to mention the many similar examples in earlier chapters.

To what, then, can we attribute this sword of Damocles that the "cold war" has suspended above our heads? Its presence *can* be explained, even though a certain amount of detail may prove necessary.

As Secretary-General I saw the hope and faith of the victorious allies sour into disillusionment and suspicion. A sharp, hard line separated two worlds—two ways of life which, apparently, could be joined no more readily than oil and water. Forces stemming from basic differences between two divergent philosophies of life and government had divided a world which the United Nations had been charged with holding together.

The first postwar years of Soviet expansion were all that were needed to reveal two bitter and basic truths: that the Communist "dictatorship of the proletariat" was no less susceptible to the evils which had damned the dictatorships so recently defeated; and that Soviet Communism was definitely designed for export. While it is true that Stalin and the other Communist leaders have declared the opposite, the facts still speak an incontrovertible language. If these truths were not recognized at San Francisco, they soon emerged with a force and a clarity which shocked the West into action and stretched a "front line" that could soon be traced along a half-circle from the Arctic Ocean in the north to the China Sea in the east. The world which twentieth century technology had drawn together into one was still two in the minds of men, and the dividing line was subject to change at any moment.

My own thoughts on Communism, both as a form of government and as a philosophy of life, do not admit the possibility of a merger with what we in the West have come to know as democracy. The basic precepts of the one defy those of the other. In the one, force media—police, prisons, concentration camps—have imposed a rule of conformity and have pegged the worth of the individual to his value to the state and the party. Their interests come first, last, and always. In the other, the individual—according to the accepted philosophy, at least—is regarded less as a means than as an end unto himself. His rights are as clearly defined as his duties. For him, the state exists as a means of assuring his own well-being rather than as a determinant of his every thought and act. In a democracy—I am by no means implying that every state west of the Iron Curtain is a democracy—the governed himself sets up the ratio between rights and duties. These differences are real and basic.

I am reminded of the closing minutes of the debate on the Universal Declaration of Human Rights at the Third Session of the United Nations General Assembly at Paris in 1948. Mr. Vyshinsky had waged a losing battle that day; and, in a final effort to justify the Soviet stand, he came out with what remains for me one of the clearest expositions of the status of the individual in a Communist society: "It was stated here that the U.S.S.R. delegation wants to subordinate the personalities of the individuals to the state, so that the individual becomes just a small part of a very important government." After a refutation that was in no way convincing, he described what he termed the classless society. "Where there is no such contradiction between classes," he explained, "there can be no contradiction between the government and the individual, because the government is the collective individual." That, according to him, was the formula, and facts would have to be made to conform. "This is why you do not have the problem of the government as opposed to the individual. . . . The State and the individual in the U.S.S.R. are fully harmonized, the interests are corresponding fully, and it is expressed in a formula of which all progressive humanity is proud." Such glib self-righteousness had a depressingly familiar ring; I had heard the selfsame assuredness in Berlin and Rome during the 1930's—not to mention the Nazi-dictated broadcasts emanating from my own homeland during the years of occupation.

Soviet Communism as a form of totalitarianism, like all other dictatorships, constitutes a source of pressure which, in my opinion, can be contained, in the first instance, only through the application of force. Experience has shown that, sooner or later, every dictatorship begins to suffer from claustrophobia and before long begins to exert pressure on its neighboring states. Where the pressure has not attained the desired objectives, the result has always been war. However, coupled with this disturbing attribute, common to any and all dictatorships having the power, is yet another factor immediately complicating the containment of Communism by force: The avowed objective of the one political party controlling and influencing no less than one-third of the world is the advancement of

THE FUTURE—FOR PEACE WITH FREEDOM 439

Communism on a global scale. These two basic truths are not recalled with any sense of emotion or alarm: they are simple facts, and should be calmly recognized as such. They are as much a part of the world in which we live as the Iron Curtain or the hydrogen bomb, and, to preserve the peace in the face of the threat they represent, we must admit their existence, appraise our position, adjust our thinking to them, and lay out our objectives accordingly. What then, are the first steps we should take to preserve peace and freedom?

As I see it, that part of the task of preserving world peace and the democratic way of life which involves the containment of Communism must be tackled with two objectives in mind: the immediate stopgap measures aimed at averting open conflict for the moment, and the long-range program designed to preserve peace for the future. Let us consider the first of these.

I for one recognize the need of a strong and effective military defense. No nation or group of nations can long survive if it persists in shirking the burden of self-protection. Postwar Soviet policy—to be followed by that of Communist China—has given the Western democracies due warning that their immediate task is to build up and keep sufficient military strength to check a potential aggressor.

I consider it as imperative that the Western democracies join in the physical defense of their countries. The regional defense agreements and programs toward this end—such as the North Atlantic Treaty Organization and the Pan-American defense arrangement—are precautionary measures which any thinking people would be obliged to take under the circumstances. With the danger of fire, and in the absence of an organized fire department, it is only common sense for the neighbors to join in setting up their own volunteer fire brigades.

But here—I want to make this clear—the simile must be carried still further. A volunteer fire brigade may provide admirable short-term protection in the absence of any other. The first and most pressing requirement for the preservation of world peace and democratic freedom through the containment of Communism is met through the regional defense arrangements, it is true. Within the foreseeable future, the Western powers will have assembled protection media which the Communist world understands and respects. These may be sufficient to preserve world peace in terms of an armed truce extending over a limited period of time; but, in my opinion, the precautionary measures *alone* are no guarantee for peace in the future. And when I refer to "the future," I am not thinking of some far-off time, years distant. This second objective and the need for meeting it are already upon us. The tasks of preserving peace for the future as well as for the present are one and the same, in that, by failing to prepare for long-term protection now, we cut the very ground out from beneath our efforts and sacrifices today.

Here we run into a number of the problems included under heading B, and we had best examine closely the nature of the conflagration we are fighting as well as the area we have been called upon to protect.

In the first place, armed might alone will not stop the spread of Communism. In a sense, our volunteer firemen are now lined up to beat out the flames at any point where they might begin to spread. We have failed to realize, however, that we are fighting a fire that can suddenly climb over the heads of the helpless firemen and race vast distances through the treetops. What about the condition of the forests on our side of the line? Are we sufficiently aware that tremendous expanses of the areas we have the duty to protect are tinder-dry and can kindle with a single spark? Our firemen, outfitted with the most modern and efficient fire-fighting equipment, can at any hour find that the conflagration has leapt their defenses with ridiculous ease and taken over broad new areas which they consider to be adequately protected. Communism as an idea, knows no boundaries, and cannot be stopped by arms and force.

Here, then, is the second of two equally pressing tasks that face the free world at this very moment. Before the conflagration that menaces our existence as free peoples, we are threatened today by a tragedy of unpreparedness in the face of defense efforts and expenditures that have known no equal. Within a relatively short time, our front lines will be defended, it is true. But unless necessary measures are taken to improve the areas of potential conflagration behind our own lines, our present defense efforts and sacrifices can become a laughingstock. Our most pressing task today is the reducing of combustibility within these areas—the economically underdeveloped areas in the world we are obligated to defend. Until now, they have received a meager attention out of all proportion to their significance. Their present condition, and the menace to our security that they represent, constitute—in my opinion—a constant threat to peace by joining the Communist movement. Our degree of success in meeting that challenge, in time, will determine whether the democracies of the West will survive.

Let us not for one moment hoodwink ourselves into thinking that Communism is any less attractive to people in these areas than democracy. On the contrary, I would be inclined to feel that Communism, in its export version, has an even greater first-glance sales appeal to the perpetually hungry and underprivileged in many of these areas than has the kind of democracy they have come to know over the years. Westerners who have enjoyed the privilege of living in modern democratic societies need no convincing as to the merits of their way of life. For those of us who have experienced them, the blessings of self-government as opposed to semidemocracy, oligarchy, or totalitarianism are self-evident. I repeat, "those of us"—for in reality we are relatively few, even in that part of the world which we can describe as being on "our side" of the line.

Right here, however, a clear distinction should be drawn between the will to democracy—the faith and belief in its principles—and the capacity for attaining democracy. Governments of the West are united in their belief in these principles, but the extent to which they have given them concrete expression varies disturbingly from country to country. When evaluating our inner strength, therefore, as contrasted to that of the exponents of world Communism, we run a great risk in assuming that the expressed—even the demonstrated—allegiance of a country's leaders and government to the principles of democracy automatically implies a similar allegiance in its citizens. Going down the list of lands supporting the democratic principles, we discover at once that a major portion of our strength in terms of population, area, and natural resources is centralized in the underdeveloped areas: 51 per cent of the world's population and forty-six per cent of its area, to be more exact. Politically, these states are listed as democratic allies. But how many of the millions making up their population are aware of the fact, or would be particularly influenced even if they did know?

Since World War II, no fewer than 500,000,000 people in these underdeveloped areas have achieved independence; their world—and ours—is in ferment. After hundreds of years of silent suffering they have decided to attain for themselves a few of the values of the modern society we boast about, the fruits of the equal opportunities about which we have preached, and the full rights of man as set forth in the United Nations universal declaration. They have achieved political independence; they are free to choose—to turn to the right or to the left. Fortunately for us, most of them have chosen in favor of democracy. But for how long? That is the burning question that confronts every nation in the free world today. How long can political democracy in the underdeveloped areas last without the economic underpinnings which a true democracy requires before it can function? How long before the decades or centuries of struggle culminating in political independence are revealed to have ended in a hollow victory—before hope and enthusiasm turn into disillusionment?

What has happened is that the drive toward political democracy in a large section of our world has in fact outdistanced its capacity to provide the economic foundation upon which such democracy must rest. Here is a time-lag which, in my opinion, represents one of the most immediate threats to the security of the free world. What happens between the time when the democratic "tree" is planted and the time when it begins to bear its first fruits in the form of material benefits will determine whether or not the democracies will succeed. Armed with their new political freedom, hundreds of millions of persons have now chosen in favor of democracy. For that, we have every reason to be proud and grateful. But let us not forget that there is another side to the picture. These states have now joined ranks with the democracies; from here on they are one with *us*. What takes place in them from now on will be taking place in the name of *democracy*—whether it be progress, stagnation, or retrogression.

At this very moment, democracy as a form of government and a way of life is on trial in an area including a majority of the world's people. If, in the short time available, it can build an economic foundation under its political promises, by expanding programs like that of United Nations technical assistance, the future of our way of life is assured. The United Nations is the channel, for,

THE FUTURE—FOR PEACE WITH FREEDOM 443

unlike bilateral assistance, United Nations aid does not arouse nationalistic sensitiveness and suspicion in the underdeveloped countries. If democracy fails, I can only see one disillusioned people after another turning to the "short-cut" solutions offered by Communist totalitarianism. The appeal of Communism to a man whose sole concern is to keep his stomach reasonably full and find a warm place to sleep at night belittles any talk of democratic advantages. For hundreds of millions of our potential allies or enemies there has never been anything that faintly resembled personal freedom. When offered a form of material security in return for a personal freedom which he has never known anyway, such men will probably not think twice. An extremely active Communist propaganda network in just these areas of discontent keeps driving home *immediate* improvements offered by a Communist system of government—and certain examples can be pointed to with a degree of validity.

The underdeveloped and underprivileged two-thirds of the world and its future long ago were fitted into the Soviet scheme of things. Realizing the extent of this drive toward a greater share of the world's bounty, which has transformed and is still transforming Asia and large parts of Africa, Communist planners are willing to wait patiently while hope and faith gradually slip into impatience and then disillusionment. The Soviet Union counts on taking over these underdeveloped areas by default—thanks to anticipated inaction of a democratic world which will fail to make good on the promises its form of government implies. Nor have the Communists been slow to exploit the shocking conditions of the underprivileged of the West. The large and powerful Communist parties of Italy and France understandably flourish in the impoverished areas of democracy. If this poverty does not go, it may be that Communism, rather than democracy, will stay.

Here, then, is the vital area of conflict in the world today—where democracy either has to produce far more impressive results than heretofore or else has to give way to totalitarianism with a Third World War as a possible aftermath. If our way of life is to survive, we shall have to demonstrate its versatility, its productive capacity; we shall have to prove to these millions, who are already beginning to doubt, that our method is the best method for achieving their goals. It is for us to show that the totalitarian systems are inferior.

Time is already running out. This vital area of our defense has already been neglected too long, and the threat of a conflagration is now too immediate to be any longer ignored.

The ideological struggle between Communism and other forms of dictatorship on the one hand, and democracy on the other, will never cease. Conflicts over the seat of governmental authority and the founding principles of states are as old as history itself. But the victory of democracy over world Communism in our time is possible if we win the trust of the 1,500,000,000 underprivileged persons now living in Asia, Africa, and several parts of South America. If, on the other hand, these millions—or a great part of them—are lost to democracy, our basic principles and our very way of life, even our prospects for peace and freedom, will be exposed to the greatest of pressures.

The same will result if the democracies fail to meet with wisdom and understanding the subjugated peoples' demands for national freedom, unity, and independence. In perhaps no other area of world politics today than this area designated at the outset as category "C," is the wisdom of our statesmen put to a greater test.

And there can be room for doubt as to whether these subjugated peoples have, until now, been met with the necessary wisdom. What, for example, has been the situation in the United Nations? One has only to refer to Article 73 in Chapter XI of the Charter where it is recorded that Member states having, or assuming, responsibility for the administration of territories that have not yet attained a full measure of self-government "accept as a sacred trust the obligation to promote to the utmost . . . the well-being of the inhabitants of these territories."

But interests clashed strongly with regard to the United Nations' responsibility for dependent or "colonial" territories and the peoples living there. The provisions in the Charter made the Organization's right more than ambiguous. Neither did it prove to be possible to define clearly the related question of what "matters essentially within the domestic jurisdiction of Member states" really are.

All this can be attributed to the continuing objections of the colonial powers and to their interpretation of the Charter. The position of dependent territories has, in fact, plagued the Organization to a considerable extent in the initial years, partly because of the noted ambiguity of the relevant Charter provisions, partly because of the attitudes taken by "colonial" and "anticolonial" Member-state groupings respectively. Member states possessing colonies have contended with consistency that their stewardship in these areas is not the concern of the United Nations. Only reluctantly have they reported to a temporary or special committee, charged by the General Assembly to study the conditions in dependent territories; and to this day they have successfully resisted any attempts to make such a committee a permanent institution. At the same time the large group of Member states holding "anticolonial" feelings has never lost an opportunity to call on the Organization to intervene more decisively in such matters and, in fact, resume the full responsibility for the fate of all colonial peoples.

It is my opinion that the Charter gives the United Nations far-reaching responsibilities in this field, particularly in light of the Organization's general duty to maintain international peace.

But France, Great Britain, Belgium, and the Netherlands hold other views as to the role of the United Nations—and this point of view bodes ill when one takes up the far more significant question of national independence for colonies and for other territories that are not self-governing. I recognize the substantial benefits these four democracies have brought to overseas lands formerly or presently under their rule. Indeed, so profound a contribution as the parliamentary forms which today are embraced by the leaders of India and Indonesia and Pakistan and other Asian states, flows directly from the days of Western rule. I equally appreciate the difficulties that extreme nationalistic elements make for the colonial powers— and the world. When one considers the unresolved problems confronting us today—first and foremost those separating the Arab, and to some extent the Asian, world from the West—there are admittedly good grounds for anxiety. The list of entrenched disagreements is long. There is the case of Egypt versus Great Britain, where problems of the Suez Canal and the Sudan have made the headlines for well over six years. Differences between France and Morocco and Tunisia have been on the United Nations agenda, or have been submitted for the agenda, for some time. The South African problems of the status and treatment of the Indian minority, and of the fate of Southwest Africa, the former German colony and League of Nations

Mandate, have consistently beset the United Nations; and the South African government's policy of *apartheid*, of separation of the races, threatens to become a third. There is the British-Iranian oil dispute, which has been long ripe for settlement, and the struggle between India and Pakistan over Kashmir—a conflict between two newly independent states of Asia. And finally there are a number of border disputes among Middle Eastern and Asian countries. In most all of these quarters, the Western democracies are to some degree involved. They often feel compelled to support their protégés, and this renders the situation no less complicated.

Until now, the United Nations has managed to control and even substantially to reduce armed conflicts in three areas of the greatest friction: Palestine, Indonesia, and Kashmir. The conflict in Indonesia seems to be largely resolved, but the situations in Kashmir and Palestine still remain uneasy.

The open struggle between Israel and the Arab states was temporarily shelved with the Armistice of 1948. But the situation between Palestine and its neighboring states can still be the source of a conflict which can spread far beyond that part of the world. Great-power interests here are highly divergent, thereby increasing the element of danger. But the conflict can still be resolved—granted sufficient patience—regardless of what the Arab leaders may set forth in their official declarations. If the United Nations does not alter its position, and the United States, Great Britain, France, and the U.S.S.R. as well are brought together on a peace plan, the Arab states will probably have to bow to reason and accept the inevitable.

What then, in short, are the prospects for peace? First, there are no grounds for despair. The democracies have had a long and stony path to follow since 1946; they have expended vast sums on arms—sums which could have been used for other purposes. Hundreds of thousands of young men have offered their lives to protect values which we, and they, regarded as the most vital—namely, values most worthy of man. From 1946 to 1953, the world was engaged in a fight to win time: a balance of power had to be established. In 1946, 1947, and 1948, when the Communist offensive was launching out to take one border state after another, culminating with the fall of Czechoslovakia, the Western democracies had disarmed all but completely. China's fall in 1949 represented yet another miscalcula-

THE FUTURE—FOR PEACE WITH FREEDOM   447

tion on their part. Since then, time has been on their side. Every year that passes—after a time every month, and now every day that passes, is a unit bearing the peace-loving world in the right direction.

When I use the word "peace," I refer to peace with freedom—both words being used in the context accepted and supported by a majority of the world's populace. Anyone can enjoy peace if he is willing to accept his neighbors' conditions. But what he obtains, in the end, will probably fail to conform with the views and desires of all peace- and freedom-loving people. But I am of the opinion that we have now arrived at a point where a minority within a country can no longer force its will upon a majority—as was the case from 1946 to 1950—even though the former, a Communistic minority, might receive support from without.

In closing, I ask myself whether the technical development we have experienced will soon render war itself an impossibility. Recent technical advances in the form of high-speed long-distance bombers, bacteriological weapons, the atomic and hydrogen bombs, plus all the other instruments of mass annihilation, are so brutal and so sweeping in their destructive force that little if any human life would probably survive a new world catastrophe. The prospect they force upon us—though terrifying—may still contain a degree of hope, the price of war now being almost certain self-destruction. But we are still dealing with human beings, and nothing—no matter how reasonable—can be taken for granted. Perhaps this hope, too, may prove illusory.

In the end, then, it is probably wise to be prepared for the worst, at the same time never ceasing to struggle toward the best, in the form of lasting peace. Perhaps one, or possibly several dictators together, can suddenly abandon even a semblance of reason, and—as before in history—unleash the hell of a new war. But the danger of such an inferno is steadily being reduced, every month and every day. If the peace-loving world makes full use of the United Nations' capacity for collective security, peaceful settlement, and economic and social advance, the dangers of a Third World War will be reduced still further.

These are my thoughts as I look backward, then ahead, sharing with everyone else that uncertain position somewhere between the past and the future. On the bleak Röros Plateau of central Norway, these weeks of 1954 have been weeks of peace. Those who make their homes up here know and are a part of this peace, at the same time enjoying a freedom with only such limitations as they have imposed upon themselves. There is no great wealth here—far from it. For every single man and woman it is a year-around struggle to win enough to keep body and soul together.

But they do know a rare peace, these people; and they are free.

Were it only possible for the rest of humanity to share this simple peace and freedom of the Norwegian mountains, how much happier the world's millions would be!

INDEX

Abstention, an improvement in veto practice, 432
Acheson, Dean G., Secretary of State, 264; and Chinese representation issue, 254–255, 271; and Secretary-General's peace mission, 283, 284, 314–316; plan for "United Action for Peace," 346–347; and extension of Lie's term as Secretary-General, 371, 379, 381; and Lie's resignation, 412
Act of Chapultepec, 133, 134
Ad Hoc Committee on Headquarters, 118
Administrative Committee on Coordination (U.N.), 303, 319
Administrative Tribunal (U.N.), 390
Advisory Committee. See Headquarters Advisory Committee
Advisory Social Welfare Services, 144
Afghanistan, admitted to U.N., 100, 101; improvement of agricultural methods, 151
Akre, Helge, 292, 368
Ala, Hussein, and Iran appeal to Security Council, 74–76, 78, 79
Albania, application for U.N. membership, 100, 101, 102; accused of aiding guerrillas in Greece, 103, 105; danger from, to Yugoslavia, 244
Aldrich, Winthrop W., 72, 110
Antiforeignism, 108
Anti-intellectualism, 203
Apartheid, 446
"Appeal to the Great Powers," General Assembly resolution, 213, 294, 295
Appointments, to Secretariat, 52, 53–54, 386–387
Arab-Asian bloc, 357, 385
Arab Higher Committee, 164, 165
Arab League, 174, 178, 188
Arab Legion, 182, 186

Arab states, hostile to Palestine as Jewish national home, 159; reject partition of Palestine, 162; armed forces from, infiltrating Palestine, 165; preparing to invade Palestine, 166; belief that partition would turn them toward U.S.S.R., 170; invade Palestine, 173, 174, 175, 176, 178; British relations with, 182, 186; U.N. mediation between Israel and, 186–192; U.N. military observers in, 187; and Arab refugees from Palestine, 195–196; poverty in, 198; danger in unresolved differences with Israel, 446
Aranha, Oswaldo, 277
Arce, José, 168, 368
Argentina, 339
Armaments race, 280, 299–300, 308
Arms embargo, by U.S.A., 168, 181
Arneberg, Arnstein, 121
Asia, representation of, 433
Asia first, as Nehru's starting point, 360–361
Athens, visit of Secretary-General to, 245
Atomic energy, 26–27; General Assembly resolution, 89, 90, 279; an effective international control system for, 279–280, 288, 299, 310, 321
Atomic Energy Commission (U.N.), 1946 meeting, 89–93; receives Baruch Plan, 91–93; continued study and report on Plan, 93, 94; abolished, 95; study of peaceful uses of atomic energy, 280, 322
Atomic weapons, prohibition of, 93, 94, 280, 299, 310, 317; influence on American attitudes, 392, 447
Attlee, Clement R., 7, 26, 183, 285–286, 311–314
Auriol, President Vincent, 266, 286–287

Austin, Warren R., intermediation in Truman Doctrine, 104–105; and San Francisco Headquarters idea, 109, 111; and Rockefeller family gift of Manhattan site, 113; active work for construction of Headquarters, 115, 117–118, 124; doctrine U.N. lacked power to enforce any political settlement, 167–168; proposes Palestine trusteeship instead of partition, 169–170; and T. Lie's proposal of joint resignation, 171; warned by Secretary-General's representative of need for prompt action in Palestine, 175–177; appeal for forceful reply to aggression against Palestine, 186; dinner at Hôtel Crillon, 211; and Korean crisis, 334, 336, 337, 338, 341, 353; and extension of term for T. Lie, 374, 376, 378, 379–381

Australia, at London Gen'l Assembly, 13–14, 16; in Security Council discussion of Iranian question, 77, 79; against closed meetings of Security Council, 81; for Secretary-General's right of intervention, 87; and Greek question, 105; opposes New York as U.N. Headquarters, 114; on U.N. Special Committee on Palestine, 161, 162; suggestion of trusteeship for Palestine, 170; on U.N. Temporary Commission on Korea, 325; and U.N. army in Korea, 338, 339; doubts extension of T. Lie's term as Secretary-General legal, 385

Austria, application for U.N. membership, 101, 102; in global sharing of skills, 151; under occupation, 220; treaty with, as first step to break a deadlock, 307

Azerbaijan, Iranian province, 29, 74, 79

Azcarate, Pablo de, 187

Bakke, Ole Helge, 188
Balfour Declaration, 162
Balkan Commission (U.N.), 393. See also Commission of Investigation
Baranovsky, Anatoli M., 384

Barkley, Alben W., Vice President, 121, 277
Barkley, Mrs. Alben W., 121–122
Baruch, Bernard M., 72, 91–92
Baruch Plan, 91–95
Bassov, N. D., 116
Bayar, Celal, 246
Bebler, Ales, 239, 251, 252, 259, 352, 374
Begley, Frank M., "conversation" with Gromyko, 77–78; in Mrs. Barkley emergency, 122
Belaunde, Dr. Victor Andrés, 139
Belgium, 187, 338, 339, 445
Belgrade, 238–239, 245
Beneš, Eduard, 26; and submersion of Czechoslovakian democracy, 231, 232, 234; dies and is buried in unknown grave, 235–236
Berendsen, Sir Carl A., 172
Berg, Hans, 58
Berlin, a show window, 201; question of elections in, 306–307
Berlin blockade, imposed by U.S.S.R., 199–201; parried by Western powers with airlift, 199, 201, 203, 210, 217, 218; currency reform in Western zones of Germany alleged by U.S.S.R. as cause, 200; first efforts at a settlement failing, Western powers appeal to Security Council on ground of threat to peace, 200–201; mediation by Secretary-General, 201–218; appeal placed by Security Council on agenda, 201, 202; mediation of "neutrals" in Council led by Dr. Bramuglia, 202, 203, 209, 212, 213, 214, 216; Dr. Evatt and the General Assembly "Appeal to the Great Powers" on, 213, 215–216; declaration by Stalin that it could be settled, 217; final lifting of, 218; one of four determinative events, 221
Bernadotte, Count Folke, U.N. Mediator for Palestine, 185–192; reparation for murder of, 193–194
Berntzen, Mrs. Ingrid, 291
Beveridge, Sir William, 48
Bevin, Ernest, British Foreign Secretary, 6, 16, 26; in debate with Vy-

INDEX 451

shinsky on Greece, 31–32, 33; on Churchill's Fulton speech, 37; his Palestine position, 182, 183, 184–185, 186; in Berlin impasse, 212, 213, 214; on diplomatic relations with Communist China, 270–271; illness of, 285, 309; reaction to Secretary-General's ten-point program for peace, 309–311, 312; and extension of Lie's term as Secretary-General, 371, 373, 376
Bidault, Georges, 16, 266, 286, 287–288, 307
Big Five, and naming of U.N. Secretary-General, 12, 16; understanding on Assistant Secretaryships-General, 45–46; preferred status, and location of U.N. Headquarters, 61; uninterested in forming Palestine preparatory committee, 160; and a U.N. land force for Palestine, 166; accept Count Folke Bernadotte as U.N. Mediator for Palestine, 185
Billotte, Pierre, 96
Björnson, Björnstjerne, 231
Black, Eugene, Jr., 319
Blanchard, F., 319
Blanco, Carlos S., 251, 259
Blickenstaff, David E., 133
B'nai B'rith, 1950 address to, on East-West deadlock, 262–263, 276–277
Board of Art Advisers, 121
Board of Design Consultants, 115–116, 117
Bogomolov, Alexandre E., 19, 26
Boheman, Erik, 365, 414, 415
Bokhari, Ahmed S., 415
Bolivia, 163
Bonnet, Henri, 16, 80, 83
Boomer, Jörgine and Lucius, 71–72
Boston, as possible U.N. Headquarters site, 62, 109, 110
Bowles, Chester, 50, 51
Boycott, by Communist Bloc, of Yugoslavia, 237, 240; U.S.S.R., of United Nations, 253, 262, 263, 267, 268, 275; Bevin on U.S.S.R., 310; U.S.S.R. ends, 341; U.S.S.R., of Secretary-General, 385, 408–409, 410–411

Bramuglia, Juan A., President of Security Council and leader of "neutrals" mediation of Berlin blockade, 202, 203, 205 n., 209, 212, 213, 214, 216; dismissal by Perón, 214
Brazil, 339
British Civil Service, 41
Brunfaut, Gaston, 115
Budget, Secretary-General's first temporary, 52
Bulgaria, application for admission to U.N., 101, 102; accused of aiding guerrillas in Greece, 103, 105; Jews from, in Israel, 197; after 1945, 220; threat of, to Yugoslavia, 239, 244
Bunche, Ralph J., 160, 166; principal secretary of Palestine Commission, 163; with Count Bernadotte, U.N. Mediator for Palestine, 186, 187, 188, 190; Acting Mediator, 189, 191; Nobel Prize for Peace awarded to, 192
Burma, admitted to U.N. membership, 101, 256
Byrnes, James F., 6, 10, 47, 76, 78, 79, 85, 387

"Cabinet," Secretary-General's, 45–52, 66, 82, 198
Cadogan, Sir Alexander, British Permanent Representative to U.N., 48, 77; and Palestine problem, 160, 164, 165, 169, 178, 179–181, 182, 186; and Berlin blockade, 211, 212, 213; embarrassed by Foreign Office "leak," 213; exchange of views with, on Chinese representation issue, 258–259
Cambodia, 101
Canada, 26, 28, 61, 161, 338, 339
Canary Islands, 151
Carías Andino, Tiburcio, 129
Caribbean area, visit of Secretary-General to, 126, 127, 129, 131–133
Central America, visit of Secretary-General to, 126, 127, 128, 130, 131
Ceylon, application for U.N. membership, 101, 102; in global pooling of skills, 152
Charter (U.N.), drafting of Security Council articles, 3; on naming of

Secretary-General, 12; provisions for discussion in Security Council and Gen'l Assembly, 24–25; Churchill on, 37; on role of Secretary-General and Secretariat, 39–40, 41–42; importance given by, to "geographical basis" for Secretariat appointments, 53; regional defense arrangements under, 133–135; need for international economic and social cooperation recognized in, 143; invasion of Palestine violation of, 166; and maintenance of international peace and security, 178–179, 192; and an internationally recruited police force, 192–193; Stalin's comment on, 230; and Iron Curtain, 247; violated by Communist China, 273; review and revision of, 424–434 *passim;* practicality of liberal construction of, 424

Chauvel, Jean, 259, 353, 375, 378, 379, 381

Chiang Kai-shek, 254; lobby of, in United States, 260; position in Formosa, 265

Chiao Kuan-hua, 356

Chile, proposal of Economic Commission for Latin America, 134, 136; penicillin production, 137; host to Economic and Social Council, 138–139; in global pooling of skills, 148; opposes secret ballot for Secretary-General, 384

China (Nationalist), one of Big Five agreeing on a Secretary-General, 12, 16; appointee from, to Secretary-General's "cabinet," 49; and U.N. Military Staff Committee, 95, 96; consults on implementing Palestine partition resolution of General Assembly, 169; right to represent Chinese people in U.N. challenged by U.S.S.R., 249–272; membership in U.N. vested in the Chinese nation, not specifically in a government, 254, 257; status of, in Formosa, 254, 265; defends its position in U.N. and fights back, 260, 261–262; opposes extension as Secretary-General to Lie, 370; votes for Charles Malik,

381. See also People's Republic of China (Communist)

Chisholm, Brock, 319

Chou En-lai, 250, 270, 356, 357

Churchill, Winston, 424; his Fulton speech, 35–38, 221; desire for direct negotiations with Stalin, 261

Ciudad Trujillo, 132

Clay, Lucius D., 210

Clementis, Vladimir, 233, 235

Coexistence, 276, 296, 302

Cohen, Benjamin A., Assistant Secretary-General for Public Information, 49, 130, 133

Cohen, Benjamin V., U.S. Delegate to General Assembly, 202–203

Cold war, forewarning of, 34; need for settling, 276–289 *passim,* 308, 317, 321; influence on American attitudes, 392; conflict between international Communism and the democracies, 436–448

Colombia, 339

Colombo Plan, 155, 362

Cominform, Marshal Tito's break with, 221, 237; and the French, 287

Commission for Conventional Armaments (U.N.), 94, 95

Commission for the Unification and Rehabilitation of Korea (U.N.), 345, 365

Commission of Investigation (U.N.), in Greece, 103, 105. See also Balkan Commission

Commission of Jurists, 398, 399–400, 405

Committee on Coordination of Assistance for Korea, proposed, 333

Commission on Korea (U.N.), 327. See also Temporary Commission on Korea

Commonwealth Technical Assistance Scheme (Colombo Plan), 155, 362

Communism (international), conflict between the democracies and, 435–448

Communist Bloc, boycott of Yugoslavia, 237, 240; in Chinese representation issue, 253; finds General Assembly Korean action "illegal," 324;

INDEX 453

and extended term of T. Lie as Secretary-General, 383, 384, 385
Communists, Norwegian, 20, 390, 391; in Indonesia, 30; in Greece, 30, 103, 106; Czechoslovakian, 224, 225, 232, 233, 234, 235; in Indochina, 266; American, policy reasons for excluding them from Secretariat, 388–389, 390
Conference Area, 120
Confiscation, 154
Connecticut, as possible U.N. Headquarters site, 62, 63, 108
Conventional weapons, 95, 280
Coplon, Judith, 388
Cordier, Andrew, 175, 177, 181–182, 328, 336, 338, 373, 398, 412
Corfu Straits, mines in, 432
Cormier, Ernest, 115
Correa, José A., 138
Costa Rica, 128, 130–131, 137
Council of Foreign Ministers, first (London, 1945), 25; second (Moscow, 1945), 26, 323; to discuss four-power disputes over Germany, proposed, 202
Cripps, Sir Stafford, 183, 184
Crittenberger, Willis D., 131
Crowther, Geoffrey, 48
Cuba, 131, 257, 258, 259, 265
Cuban Association for the United Nations, 131
Currency reform, German, and the Berlin blockade, 200, 203–218 *passim*
Czechoslovakia, hopeful U.S.S.R. relations with, 25, 26; on U.N. Special Committee on Palestine, 161; on Palestine Commission, 163, 167; effort to reestablish itself, 220; Communist coup in, 221, 230–232, 234; Moscow festivities for visiting delegation from, for new trade agreement, 224–226; 1948 visit of Secretary-General to, 231, 232–234; aftermath of coup, 235–236; 1950 visit of Secretary-General, 235–236; and the abducted Greek children, 289–290; demands dismissal from Secretariat of certain of its nationals, 394

Davies, Joseph E., 72
Democracy, distinction between the will and the capacity for, 441, 442
Denmark, 121, 163, 253, 340
Department of Administrative and Financial Services, 44; naming of Assistant Secretary-General for, 46–47, 49–50
Department of Conference and General Services, 44; naming of Assistant Secretary-General for, 49–50
Department of Economic Affairs, 44; naming of Assistant Secretary-General for, 48
Department of Public Information, 44; naming of Assistant Secretary-General for, 47–48, 49
Department of Security Council Affairs, 44; naming of Assistant Secretary-General for, 45–46, 51; Korean affairs separately handled, 343
Department of Social Affairs, 44; naming of Assistant Secretary-General for, 48, 51
Department of Trusteeship, 44; naming of Assistant Secretary-General for, 48–49
Dewey, Thomas E., 63, 67, 120
"Dictatorship of the proletariat," 437
Dimidoff, Dr., 291
Disarmament Commission (U.N.), 95
Disarmament resolution (1946), 89, 94, 95
Discrimination, 302–303, 316, 317
Dodd, Norris E., 319
Domestic jurisdiction, 335, 336
Dominican Republic, 129
Drummond, Sir Eric, pioneer in international civil service, 41–42, 43, 44
Dumbarton Oaks Proposals, 23
Dutch East Indies, 30. *See also* Indonesia

Ecker, Frederick H., 72, 110
Economic and Social Council (U.N.), elections to, 27, 28; rule permitting Secretary-General to speak, 87, 88; Chamber decorated and furnished by Sweden, 121; sets up Economic Commission for Latin America, 132,

134, 135–136; session at Santiago, Chile, 138–139; as "General Staff for Peace," 143–144, 145, 154
Economic Commission for Asia and the Far East, 136
Economic Commission for Eur., 136, 144
Economic Commission for Lat. America, 134, 135–136, 144
Economic Cooperation Administration, 245, 340
Economy, pressure for, 52
Ecuador, 136, 137; visit of Secretary-General to, 139–140; and Chinese representation issue, 250, 257, 258, 259, 265
Eden, Anthony, 11–12, 13, 14, 19, 21, 261, 412, 413
Egypt, 148; rejects Palestine partition, 162; invades Palestine, 173, 174, 175, 176, 178, 179; negotiations ending in armistice with Israel, 189, 191–192; hatred of Israel, 195; Palestine Arab refugees in, 196; Jewish refugees from, 197; visit of Secretary-General to, 198; and Chinese representation issue, 255, 257, 258, 259, 261, 265; supports Indian plan in deadlock over Secretary-General, 378; differences with Great Britain, 445
Einstein, Albert, 277
Eisenhower, Dwight D., suggested for Secretary-General, 12–13, 61; wartime relations with Lie, 18, 19; new approach in 1953 to international problem of atomic energy, 95, 321; 1953 evaluation of United Nations, 423–424
Eisenhower, Milton S., 47, 50–51
el-Khouri, Faris, 33
England. *See* Great Britain
Entezam, Nasrollah, 355, 356, 365, 373, 379, 414
Equality for all peoples, 281–282
Estimé, Dumarsais, 129
Ethiopia, 339
Europe, vs. U.S. as site for U.N. Headquarters, 55–62, 109; time of greatest war danger, 201

Evatt, Herbert V., 14, 64, 87; mediation as President of General Assembly in Berlin blockade, 212–216 *passim;* joint letter with Secretary-General to four powers, 215–216, 294, 295; supports Secretary-General's B'nai B'rith speech, 277
Expanded Technical Assistance Program, 137, 144, 146, 153, 156, 322
Exploitation, 155
Expropriation, 155

FBI, 389, 401, 402
Fawzi Bey, Mahmoud, 259, 277, 329, 332
Federal Bureau of Investigation, 389, 401, 402
Feldmann, Prof., 291
Feller, Abraham H., Gen'l Counsel to U.N., 64–65, 66, 387; collaboration with Secretary-General in precedent-setting memorandum to President of Security Council, 82, 87; negotiates transfer of Headquarters site title to U.N., 116; work on promised loan from U.S., 119; high credit due to, 124; in "council of war" on Palestine, 175; consulted on Palestine action to be taken, 177; memorandum on U.N. as an "international person," 193; in Berlin blockade mediation, 201, 202, 203, 204, 207–214 *passim;* memorandum on Berlin situation, 205–207; with Secretary-General at Belgrade, 238; Legal Department memorandum on Chinese representation issue, 256–257, 261; helps in Secretary-General's North Korean aggression statement to Security Council, 328, 329; and T. Lie's 1950 unsent letters about retiring, 373; death, 399; and Lie's resignation as Secretary-General, 412
Fierlinger, Zdenek, 224, 225
Fifth Amendment, pleas of, by Secretariat members, 395–400
Fingerprinting, 402
Finland, 20, 26; application for membership in U.N., 101, 102; finds its natural place after 1945, 220

INDEX 455

Flushing Meadow, 68, 107, 108, 110, 112
Food and Agriculture Organization, 136, 147, 151, 303, 304
Foote, Wilder, 238, 373, 412
Foreign Office (British), leak from, 212, 213; not interested in a compromise, 216
Forest Hills, 418–419
Formosa, controlled by Chiang Kaishek, 254, 264–265; danger from Communist China, 265; proposed U.N. trusteeship for, 265, 266; United States Seventh Fleet ordered to protect, 332; and Communist China, 351, 355, 356, 357, 359, 361, 363
France, as one of Big Five in choosing U.N. Secretary-General, 12, 16; troops in Syria and Lebanon, 33–34; appointee from, to Secretary-General's "cabinet," 48, 51; for Europe as U.N. Headquarters site, 60, 61; and U.N. Military Staff Committee, 95–97; and implementing of General Assembly partition resolution, 169; on Security Council's Palestine Truce Commission, 187; and Chinese representation issue, 255, 257, 258, 259, 266, 269, 270; and the cold war, 288, 308; and U.N. army in Korea, 338, 339; and extension in term as Secretary-General to T. Lie, 371–372, 373, 375, 378; Communist party of, 443; as a colonial power, 445. *See also* Western powers
Fraser, Peter, 14, 15
Freitas-Valle, Cyro, 375

Galagan, Andrei I., 250
Gallagher, Manuel, 139
Ganem, André, 371–372
García Robles, Alfonso, 161
Garrod, Sir Guy, 95–96
Gavrilović, Stoyan, 62, 112
General Assembly (U.N.), naming of first President, 2–11; naming of Secretary-General, 11–17; debate on Preparatory Commission report, 22; its Charter right of discussion, 24; establishes Atomic Energy Commission, 27, 89, 90; revises rules to give Secretary-General unrestricted rights of intervention, 88; disarmament resolution, 89, 95; deadlocked on control of atomic energy and armaments, 93–94, 95; establishes Special Commission on the Balkans, 105; concluding argument over location of permanent Headquarters, 107–114; Secretary-General's report on Headquarters financing and promised loan, 117–119; votes supplementary Headquarters appropriation, 123; occupies its hall in permanent Headquarters, 123; its Expanded Technical Assistance Program, 137, 146; special session appoints U.N. Special Committee on Palestine, 160, 161; adopts partition and authorizes Palestine Commission, 162–163; recommendation that mandatory power evacuate Palestine seaport and hinterland, 165; relief program for Arab refugees, 191; establishes Conciliation Commission, 191; authorizes U.N. Field Service, 192–193; in Berlin impasse, 212, 213, 214, 218; Yugoslav complaints against satellite states brought to, 242; and Greek children in Yugoslavia, 243; discussion of Secretary-General's ten-point program, 320–321; and independence of Korea, 324–325; recognizes Republic of (South) Korea and establishes U.N. Commission on Korea, 326–327; and "Suggested Terms of Settlement," 344; establishes Commission for Relief and Rehabilitation of Korea, 345; adopts Acheson Plan, 346; Cease-Fire Committee of, and the delegation from Communist China, 354–357, 363; and extension in term as Secretary-General of T. Lie, 372, 373, 374, 377, 379, 381–385; on conduct of Secretariat members, 396; Secretary-General's report to, on personnel policy, 403–405; Lie's resignation to, as Secretary-General, 406–407, 409–411, 413; its "Uniting for Peace" resolution, 432

General Convention on Privileges and Immunities, 126, 128, 129

Geneva, proposed U.N. Headquarters site, 59, 60; transfer to U.N. of League of Nations buildings in, 125; as place for first of Security Council periodic meetings, 296

Geneva Conventions, 340, 354

Genocide Convention, 282

"Geographical basis," in appointments to Secretariat, 53

Georges-Picot, Guillaume, Assistant Secretary-General for Social Affairs, 51

Germ warfare, 365

Germany, division and occupation of, 25; zone rule of, by occupying powers, 199–218 *passim;* political vacuum under occupation, 220; admission to U.N., 280; plan for a united neutral, 300

Gjesdal, Tor, 58, 138, 175, 231, 373, 412

González Videla, Gabriel, 138

Gottwald, Klement, 224, 225, 233

Gousev, Feodor T., and election of first Gen'l Assembly President, 5, 6

Grafstrom, Sven, 353

Great Britain (United Kingdom, England), and choice of first Gen'l Assembly President, 4, 5, 6; and choice of first U.N. Secretary-General, 11–12, 16–17, 20; in League of Nations, 12; wartime relations with Norway, 17, 19, 20–21; supports creation of U.N. commission on atomic energy, 26–27; Soviet suspicions of, in complaint by Iran, 29–30; charged by U.S.S.R. with interference in Greece and Indonesia, 30, 31–33; troops in Syria and Lebanon, 33–34; appointee from, to Secretary-General's "cabinet," 47–48; for Europe as U.N. Headquarters site, 60, 61; shifts to favor Secretary-General's right of intervention, 87; participation in work and report of Military Staff Committee, 95–97; and deadlocks over admitting new members to U.N., 101, 102; reaches its limit in Greece and Palestine, 103–104; opposes San Francisco as Headquarters site, 111; as mandatory power requests Palestine be placed on General Assembly agenda, 159–161; early termination of its mandate recommended by UNSCOP, 161; abstains from voting on partition of Palestine, 162; while accepting partition cannot implement it, 163, 164, 167, 169; insists on abrupt, not progressive, turning over of Palestine authority, 164–165, 169; difficulties in agreement with U.S. on Palestine, 180, 182; legalistic attitude in Security Council, 182; Government, exchange of views with R. G. A. Jackson representing Secretary-General, 183–185; shifts from inaction and backs U.N. truce order in Palestine, 186; supports Security Council threat of sanctions, 188; "defeatism" in Czechoslovakia, 233; benevolence toward Yugoslavia, 240; and Chinese representation issue, 252, 253, 255, 258–259, 269, 270–271; urged to participate more actively in U.N., 285, 314; opposed to periodic meetings of Security Council, 309; gives first importance to North Atlantic Treaty Organization, 309, 311; finds fault with U.N. handling of colonial question, 310; and U.N. army in Korea, 338, 340; and extension in term as Secretary-General to T. Lie, 372, 373, 375, 376, 379; resistance as a colonial power to U.N., 445. *See also* Western powers

Greece, 61; Vyshinsky charges British interference in, 30–33, 89, 103; Great Britain ends aid to, 103–104; beginning of American aid to, 104–105, 220; Security Council deadlock on, ends in transfer of issue to General Assembly, 105; peace restored to, 106; civil war in, 220; visit of Secretary-General to, 221, 237, 245–246; possible defense cooperation among Yugoslavia, Turkey, and, 242, 245, 246; combat forces in Korea, 339

INDEX

Greek children, kidnaped, 235, 243, 245, 289–290, 304–305
"Greek Children in Yugoslavia," Yugoslav propaganda film, 212
Gromyko, Andrei A., at first Gen'l Assembly, 8, 9, 16; in San Francisco fight over veto, 24; for United States as U.N. Headquarters site, 60; requests Secretary-General to postpone Security Council meeting, 76; walks out from Security Council, 76–78; charges Security Council with "illegality," 79; broad interpretation of Secretary-General's powers, 84, 86; and Baruch Plan, 91, 93, 94; and admission of new members to U.N., 101; denounces U.S. Truman Doctrine, 105; advises T. Lie against resignation, 171; suggests visit by Secretary-General to Moscow, 222; on World Health Organization, 304; on "scandalous" Korean resolution of Security Council, 335, 336; and beginning of Korean cease-fire talks, 364; protest against White Russians in Secretariat, 394
Gross, Ernest A., 252, 259, 328, 333, 336, 338, 353, 354, 368, 369, 371, 373
Gross, Gerald C., 319
Guatemala, 128, 136, 138, 161
Guatemala City, 130
Guayaquil, Ecuador, 140–141
Gubitchev, Valentin, 388
Gurion, David Ben, 195

Haiti, 129, 132, 136, 150
Hammarskjöld, Dag, second Secretary-General, 416, 417, 418
Harrison, Wallace K., 113; Director of Planning, U.N. Headquarters, 115–119, 122, 124
Harvard University, T. Lie's commencement address at, 98–99
Havana, 131–132
Headquarters (U.N.), battle over Europe or United States as site for, 13, 55–62, 109; problems of permanent site in U.S., 62–63, 69, 108–112; temporary, at Lake Success, Flushing Meadow, and Hunter College Bronx campus, 64–70, 71, 107, 108; establishment and construction of, in Manhattan, 112–124; completion of, 411
Headquarters Advisory Committee, 115, 117, 118
Headquarters Building (U.N.), 115–116, 119, 120–121, 122–123
Headquarters Commission, report of, 107–108
Headquarters Committee (Assembly), 110–112, 113–114, 115
Herbert, Sir Edwin, 398
Hewitt, H. Kent, 95
Hickerson, John D., 263, 271, 314, 315, 327, 328, 338, 339, 368
Hiss, Alger, 392–393
Ho Chi Minh, 266, 269
Ho, Ying-chin, 96
Hodgson, W. R., 13, 64
Holy Places (Palestine), 159, 161, 172
Honduras, 128–129, 130
Hoo, Victor Chitsai, Assistant Secretary-General for Trusteeship, 48–49, 66; personal representative of Secretary-General to UNSCOP, 161; to Temporary Commission on Korea, 325
Hoover, Herbert, 72
Hopkins, Harry, 18, 24
Houdek, Vladimir, 394
Huleh Lake, land reclamation, 195
Human rights, issue of, 158, 281, 438, 442
Human Rights Commission, 88
Hungary, application for admission to U.N., 101, 102; Jews from, in Israel, 197; after 1945, 220; threat of, to Yugoslavia, 239, 244
Hunter College, Bronx campus temporary answer to U.N. needs, 66–67
Hutson, John B., Assistant Secretary-General for Administrative and Financial Services, 47, 50

Iceland, admitted to U.N., 100, 101
Illegality, U.S.S.R. charges of, 432
Immigration, to Israel, 165, 197
Immunity, United Nations, 395
Impellitteri, Vincent R., 72

India, 50, 148, 151, 152, 161; and Chinese representation issue, 250, 252, 255, 259; on U.N. Temporary Commission on Korea, 325; cease-fire proposal for Korea, 359; under Nehru, 361-362; candidacy for Permanent Membership in Security Council, 433; political contribution to, by former Western rule, 445; conflict with Pakistan over Kashmir, 446

Individual, status of, in a Communist society, 437-438

Indo-China, 287, 332

Indonesia, interference in, 30, 32; admitted to U.N. membership, 101, 257; in global pooling of skills, 149-150; political contribution to, by former Western rule, 445; friction in, 446

Inter-American Conference on Peace and Security, 133-135

Inter-American Economic and Social Council, 136

Internal security, 1952-1953 furor over, 386, 390-393, 396-397, 401

International Atomic Development Authority, proposed, 91, 92, 93

International Bank for Reconstruction and Development, 147, 153, 240

International Children's Emergency Fund (UNICEF), 126, 128, 137, 152, 245

International Civil Aviation Organization, 147

International civil service, U.N. Secretariat as, 40, 41, 42-43, 53-54; Sir Eric Drummond a pioneer in, 41

International Court of Justice, 102, 193-194, 256, 282, 432-433

International Finance Corporation, proposed, 153-154

International Labor Office, 145, 147, 151, 304

International law, development of, 282

International Monetary Fund, 147

International Red Cross, 299, 304, 305, 340, 354

International Refugee Organization, 126, 128-129

International Telecommunication Union, 145, 303

International trade, 281, 284, 302, 309, 317

International Trade Organization, 281, 302, 309, 316

Iran, complaint in Security Council of interference by U.S.S.R., 28-31; new appeal through Ambassador at Washington and its sequels, 74-88; in global sharing of skills, 151; on U.N. Special Committee on Palestine, 161; Turkish anxiety over, 246; oil dispute with Great Britain, 446

Iraq, 162, 197, 385

Ireland, application for U.N. membership, 100, 101, 102, 256

Iron Curtain, 230, 231, 233, 235

Isolationism, combating American, on the spot, 57, 131; in American newspapers, 261, 262

Israel, admitted to U.N. membership, 101, 194, 257; in global pooling of skills, 149-150; existence proclaimed, 173; *de facto* recognition by President Truman, 173, 184; U.N. military observers in, 187; working suggestions for accord with Arabs rejected by, 188; horror at assassination of Count Bernadotte, 190; conclusion of armistices with Arab states, 191-192; reparation for deaths of Bernadotte and U.N. military observers in attacks, 193-194; visit of Secretary-General to, 195, 196-198; Turkish friendliness toward, 247; recognition of Communist China, 253; danger in unresolved differences with Arab states, 446. *See also* Palestine

Italy, application for membership in U.N., 101, 102

Jackson, R. G. A., Assistant Secretary-General for General Coordination, and Palestine problem, 175-178, 179-181, 183-185, 394

Jamaica, 137

Japan, application for admission to U.N., 101, 280

INDEX

Jebb, (Sir) Gladwyn, head of London temporary Secretariat, 8, 42; in charge U.N. affairs, British Foreign Office, 183, 184; and crisis over Chinese membership in U.N., 265–266; argues that 1950 membership of Communist China in U.N. might have headed off Korean War, 273; answers Yakov Malik in Security Council Korean debate, 341; and Chinese Communist delegation, 353; and extension in term as Secretary-General of T. Lie, 372–379 *passim*

Jerusalem, UNSCOP recommendation for, 162; temporary international regime proposed for, 173; demilitarization of, 189; murder of Count Bernadotte in, 190–191; Government House in, 193

Jessup, Philip C., U.S. Ambassador at large, 201; discusses with Secretary-General ways through Berlin impasse, 202–204, 209; reports Americans in Germany inclined to carry the "show" through, 210; advises Secretary-General French and British must be informed, 211; approves joining of efforts by Secretary-General and Bramuglia, 214; asks Malik about Stalin's reported statement Berlin dispute could be settled, 217

Jewish Agency, 164, 165

Jews, age-old persecution of, climaxed by Hitler, 158–159; Palestine as national home for, 159–160; displaced persons, 162, 163; refugee, from Arab states, 196–197

Jiminez, Enrique A., 131

Johnson, Herschel V., 100, 101

Johnson, Joseph E., 87

Jones, Arthur Creech, 163, 167, 310

Jordan, application for admission to U.N., 100, 101; intervention in Palestine, 174, 182; Agreement with Israel, 192; fear of Israel, 195; Palestine Arab refugees in, 196

Juell, Finn, 121

Kaldor, Dr. N., 216
Kashmir, 446
Katz-Suchy, Juliusz, 384

Katzin, Col. Alfred G., on liaison service for Secretary-General in Korea, 334–335, 340, 343–344, 348

Kerno, Dr. Ivan, at first Gen'l Assembly, 8; Assistant Secretary-General for Legal Affairs, 49, 256

Khalidy, Awni, 64

Kilpatrick, John R., 117

King, W. L. Mackenzie, 26

Klaveness, Kristen, 222, 223, 225

Koo, V. K. Wellington, 261

Köprülü, Fuad, 246

Korea (Republic of), application for U.N. membership, 101; case against U.N. unifying, by force, 167; invaded by North Korea, 318, 320; Secretary-General's stand on, attacked, 320; U.N. army in, 322; history to the North Korean aggression, 323–327. *See also* North Korea

Korean War, Yugoslavia and, 243–244; Turkey and, 247; and Chinese representation issue, 271–273, 335, 357, 359, 360, 363; background of, 323–327; U.N. participation in, 327–366; confirmation by U.N. Temporary Commission of North Korean attack, 328–329; Secretary-General's statement of situation to Security Council, 329–330; Security Council calls vainly on North Korea to cease fire and withdraw its forces, then authorizes Unified Command in Korea with MacArthur as U.N. Commander, 331–334; organization of U.N. effort, 337–340; prisoners of war in, 340; relief assistance and medical aid in, 340–341; U.S.S.R. attacks on Secretary-General's acts in, 341–343; sudden flight of North Koreans brings pursuit into North Korea, 343–346; establishment of U.N. Commission for Unification and Rehabilitation of Korea, 345; entry of Communist China brings disaster, 349–351, 357; fruitless New York talks on a cease-fire with a delegation from Communist China, 351–357; U.N. intentions in, 358–359; conversation with Nehru on,

359–362; negotiation of an armistice, 362–366
Kuo, Ping Cha, 87
Kyron, Alexis, 115, 118, 237, 413

Lake Success, 68, 69, 108, 110, 120
Lall, Shamaldharee, Assistant Secretary-General for Conference and General Services, 50
Lange, Oscar, 77, 80–81, 83
Laos, 101
Laugier, Henri, Assistant Secretary-General for Social Affairs, 48, 51, 266
League of Nations, Great Britain in, 11, 12; Secretary-General and Secretariat of, 41–42, 43–44, 54; tragedy of, repetition not to be permitted, 57; transfer of its Geneva buildings to U.N., 125; Latin-American resentment at status in, 126; mandate over Palestine to Great Britain, 159; collapse of, 180, 182; anecdote about committee of, 216
Lebanon, 33–34; rejects Palestine partition, 162; hatred of Israel, 195; Armistice with Israel, 192; Palestine Arab refugees in, 196
Le Corbusier, Charles E., 116
Legal Department, 44; naming of Assistant Secretary-General for, 49; opinion on rights of Security Council in Palestine question, 168; memorandum to Secretary-General and draft letter to President of the Council on armed invasion of Palestine, 174; memorandum on Chinese representation issue, 256–257, 261; memorandum on "Legal Aspects of Security Council Action on Korea," 335–336; memorandum on Unified Command authority to negotiate cease-fire, 364; constitutes Commission of Jurists, 398
Lend-Lease, 29, 36
Liang, Ssu-ch'eng, 115
Libya, application for U.N. membership, 101; in global pooling of skills, 151
Lie, Trygve, a family Christmas, 1–3; and the U.N. General Assembly presidency, 2–11; in Norwegian Cabinet, 2, 3–4, 17–20, 23, 43; at San Francisco Conference, 22–24; resignation as Secretary-General, 406–414; farewell speech to General Assembly, 416–417; farewell to New York, 418–419. See also Secretary-General
Lima, Peru, 139
Lisický, Karel, 166
Literaturnaya Gazeta, 369
Lodge, Henry Cabot, 415
Lokanathan, Palamadais, 144
London, and first U.N. Gen'l Assembly, 3, 4, 6, 7, 14, 21; as possible U.N. Headquarters site, 59
Lovett, Robert A., 176, 177, 178
Lund, Col. Roscher, 394
Luxembourg, 339

MacArthur, Gen. Douglas, 272; United Nations Commander in Korea, 334, 335; advises formation of permanent supreme U.N. military command, 347–348; disaster of Communist Chinese intervention, 349–351
McCarran, Senator Pat, 401
McCarthy, Senator Joseph R., 393
McCormick, Col. Robert R., 131
McNeil, Hector, 119
Madariaga, Salvador de, 216
Makin, Norman J. O., 13, 17, 32, 64
Malaria, control of, 149
Malik, Charles, 33, 380, 381, 414
Malik, Yakov A., Soviet Deputy Foreign Minister, 102, 217; calling Communist People's Republic sole legal representative of Chinese people, he refuses for Soviet delegation to participate in Security Council until Kuomintang representation is ended, and conducts second Soviet walkout, 249–251; declares U.S.S.R. will not be bound by any Council decision reached with Kuomintang participation, 252; sensational return to Council, 271–272; on ten-point memorandum and covering letter, 317; maintains boycott, 333; ends boycott by assuming presi-

INDEX 461

dency of Security Council, 341; indicates possibility of Korean cease-fire and armistice, 363, 364; noncommittal on extension of Secretary-General's term, 370, 371, 373; opposes prolonging term, 374; nominates Modzelewski, 376; delaying tactics, 377, 379, 380; baits Austin for talk of veto by U.S., 380–381; final threat "if the appointment of Mr. Lie is imposed," 381–382

Managua, 130

Manhattan, housing crisis, 65, 68, 69

Manuilsky, Dmitri Z., at first Gen'l Assembly, 9, 11; complains in Security Council against British interference in Indonesia, 30; suggests Oslo as U.N. Headquarters site, 61; in propaganda debate on Greece, 103; raises again idea of Headquarters in Europe, 109

Mao Tse-tung, 259, 260, 261, 266, 270

Markelius, Sven, 116, 121

Marshall, George C., 18, 176, 177, 178, 211, 394

Marshall Plan, 37, 98, 284, 368, 370; and Czechoslovakia, 231, 233, 236

Märtha, Norwegian Crown Princess, 17

Masaryk, Jan, 14, 26, 49; on 1946 Czechoslovak trade agreement with U.S.S.R., 224–225; and submersion of Czechoslovakian democracy, 231–234, 236; "suicide" of, 235; grave not to be found, 235–236

Mass destruction weapons, 95, 280, 308, 310, 317, 447

Massachusetts, 62

Maxwell, Elsa, 70

Mediation, need for development of, by U.N., 279

"Memorandum of Points for Consideration in the Development of a Twenty-Year Program for Achieving Peace Through the United Nations," text as handed to the leaders of the four great powers, 277–283; offered for examination—in Washington, 283–285, in London, 285–286, in Paris, 286–288, in Moscow, 291–297; criticism and discussion of, in Moscow, 297–307, in Paris, 307–309, in London, 309–314, in Washington, 314–316; published, with letter of transmittal, 316–318; public reception of, 318–319; discussion in General Assembly, 320–321; some straws in the wind since, 321–322

Menderes, Adnan, 246

Menon, K. P. S., 325–326

Merchant, Livingston T., 338

Mexico, visit of Secretary-General to, 126, 128, 129–130; requests technical advice, 136; UNESCO and International Children's Emergency Fund activities in, 137, 138; in global pooling of skills, 148

Mexico City, 129

Middle East, visit of Secretary-General to, 195–198

Military Staff Committee (U.N.), 34–35, 95–98, 300, 431

"Miss" and "Mrs.," 70–71

Mitchell, William D., 398

Modzelewski, Zygmunt, 376

Moe, Finn, 58, 112, 115, 118

Mohn, Paul, 187

Molotov, Vyacheslav M., 22, 267; rigidity on veto right in Charter, 24–25; against San Francisco as Headquarters site, 109; Moscow luncheon in honor of Secretary-General, 223; participant in Secretary-General's 1950 interview with Stalin, 291, 293, 294, 296, 297–299, 300, 305

Mongolian People's Republic, application for U.N. membership, 100, 101, 102

Montreux Convention, 104

Morgenstierne, Wilhelm, 17

Morocco, 445

Morse, David A., 319

Moscow, 1946 visit of Secretary-General to, 221–230; 1950 visit to, 266–270, 291–292, 294, 307

Moses, Robert, 69, 72, 110, 112, 113, 116, 118, 124

Motorcycle police escort, 71

Mowinckel, Johan Ludwig, 19

Mudaliar, Sir Ramaswami, 14, 365

Murphy, Robert D., 210

Myrdal, Gunnar, 144, 216, 317

Nansen, Fridtjof, on the difficult and the impossible, 54
Nationalism, 158, 162
Nationalization, 154
Nehru, Jawaharlal, 359–362
Nelson, Otto L., 117
Nepal, application for U.N. membership, 101, 102, 256
Netherlands, 61, 101, 136, 161, 253, 340, 445
New York City, considered for U.N. permanent Headquarters, 60, 63; setting up temporary Headquarters in, 64–70, 71; first impressions and new friends in, 70–73; early doubts as to, for Headquarters, 108, 110–112; Turtle Bay and Rockefeller gift bring Headquarters to, 112–124
New York State, 62–63, 116
New Zealand, 172, 253, 338, 340
Newspapermen, 215
Nicaragua, 128, 130
Niemeyer, Oscar, 115
Nobel Prize for Peace, to Ralph Bunche, 192
Noel-Baker, Philip, 6, 12, 13, 60, 62, 64
North Africa, 197
North Atlantic Treaty, 37, 232, 241, 245, 246, 368
North Atlantic Treaty Organization, Western-power concentration on, 275, 309, 311; importance of, 439
North Korea (Democratic People's Republic of Korea), application for membership in U.N., 101; case against forcible unifying with Korea by U.N., 167; aggression against Korea, 318, 320, 323, 327–366; sharp defeat ending at the Yalu, 343–346, 349–350; day saved by heavy Communist Chinese reenforcement, 349, 350–351, 357; negotiations ending in armistice, 362–366
Norway, first freedom after war, 1–2; wartime relations with U.S., 17–18; liberation of, 18–19, 22; historical relations with Russia, 19–20; attitude toward United Nations, 22–23; global slant on world affairs, 56–57; sentiment on U.N. Headquarters site, 60; U.N. Security Council Chamber decorated and furnished by, 121; problems of poverty in, 143; Jews in, 159; Stalin's praise of, 227–228; and Czechoslovakia, 231; and Chinese representation issue, 252, 253, 254, 255, 259; supporter of U.N. action in Korea, 329, 340; Communists in, 390, 391
Norwegian Cabinet, T. Lie in, 3–4, 17–20, 23, 43

Oath of office, of Secretariat members, 53
Objectivity, importance of, 342–343, 388, 393
O'Dwyer, Mayor William, and U.N. temporary Headquarters, 65, 66–67, 68, 69; and permanent Headquarters, 110, 112, 113, 116, 124
Oil concessions, 158, 170, 446
Olav, Norwegian Crown Prince, 17
Ording, Arne, 58
Organization of American States, 126
Oshanin, Lev, 369
Osvik, Osvald, 140
Overby, Andrew N., 319
Owen, Arthur David K., Assistant Secretary-General for Economic Affairs, 48, 64, 135; Executive Chairman of U.N. Technical Assistance Board, 147, 148

Padilla Nervo, Dr. Luis, 8, 49, 213, 368, 380, 381, 414
Pakistan, admitted to U.N. membership, 101; in global pooling of skills, 151; political contribution to, by former Western rule, 445; conflict with India over Kashmir, 446
Palestine, outbreak of hostilities, 98, 99; problem turned over by Great Britain to U.N., 103; General Assembly authorizes a U.N. Mediator for, 172, 178; appointment as Mediator declined by P. van Zeeland, 181, 185; Mediator appointment and service of Count Bernadotte, 185–186, 186–191, 192; Ralph Bunche, Acting Mediator, 191–192; friction

INDEX 463

in, 446. *See also* Israel; Partition of Palestine
Palestine Arabs, 158, 159, 161, 162; assault Jewish community, 163; intention to resist partition, 163; as refugees in Arab states since partition, 189, 191, 195–196
Palestine Commission, 163–167, 168–169, 172
Palestine Jews, 161, 162; retaliate for Arabs' assaults, 163
Pan American Union, and United Nations, 126–127, 133
Panama, 131, 163
Panama Canal Zone, 131
Pandit, Vijaya Lakshmi, 360, 414
Parodi, Alexandre, 211, 213, 266, 412
Partition of Palestine, 158; voted by U.N. General Assembly, 161–162, 164; Great Britain accepts but cannot implement, 163, 164, 167, 169; resistance by Arabs to, 163, 164, 166, 167; division in Big Five on, 169; vs. trusteeship, 169–170, 172; United States reversal on, a rebuff to U.N. and Secretary-General, 169–171; failure to meet armed defiance of, 194
Pátzcuaro, Mexico, 138
Paul-Boncourt, Joseph, 16
Pavlov, interpreter, 207, 208, 292, 294, 297, 304
Pearson, Lester B., 15, 16, 355, 356, 363; refutes Vyshinsky charge against Secretary-General of illegality, 383–384; and Lie's resignation as Secretary-General, 406, 412; vetoed by U.S.S.R. as successor, 414, 415
Peissel, Georges, 238
Pelt, Adrian, Assistant Secretary-General for Conference and General Services, 49–50, 64, 66
Pentagon, 334
People's Republic of China (Peking government, Communist China), right as sole legal representative of Chinese people to represent it in U.N. asserted by U.S.S.R., 249–272; treaty negotiations with U.S.S.R., 253, 260–261; nations recognizing, 253–254, 255; dangers in isolating, 254, 264; United States denial of recognition to, and resistance to its entrance into U.N., 255, 261, 263, 269, 271; international repercussions of its treatment of foreign nationals and recognition of Viet-Minh movement, 255, 257, 258, 263, 266, 269; efforts to ease crisis over, 255–271; conversation of Secretary-General with Moscow Ambassador of, 267–270; in Korean War, 272–273; and U.N. Charter, 273–274; alliance with U.S.S.R., 275; intervention in Korean War, 349, 350–351, 357–359; delegation to Lake Success *re* U.S. "armed invasion" of Formosa, 351–357
Perón, Juan D., 214
Peru, 136; visit of Secretary-General to, 139; on U.N. Special Committee on Palestine, 161
Petitpierre, Max, 305
Philadelphia, as possible U.N. Headquarters site, 109, 110, 111, 112, 113
Philippines, 163, 325, 332, 340
Plaza Lasso, Galo, 140
Plimsoll, James, 351
Point Four program, 146, 155
Poland, 25, 61, 80–81, 103, 105, 220
Ponce, Neftalí, 140
Portugal, application for U.N. membership, 100, 101, 102, 256
Potsdam Conference (1945), 25
Poverty, challenge of our time, 132, 137, 139, 140, 142–157, 198, 443; of India, 361–362
Pravda, 370
Prebisch, Raúl, 144
Preparatory Commission (U.N.), 2, 4, 5, 12, 13, 22, 27–28, 43, 44, 60–62
Price, Byron, Assistant Secretary-General for Administrative and Financial Services, 50, 51, 116, 117, 119, 122, 124, 254, 264, 389, 394, 397
Prisoners of war, 340
Protein deficiency, 149
Protitch, Dragon, 87, 175, 328, 412
Publicity, weakness for, 214

Quito, Ecuador, 139–140
Quo Tai-chi, 83

Radice, Fulke R., 319
Ræstad, Arnold, 58
Rasmussen, Gustav, 9, 365
Rau, Sir Benegal, 251, 252, 259; and North Korean aggression, 328, 329, 331, 332; and the delegation from Communist China, 353, 354, 355, 356; offers a "possible procedure" in deadlock on Secretary-General, 377; proposed by U.S.S.R. for Secretary-General, 380; withdraws, 381; considered again for Secretary-General, 414
Reedman, John, 187, 189
Refugees, Jewish, 160, 161, 196–197; Arab, 189, 195–196; Korean, 335
Reid, Helen Rogers (Mrs. Ogden M.), 413
Reid, Ogden Mills, 72
Rhee, Syngman, 326
Rhode Island, 63
Ridgway, Matthew B., 95, 364
Robertson, Howard, 116
Rockefeller, John D., Jr., 113–114, 124
Rockefeller, Nelson A., 72, 113
Rockefeller Center, 66
Rockefeller family, gift of U.N. Headquarters site, 112–114
Romulo, Carlos P., 277, 368, 380, 381, 414, 415
Roosevelt, Mrs. Eleanor, at London Gen'l Assembly, 8–9
Roosevelt, Franklin D., 8–9, 17, 57
Roschin, Alexis A., 46
Ross, John C., 113, 259, 336, 369
Rueff, Jacques, 48
Rumania, application for admission to U.N., 101, 102; Jews from, in Israel, 197; after 1945, 220; arming of, 239, 244
Rusk, Dean, 177, 181, 182, 202, 209, 263
Russia. See U.S.S.R.
Russo-Finnish War (1939–1940), 20
Rytter, Olav, 291
Rzymowski, Wincenty, 9, 16

SUNFED, proposed, 154
Saksin, Georgi Filipovich, 111

Salter, Sir Arthur, 48
Salvador (El), opposes New York as U.N. Headquarters, 114; health assistance to, 137
San Francisco, as possible U.N. Headquarters site, 63, 109–112, 113
San Francisco Conference (1945), 3, 7, 22–25, 45, 60
Santa Cruz, Hernán, 137
Sargent, Sir Orme, 183, 184
Sarper, Selim, 237
Saudi Arabia, 151; rejects Palestine partition, 162
Schmidt, Petrus J., 325
School children, American, 121
Schuman, Robert, French Foreign Minister, 211, 266; on London decision to postpone discussion of Chinese issue, 270; and Secretary-General's peace mission, 286–287, 288, 307–309; and extension of Lie's term as Secretary-General, 371, 373; hears of Lie's resignation, 412
Screening of applications for Secretariat appointments, 54
Secretariat (U.N.), London temporary, 7, 8, 42, 54; organization of permanent (New York), 27, 39–54; as an international civil service, 40, 41, 42–43, 53–54; eight departments, each headed by an Assistant Secretary-General, 44–52; problem of staffing, 52–54; discontent in, with temporary Headquarters, 108; moves into permanent Headquarters, 120; volunteers from, for guard service in Palestine, 187–188; U.N. Field Service a branch of, 193; members killed in Palestine conflict, 194; Russians in, 230; review of initial recruitment problems, 386–387; policy exclusion of American Communists from employment explained, 387–389; Gubitchev sole official accused in court of espionage, 388; difficulty of checking American personnel and establishing reasons that would permit termination of service, 389–390; 1947 charges against Balkan Commission staff members, 393–394; Gromyko protest against White Rus-

sian personnel, 394; 1948 Czechoslovak demand for dismissals, 394; distorted and exaggerated stories about, 394–395; no U.N. immunity for Fifth Amendment pleas against self-incrimination, 395–400; strange "presentment" of a federal grand jury against, 400–401; Senator McCarran's bill on, 401; President's executive order affecting, 401–403; Secretary-General's report to General Assembly on, 403–405

Secretary-General (U.N.), first election of, 10–17; constitutional and practical differences from League of Nations counterpart, 12, 39–42; T. Lie in office, and his aims, 30, 38; presented with table of organization to be filled, 43–45; search for department heads as a "cabinet," 45–52; creation of Secretariat staff, 52–54; directing establishment of New York temporary Headquarters, 64–70, 71; advice requested, then disregarded, in second Iran appeal to Security Council, 74–76; obtains answers from Teheran and Moscow on status of negotiations, 78–79; opinion of status of Iran's request, at odds with majority of Security Council, 79–82; memorandum to President of Council, a new form of intervention thenceforth regularized, 82–88; and Baruch Plan, 91; trial balloon for an armed force to be used by Security Council, 98–99; urges on Council wisdom of universality in U.N. membership as goal, 100–101; Truman Doctrine a complete surprise to, 104; address to General Assembly on coming to Flushing Meadow, 107; defends New York site to Headquarters subcommittee, 110; stirs O'Dwyer and Moses to improve New York's case for Headquarters site, 112–113; legal and financial spadework preceding construction, 115, 116–120; lays cornerstone, 120; obtains supplementary appropriation from General Assembly for building costs, 122–123; welcomes Assembly to permanent Headquarters, 123; visit to Mexico, Central America, and Caribbean area, 125, 126–132; visit to Brazil and Inter-American Conference on Peace and Security, 133–135; visit to Chile, Peru, and Ecuador, 138–141; support of partition in Palestine, 162, 165, 194; reply to José Arce's criticism, 168; answer to Austin's trusteeship proposal, 170; discusses resignation with Austin and Gromyko, 171; letter to permanent members of Security Council, 178–179, 181; suspicion in British Government of Jackson as representative of, 183–184; suggests Bernadotte as U.N. Mediator in Palestine, 185; declines proposal to fly to Rhodes, 188; and U.N. Field Service, 192–193; visit to Middle East, 195–198; mediation by, in Berlin blockade, 201–218; 1946 visit to Moscow, 221–230; luncheon guest of Molotov, 223; a meeting with Jan Masaryk, 224–225, 226; conversation with Stalin, 226–230; 1948 talks with Masaryk and Beneš, 232–234; 1950 vain search for their graves, 235–236; 1951 visit to Yugoslavia, 237–245, and Greece, 245–246, and Turkey, 246–247; mediation efforts after U.S.S.R. walkout on Chinese representation issue, 254–271; B'nai B'rith speech and ten-point peace program, 262–263, 276–292; peace mission to the four great-power capitals, 283–316; program published with covering letter, 316–318; general reception of program, 318–320; program discussed and commended by General Assembly, 320–321; receives notice of North Korean aggression and summons Security Council for emergency meeting, 327–328; states situation to Council, 329–330; organizer of U.N. military and nonmilitary effort, 333–335, 336–340; answers propaganda attack by Gromyko, 335–336; and prisoners of war, 340; objectivity, not neutrality, the duty of, 342–343; "Suggested Terms of Settlement," 344–345; relations with Gen. MacArthur, 347–348, 350–351; conversations in N.Y. with a Communist Chinese delegation, 351–357; statement of U.N. position toward Communist China, 358–359; conversation with Nehru, 359–362; and armistice negotiations, 363–366; dispute ending in extension of term to first, 367–385; appointment practice in Secretariat, 386–388; policy toward American members of Secretariat, 388–390, 391, 394–400, 402–405; called a Communist tool, 394; resignation of T. Lie as, 406–414; finding a new, 414–416; farewell speech of Lie as, 416–417

Security Council (U.N.), drafting of Charter articles on, 3; and naming of Secretary-General, 12, 16, 17; role of great powers in, 22–23; Charter right of veto in, 22, 24–25; elections to, 27, 28; first meeting (London, Jan., 1946), 28–34; obstacle to making Switzerland U.N. Headquarters site, 59; at Hunter College, 67; considers second Iran appeal against U.S.S.R., 74–79; absurdity of Gromyko's charge of "illegality," 79–80; precedent-setting memorandum of Secretary-General to, 81–88; Committee of experts of, 83–85, 86, 87–88; and control of atomic energy and armaments, 94; study of armed forces for, 95–99, 166, 192, 280, 300, 322; deadlocked on admission of new members to U.N., 100–102; names Commission of Investigation on Greek complaint of outside interference, 103, 105; considers Truman Doctrine and Greece, 105; Chamber of, decorated and furnished by Norway, 121; and Palestine Commission, 164, 165, 166–170; U.N. trusteeship for Palestine proposed to, 169–170; Truce Commission of, 172, 178, 187; Egyptian formal notice to, of armed intervention in Palestine, 173; inaction of, 175, 180, 186; Secretary-General's letter to Permanent Members of, 177–179, 181; renewed firmness of United States in, 182; Arab complaints to, against Israel, 195; places Berlin blockade on agenda as threat to peace, 200–202; mediation of "neutrals" in, led by Dr. Bramuglia, 202, 203, 207, 209, 212, 213, 214, 216; relations in, between United States and U.S.S.R., 205; notified of agreement between Western powers and U.S.S.R., 218; issue of Chinese representation in, 249–261 *passim*, 266–274 *passim*, 335; need for periodic meetings of, 279, 300, 303, 308, 309, 311, 312, 313, 314, 321, 431; emergency meeting to deal with North Korean aggression, 328, 330, 331; organizing the Unified Command for, 337–340; Secretary-General and, 342; six-power draft resolution reassuring Communist China vetoed by U.S.S.R., 350; and Peking's complaint of United States "armed intervention" in Formosa, 351; deadlock in, over Secretary-General, 374–382; change in number of Permanent Members, 433

Sekaninova-Cakrtova, Madame, 289, 290

Serot, Col. André Pierre, 190, 191

Sharapov, A. R., 95

Shertok (later, Sharett), Moshe, 164 and n., 165, 190, 195, 353

Silva Pena, Eugenio, 128

Simič, Stanoje, 15, 16

Sinatra, Frank, 70

Siroky, Viliam, Czech Minister for Foreign Affairs, 235; 1950 interview with, 288–290; and the abducted Greek children, 289–290, 305; views on peace in Korean conflict, 345, 353

Skills, global pooling of, 137–138, 146–152, 155, 156

Skrzeszewski, Stanislaw, 415

Snyder, John W., 70

Sobolev, Arkady A., Assistant Secretary-General for Security Council

Affairs, 37, 46, 51, 75, 82, 86, 87, 88; in Berlin blockade mediation, 201–210 *passim*, 213; expresses U.S.S.R. support of second term for T. Lie as Secretary-General, 368
Sokolovsky, Vasili, 200, 206
Soilleux, G. A., 115
Somoza, Anastasio, 128, 130
South Africa, 340, 445–446
Soviet Union. See U.S.S.R.
Spaak, Paul-Henri, election as General Assembly President, 4–10; for Europe as U.N. Headquarters site, 61; refusal of the floor to Secretary-General, 87; considered for Secretary-General, 414
Spargo, George, 117
Special Commission on the Balkans (U.N.), 105
Special United Nations Fund for Economic Development, proposed, 154
Specialized Agencies, 130, 132, 136; technical assistance projects of, 145–146, 146–153, 281, 301; call for greater use of, by member governments, 281, 302, 303–304; statement by leaders of, supporting Secretary-General's peace mission, 318–319
Sperry plant (Lake Success), 68–69
Stalin, Joseph, and veto crisis, 24–25; statement that Americans and British did not want an understanding, 208; failure to mention currency in saying Berlin dispute could be settled, 217; 1946 visit of Secretary-General to, 221, 226–230; at a sports event, 226; his praise of Norway, 227–228; his reading of American newspapers, 229; Teheran bon mot about the Pope, 242; 1950 visit to, 267, 291, 292, 293–307; and Truman, 295, 303; reply to United States charge against U.S.S.R. of discrimination, 302; and the abducted Greek children, 304–305
State Department (U.S.), applications through, for Secretariat appointments, 54; offended by Secretary-General, 75; slip by, in Truman Doctrine, 104; conversations on Palestine with Secretary-General's representative, 181–182; not interested in compromise in Berlin impasse, 216; and Czechoslovakia, 233; and Chinese representation, 261; early stand-aside attitude in appointments to U.N. Secretariat, 387; agrees to examine government records on American applicants and holders of Secretariat positions, 389
Stavropoulos, Constantin A., 187, 189, 351
Stein, Boris, 87
Stepinac, Bishop Aloysius, 242–243
Stettinius, Edward R., Jr., U.S. Chief Delegate to U.N., suggests Presidency of Gen'l Assembly to T. Lie, 3; compromises with Gromyko to make Lie Secretary-General, 15–17; leads in overcoming veto crisis, 24; moderating influence in Iran and Greece debates, 30, 33; on Big Five understanding on Assistant Secretaryships-General, 45–46; proposes an American be appointed to Administrative and Financial Services, 46–47; his sole recommendation for Secretariat appointment, 65; and Iranian question, 76; complains of Secretary-General's memorandum, 85; preference of San Francisco for U.N. Headquarters, 109
Stevenson, Adlai E., and T. Lie candidacy for General Assembly President, 2, 10; on proposal of Gen. Eisenhower for Secretary-General, 13; considered for Assistant Secretary-General for Administrative and Financial Services, 47, 50, 51; expresses welcome of United States to U.N., 61, 62; at U.N. luncheon to Vice President and Mrs. Barkley, 121–122
Stikker, Dirk, 414
Stoneman, William H., 14, 133, 187; in Berlin blockade mediation, 201, 202, 210; accompanies Secretary-General to Moscow, 222, 225; investigates staff work of Balkan Commission, 394; anecdote of the English banker-visitor to U.N., 421
Sulzberger, Arthur Hays, 72

Sunde, Arne, 259, 329, 333, 336, 369, 378

Sweden, admitted to U.N., 100, 101; Economic and Social Council Chamber decorated and furnished by, 121; on U.N. Special Committee on Palestine, 161; recognition of Communist China, 253; aid to U.N. effort in Korea, 340

Switzerland, qualified welcome to United Nations, 59; transfer of League of Nations buildings in, to U.N., 125; in global sharing of skills, 151

Syria, 33–34, 162, 192, 195, 196, 198, 325

Taiwan. *See* Formosa

Technical Assistance Administration (UNTAA), 147, 151

Technical Assistance Board (U.N.), 147, 151

Technical assistance projects, U.N., 145–157, 280–281, 284, 301, 442

Tegucigalpa, 130

Temporary Commission on Korea (U.N.), 324–326, 328, 329, 330, 331, 338, 344, 351, 353. *See also* Commission on Korea

Terrorism, in Palestine, 160, 190

Thailand, admitted to U.N. membership, 101; in global pooling of skills, 151; combat forces in Korea, 340

"Third force," 36

Tito, Marshal, 15; break with Cominform, 221, 237, 241; contrasting status of, in Yugoslavia and Stalin in U.S.S.R., 238; visit of Secretary-General to, 239–245

Torres Bodet, Jaime, 128, 129, 138, 319

Transjordan, application for admission to U.N., 102, 256; fear of Israel, 195

Trieste, 167–168

Trinidad, 137

Trotsky, Leon, 20

Trucco, Manuel, 351

Trujillo Molina, Rafael, 130, 132

Truman, Harry S., 24, 26, 47; and Churchill's Fulton speech, 35, 37; helps in U.N. housing problem, 69–70; courageous leadership, 104; welcomes General Assembly to Flushing Meadow, 107; not keen for N.Y. as U.N. Headquarters site, 109, 111; obtains U.S. loan for Headquarters construction, 118, 120; at cornerstone laying, 120; credit due to, 124; gives new life to technical assistance concept, 146; *de facto* recognition of Israel, 173, 184; exchange of views with, on Chinese representation and Formosa, 264–265; orders fleet to protect Formosa, 265; visits by Secretary-General on peace mission, 283–285, 315–316; and Stalin, 284, 295, 316; orders Seventh Fleet to protect Formosa, 332; appoints MacArthur United Nations Commander in Korea, 334; and deadlock over Secretary-General, 379; executive order making available to Secretary-General government information on American applicants and holders of Secretariat positions, 401–402, 403

Truman Doctrine, 37, 104–105, 220–221, 394

Trusteeship Council, 88; Chamber decorated and furnished by Denmark, 121

Tsiang, T. F., right to represent China in Security Council challenged, 249–252, 272; as President of Council, 250–251; possible unseating of, 258, 264; conversation with Secretary-General, 260; reaction to Secretariat Legal Department memorandum, 261–262; assailed by Gromyko, 335

Tunisia, 445

Turkey, U.S. aid to, 104, 221, 246; escape from World War II, 220; visit of Secretary-General to, 237, 246–248; concern with danger from U.S.S.R., 246, 247; friendly to U.N., 247; combat forces in Korea, 340

Turner, Lana, 71

Turtle Bay, site of U.N. Headquarters, 112, 120

INDEX

UNESCO. See United Nations Educational, Scientific and Cultural Organization
UNRRA, 128, 233, 245
U.S.S.R. (Soviet Union, Russia, Kremlin), and first Gen'l Assembly President, 4, 5–11 *passim;* and choice of first Secretary-General, 12, 15, 16, 18, 26; historical Norwegian relations with, 19–20; in San Francisco fight over veto, 24–25; military control over Eastern Europe, 25; relations with Czechoslovakia, Finland, Norway as hopeful sign, 26; supports creation of U.N. commission on atomic energy, 26–27; accused by Iran of interference, 28–29, 30–31; charges British interference in Greece and Indonesia, 30, 31–33; first use of veto, 34; developing split with West, 35–38; key post among Assistant Secretaryships-General accorded to, 45, 51; for placing U.N. Headquarters in U.S. on east coast, 58–59, 60, 61, 109–110, 111; renewed Iranian complaint against, 74–86; degree of openness to persuasion, 75; intransigence of, 77; assures Security Council it is withdrawing its troops, 78–79; and Secretary-General's intervention in Security Council, 86; signs of developing cleavage with West, 89; and the Baruch Plan (International Atomic Development Authority), 92–95; participation in Military Staff Committee work and report, 95–97; and deadlock over admitting new members to U.N., 100, 101, 102; and Greek question, 103, 105; war of nerves on Turkey, 104; and the Rio Inter-American Conference on Peace and Security, 134, 135; membership in U.N. Specialized Agencies, 145; supports Palestine partition, 160, 164, 169; opposes an international force for U.N., 192–193; imposes Berlin blockade, alleging currency matters as reason, 199–201; proposes Council of Foreign Ministers convene to discuss disputes over Germany, 202; vetoes resolution of "neutrals" in Security Council, 202, 205 n.; relations with United States in Security Council, 205; accepts idea of "immediate conversations," 215; reaches agreement on Berlin with Western powers, 218; promise of free secret elections in border states, 220; 1946 visit of Secretary-General to, 221–230; reconstruction problem of, 228, 229; Czechoslovakian dependence on, 233; economic and military pressure on Yugoslavia, 237, 239–240, 241; Tito insists on Yugoslav equality with, 241; Greek and Turkish concern with danger from, 246, 247; insists on removal from Security Council of Kuomintang representative, 250; second walkout from Council, 251; will not recognize as legal any decision made with participation of Kuomintang representative, 252; negotiations with Communist China, 253, 260–261; further boycott of U.N., 253; isolation of, by West in 1920's, 254, 264; importance of participation by, in U.N., 265; recognition of Ho Chi Minh, 266; intransigence of, criticized by Secretary-General to Vyshinsky, 267; return to Security Council, 271–272; concentration on alliance with Communist China with continuance of boycott, 275; urged to join more of Specialized Agencies, 281, 302, 303–304; non-cooperative attitude of, 284, 286, 287, 317; and Cominform, 287; and the veto, 298–299; and the kidnaped Greek children, 304–305; return to U.N., 320; first pledge to U.N. technical assistance program, 322; joint commission with United States for Korea, 323; opposes U.N. Temporary Commission on Korea, 324–325; absent from Security Council when North Korean aggression was considered, 330–331, 335; furnishes large tanks to North Korea, 332; attacks on Secretary-General, 335, 341–342; initial support for reelec-

tion of T. Lie as Secretary-General, 368; efforts to defeat Lie, 369–370, 374–385; use of outside Communist parties, 392; boycott of Secretary-General, 408–409, 410–411; interpretation of his resignation, 413–414; and choice of new Secretary-General, 415; abuse of veto privilege, 425; abstention practice, 432; its charges of illegality, 432; immediate task of democracies toward, 439; and the underdeveloped and underprivileged two-thirds, 443

Ukraine (S.S.R.), 325

Unanimity rule, 428. *See also* Veto

Underdeveloped areas and countries, 126, 127, 135, 144, 146, 147–156, 281, 304, 436, 440–443

Underprivileged, 443, 444

Unified Command (in Korea), 334–340 *passim*, 355, 357

United Kingdom. *See* Great Britain

United Nations, flag, 7, 322, 333, 334; Norway's attitude toward, 22; six principal organs, 40; an army for, 95–99, 166, 192, 280, 300, 322; disputes over admission of new members, 99–103; Latin-American misgivings on United States support of, 127, 133; harmony of regional defense agreements with, 133–135; doctrine that it has no power to enforce any political settlement, 167; Arab invasion of Palestine a death threat to, 174, 183, 184; cease-fire its first major success in Palestine, 187; military observers for, in Palestine and Arab states, 187, 190, 194; and problem of Arab refugees, 195–196; British Foreign Office coolness toward initiative by, 211; role in Berlin blockade mediation, 218; Yugoslav feeling toward, 238, 241; border lands in cold war a challenge to, 247–248; Chinese representation issue and Communist Bloc 1950 walkout, 252–253, 262–263; lasting, central significance of, emphasized by "Memorandum of Points . . . in the Development of a Twenty-Year Program for Achieving Peace," 263, 275–282; war of Communist China against, 272, 273, 349–351, 357; exercise by Great Britain and France of moderating influence in, urged, 285, 288, 314; importance of settling Chinese representation issue in, 316; and the Korean aggression, 320, 323–366; army of, 322, 323, 331–334, 337–340; nonmilitary services in Korea, 340; attitude toward Communist China, 358–359; in Korea after the truce, 366; Bevin on, 371; and 1946–1952 preservation of world peace, 420–422; the veto right in, 422–432 *passim;* voluntary character of, 422–423; evaluation by President Eisenhower, 423–424; advantage over other channels in technical assistance to underdeveloped countries, 442–443; and the colonial powers, 444–445; South African problems in, 445–446; and the resolution of the Israel and Arabs conflict, 446

United Nations Correspondents Association, 331

United Nations Day, 120

United Nations Educational, Scientific and Cultural Organization (UNESCO), 137, 138, 145, 147, 152, 303, 304

United Nations Field Service, 192–193

United Nations Library, 399

United Nations Relief and Works Agency, 196

United Nations Special Committee on Palestine (UNSCOP), 161–162, 170

United States, and election of first U.N. Gen'l Assembly President, 2–10 *passim;* and choice of first Secretary-General, 12–13, 15–16; and resolution of Charter veto crisis, 24; and creation of U.N. atomic energy commission, 26–27; troops in Iran, 29; appointee from, in Secretary-General's "cabinet," 46–47, 50–51; battle over choice of, as U.N. Headquarters site, 55–62; reaction to Secretary-General's intervention in Security Council, 85, 86; proposal of Baruch Plan (International Atomic

Development Authority), 91–95; participation in work and report of Military Staff Committee, 95–97; and deadlocks over admitting new members to U.N., 100, 101, 102; proclamation of Truman Doctrine and U.N., 104–105; exempts Rockefeller grant and U.N. property from taxes, 116; interest-free loan of $65,000,000 to U.N., 118–120; Latin-American misgivings on United States support of U.N., 127, 133; General Convention on Privileges and Immunities not yet ratified by, 128; wavering support of Palestine partition, 162, 164, 167, 168, 169–172; *de facto* recognition of Israel, 173, 184; silence on Arab states' invasion of Palestine, 174–175; difficulties with Great Britain, 177, 178; divergencies in view between Great Britain and, 179, 180; prepared to nominate van Zeeland as U.N. Mediator in Palestine, 181; other steps considered, 181; again ready for firm action in Security Council, 182, 186; assigns officers as U.N. military observers in Palestine and Arab states, 187; yields alphabetical right to preside over Security Council, 202; relations in Security Council with U.S.S.R., 205; desires agreement on Berlin, 207, 214; its Truman Doctrine a determinative event, 220–221; and reconstruction aid to U.S.S.R., 228, 229; its "defeatist" policy toward Czechoslovakia, 233–234; and Yugoslavia, 240; military and economic aid in Greece, 245; military aid in Turkey, 246; and Chinese representation issue, 255, 261, 263, 271; Chiang Kai-shek lobby in, 260; isolationist press in, 261; support of U.N. technical assistance, 301; its charge against U.S.S.R. of discrimination answered by Stalin, 302; Truman and Acheson deny discrimination by, 316; joint commission with U.S.S.R. for Korea, 323; and Security Council action on North Korean aggression, 331, 332; complaint at burden it has to carry, 334; and the Unified Command, 336–340; proposes all-Korean elections under U.N. auspices, 345; Communist Chinese complaint against, of "armed invasion" of Formosa, 351, 352, 355, 356, 357; and extension of term of T. Lie as Secretary-General, 368–381 *passim*; furor in, over internal security, 386, 390, 391–395, 396–397, 399, 401; extreme restraint about influencing U.N. Secretariat appointments, 386–390; Communist party in, 388, 390, 392; executive order authorizing federal cooperation in Secretariat personnel check, 401–402

United States Mission to the U.N., 336, 337, 338

United States Senate, attack on Dr. Jessup in, 203; 1952 New York hearings of its Internal Security Subcommittee, 396, 397

Universal Declaration of Human Rights, 281, 438, 442

Universal Postal Union, 145, 303

Universality, 50; of membership, as a goal for U.N., 100–101, 102, 254, 280, 301, 319, 428

Uruguay, 137, 161

van Kleffens, Eelco, Dutch Foreign Minister, 4, 15, 33, 77
van Roijen, J. H., 365
van Zeeland, Paul, 181, 185
Vandenberg, Arthur H., 24, 104
Vasiliev, A. F., 95
Vaughan, David B., 64
Vavilov, Michael, 291, 292
Veldekens, Paul, 398
Venizelos, Sophocles, 245, 246
Vesugar, M. J., 117
Veto, fight over Charter right of, 22, 24; the first, 34; barred in Baruch Plan, 92, 94; as a means of bargaining, 102; in Berlin impasse, 202, 205 n., 209; proposed limitation on use of, 279, 298–299, 308; general discussion, 422–432 *passim*
Viet-Minh movement, 257, 258, 287

472 INDEX

Vietnam, two applications from, for membership in U.N., 101
Vigier, Henri, 187
Vilamajó, Julio, 116
Vilfan, Joze, 239, 243
Viteri Lafronte, Homero, 259
Vyshinsky, Andrei Y., at London Gen'l Assembly, 15, 26; complains in Security Council against British interference in Greece, 30, 31, 32, 33; casts first veto, 34; seeks appointment of Soviet national as Assistant Secretary-General for Security Council Affairs, 45–46; critical of Rio Agreement (1947), 135; exchange of views with Secretary-General on Berlin impasse, 204, 207–209; in second meeting authorizes Secretary-General to continue efforts, 209–210; and 1946 visit by Secretary-General to Moscow, 221, 223; 1949 resistance to election of Yugoslavia to Security Council, 252; exchange with Secretary-General on Malik walkout, 267; participant in Secretary-General's 1950 interview with Stalin, 291, 293, 297, 300, 305; attack in General Assembly on Secretary-General, 320–321; on Soviet equipment to North Korea, 327; ridicule of Acheson Plan for "United Action for Peace," 346–347; initial support for reelection of T. Lie as Secretary-General, 368; noncommittal, 371; assails Lie as violator of Charter, 382–383; answered by Lester Pearson, 383–384; last interchange with Secretary-General Lie, 416; accepts Hammarskjöld as Secretary-General, 416; on status of the individual in U.S.S.R., 438

Wagner, Robert F., Jr., 72
Waithayakon, Prince Wan, 415
Waldorf-Astoria Hotel, 66, 71
Walker, Horacio, 138
Walkout, first Soviet, 77–79; by Arab states, 162; second Soviet, 251, 252; harmful, 262, 263, 267, 268, 271; a backward look at the 1950 Soviet, 272; Bevin on, 310
Wallace, Henry A., 341
Wang Chia-hsiang, Communist Chinese Ambassador to U.S.S.R., conversation with, 267–270
Warner, Edward, 319
Watson, Thomas J., 72
Weapons. See Atomic; Conventional; Mass destruction
Weizmann, Chaim, 195
Wergeland, Henrik, 159
Westchester County (N.Y.), as possible U.N. Headquarters site, 62, 63, 108, 111
Western powers, answer Berlin blockade with airlift, 199, 201, 203, 210, 217, 218; their reform of German currency in Western zones the U.S.S.R. pretext for blockade, 200; appeal to Security Council on ground of threat to peace, 200–201; announce to Security Council agreement with U.S.S.R., 218
Whalen, Grover, 71, 419
White, E. Wyndham, 319
White Russians, 394
Williams, Francis, 47–48
Wilson, Harold, 309
Winant, John G., 15
World Economic Report, annual volumes of, 136, 144
World Health Organization, 145, 147, 152, 303, 304
World Meteorological Organization, 145
Wright, Michael R., 183, 184
Wu Hsiu-chuan, 351–357
Wyatt, Wilson W., 50, 51

Yalta agreements, for free elections, 25, 220, 248
Yalta formula on veto, 24
Yemen, admitted to U.N. membership, 101, 256; rejects Palestine partition, 162; Jewish refugees from, 197
Younger, Kenneth G., 64, 111, 355, 363
Yugoslavia, and Greek guerrillas, 103, 105; on U.N. Special Committee on

Palestine, 161; self-liberated, 220; visit of Secretary-General to, 221, 237–245; breach with Cominform and U.S.S.R., 237, 240, 241; economic and military pressure by U.S.S.R. and Communist Bloc, 237, 239–240, 241; and United Nations, 238, 241, 242; need of capital, 240–241; defense cooperation with Greece and Turkey considered by, 242; and Bishop Stepinac, 242–243; Greek children in, 243, 245; and Korean War, 243–244; army second largest in Europe, 246; election to Security Council, 252, 368; and Chinese representation issue, 253, 255, 259; abstains in Security Council vote on North Korean aggression, 331; and U.N. effort in Korea, 339; and extension of term as Secretary-General of T. Lie, 376, 378

Zafrulla Khan, Sir Muhammad, 353, 413

Zinchenko, Constantin E., Assistant Secretary-General for Security Council Affairs, 51, 236, 291, 333, 335, 341, 343, 344, 363, 368, 371

Zuleta Angel, Dr. Eduardo, chairman of London Gen'l Assembly, 5, 7, 8, 9; on Manhattan for U.N. Headquarters, 114; proposed for Secretary-General, 415